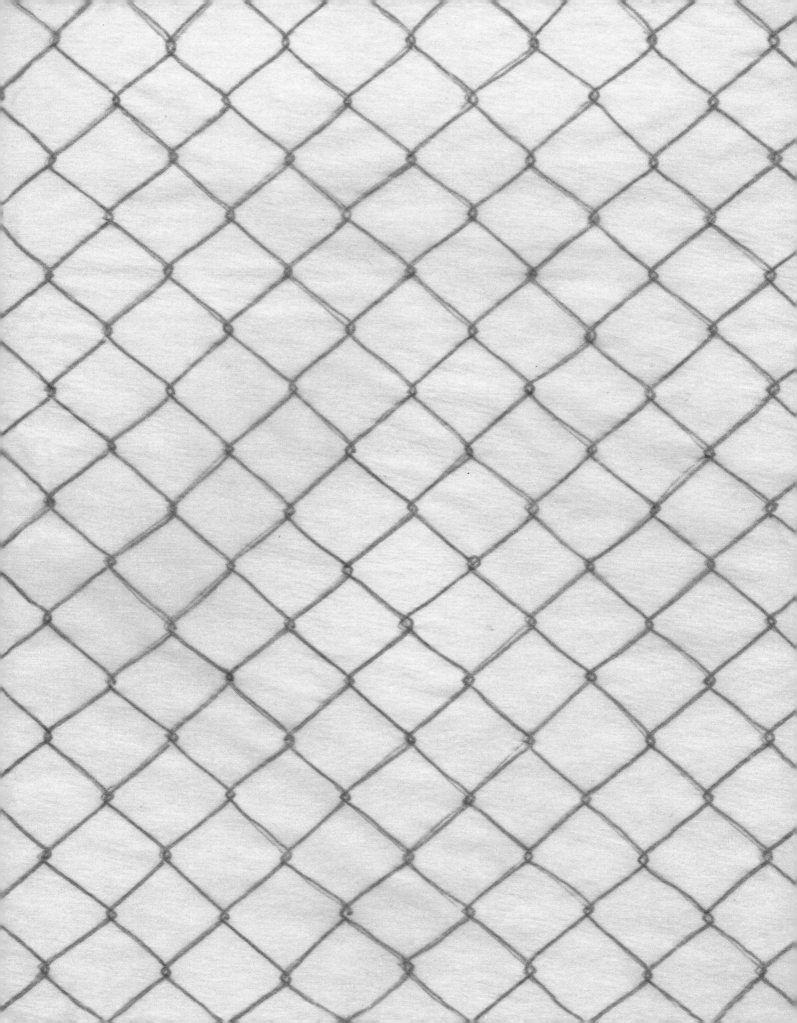

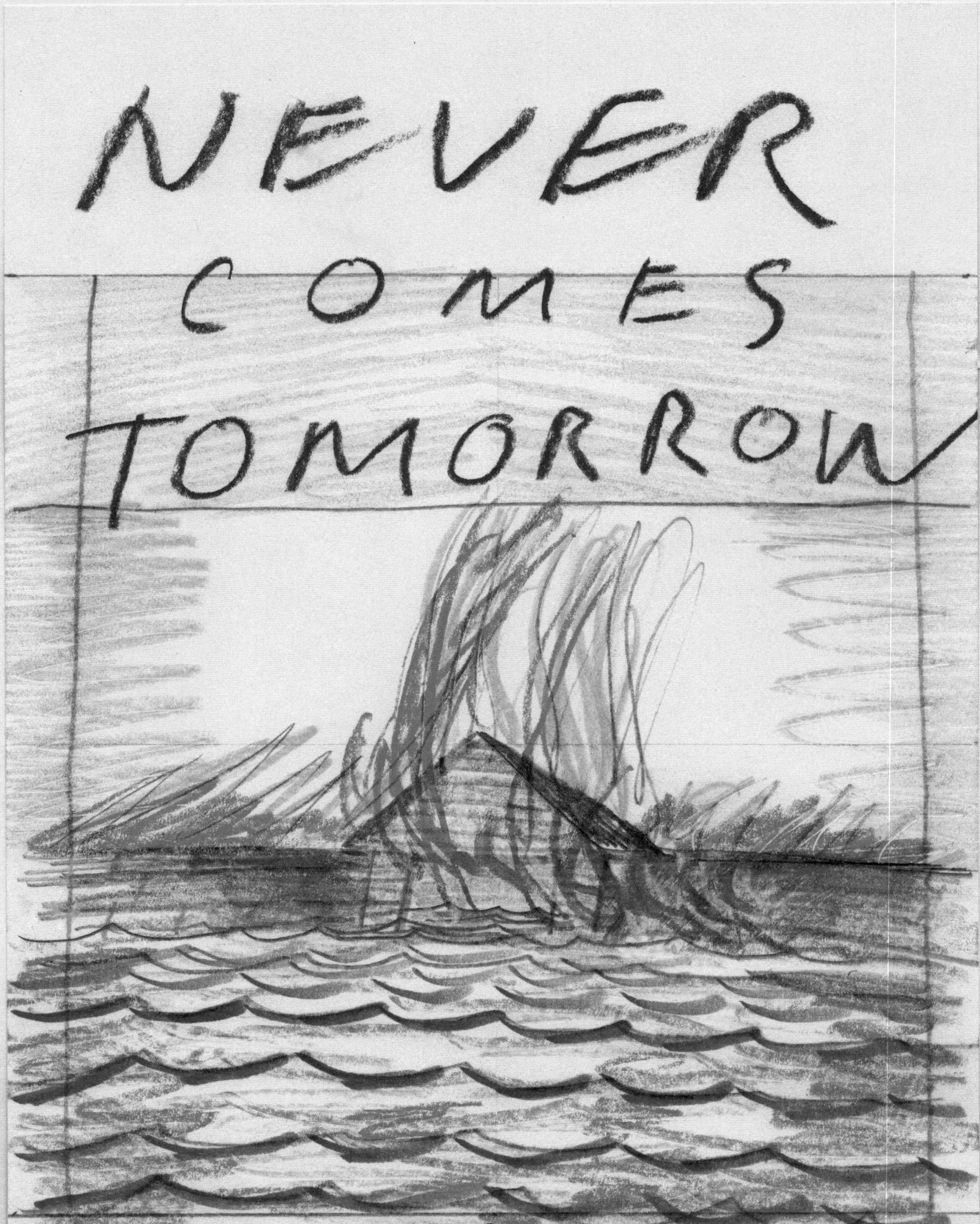
NEVER
COMES
TOMORROW
FRANK SANTORO

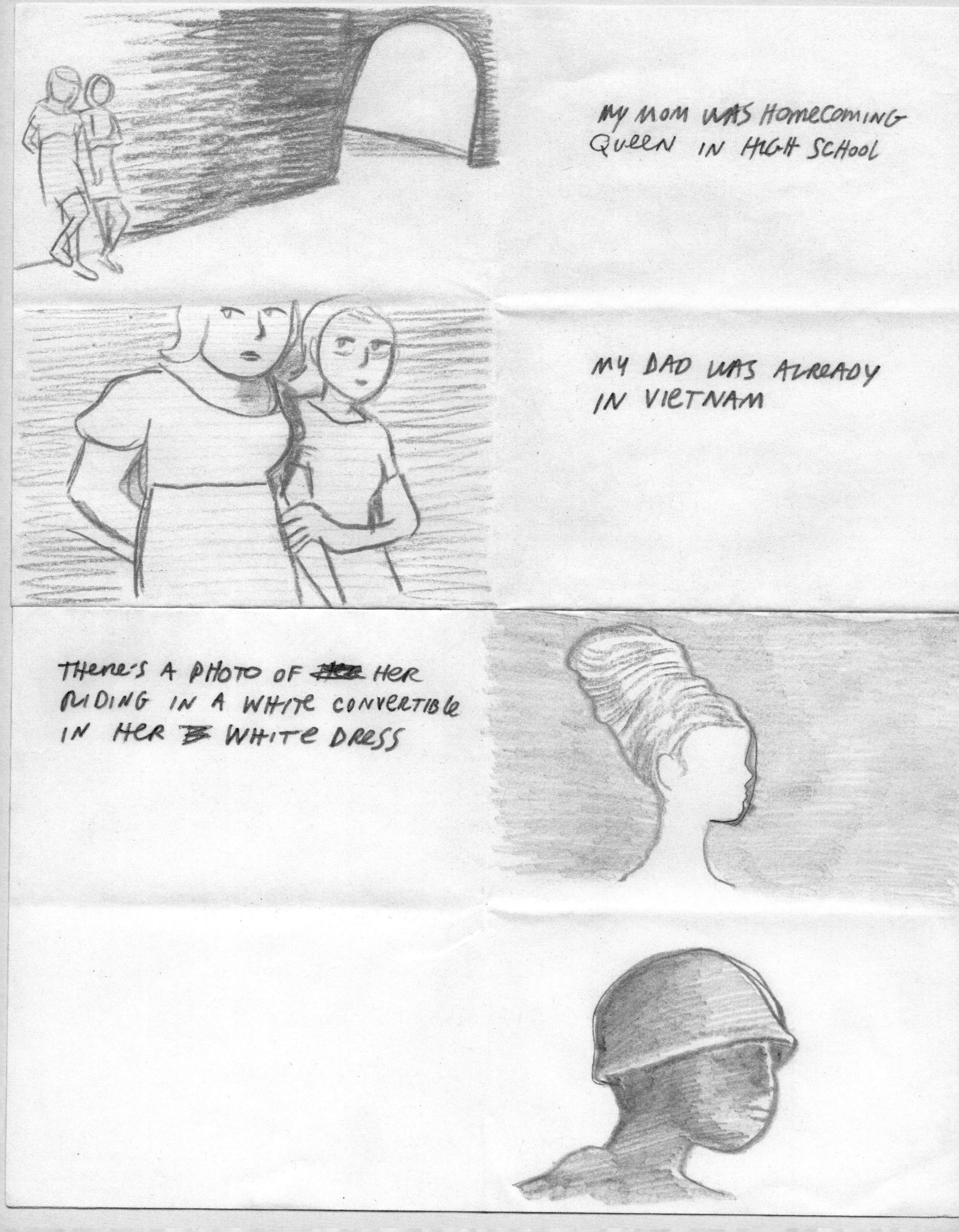
MY MOM WAS HOMECOMING QUEEN IN HIGH SCHOOL
MY DAD WAS ALREADY IN VIETNAM
THERE'S A PHOTO OF HER RIDING IN A WHITE CONVERTIBLE IN HER WHITE DRESS

MY DAD SAID THAT
WHEN MOM WAS
HOMECOMING QUEEN
SHE GOT A TON OF
PHOTOS MADE —

AND MAILED THREE THICK
ENVELOPES FULL OF THEM
TO HIM IN VIETNAM

AT MAIL CALL, THE
COMMANDING OFFICER WAS
~~SO~~ ANNOYED THAT MY DAD
GOT THREE BIG LETTERS —
AND THREW THE ENVELOPES
~~AT MY DAD~~ AT HIM

THE SHARP CORNER OF ONE
OF THEM HIT MY DAD HARD,
SQUARE BETWEEN THE EYES

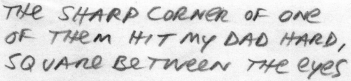

NOW DO
20 PUSHUPS
FOR EACH
LETTER

MY PARENTS
WHO HAVE BARELY SPOKEN
TO EACH OTHER
IN 20 YEARS,
DIVORCED FOR 20 YEARS —
NOW BOTH WORK FOR THE
SAME HOSPITAL
IN PITTSBURGH —
THE NEW FACTORY IN TOWN

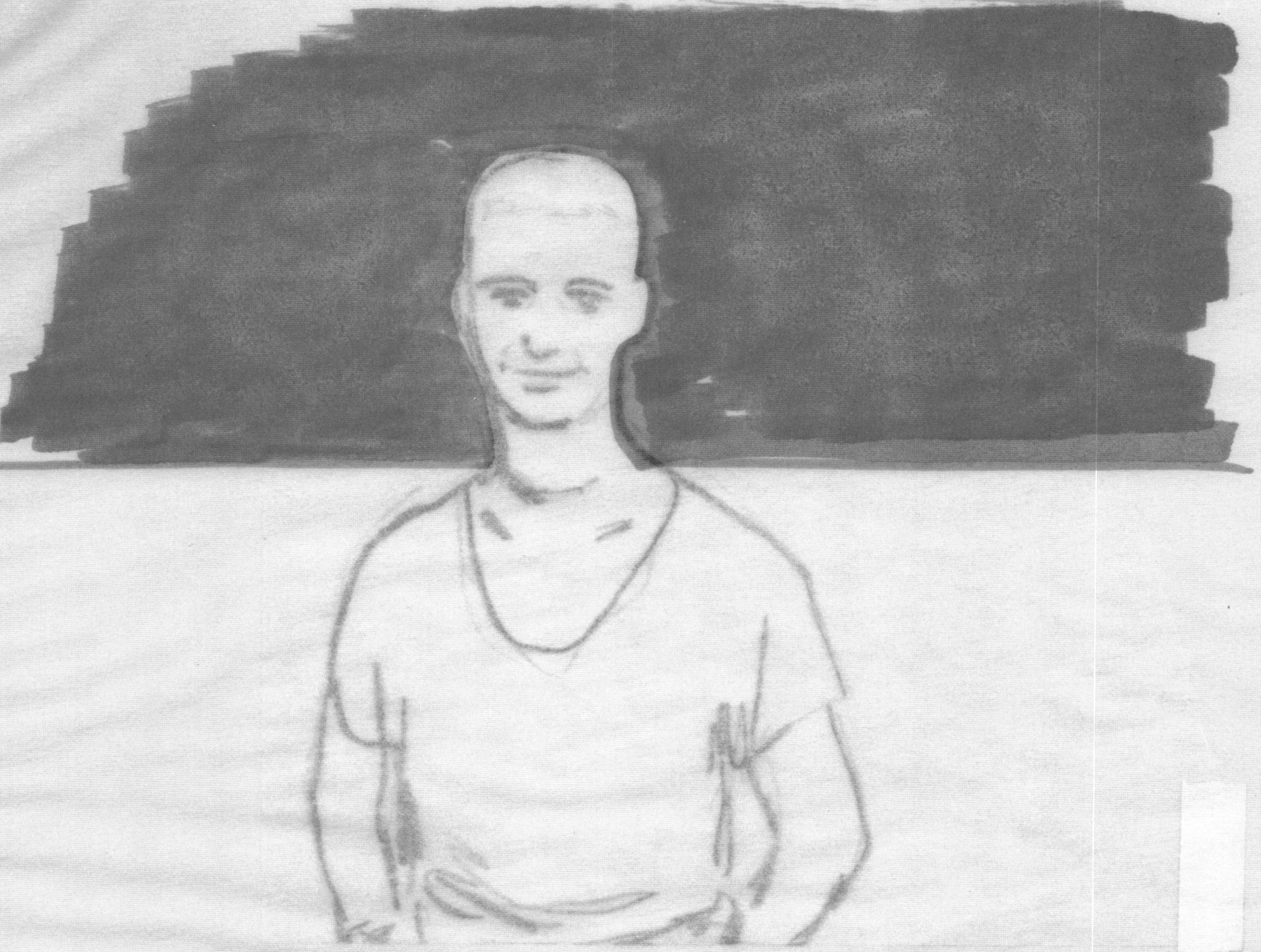

SO, AFTER 20 YEARS
THEY OCCASIONALLY
RUN INTO EACH OTHER
AT WORK,
AND PRETEND NOT TO SEE
EACH OTHER

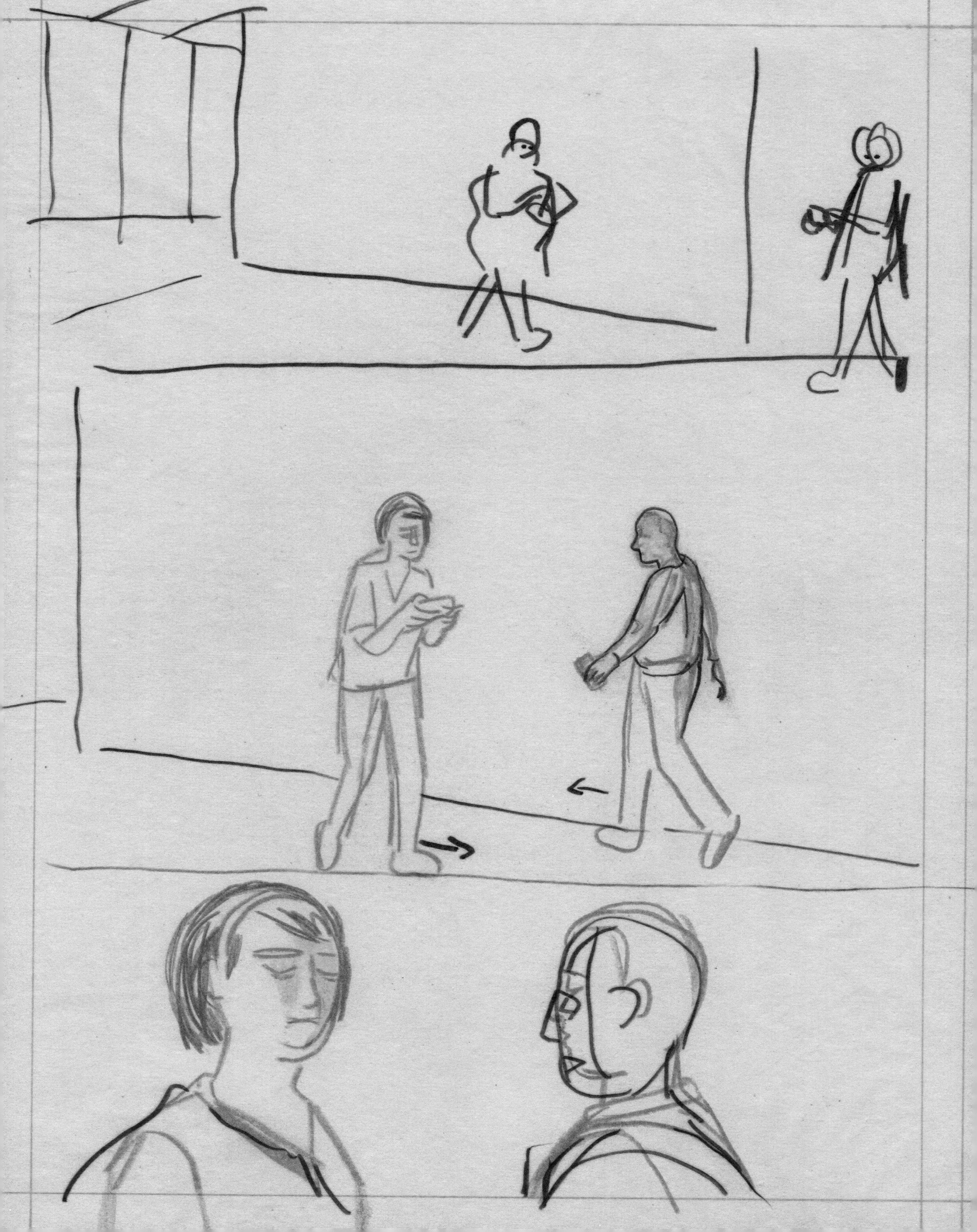

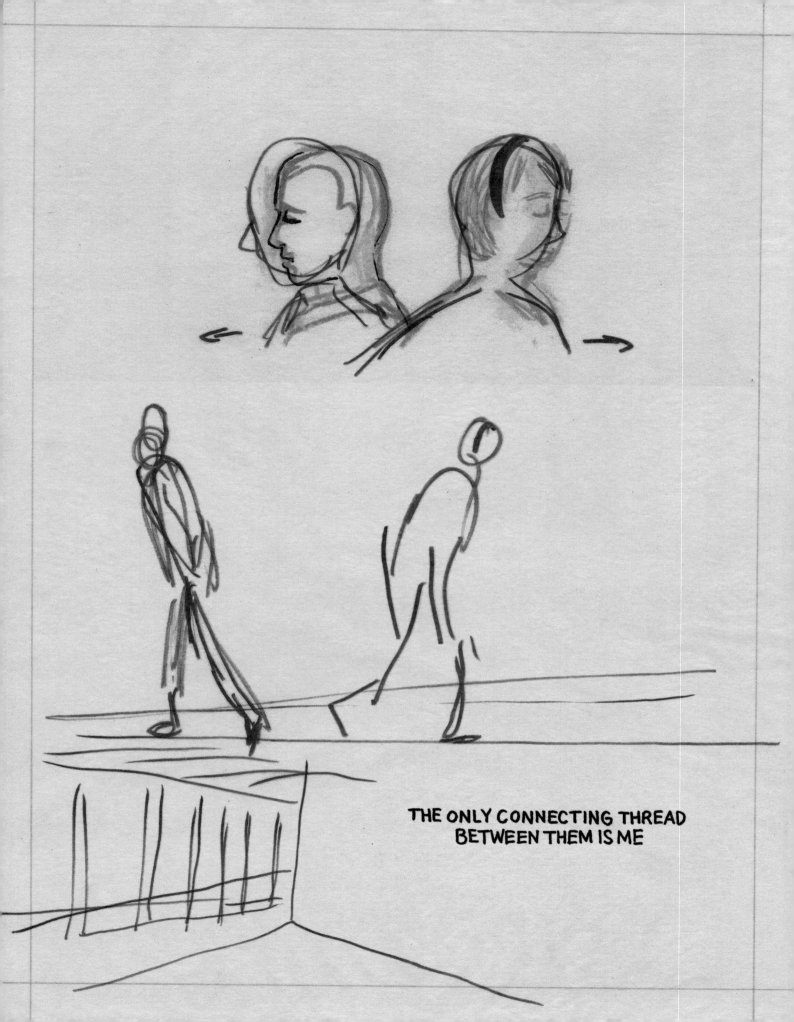

THE ONLY CONNECTING THREAD
BETWEEN THEM IS ME

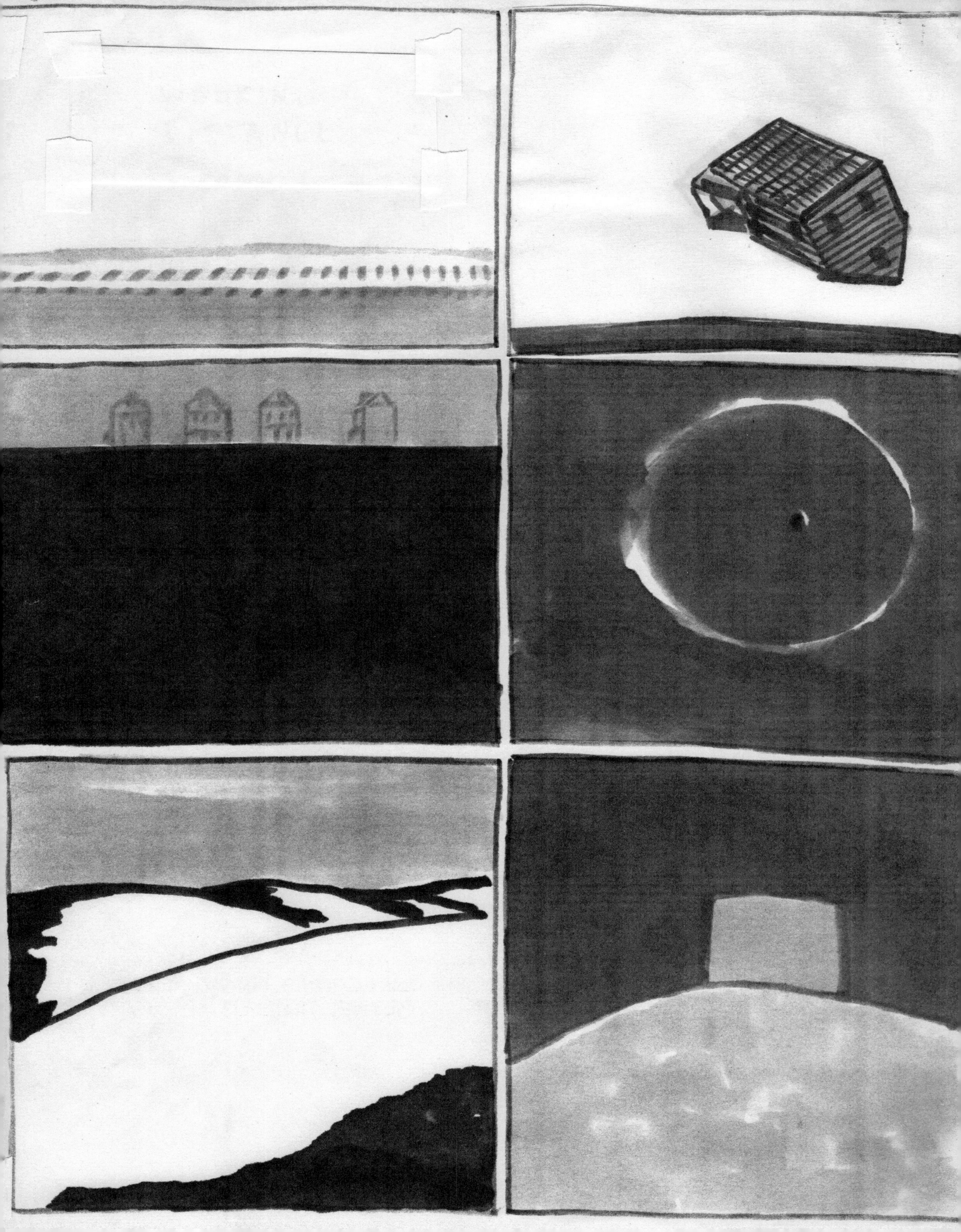

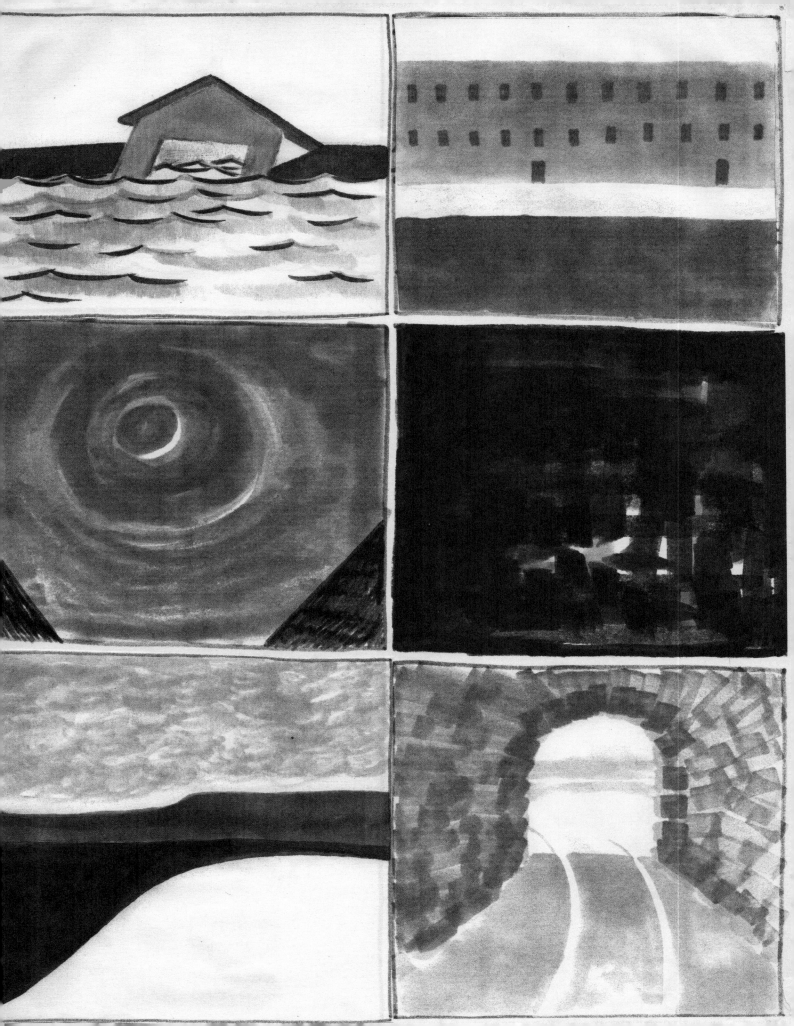

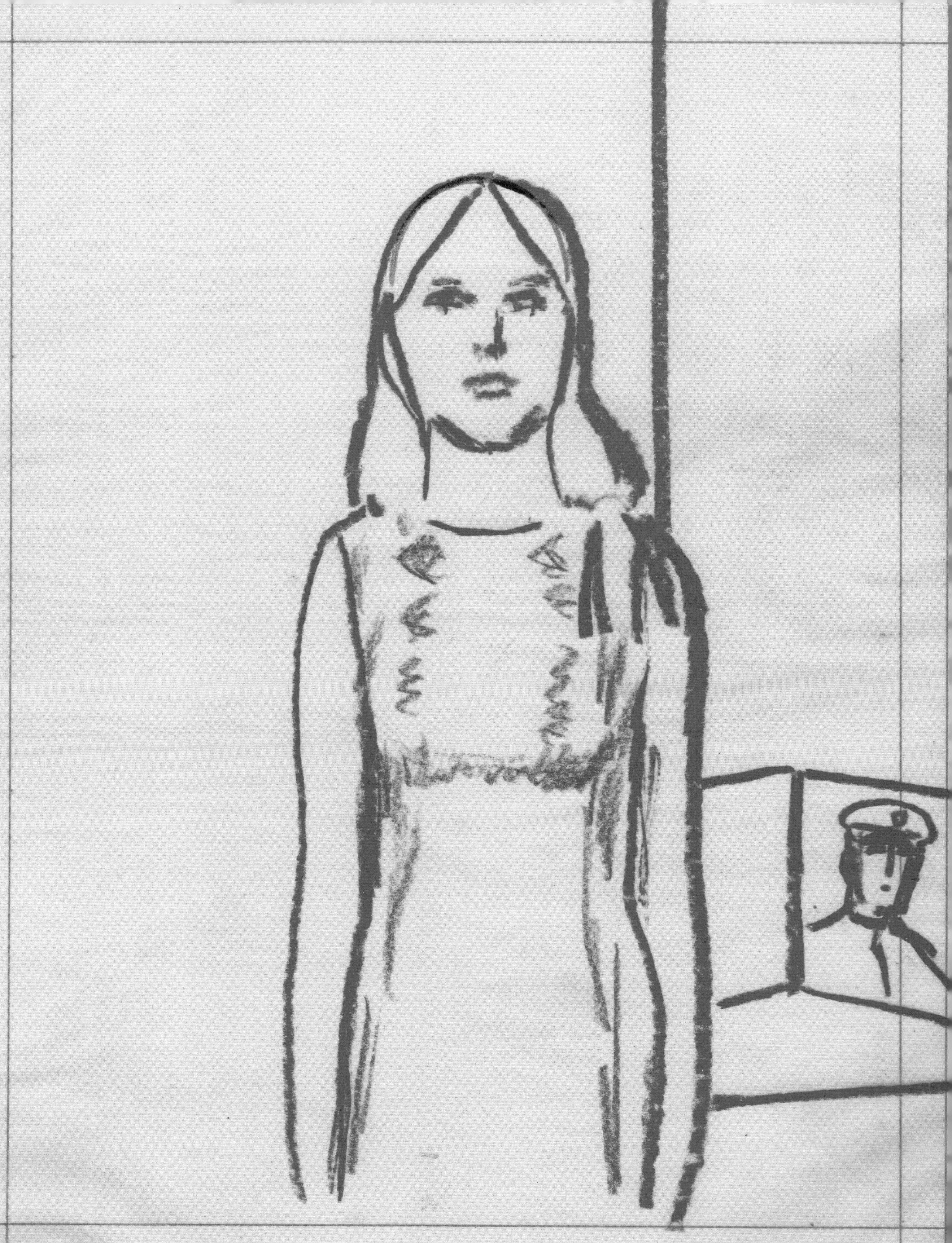

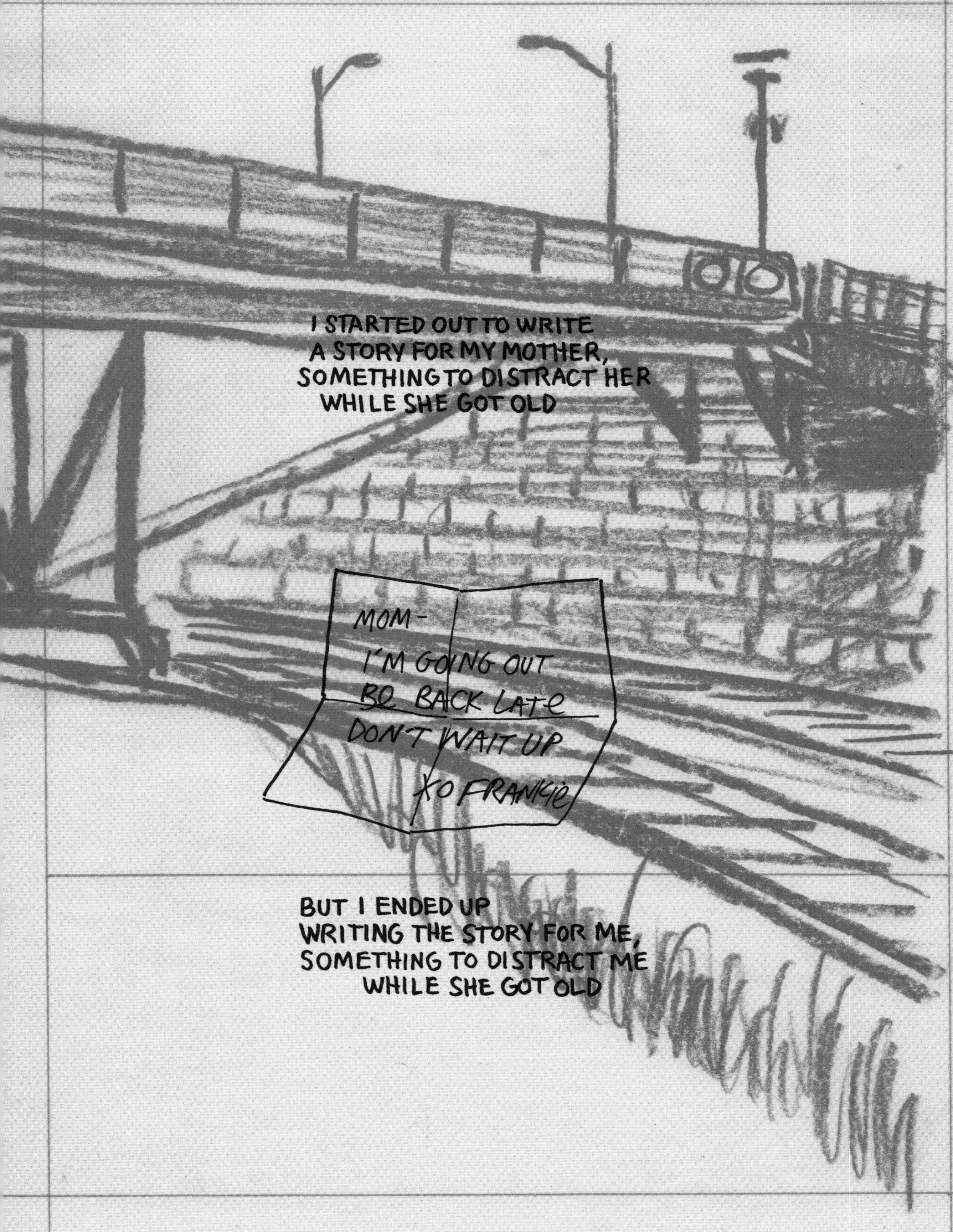
I STARTED OUT TO WRITE A STORY FOR MY MOTHER, SOMETHING TO DISTRACT HER WHILE SHE GOT OLD
MOM- I'M GOING OUT BE BACK LATE DON'T WAIT UP XO FRANKIE
BUT I ENDED UP WRITING THE STORY FOR ME, SOMETHING TO DISTRACT ME WHILE SHE GOT OLD

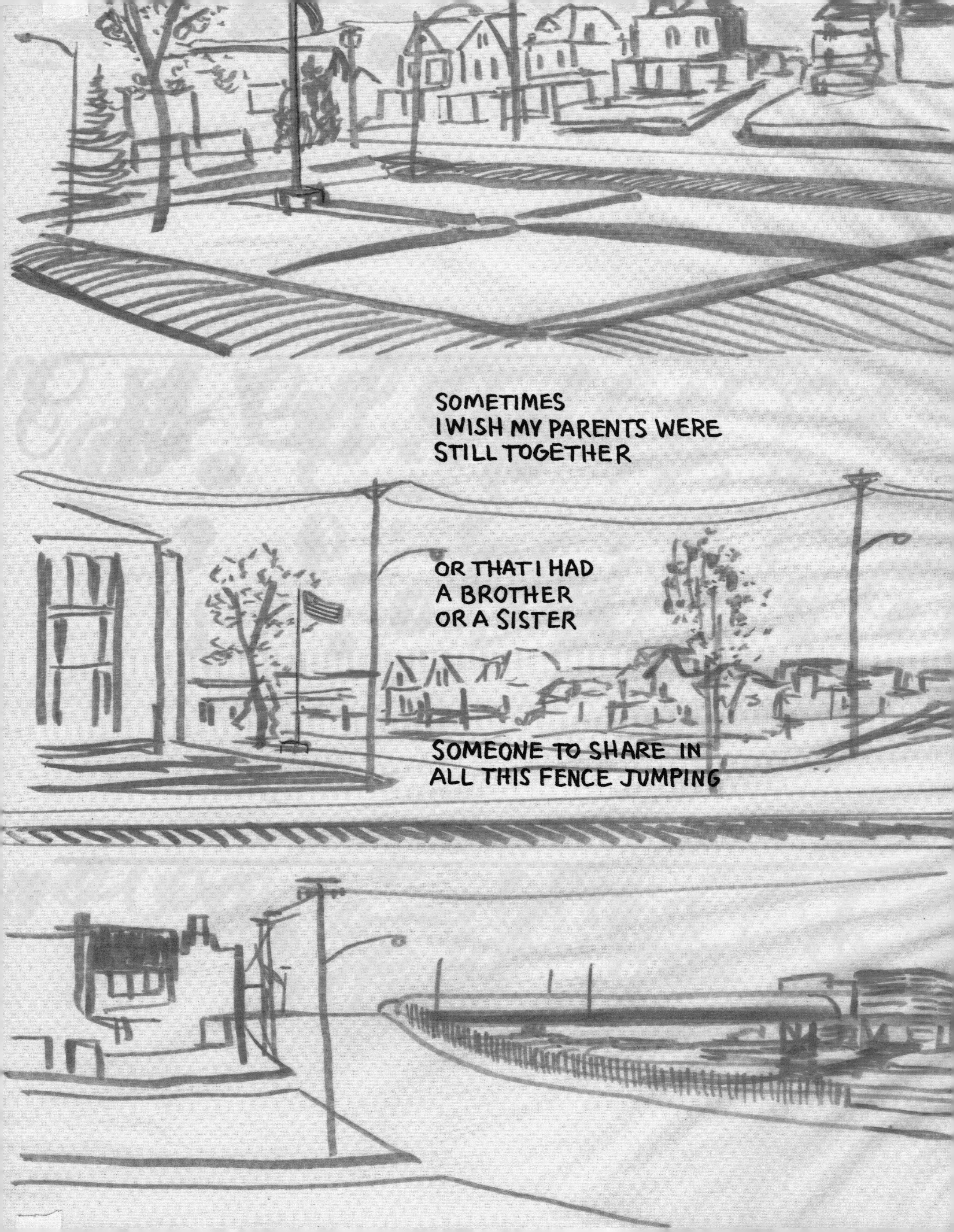
SOMETIMES
I WISH MY PARENTS WERE
STILL TOGETHER
OR THAT I HAD
A BROTHER
OR A SISTER
SOMEONE TO SHARE IN
ALL THIS FENCE JUMPING

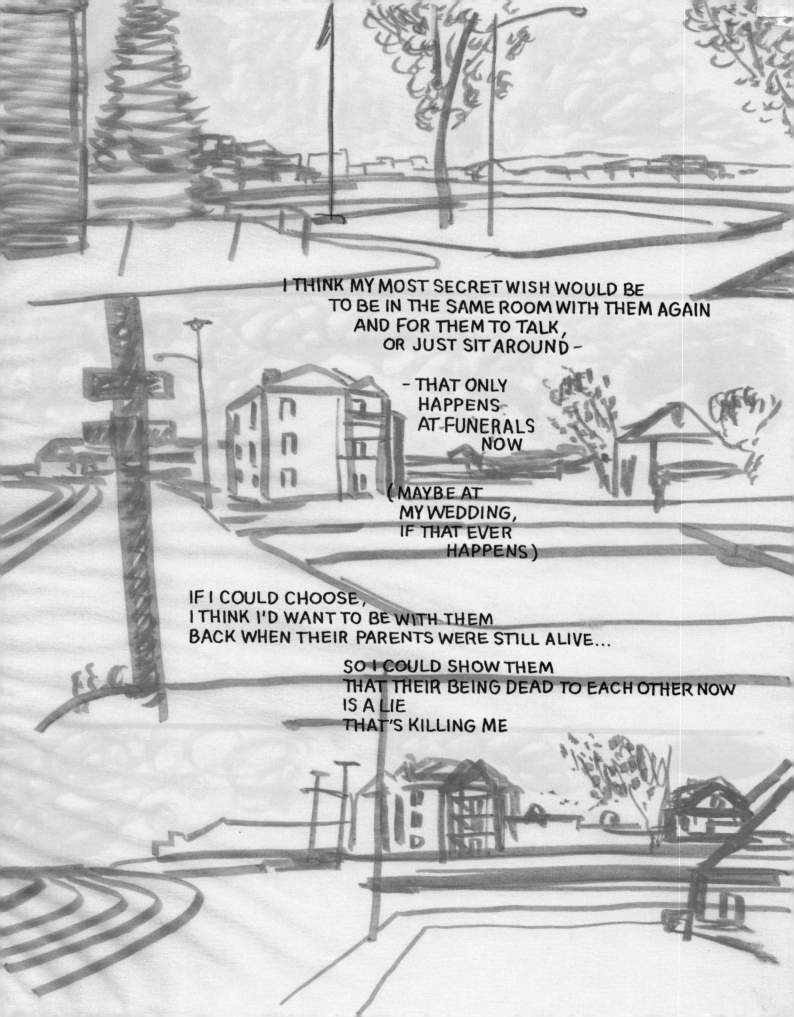

I THINK MY MOST SECRET WISH WOULD BE
TO BE IN THE SAME ROOM WITH THEM AGAIN
AND FOR THEM TO TALK,
OR JUST SIT AROUND —

— THAT ONLY
HAPPENS
AT FUNERALS
NOW

(MAYBE AT
MY WEDDING,
IF THAT EVER
HAPPENS)

IF I COULD CHOOSE,
I THINK I'D WANT TO BE WITH THEM
BACK WHEN THEIR PARENTS WERE STILL ALIVE...

SO I COULD SHOW THEM
THAT THEIR BEING DEAD TO EACH OTHER NOW
IS A LIE
THAT'S KILLING ME

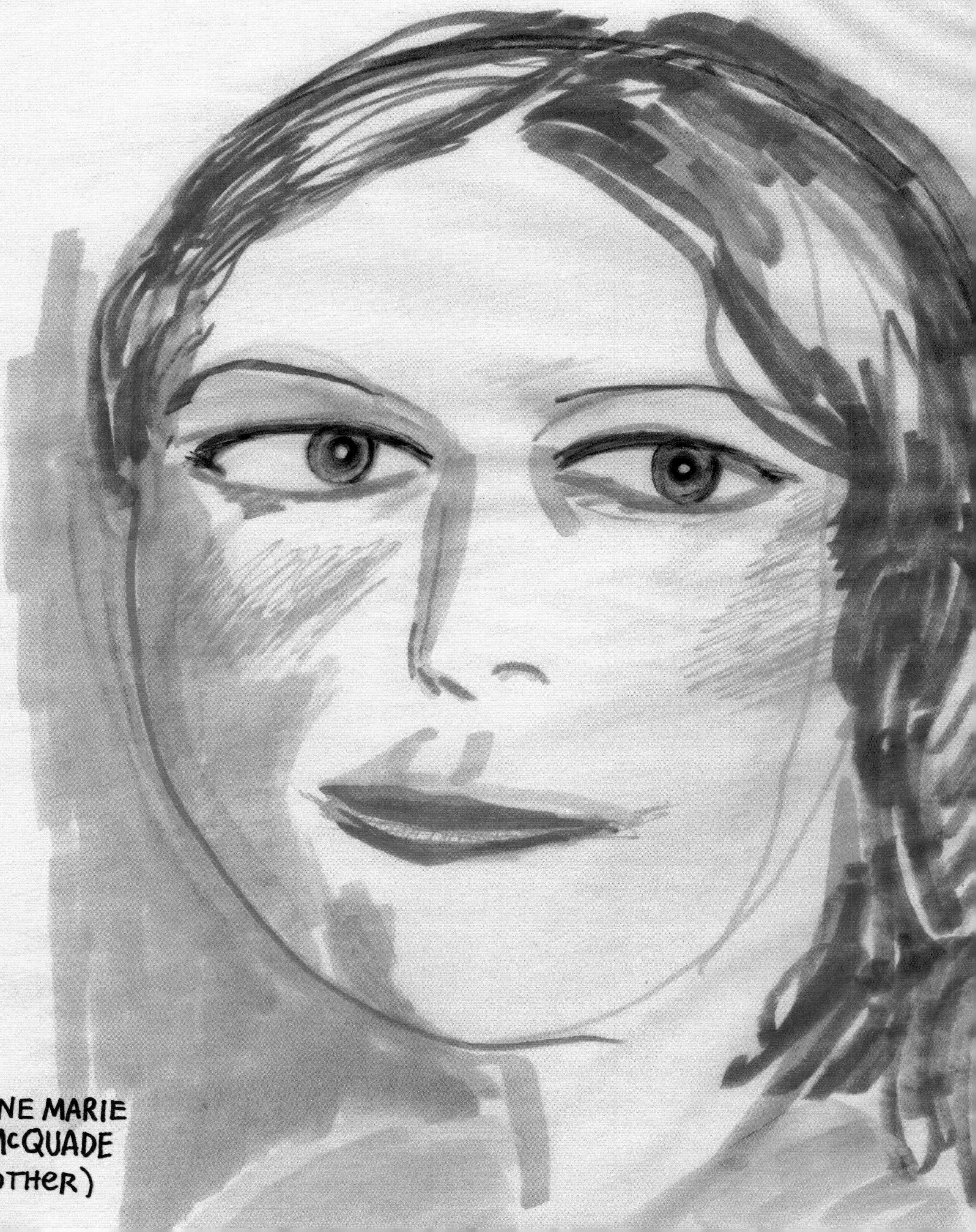

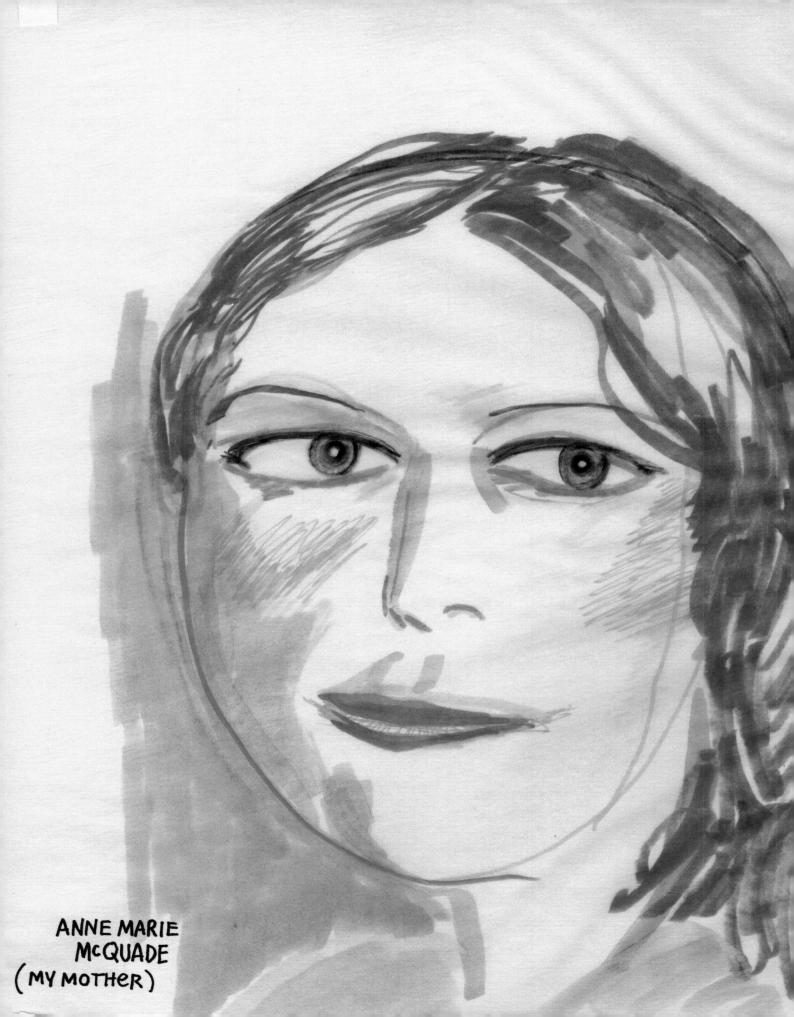

ANNE MARIE
McQUADE
(MY MOTHER)

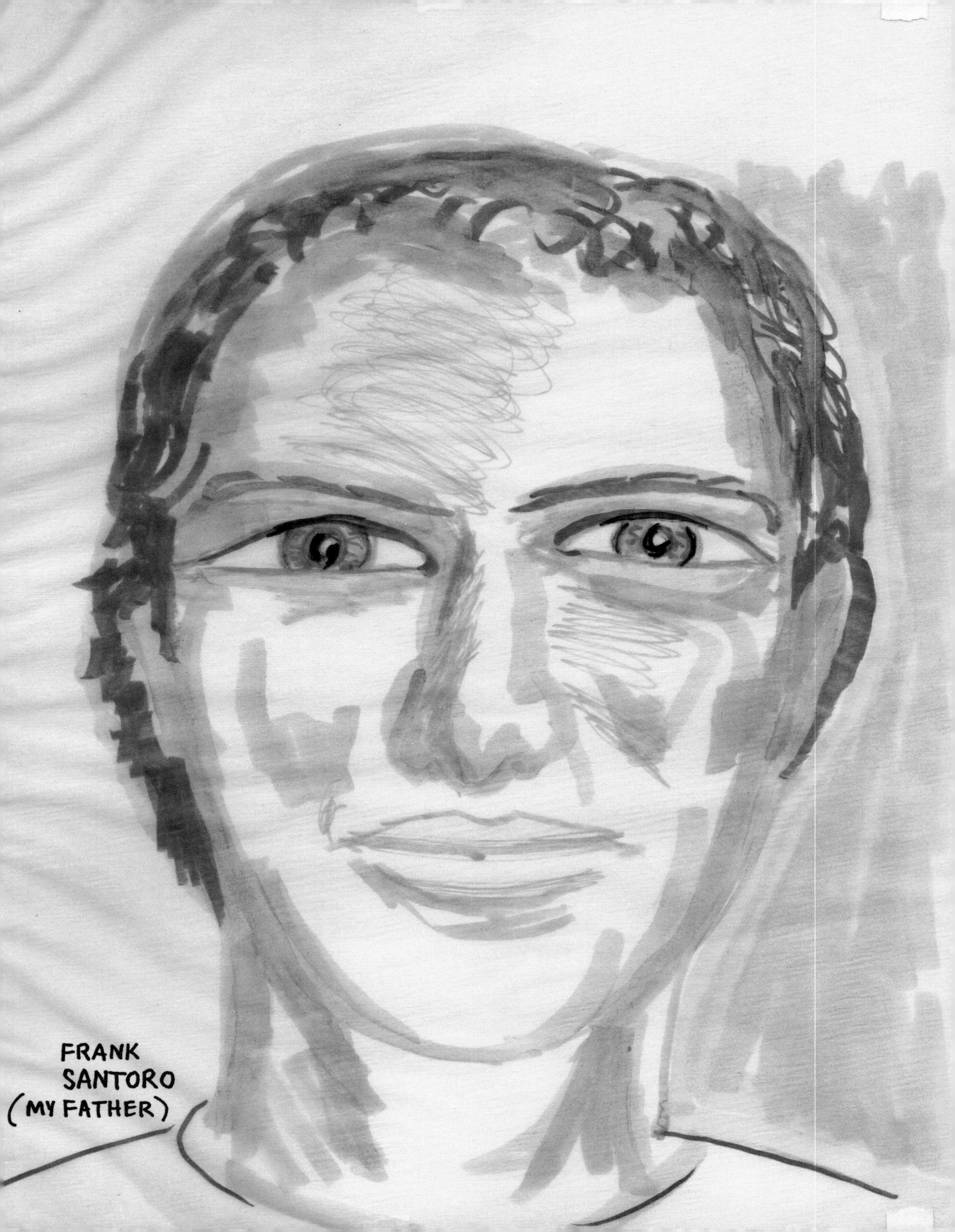
FRANK
SANTORO
(MY FATHER)

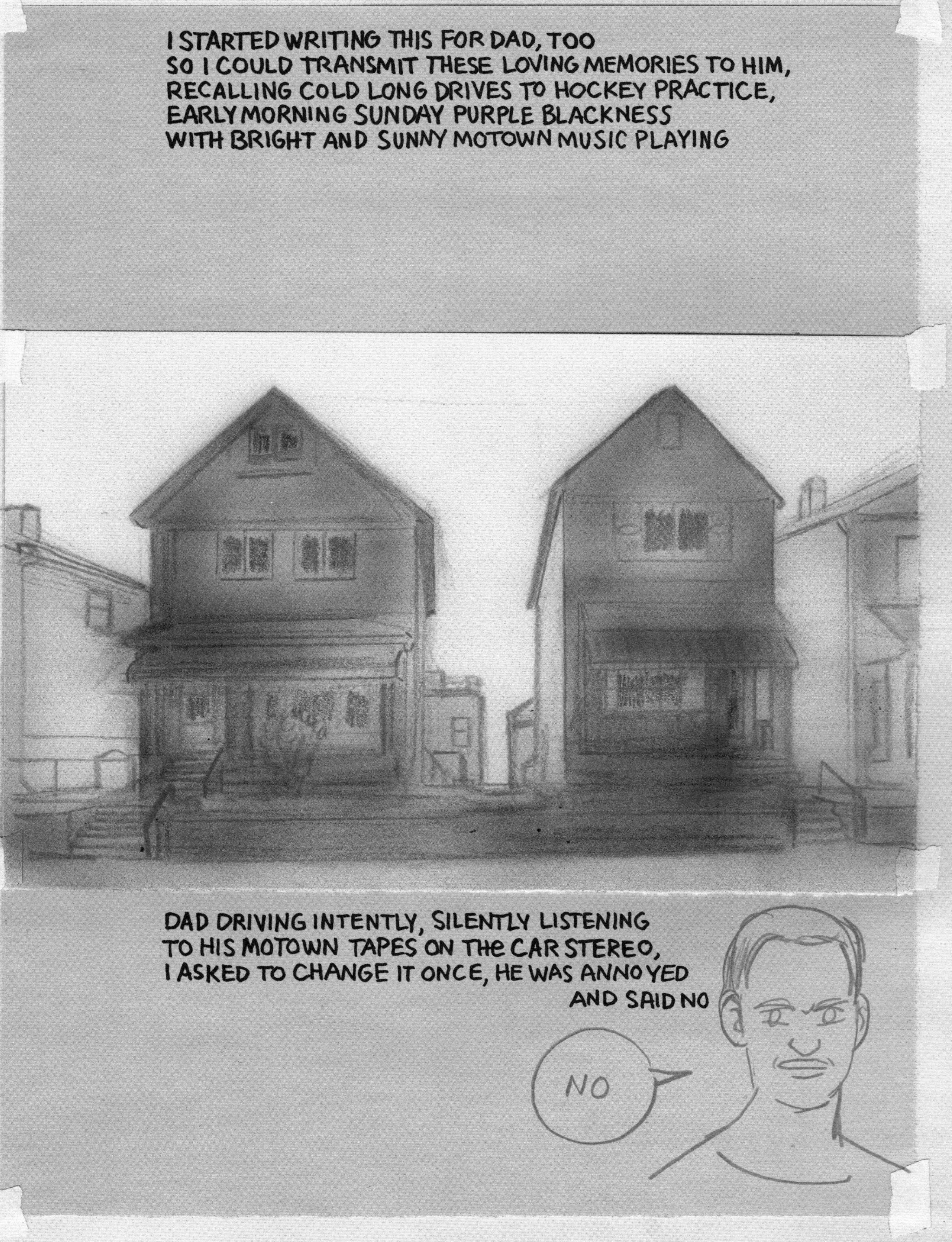
I STARTED WRITING THIS FOR DAD, TOO
SO I COULD TRANSMIT THESE LOVING MEMORIES TO HIM,
RECALLING COLD LONG DRIVES TO HOCKEY PRACTICE,
EARLY MORNING SUNDAY PURPLE BLACKNESS
WITH BRIGHT AND SUNNY MOTOWN MUSIC PLAYING
DAD DRIVING INTENTLY, SILENTLY LISTENING
TO HIS MOTOWN TAPES ON THE CAR STEREO,
I ASKED TO CHANGE IT ONCE, HE WAS ANNOYED
AND SAID NO
NO

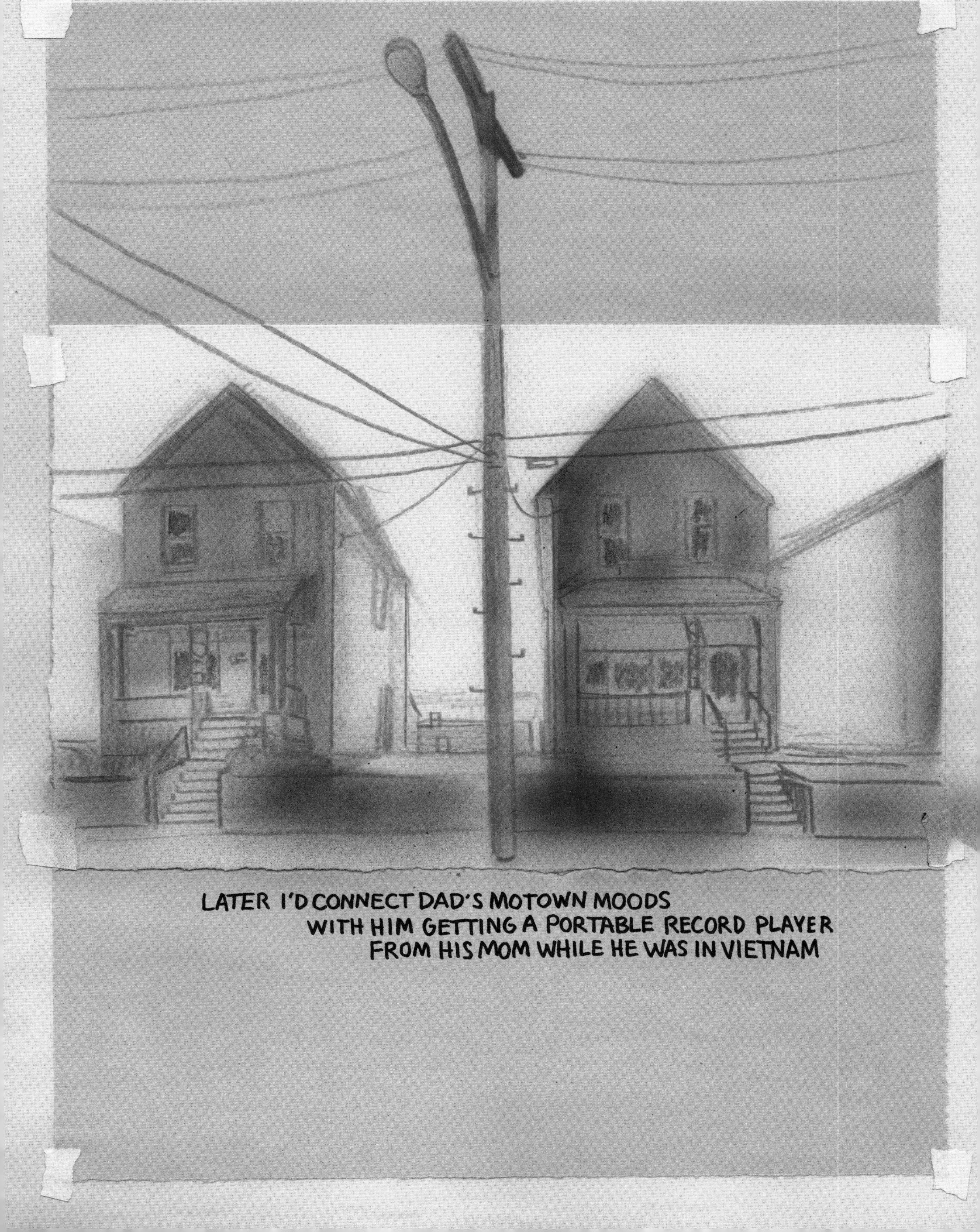

LATER I'D CONNECT DAD'S MOTOWN MOODS
WITH HIM GETTING A PORTABLE RECORD PLAYER
FROM HIS MOM WHILE HE WAS IN VIETNAM

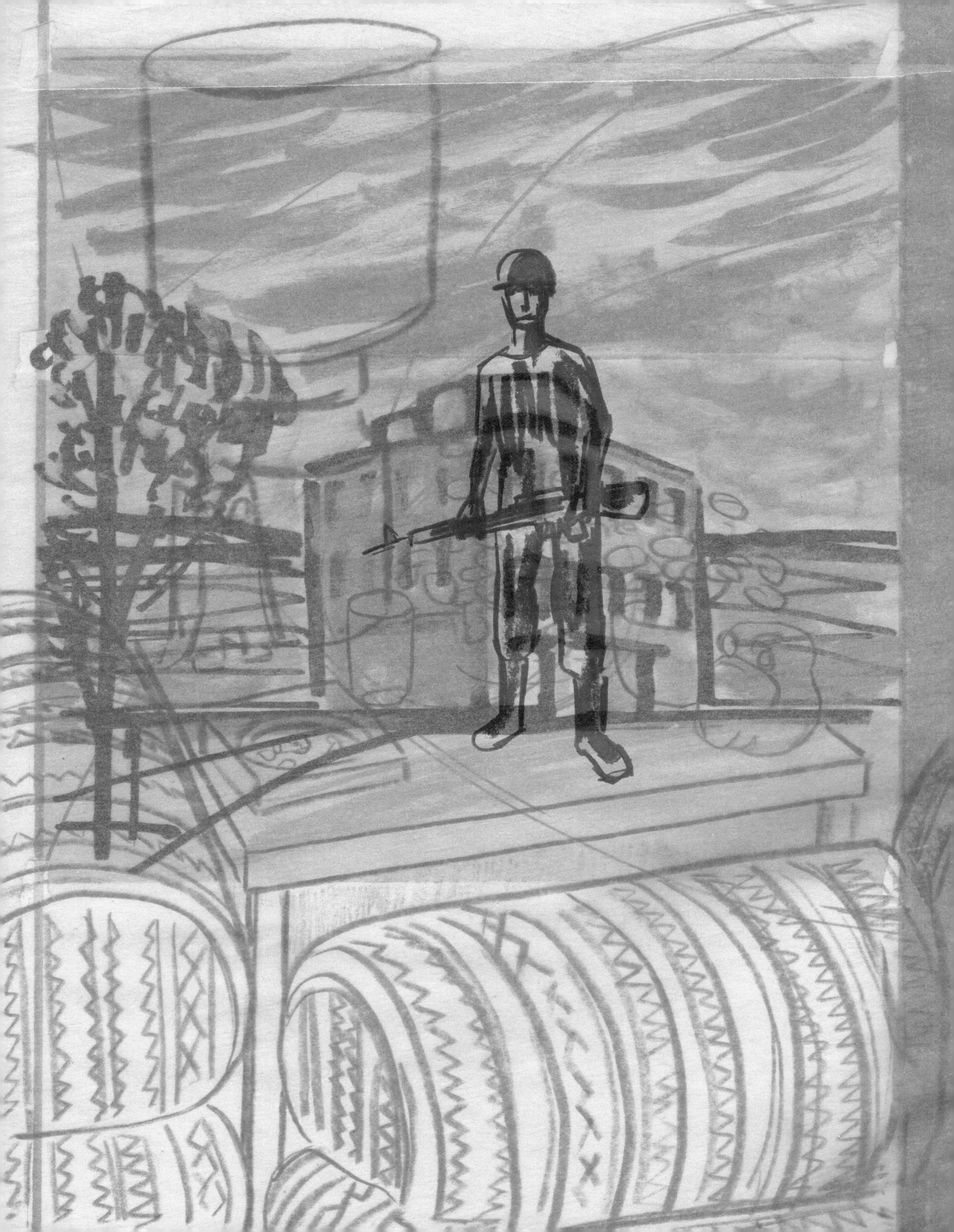

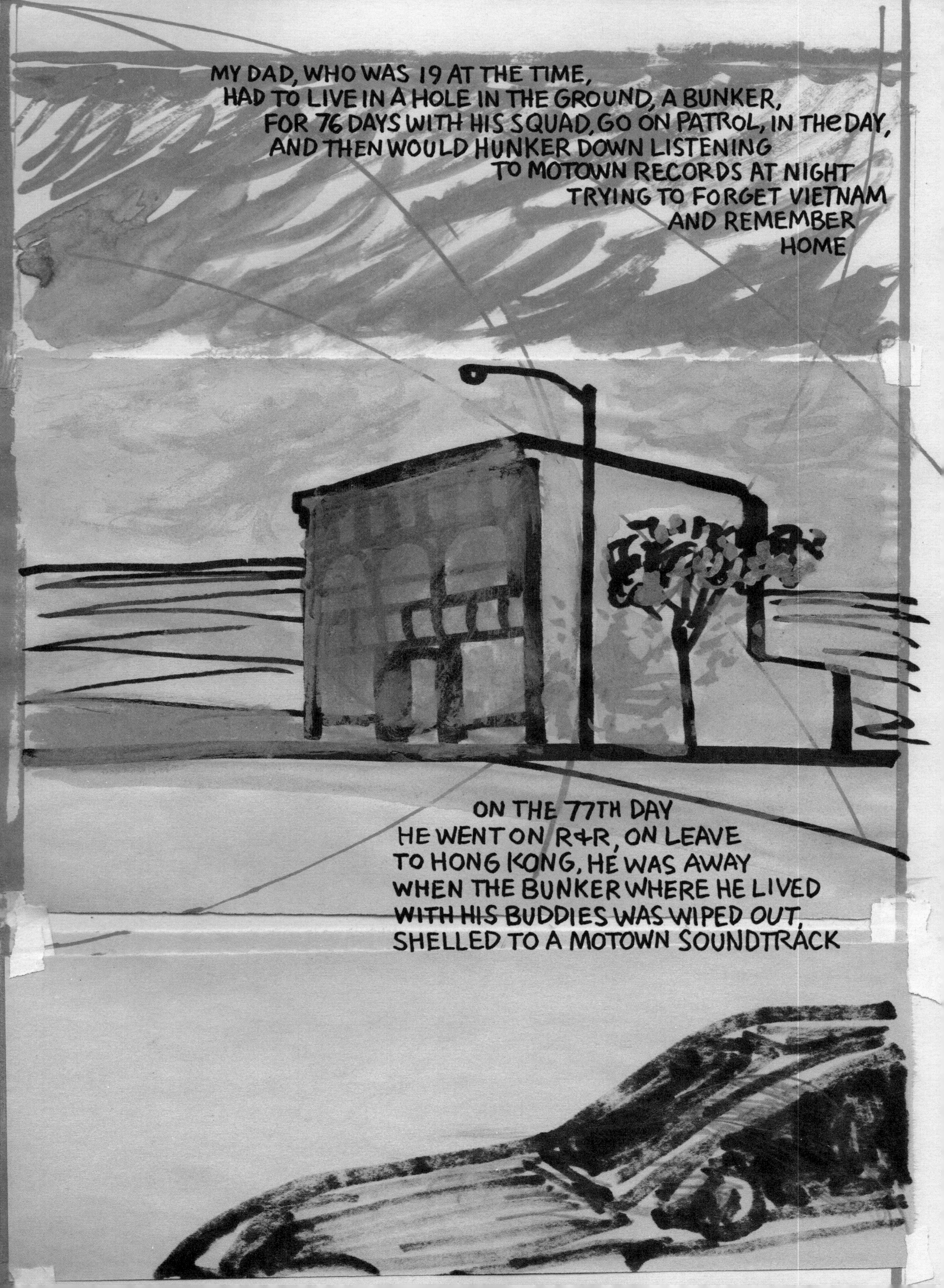
MY DAD, WHO WAS 19 AT THE TIME, HAD TO LIVE IN A HOLE IN THE GROUND, A BUNKER, FOR 76 DAYS WITH HIS SQUAD, GO ON PATROL, IN THE DAY, AND THEN WOULD HUNKER DOWN LISTENING TO MOTOWN RECORDS AT NIGHT TRYING TO FORGET VIETNAM AND REMEMBER HOME
ON THE 77TH DAY HE WENT ON R&R, ON LEAVE TO HONG KONG, HE WAS AWAY WHEN THE BUNKER WHERE HE LIVED WITH HIS BUDDIES WAS WIPED OUT, SHELLED TO A MOTOWN SOUNDTRACK

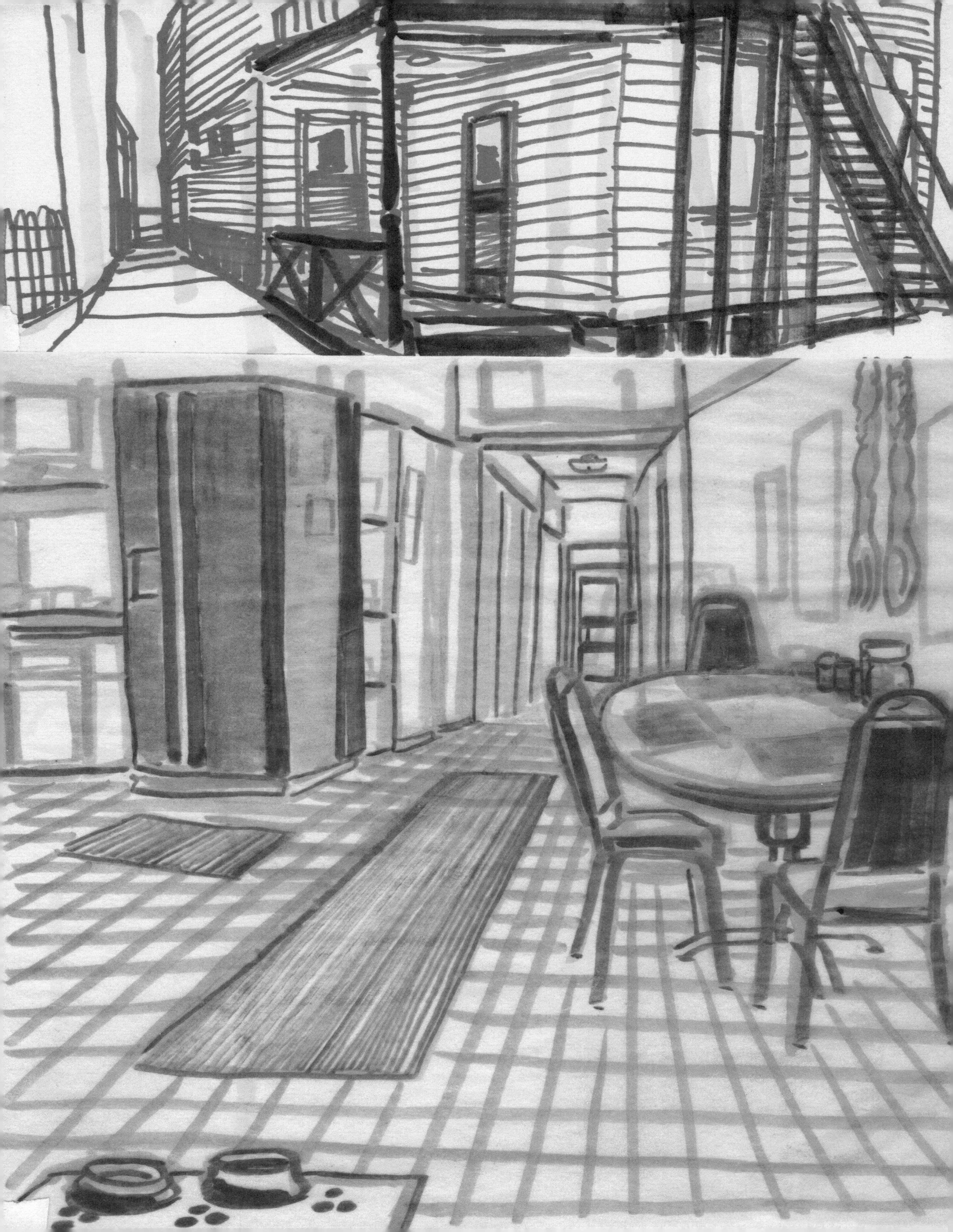

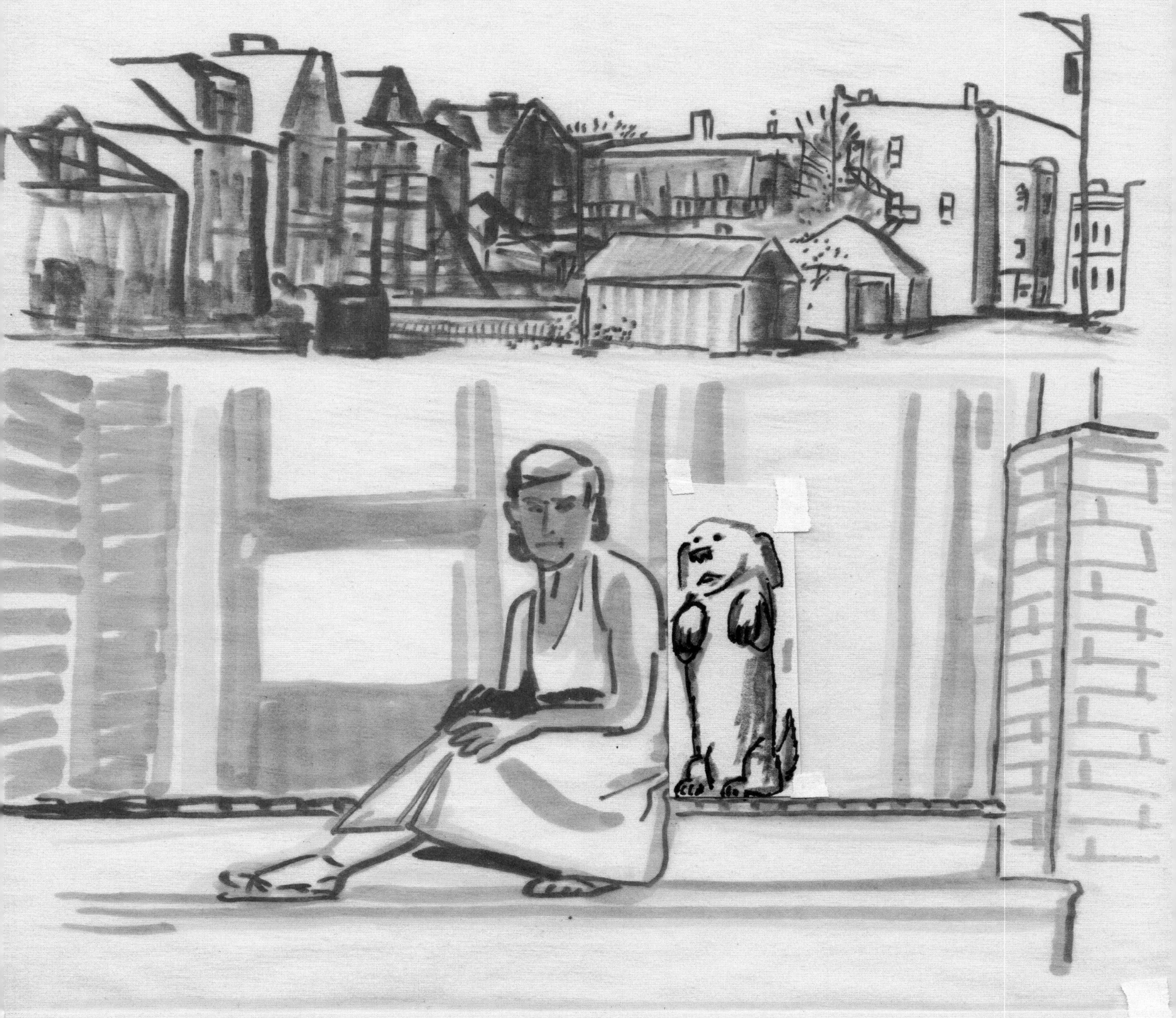

♫ All the Things You Are ♪♫

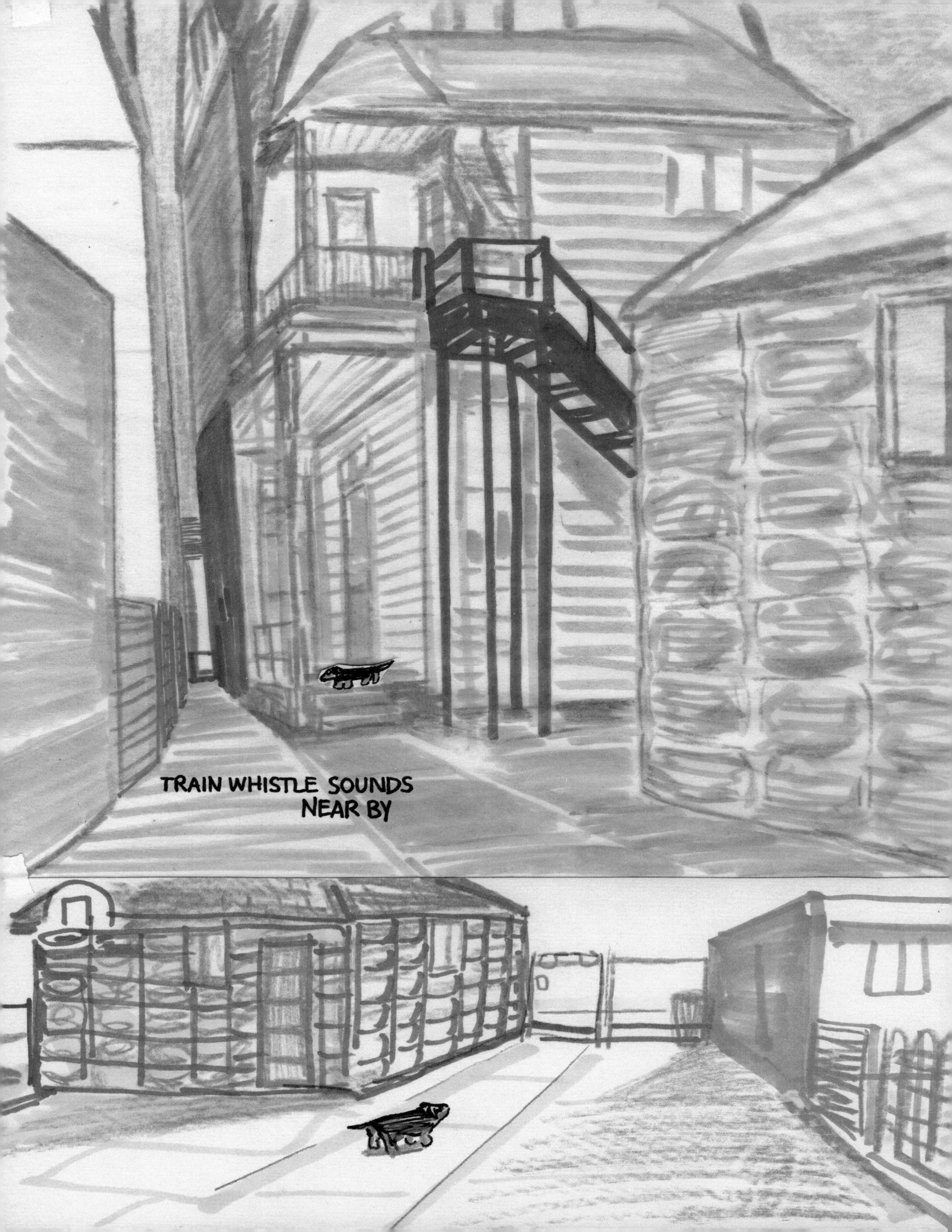
TRAIN WHISTLE SOUNDS
NEAR BY

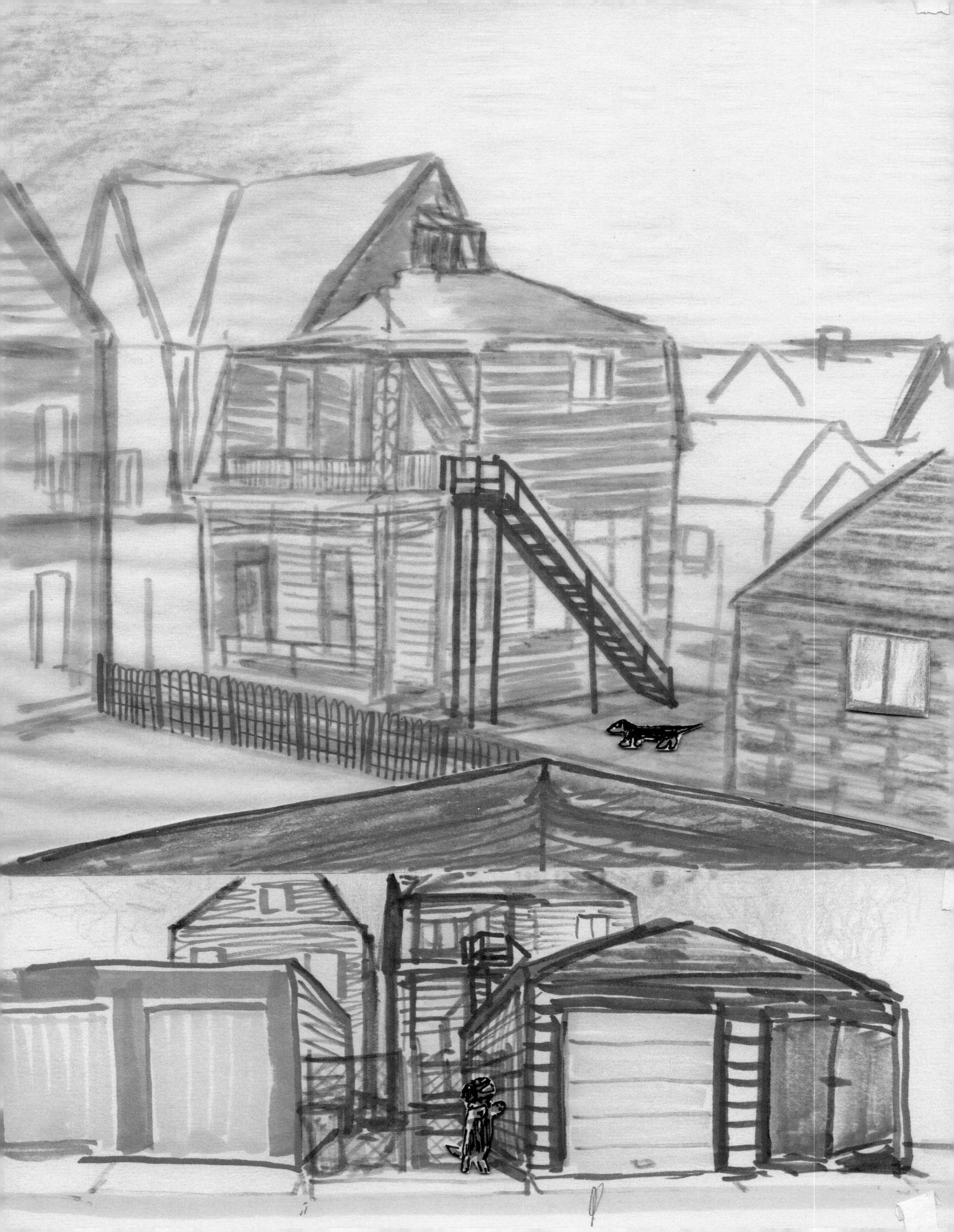

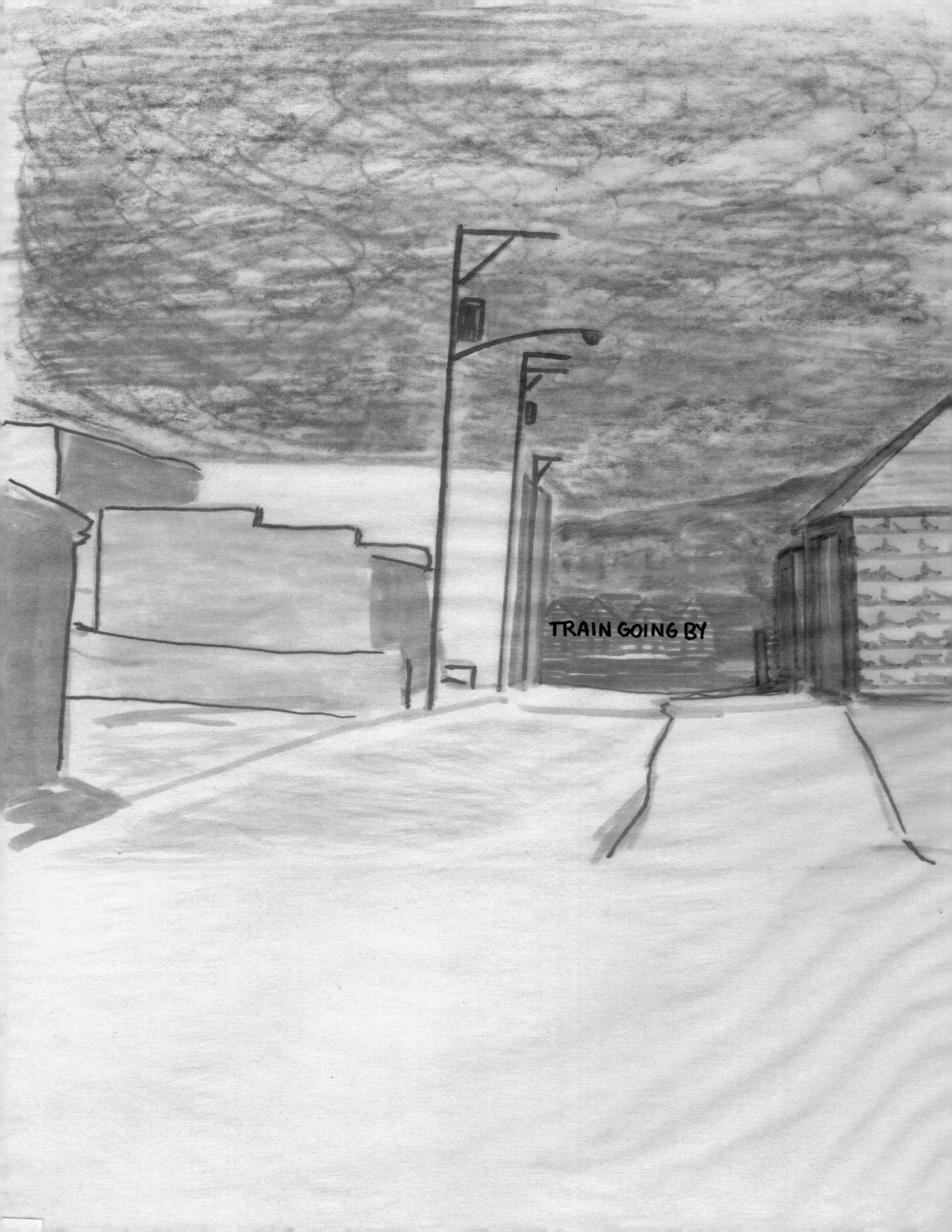
TRAIN GOING BY

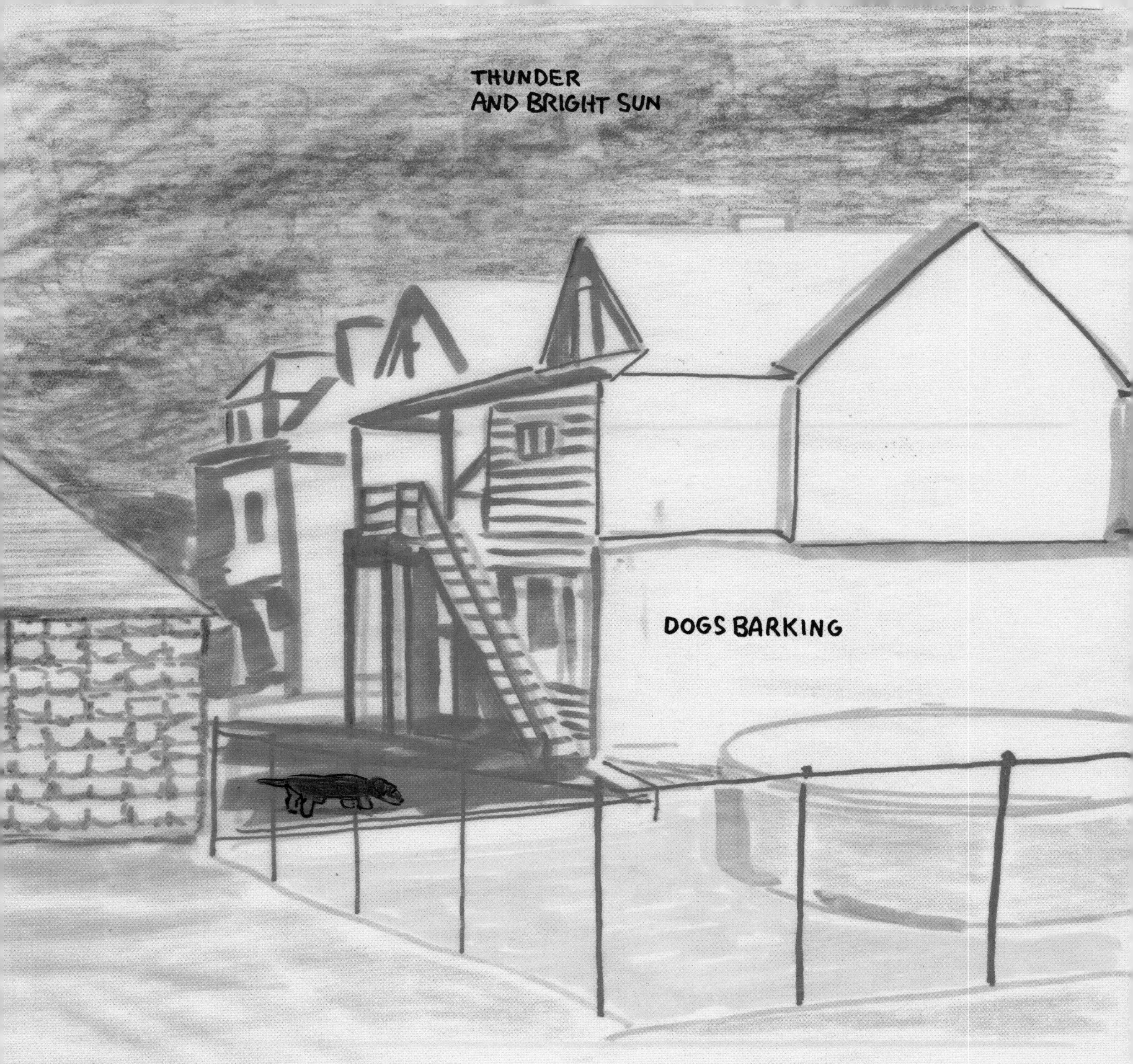
THUNDER
AND BRIGHT SUN
DOGS BARKING

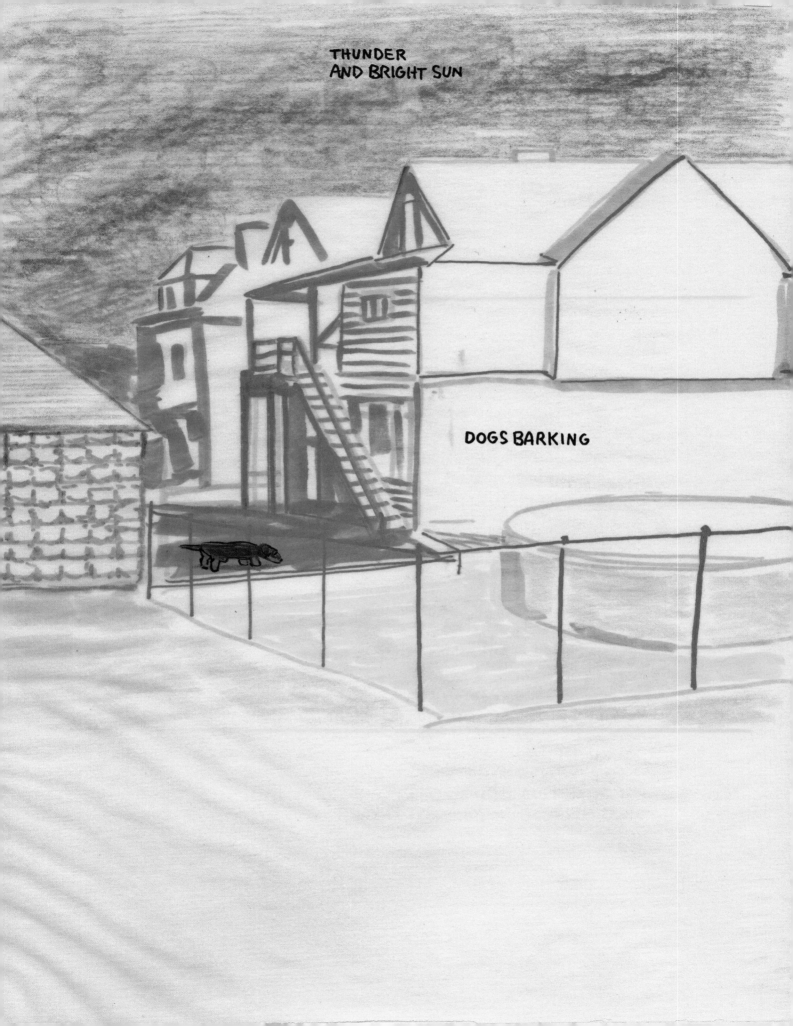

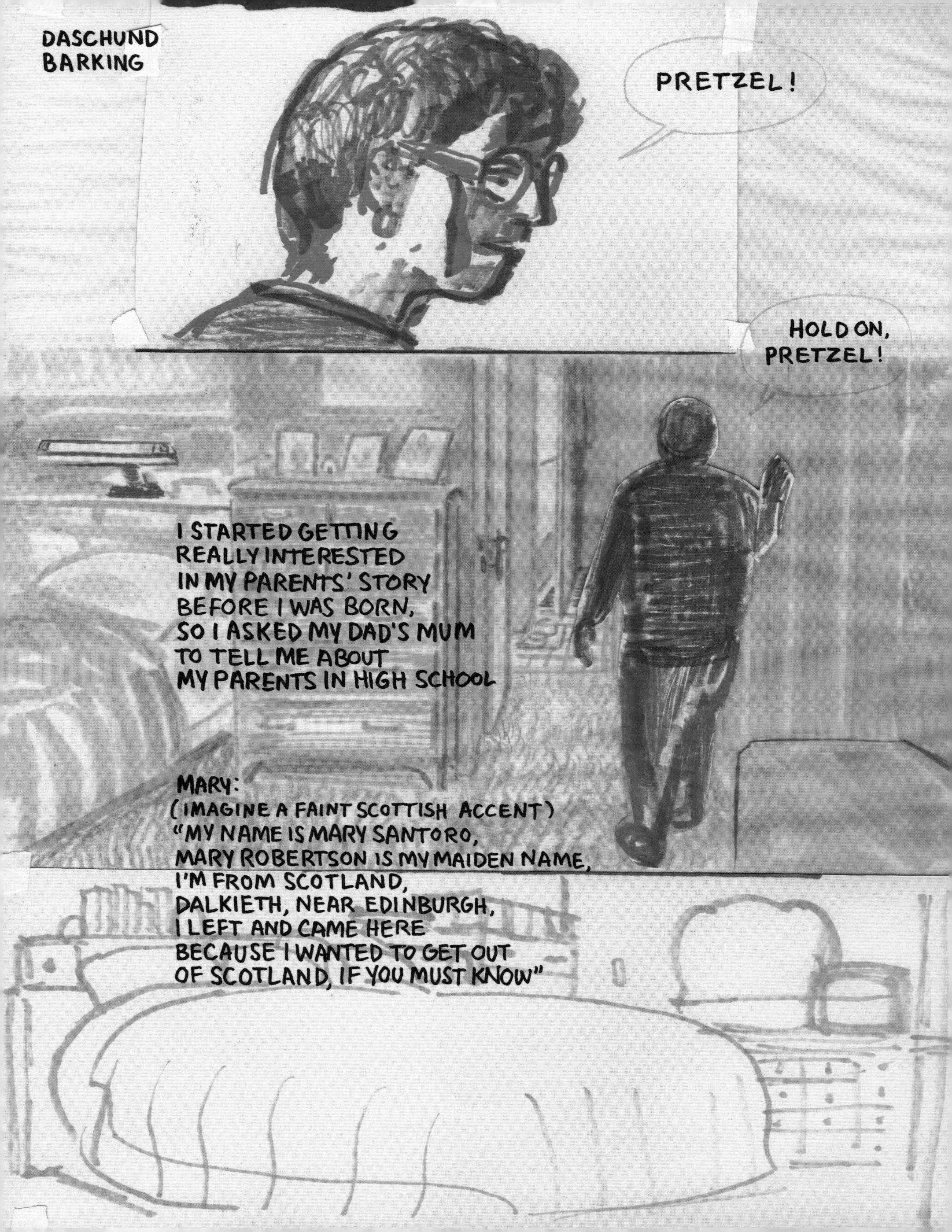
DASCHUND BARKING
PRETZEL!
HOLD ON, PRETZEL!
I STARTED GETTING REALLY INTERESTED IN MY PARENTS' STORY BEFORE I WAS BORN, SO I ASKED MY DAD'S MUM TO TELL ME ABOUT MY PARENTS IN HIGH SCHOOL
MARY:
(IMAGINE A FAINT SCOTTISH ACCENT)
"MY NAME IS MARY SANTORO, MARY ROBERTSON IS MY MAIDEN NAME, I'M FROM SCOTLAND, DALKIETH, NEAR EDINBURGH, I LEFT AND CAME HERE BECAUSE I WANTED TO GET OUT OF SCOTLAND, IF YOU MUST KNOW"

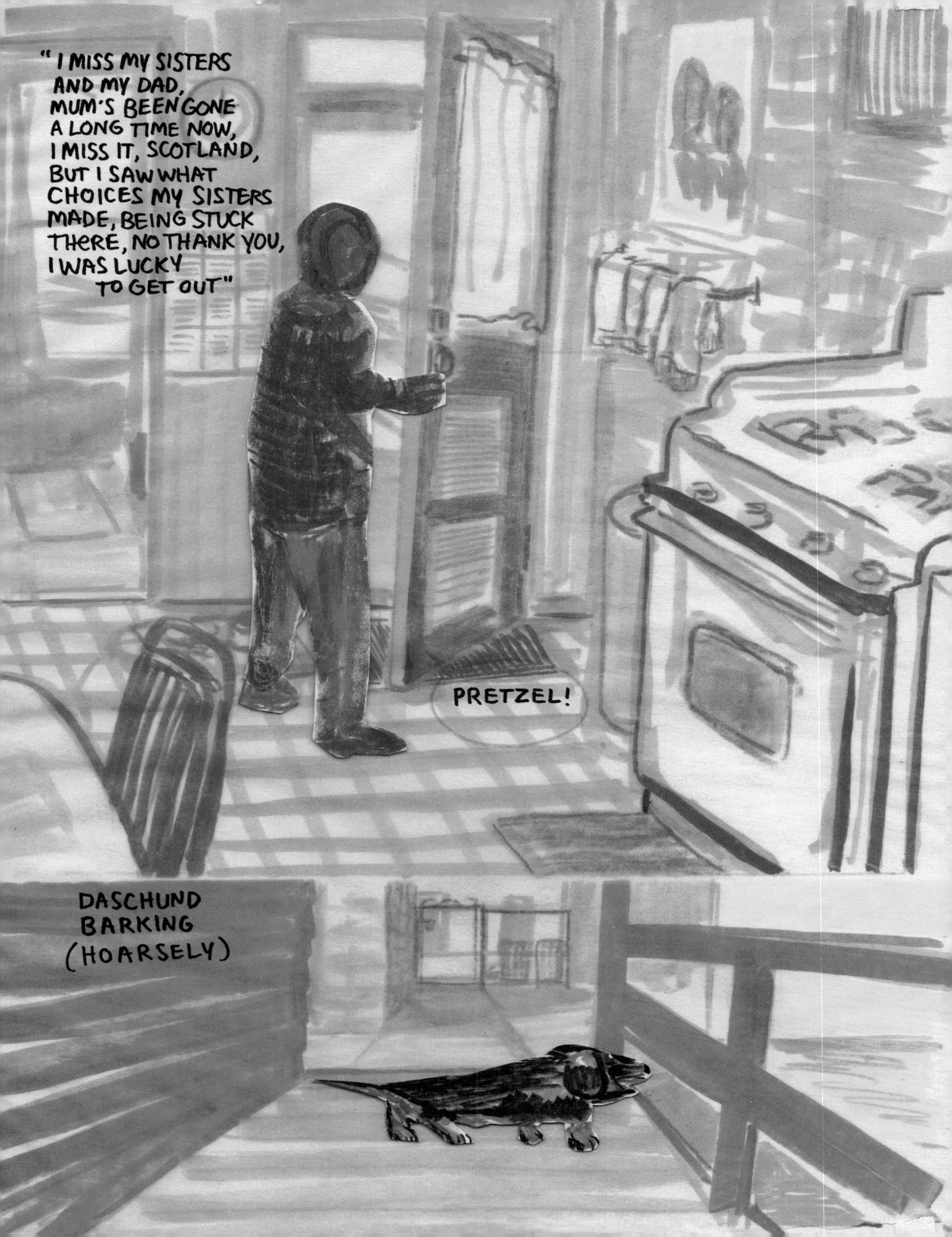
"I MISS MY SISTERS AND MY DAD, MUM'S BEEN GONE A LONG TIME NOW, I MISS IT, SCOTLAND, BUT I SAW WHAT CHOICES MY SISTERS MADE, BEING STUCK THERE, NO THANK YOU, I WAS LUCKY TO GET OUT"
PRETZEL!
DASCHUND BARKING (HOARSELY)

EARLY MORNING
BRIGHTSUN

" I WAS LUCKY BECAUSE IT
WAS THE WAR AND I MET SAM
AT A SOCIAL DANCE,
HE WAS AN AMERICAN SERVICEMAN
AND A DUMB DAGO, HAHAHA, AND SO
HERE I AM, HONESTLY JUNIOR,
WHAT DO YOU WANT ME TO SAY?
MY FATHER HAD TO MARRY US OFF
AND SOMEHOW HE LIKED SAM "

(TO ESCAPE THE AIR RAIDS
OF LONDON
MANY AMERICAN SOLDIERS
WERE STATIONED
IN SCOTLAND
DURING WORLD WAR TWO)

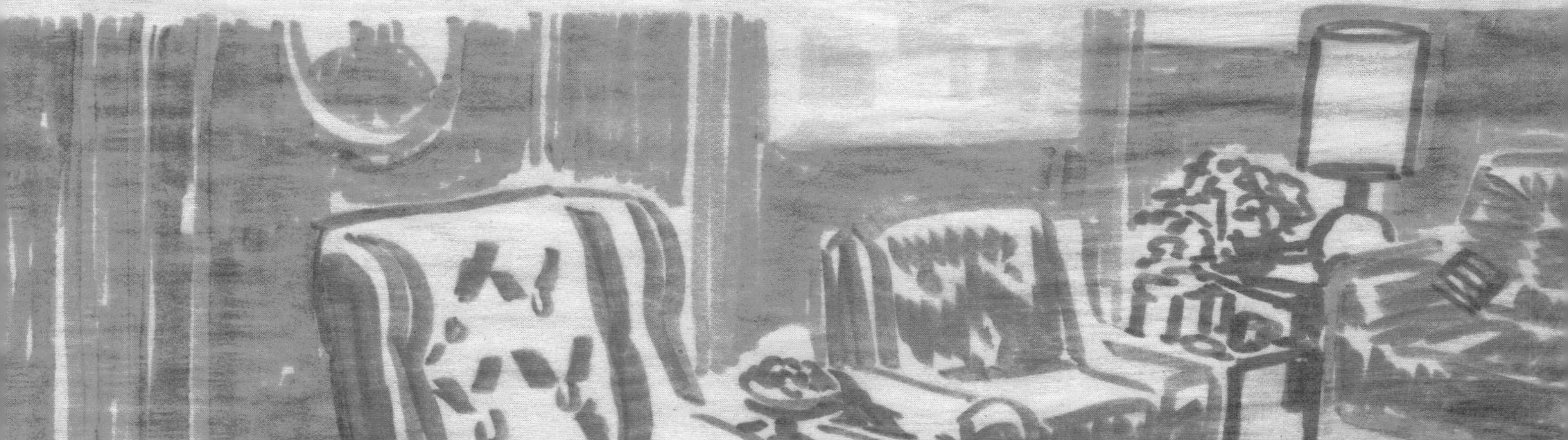

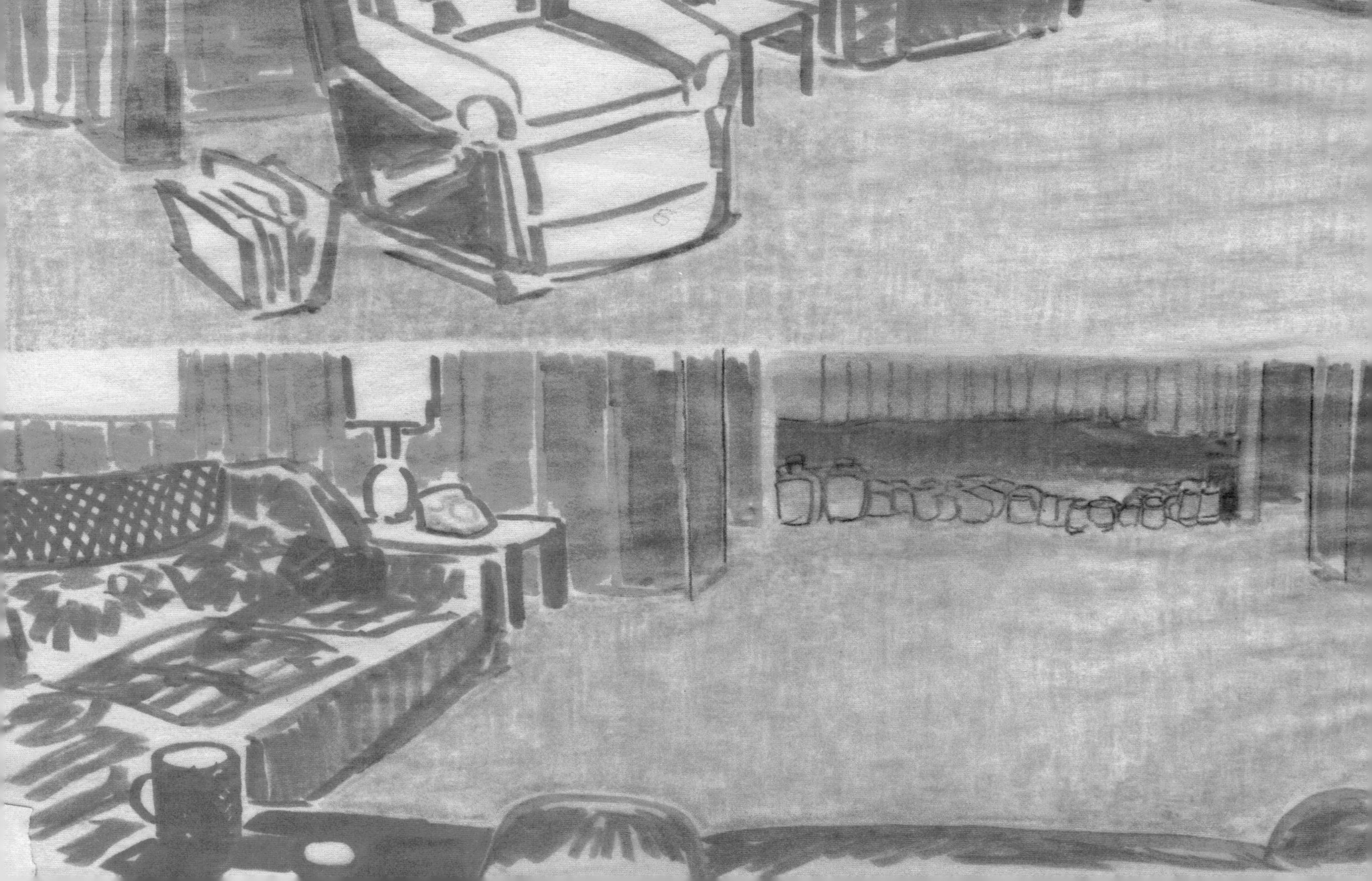

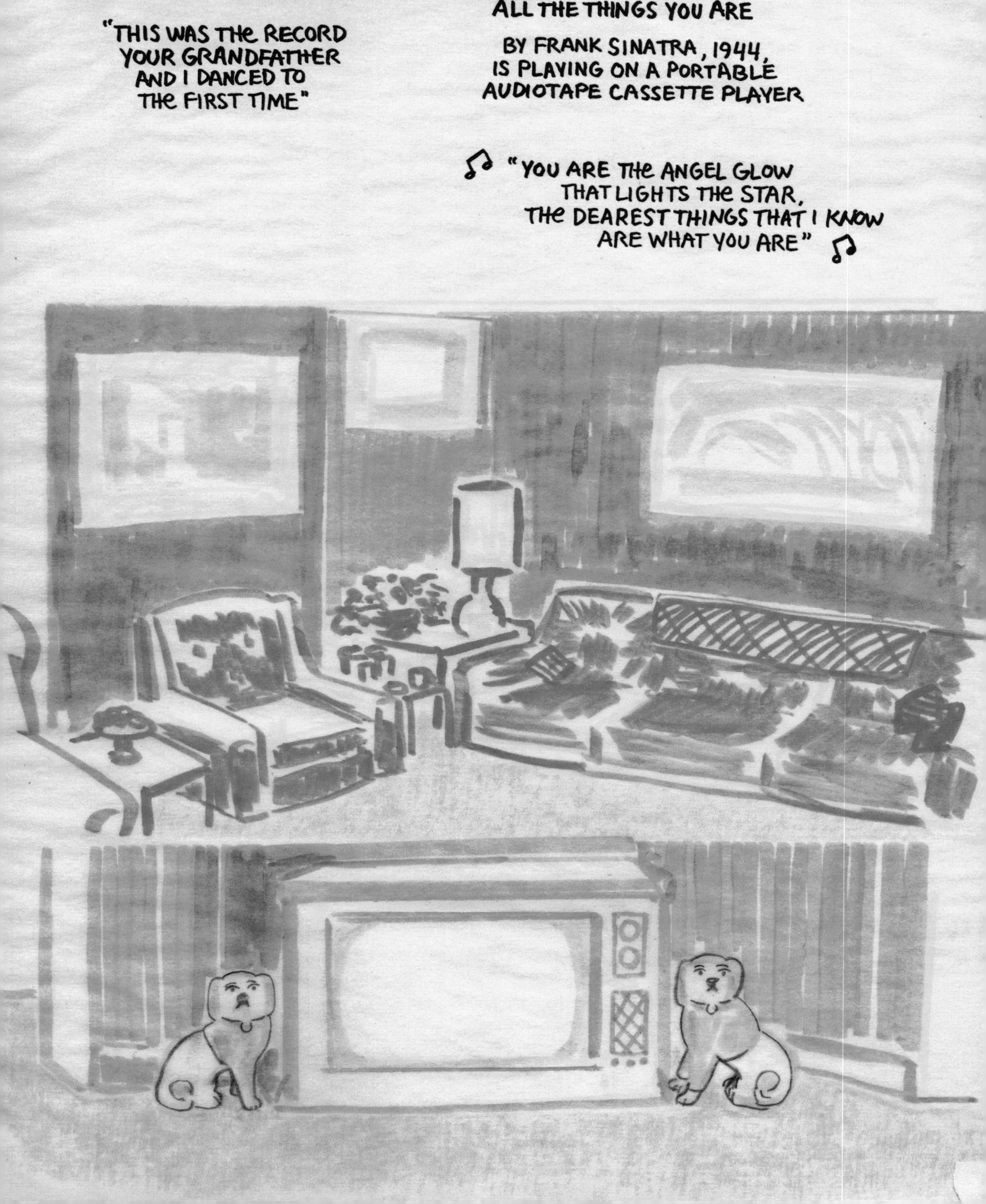
"THIS WAS THE RECORD YOUR GRANDFATHER AND I DANCED TO THE FIRST TIME"
ALL THE THINGS YOU ARE
BY FRANK SINATRA, 1944, IS PLAYING ON A PORTABLE AUDIOTAPE CASSETTE PLAYER
"YOU ARE THE ANGEL GLOW THAT LIGHTS THE STAR, THE DEAREST THINGS THAT I KNOW ARE WHAT YOU ARE"

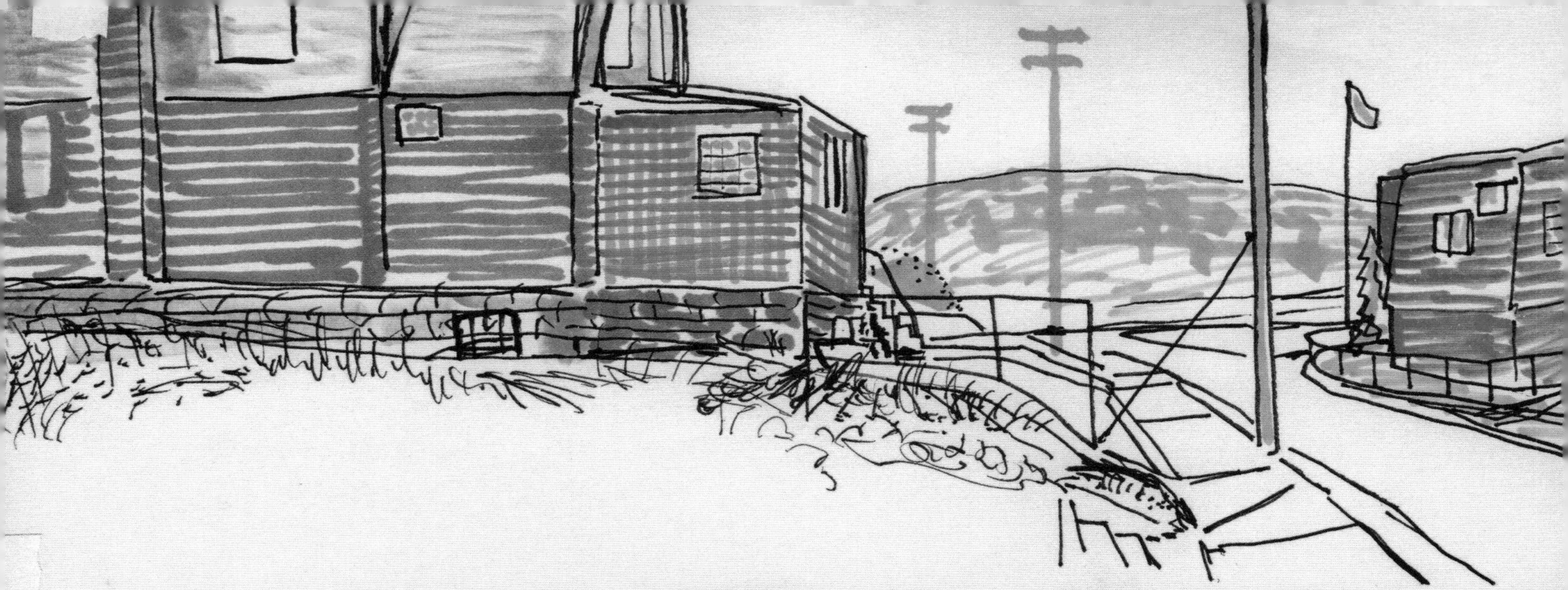

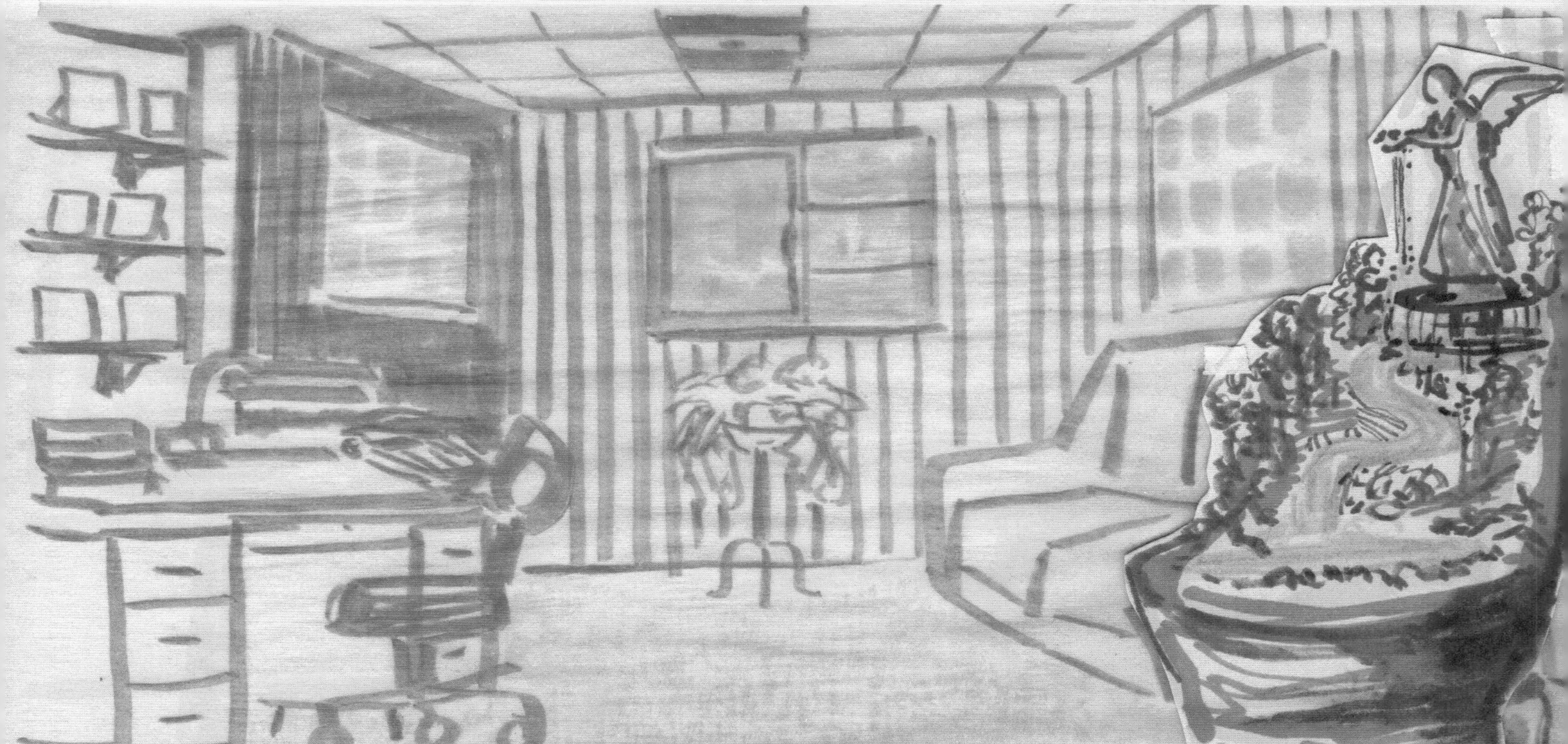

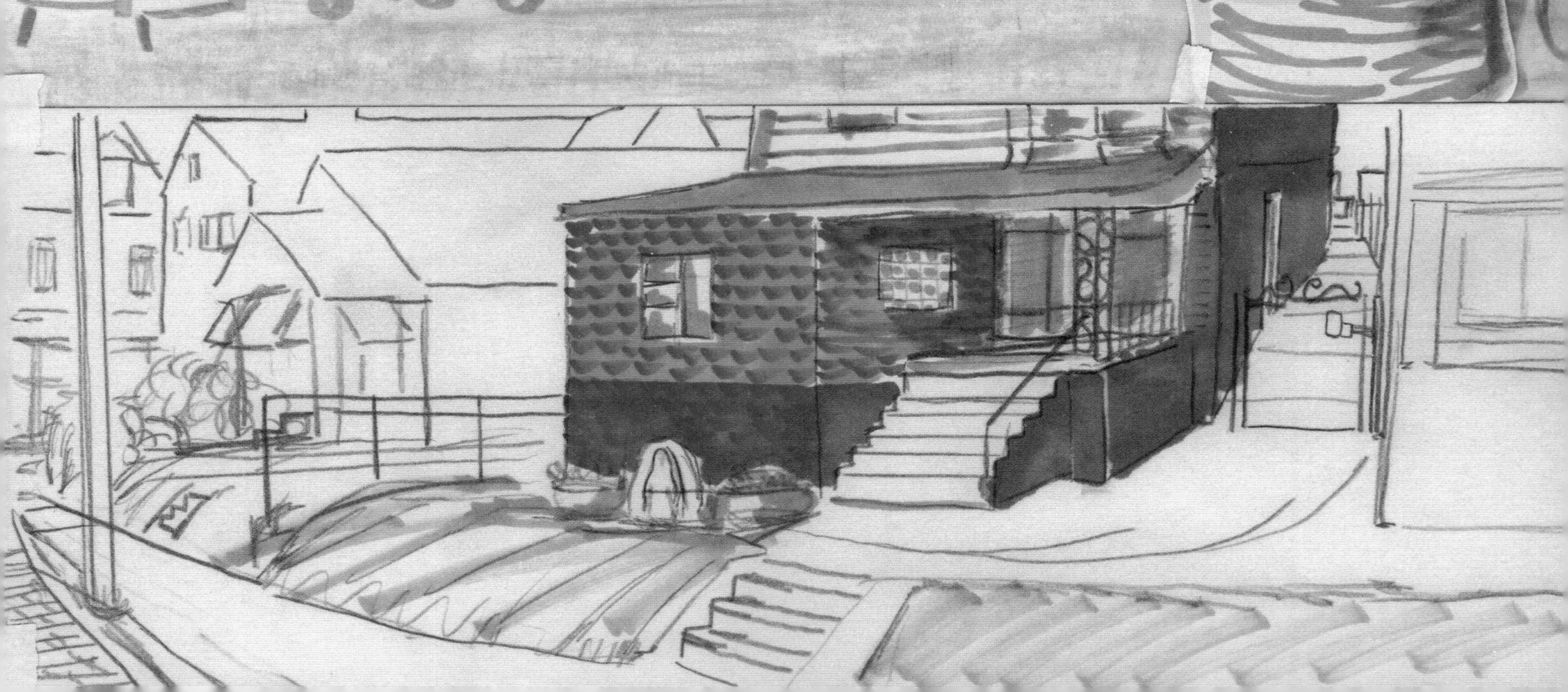

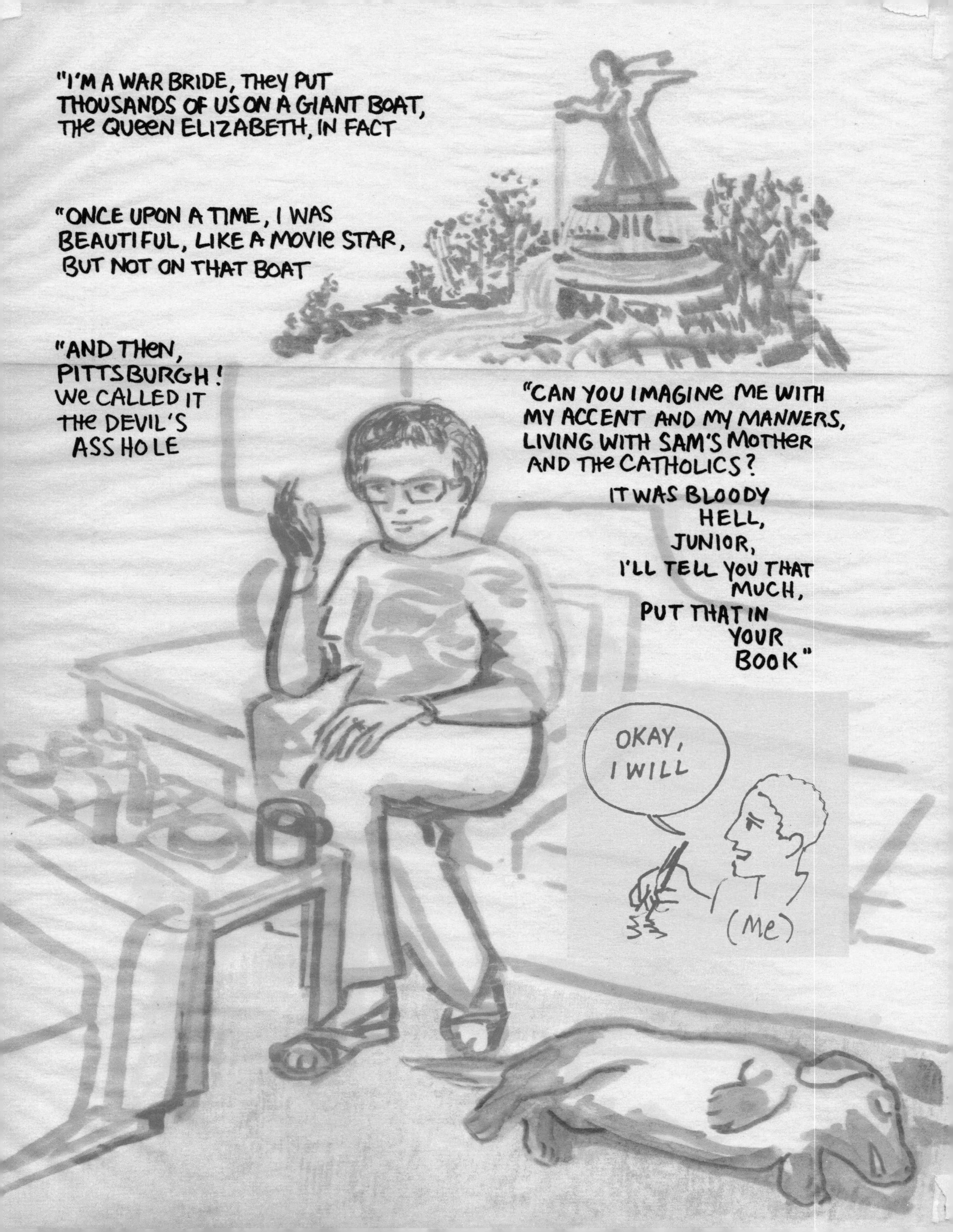
"I'M A WAR BRIDE, THEY PUT THOUSANDS OF US ON A GIANT BOAT, THE QUEEN ELIZABETH, IN FACT
"ONCE UPON A TIME, I WAS BEAUTIFUL, LIKE A MOVIE STAR, BUT NOT ON THAT BOAT
"AND THEN, PITTSBURGH! WE CALLED IT THE DEVIL'S ASSHOLE
"CAN YOU IMAGINE ME WITH MY ACCENT AND MY MANNERS, LIVING WITH SAM'S MOTHER AND THE CATHOLICS?
IT WAS BLOODY HELL, JUNIOR, I'LL TELL YOU THAT MUCH, PUT THAT IN YOUR BOOK"
OKAY, I WILL
(ME)

MARY:

"SAM'S MOTHER PICKED THE HOUSE, EVEN,
WE DIDN'T HAVE TO LIVE WITH HER ANYMORE,
THANK GOD, BUT SHE WAS STILL RIGHT
DOWN THE STREET

"THAT'S WHEN I STARTED WORKING
FOR THE BOROUGH AS A TRAFFIC COP
OVER BY THE SWITCH & SIGNAL*
AND THEY PUT ME THERE TO STOP TRUCKS
FROM THE MILL RUNNING INTO THE
RAILROAD OVERPASS AT BRADDOCK AVENUE"

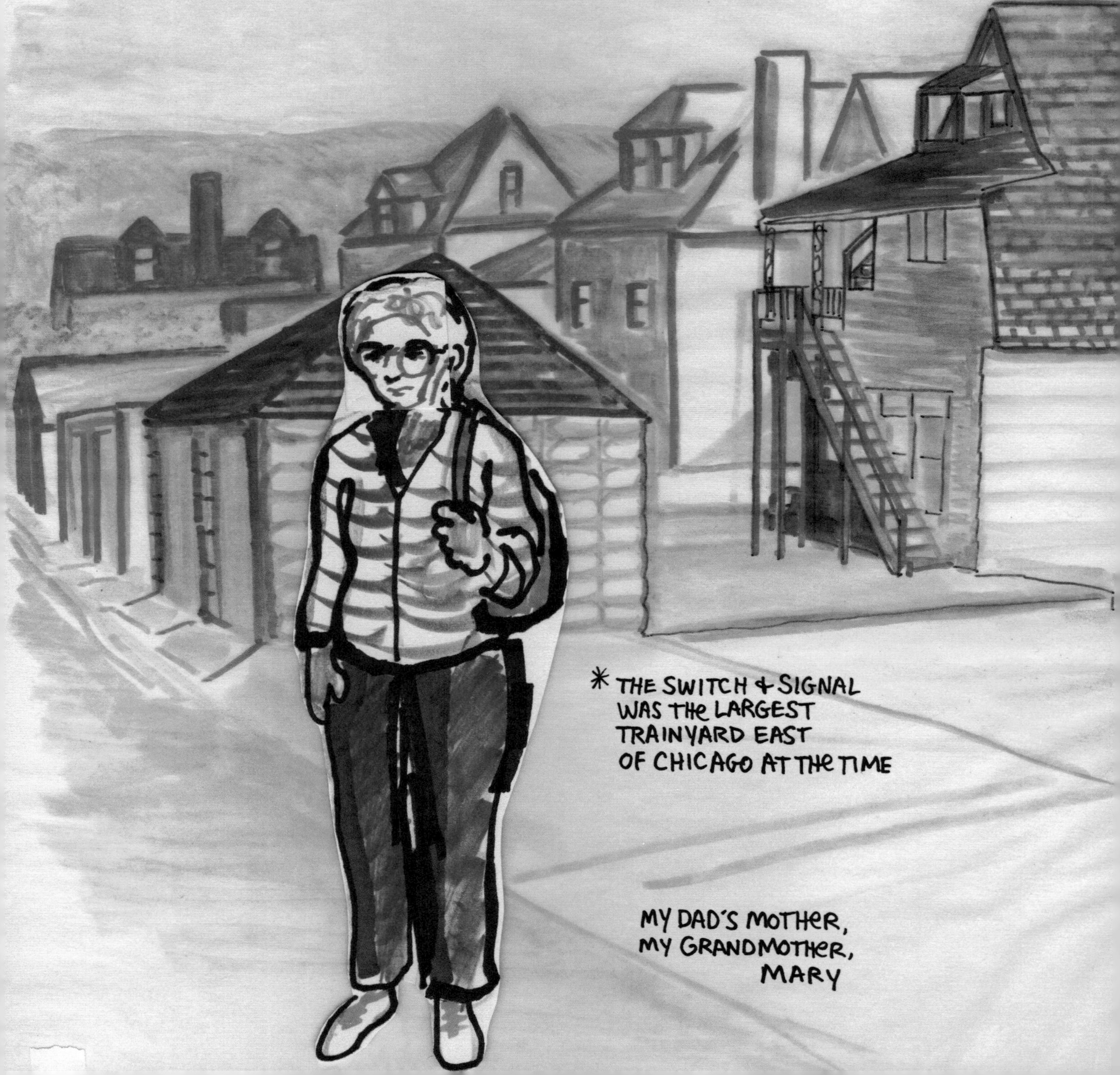
* THE SWITCH & SIGNAL
WAS THE LARGEST
TRAINYARD EAST
OF CHICAGO AT THE TIME
MY DAD'S MOTHER,
MY GRANDMOTHER,
MARY

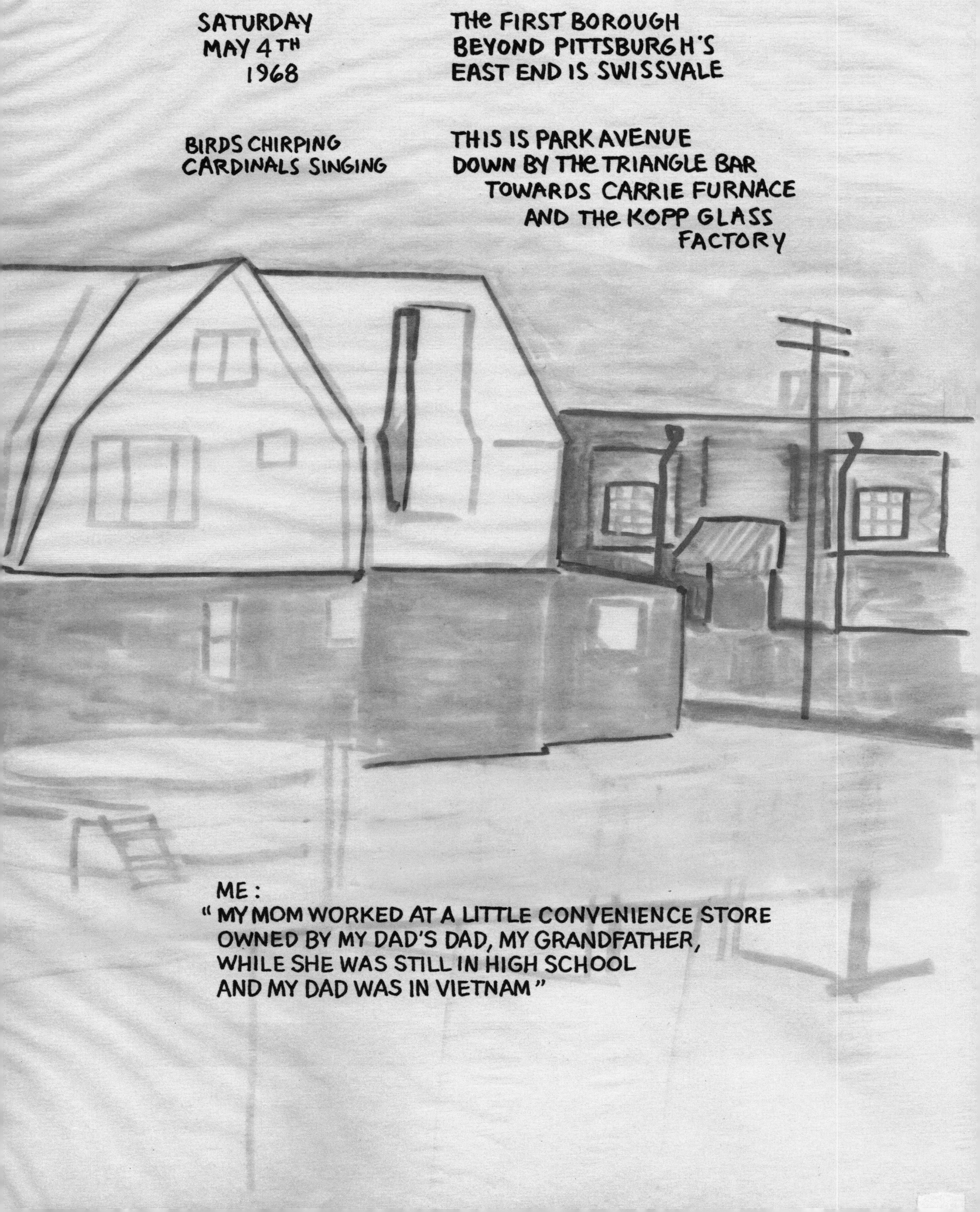
SATURDAY
MAY 4TH
1968
THE FIRST BOROUGH
BEYOND PITTSBURGH'S
EAST END IS SWISSVALE
BIRDS CHIRPING
CARDINALS SINGING
THIS IS PARK AVENUE
DOWN BY THE TRIANGLE BAR
TOWARDS CARRIE FURNACE
AND THE KOPP GLASS
FACTORY
ME:
" MY MOM WORKED AT A LITTLE CONVENIENCE STORE
OWNED BY MY DAD'S DAD, MY GRANDFATHER,
WHILE SHE WAS STILL IN HIGH SCHOOL
AND MY DAD WAS IN VIETNAM "

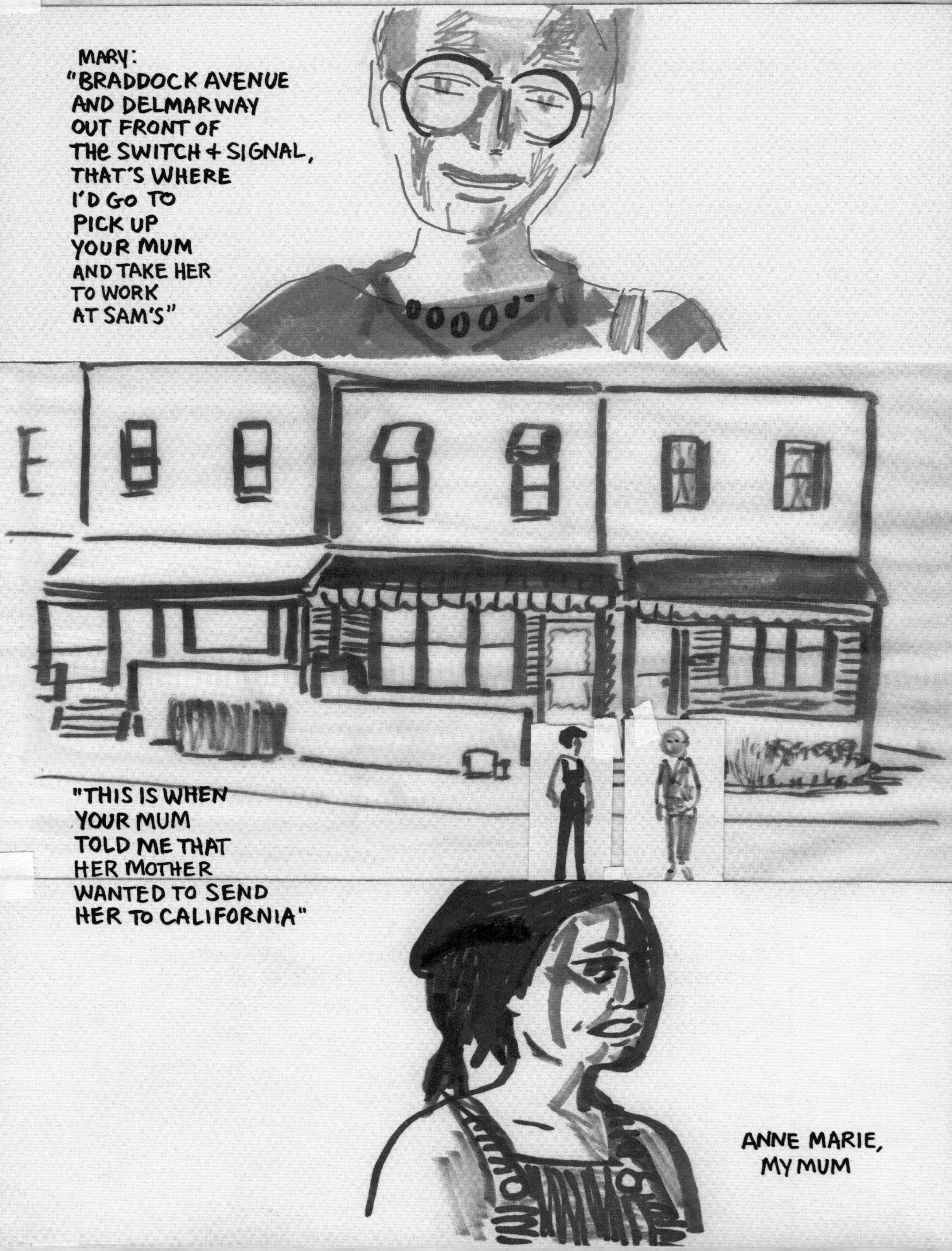
MARY:
"BRADDOCK AVENUE AND DELMAR WAY OUT FRONT OF THE SWITCH & SIGNAL, THAT'S WHERE I'D GO TO PICK UP YOUR MUM AND TAKE HER TO WORK AT SAM'S"
"THIS IS WHEN YOUR MUM TOLD ME THAT HER MOTHER WANTED TO SEND HER TO CALIFORNIA"
ANNE MARIE, MY MUM

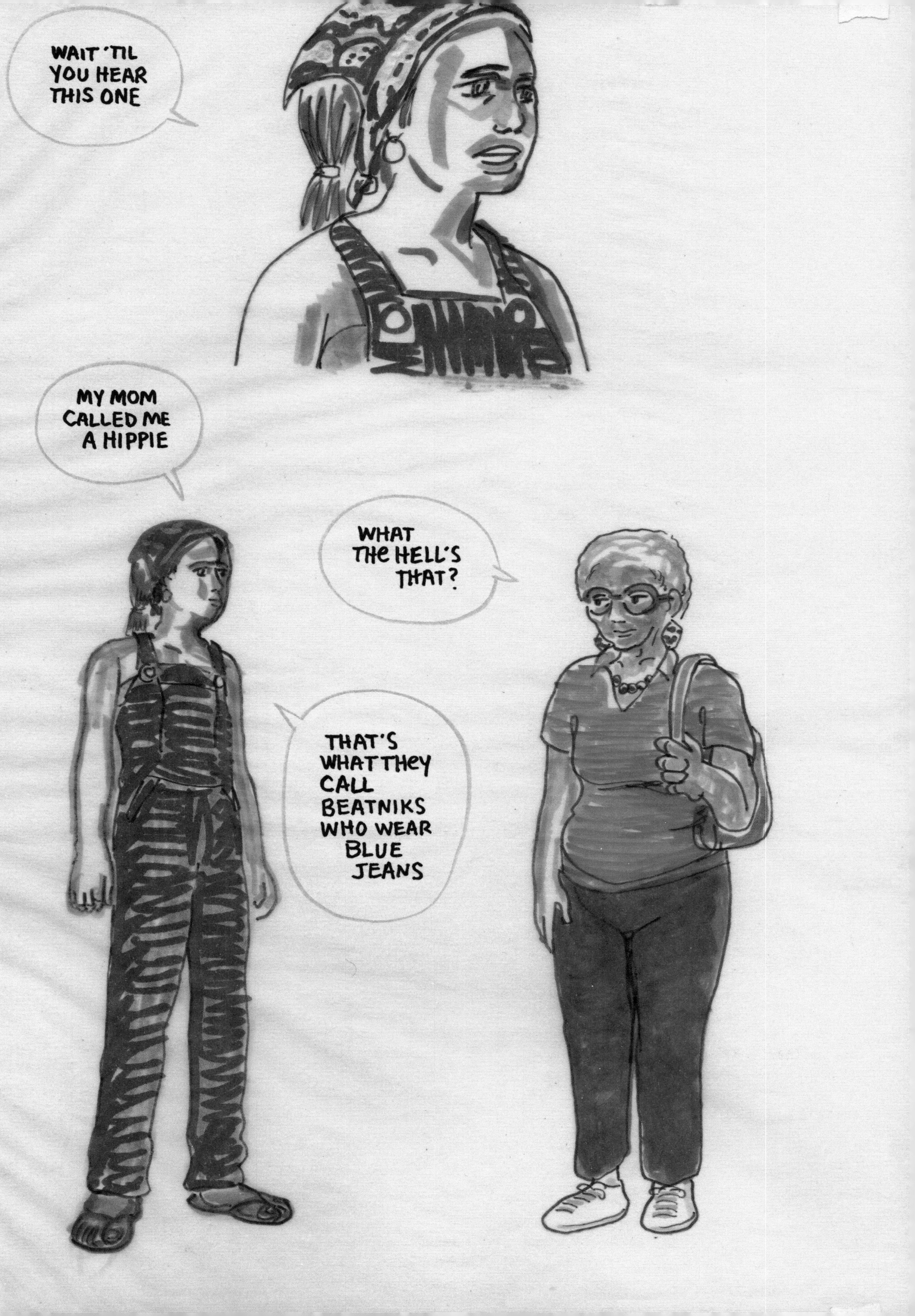
WAIT 'TIL YOU HEAR THIS ONE
MY MOM CALLED ME A HIPPIE
WHAT THE HELL'S THAT?
THAT'S WHAT THEY CALL BEATNIKS WHO WEAR BLUE JEANS

MY MUM'S PARENTS

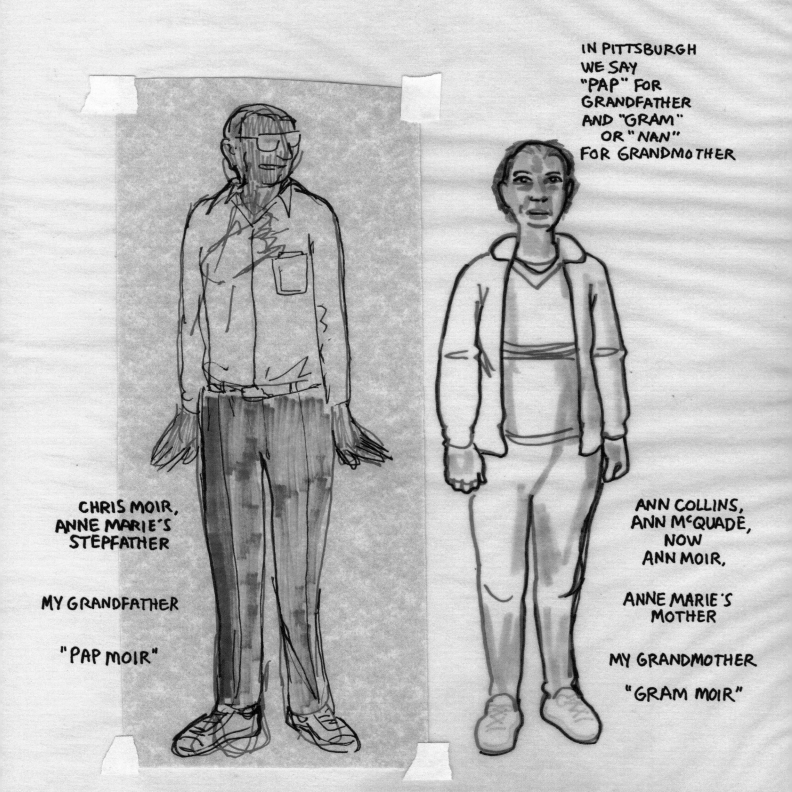

IN PITTSBURGH WE SAY "PAP" FOR GRANDFATHER AND "GRAM" OR "NAN" FOR GRANDMOTHER

CHRIS MOIR, ANNE MARIE'S STEPFATHER

MY GRANDFATHER

"PAP MOIR"

ANN COLLINS, ANN McQUADE, NOW ANN MOIR,

ANNE MARIE'S MOTHER

MY GRANDMOTHER

"GRAM MOIR"

MY DAD'S PARENTS

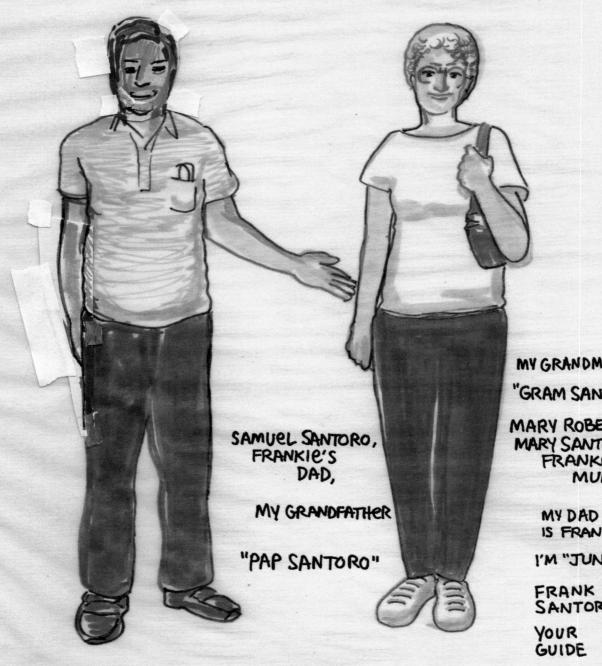

SAMUEL SANTORO,
FRANKIE'S
DAD,

MY GRANDFATHER

"PAP SANTORO"

MY GRANDMOTHER

"GRAM SANTORO"

MARY ROBERTSON,
MARY SANTORO,
FRANKIE'S
MUM

MY DAD
IS FRANKIE,

I'M "JUNIOR"

FRANK
SANTORO, JR

YOUR
GUIDE

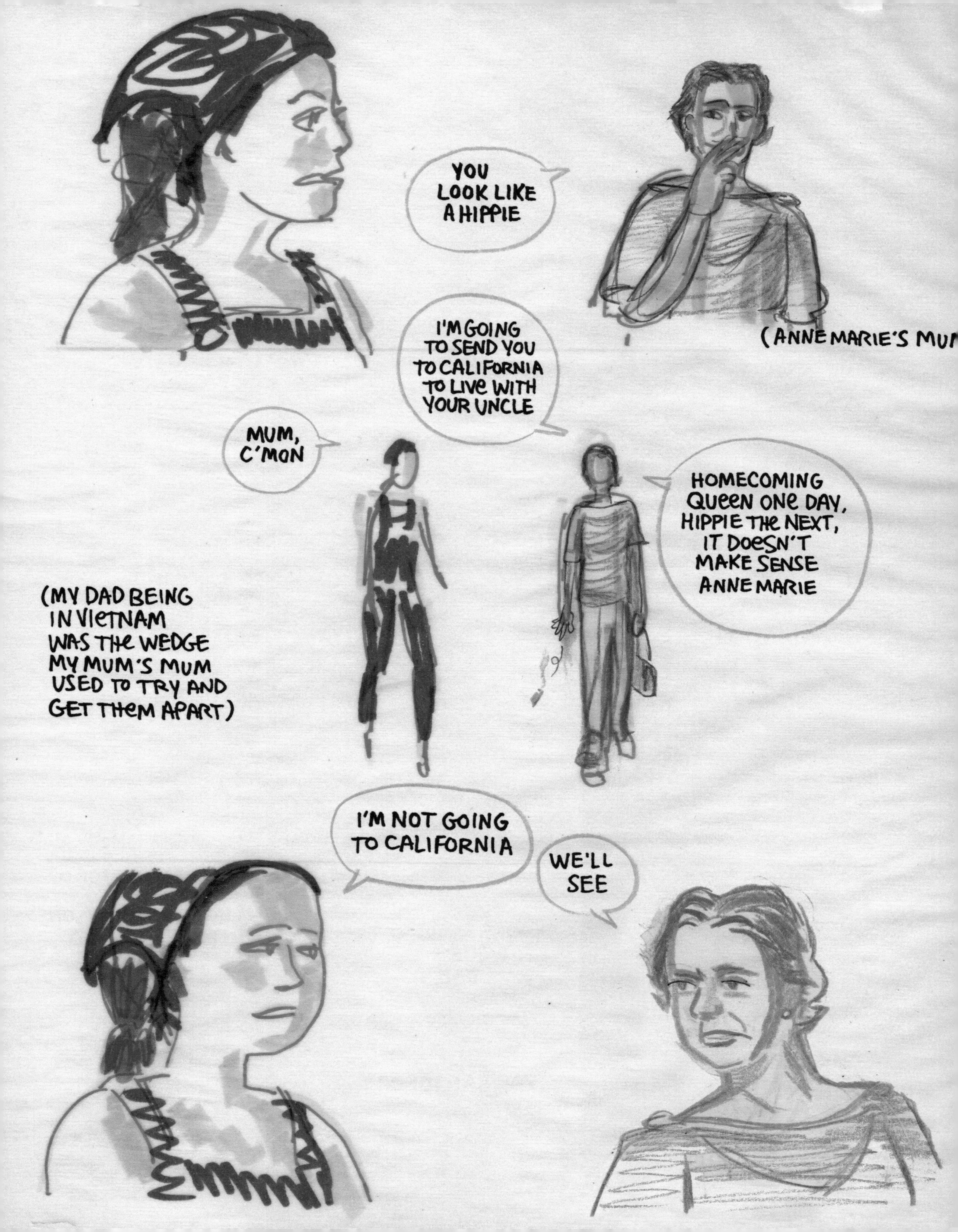
YOU LOOK LIKE A HIPPIE
(ANNE MARIE'S MU
I'M GOING TO SEND YOU TO CALIFORNIA TO LIVE WITH YOUR UNCLE
MUM, C'MON
HOMECOMING QUEEN ONE DAY, HIPPIE THE NEXT, IT DOESN'T MAKE SENSE ANNE MARIE
(MY DAD BEING IN VIETNAM WAS THE WEDGE MY MUM'S MUM USED TO TRY AND GET THEM APART)
I'M NOT GOING TO CALIFORNIA
WE'LL SEE

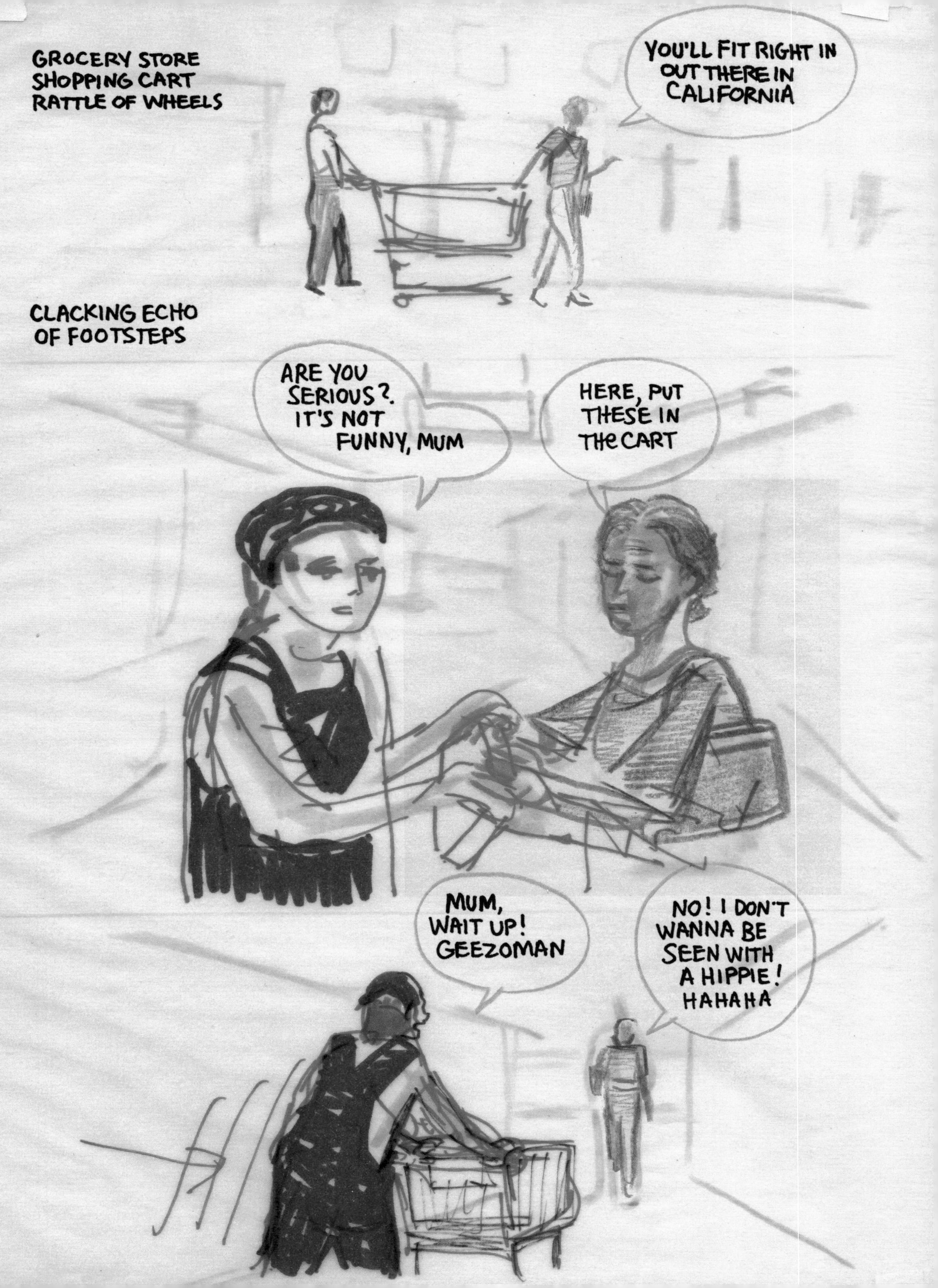
GROCERY STORE
SHOPPING CART
RATTLE OF WHEELS
YOU'LL FIT RIGHT IN OUT THERE IN CALIFORNIA
CLACKING ECHO
OF FOOTSTEPS
ARE YOU SERIOUS?. IT'S NOT FUNNY, MUM
HERE, PUT THESE IN THE CART
MUM, WAIT UP! GEEZOMAN
NO! I DON'T WANNA BE SEEN WITH A HIPPIE! HAHAHA

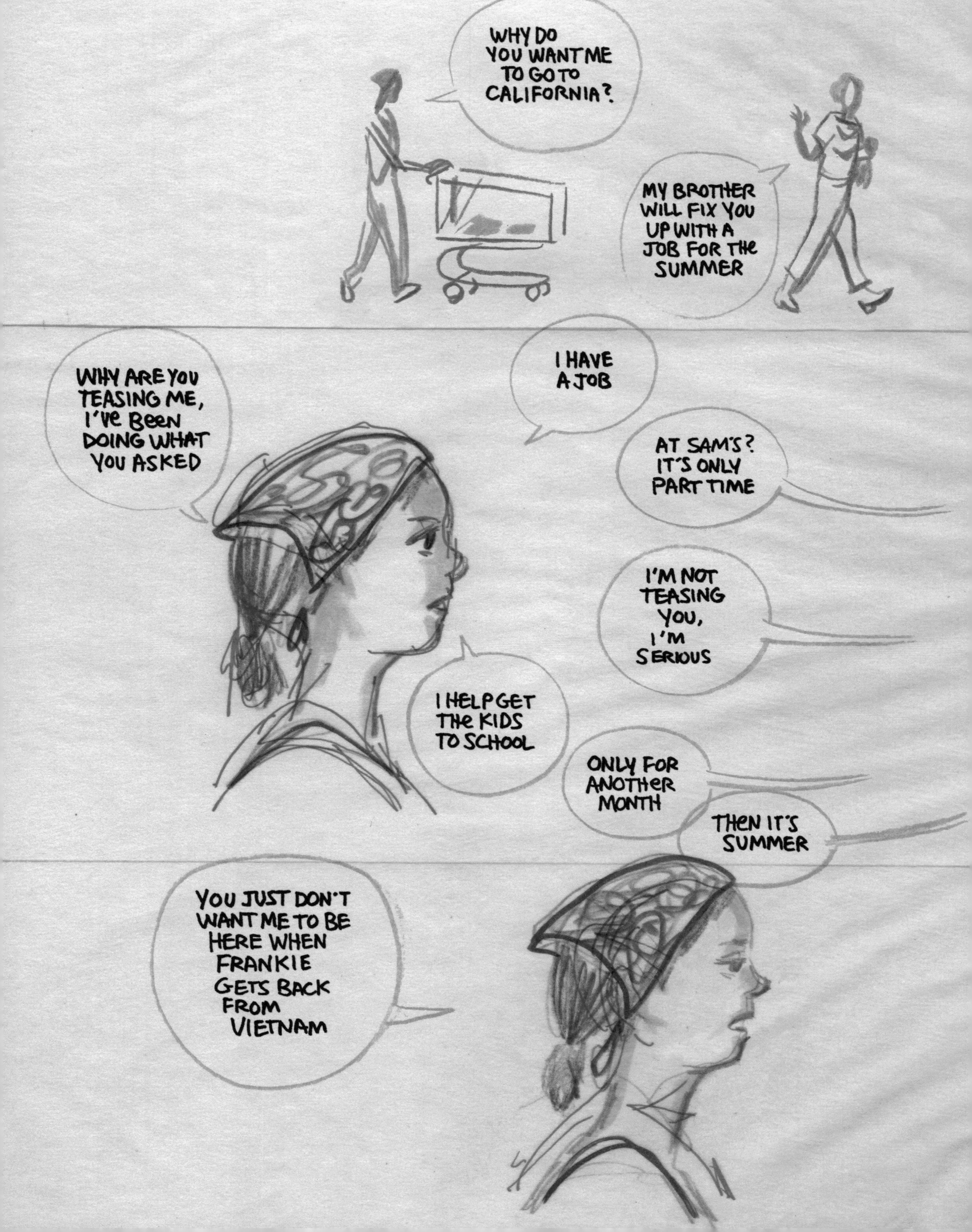
WHY DO YOU WANT ME TO GO TO CALIFORNIA?
MY BROTHER WILL FIX YOU UP WITH A JOB FOR THE SUMMER
WHY ARE YOU TEASING ME, I'VE BEEN DOING WHAT YOU ASKED
I HAVE A JOB
AT SAM'S? IT'S ONLY PART TIME
I'M NOT TEASING YOU, I'M SERIOUS
I HELP GET THE KIDS TO SCHOOL
ONLY FOR ANOTHER MONTH
THEN IT'S SUMMER
YOU JUST DON'T WANT ME TO BE HERE WHEN FRANKIE GETS BACK FROM VIETNAM

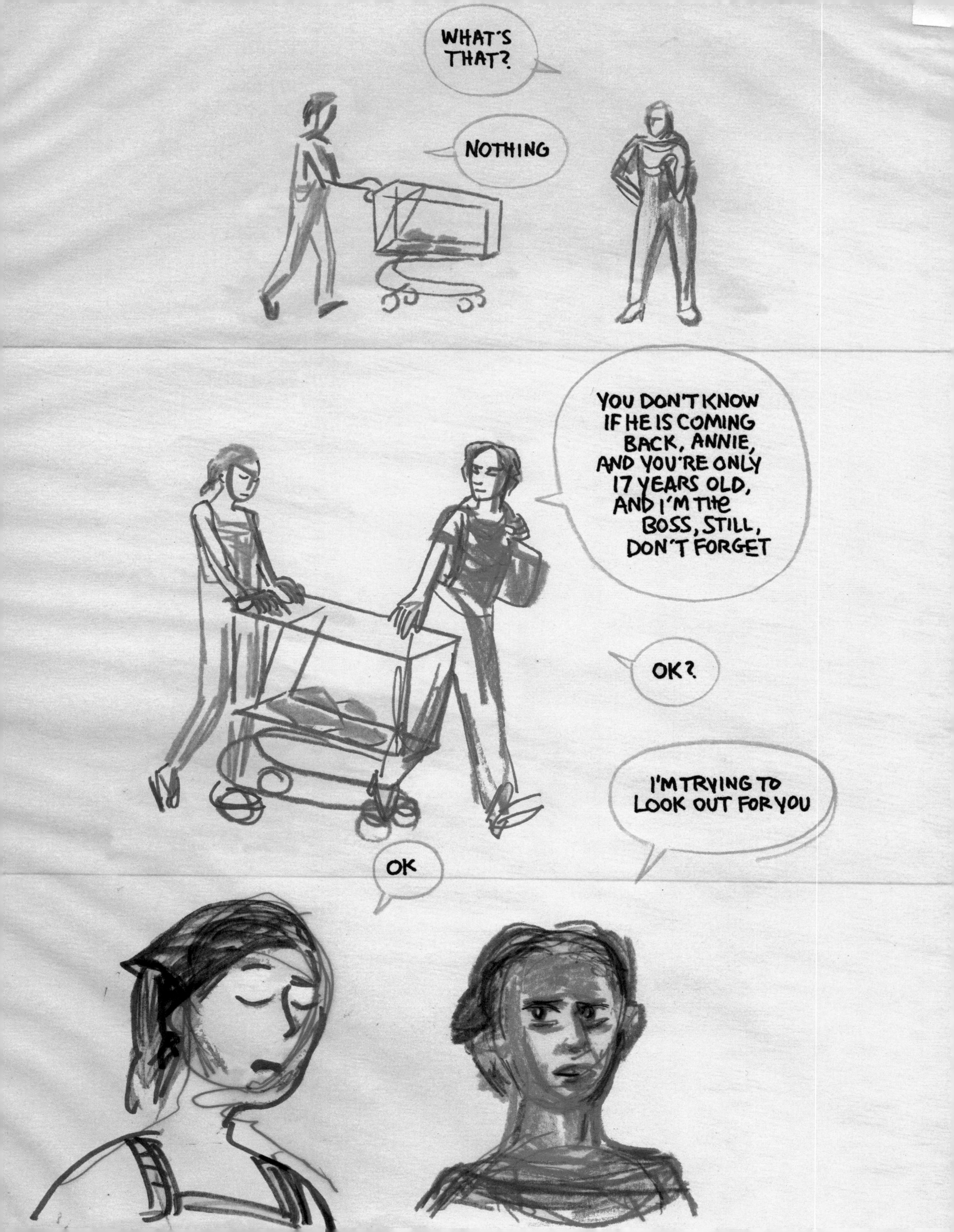
WHAT'S THAT?
NOTHING
YOU DON'T KNOW IF HE IS COMING BACK, ANNIE, AND YOU'RE ONLY 17 YEARS OLD, AND I'M THE BOSS, STILL, DON'T FORGET
OK?
I'M TRYING TO LOOK OUT FOR YOU
OK

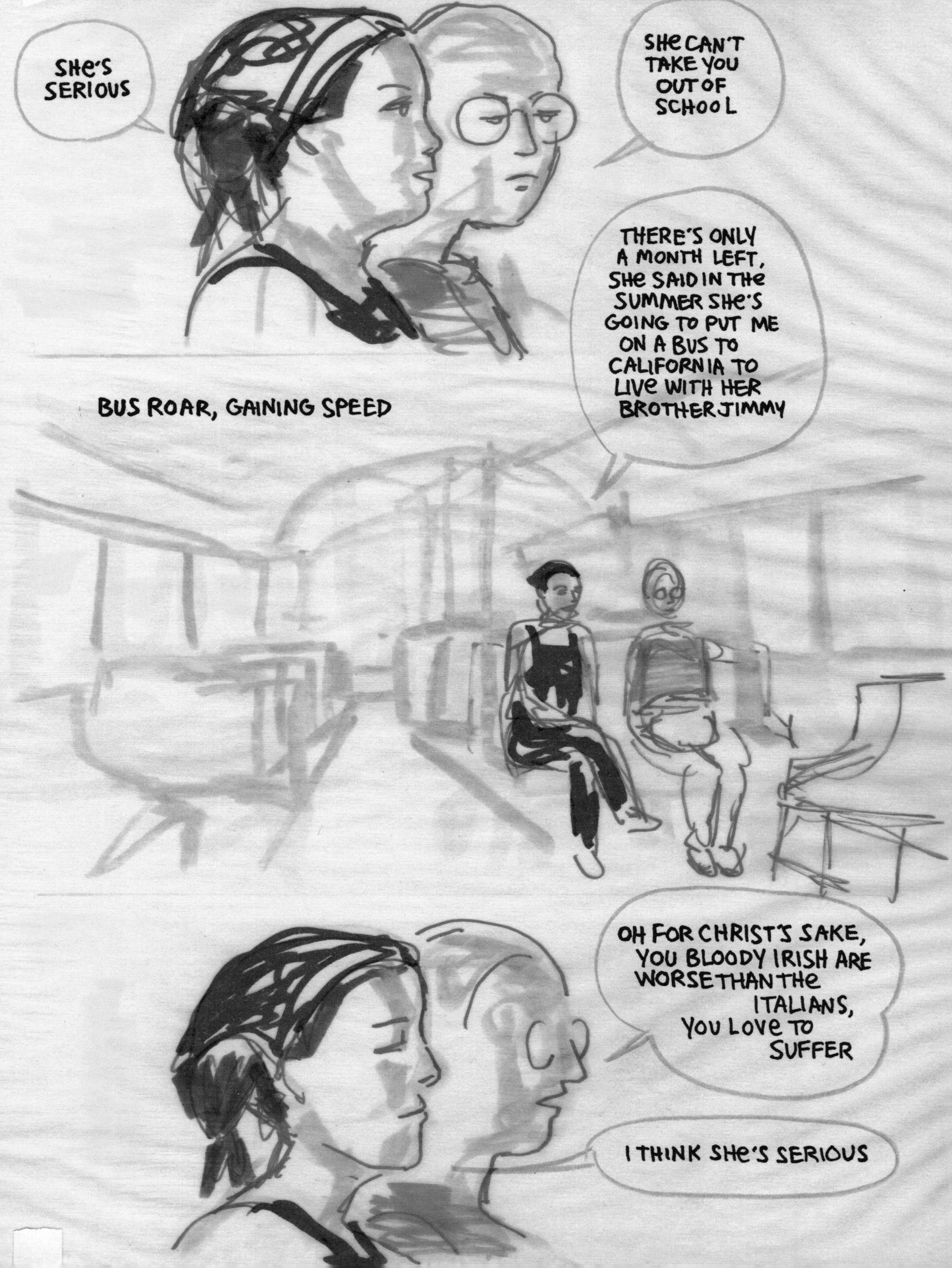
SHE'S SERIOUS
SHE CAN'T TAKE YOU OUT OF SCHOOL
THERE'S ONLY A MONTH LEFT, SHE SAID IN THE SUMMER SHE'S GOING TO PUT ME ON A BUS TO CALIFORNIA TO LIVE WITH HER BROTHER JIMMY
BUS ROAR, GAINING SPEED
OH FOR CHRIST'S SAKE, YOU BLOODY IRISH ARE WORSE THAN THE ITALIANS, YOU LOVE TO SUFFER
I THINK SHE'S SERIOUS

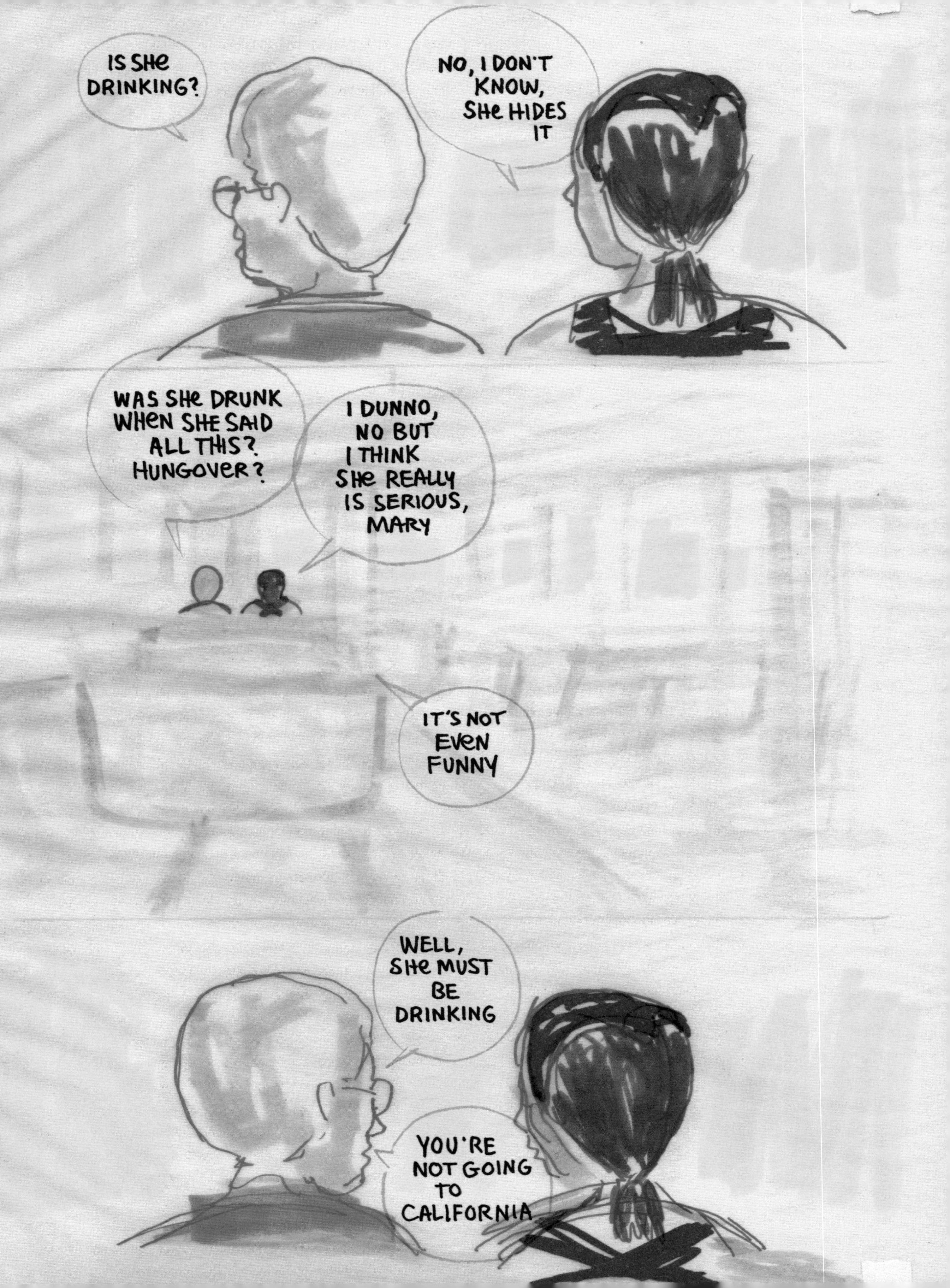
IS SHE DRINKING?
NO, I DON'T KNOW, SHE HIDES IT
WAS SHE DRUNK WHEN SHE SAID ALL THIS? HUNGOVER?
I DUNNO, NO BUT I THINK SHE REALLY IS SERIOUS, MARY
IT'S NOT EVEN FUNNY
WELL, SHE MUST BE DRINKING
YOU'RE NOT GOING TO CALIFORNIA

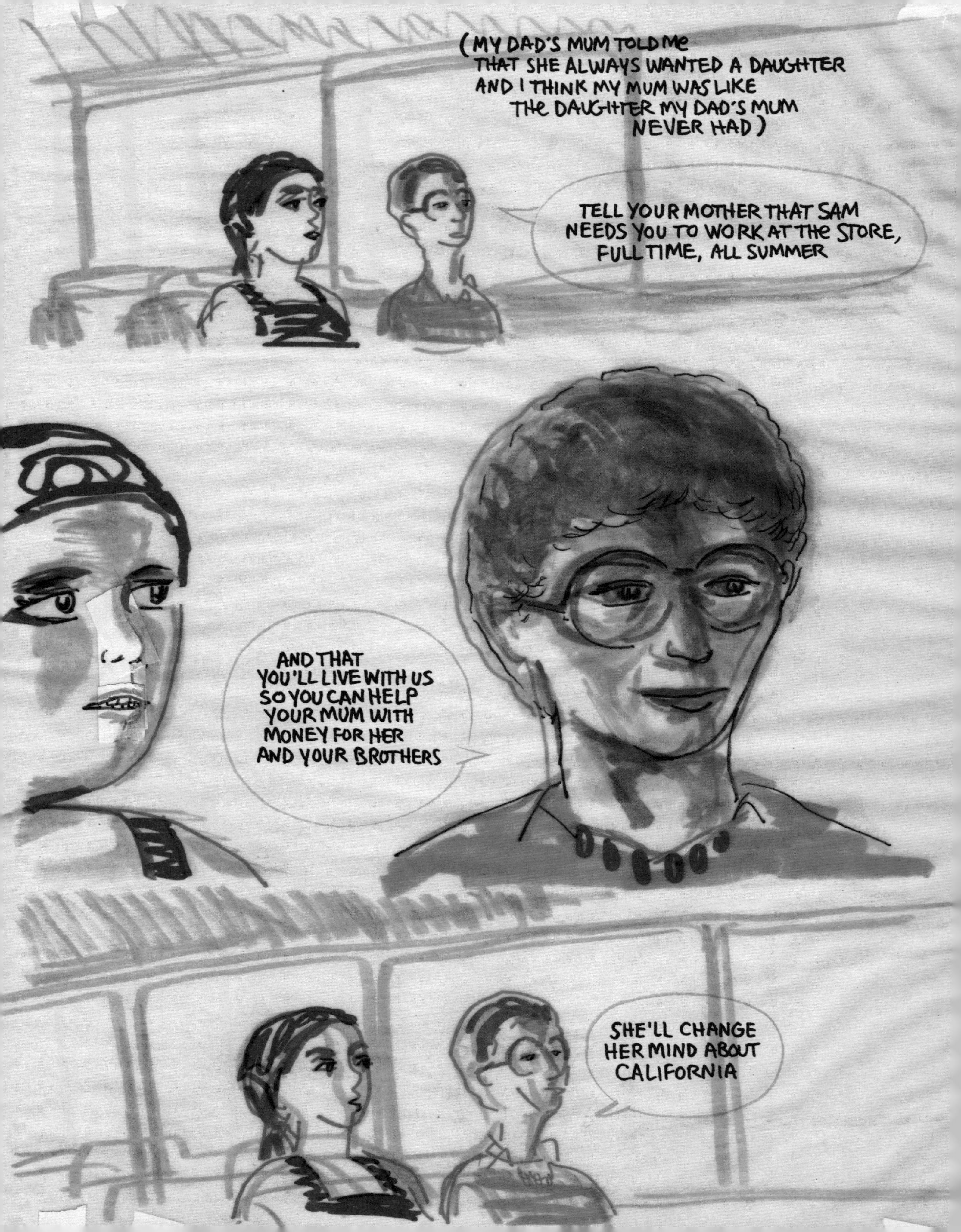
(MY DAD'S MUM TOLD ME THAT SHE ALWAYS WANTED A DAUGHTER AND I THINK MY MUM WAS LIKE THE DAUGHTER MY DAD'S MUM NEVER HAD)
TELL YOUR MOTHER THAT SAM NEEDS YOU TO WORK AT THE STORE, FULL TIME, ALL SUMMER
AND THAT YOU'LL LIVE WITH US SO YOU CAN HELP YOUR MUM WITH MONEY FOR HER AND YOUR BROTHERS
SHE'LL CHANGE HER MIND ABOUT CALIFORNIA

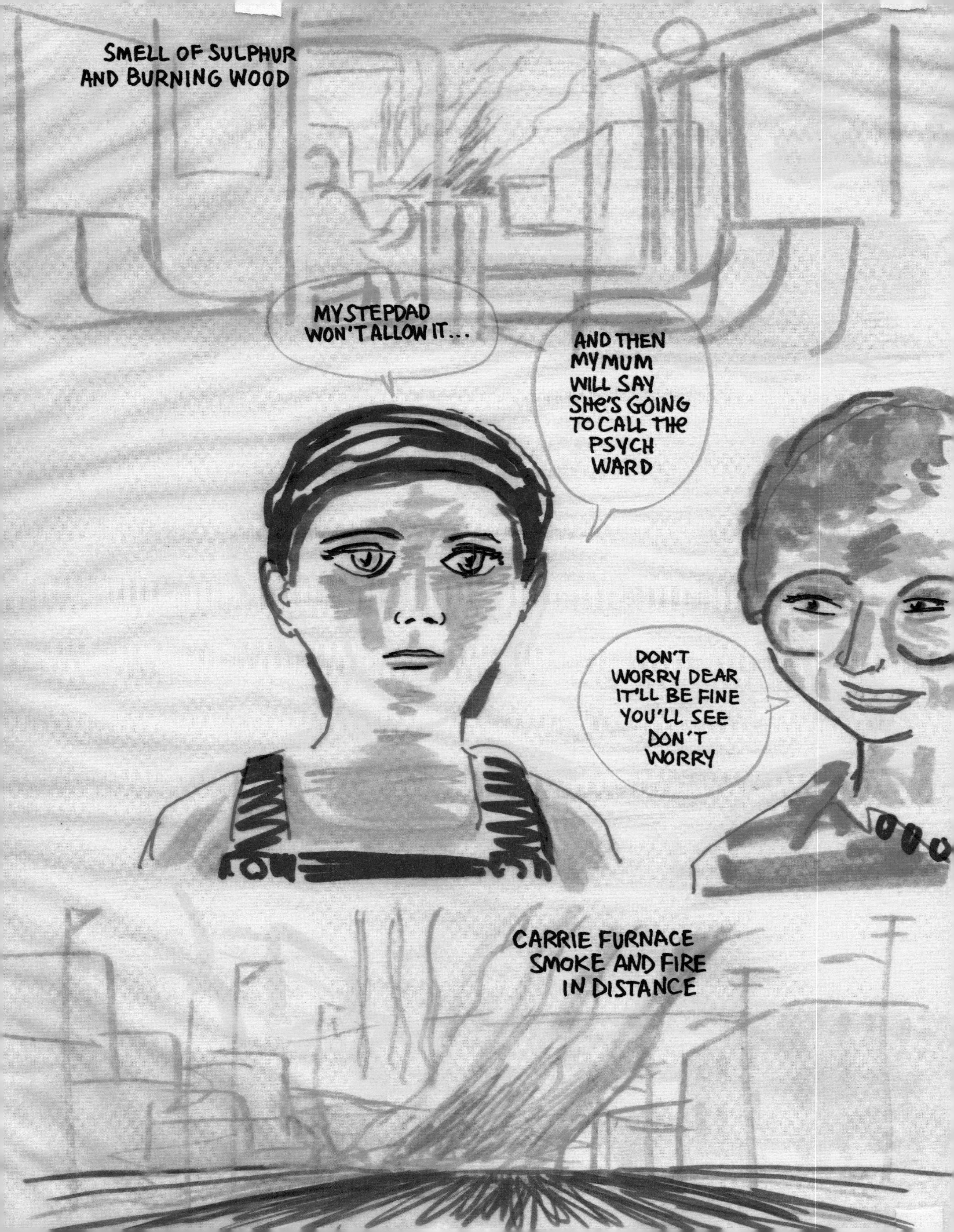
SMELL OF SULPHUR AND BURNING WOOD
MY STEPDAD WON'T ALLOW IT...
AND THEN MY MUM WILL SAY SHE'S GOING TO CALL THE PSYCH WARD
DON'T WORRY DEAR IT'LL BE FINE YOU'LL SEE DON'T WORRY
CARRIE FURNACE SMOKE AND FIRE IN DISTANCE

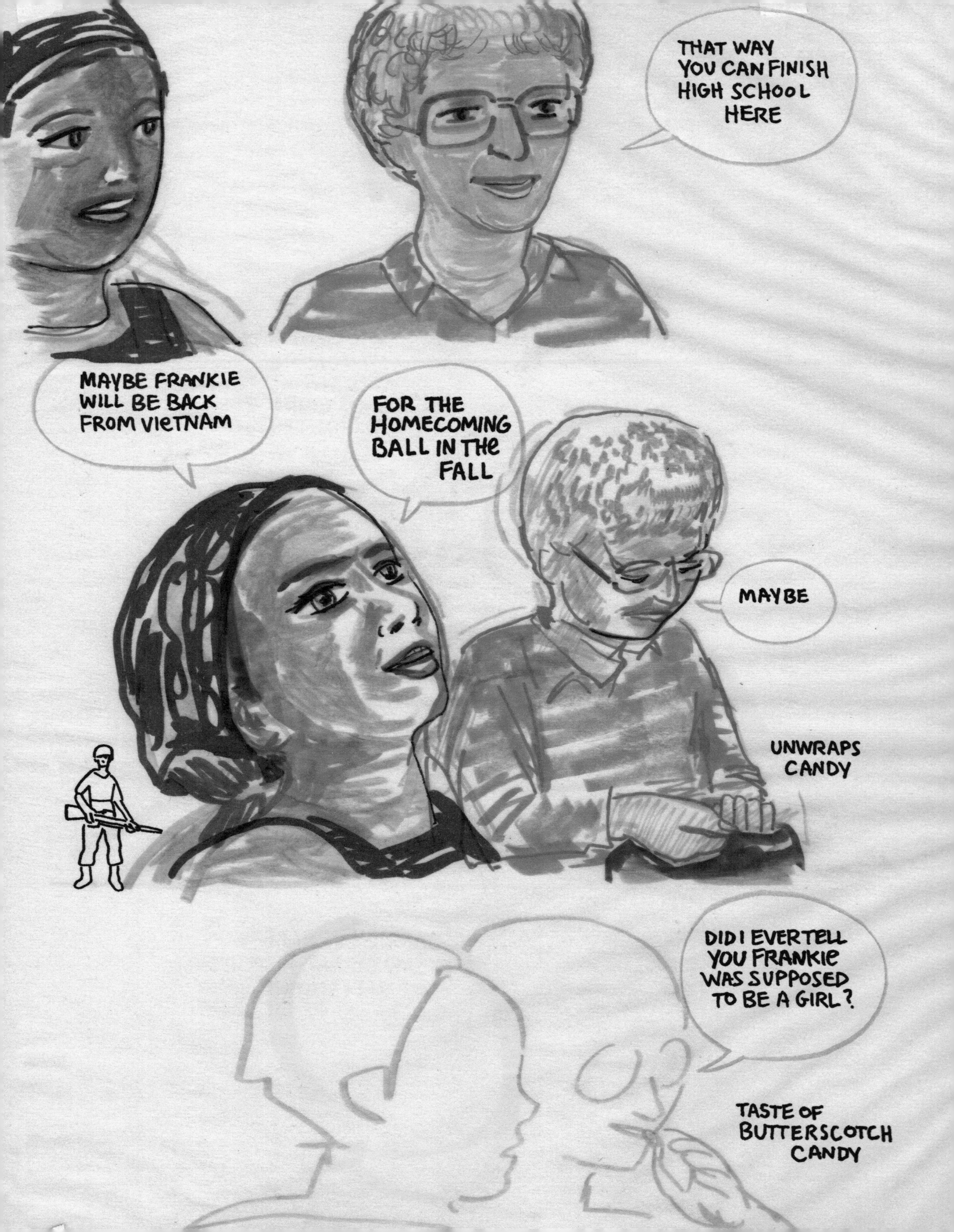
THAT WAY YOU CAN FINISH HIGH SCHOOL HERE
MAYBE FRANKIE WILL BE BACK FROM VIETNAM
FOR THE HOMECOMING BALL IN THE FALL
MAYBE
UNWRAPS CANDY
DID I EVER TELL YOU FRANKIE WAS SUPPOSED TO BE A GIRL?
TASTE OF BUTTERSCOTCH CANDY

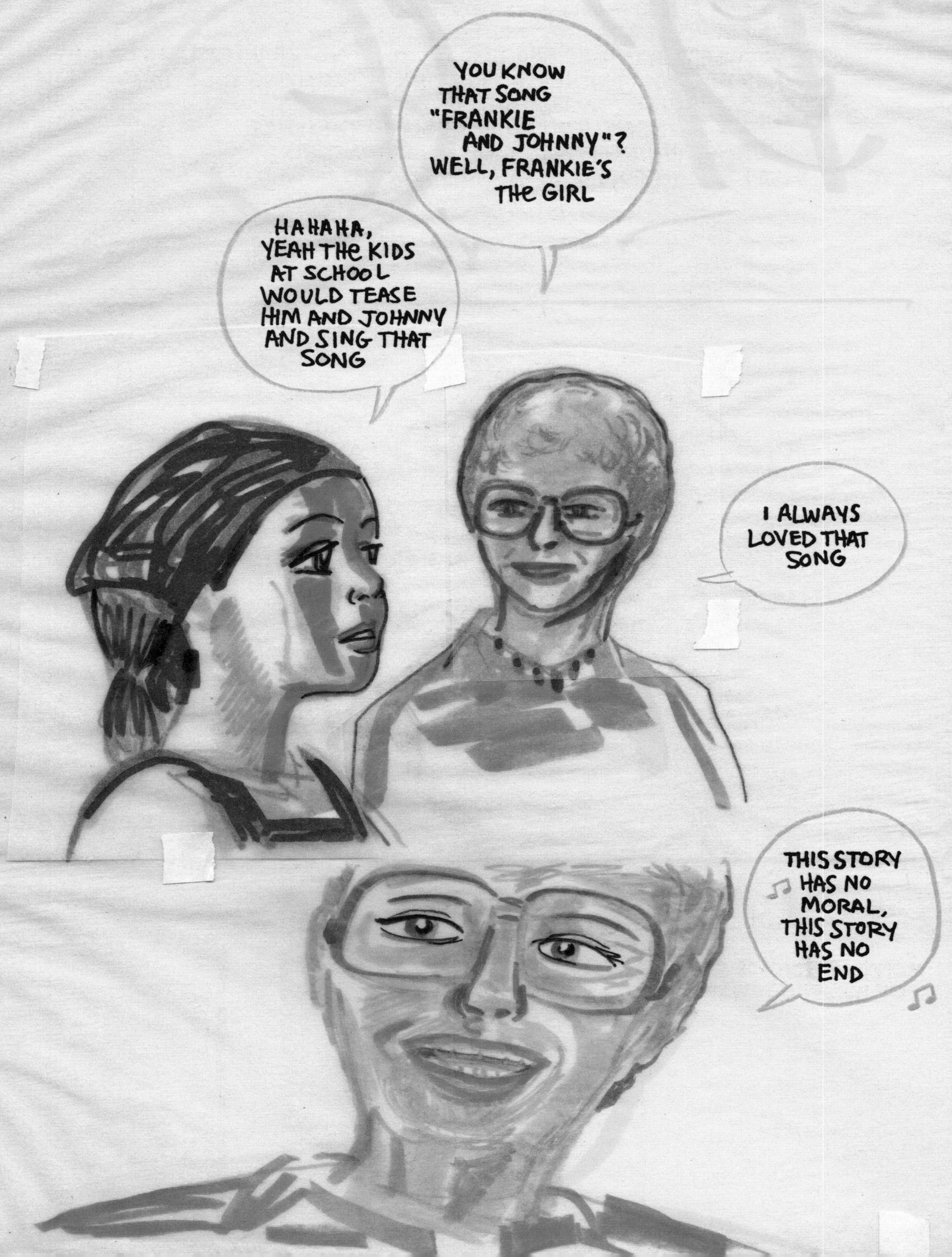
YOU KNOW THAT SONG "FRANKIE AND JOHNNY"? WELL, FRANKIE'S THE GIRL
HAHAHA, YEAH THE KIDS AT SCHOOL WOULD TEASE HIM AND JOHNNY AND SING THAT SONG
I ALWAYS LOVED THAT SONG
THIS STORY HAS NO MORAL, THIS STORY HAS NO END

WHEN I ASKED MOM ABOUT THIS TIME,
SHE REMINDED ME THAT ALL FOUR OF HER
YOUNGER BROTHERS AND HER YOUNGER SISTER WERE LIKE HER KIDS,
AND HER MOM AND HER STEPDAD WERE ALL LIVING TOGETHER
IN ONE HOUSE, AND THAT HER MOTHER WAS
STUCK BETWEEN NEEDING HER HELP IN THE HOUSE,
BUT NOT HAVING ENOUGH ROOM AND WANTING
TO KEEP MY FUTURE MOM AWAY FROM MY FUTURE DAD

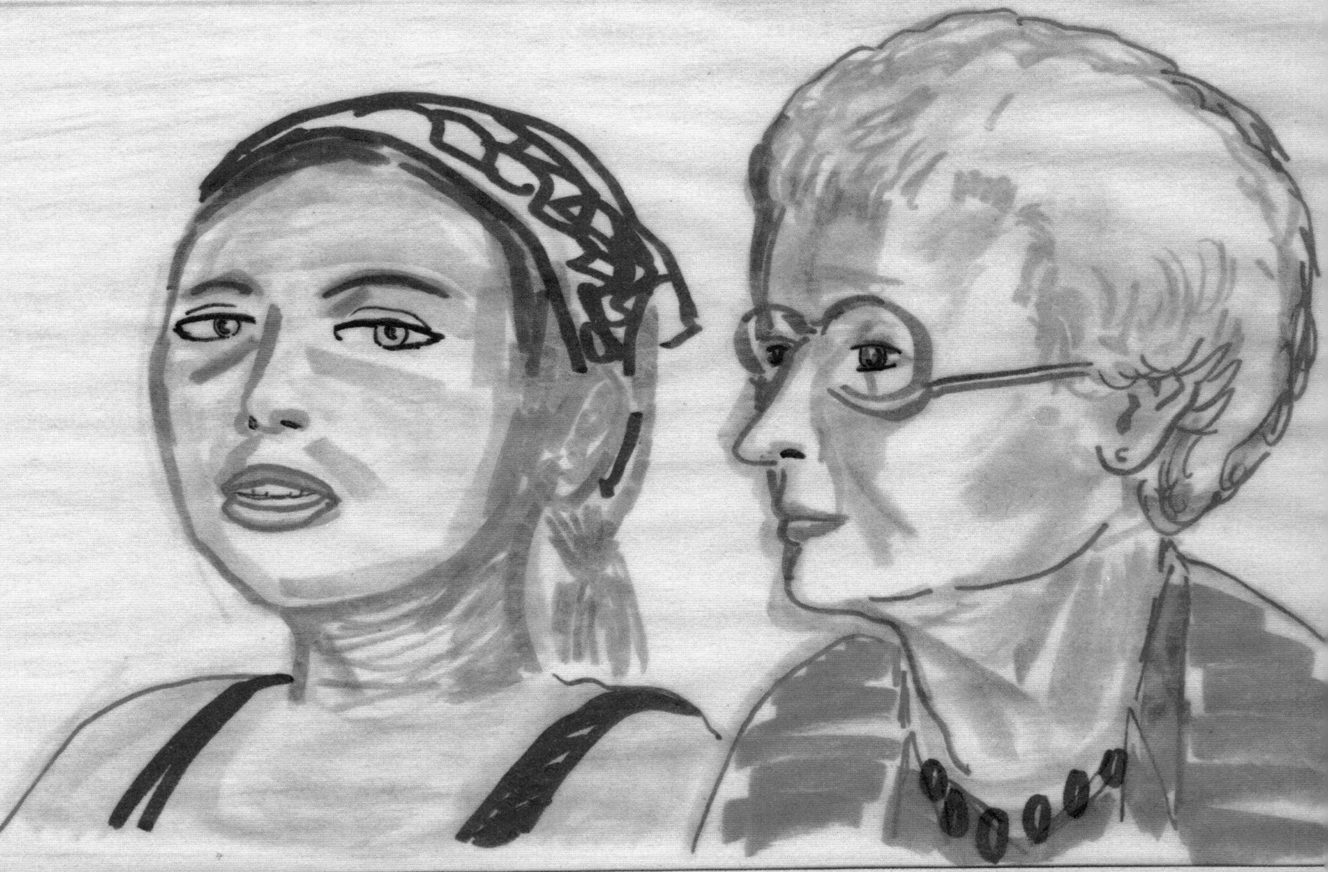

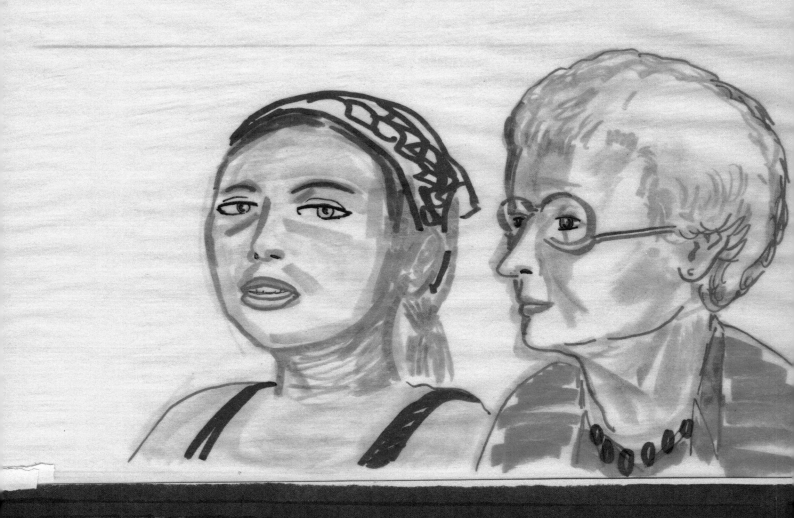

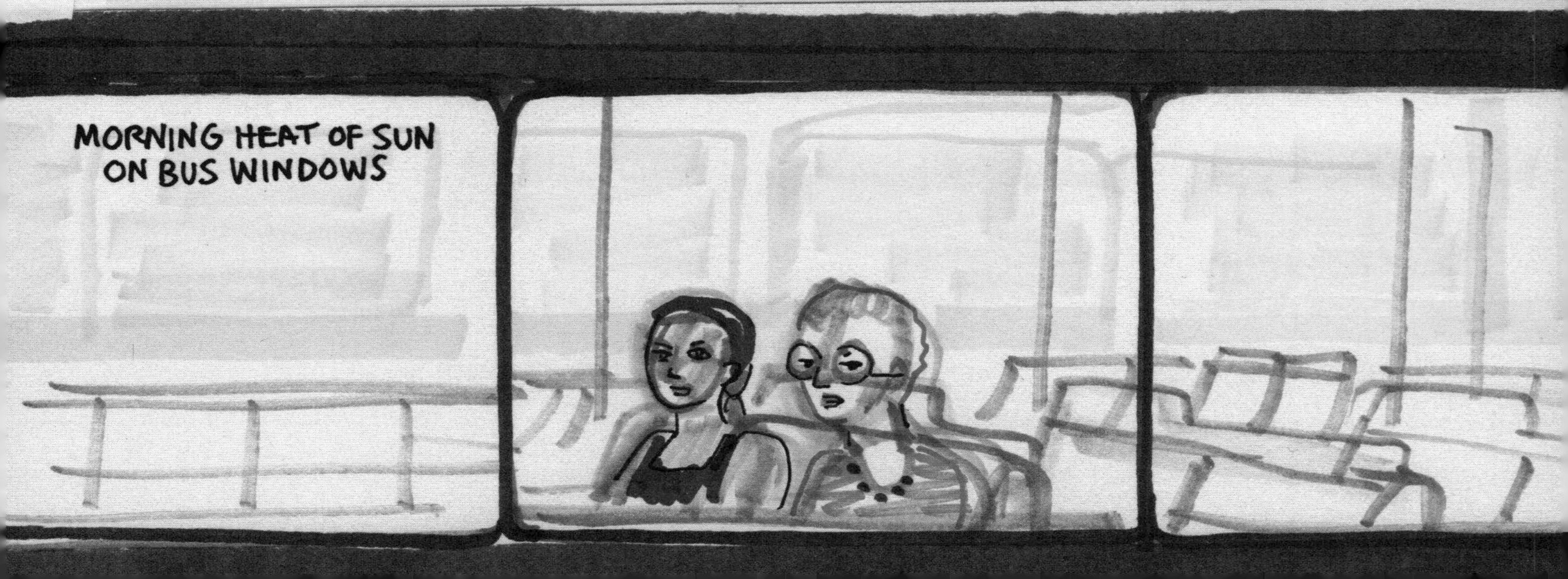
MORNING HEAT OF SUN
ON BUS WINDOWS

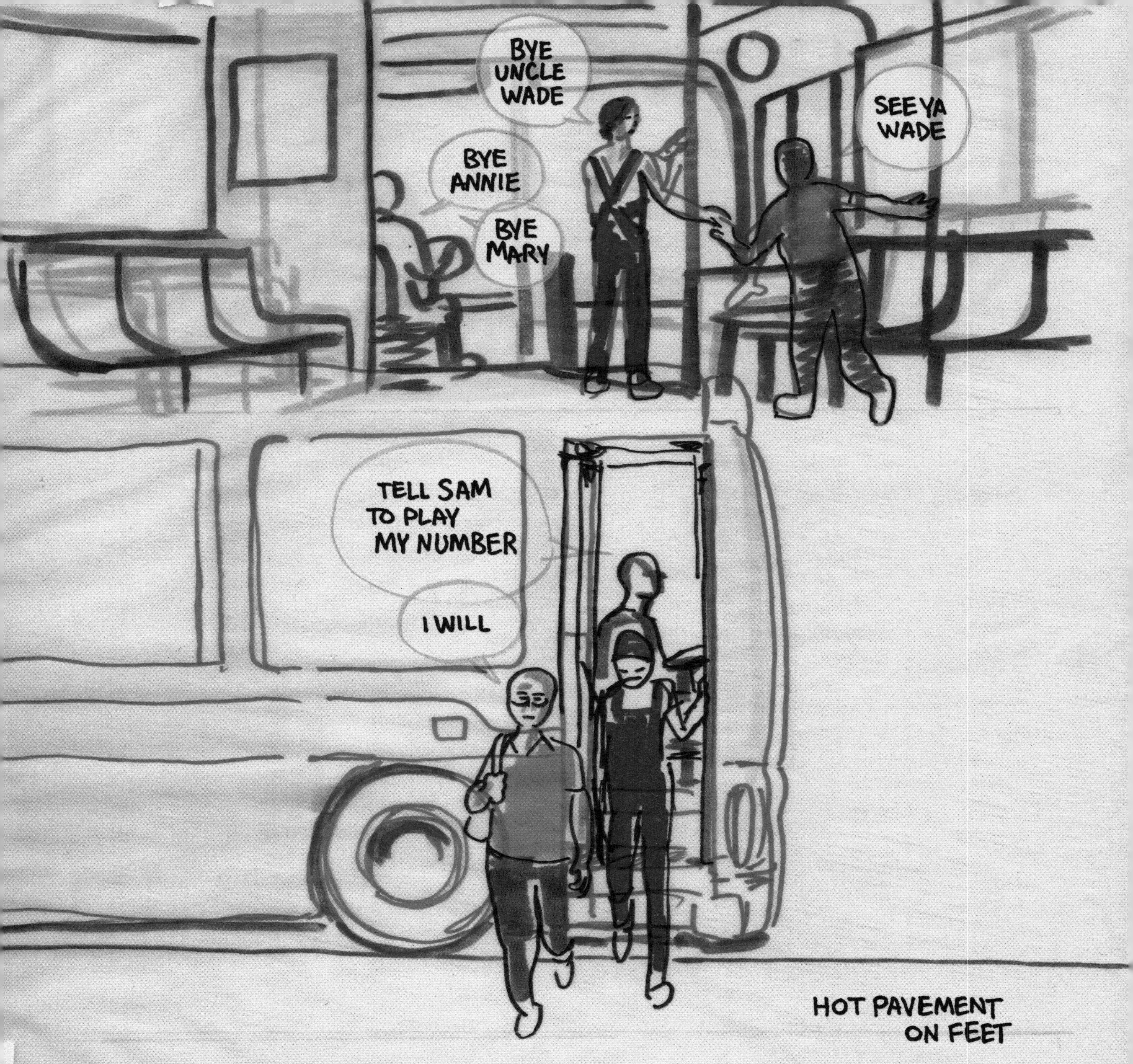
BYE UNCLE WADE
SEE YA WADE
BYE ANNIE
BYE MARY
TELL SAM TO PLAY MY NUMBER
I WILL
HOT PAVEMENT ON FEET

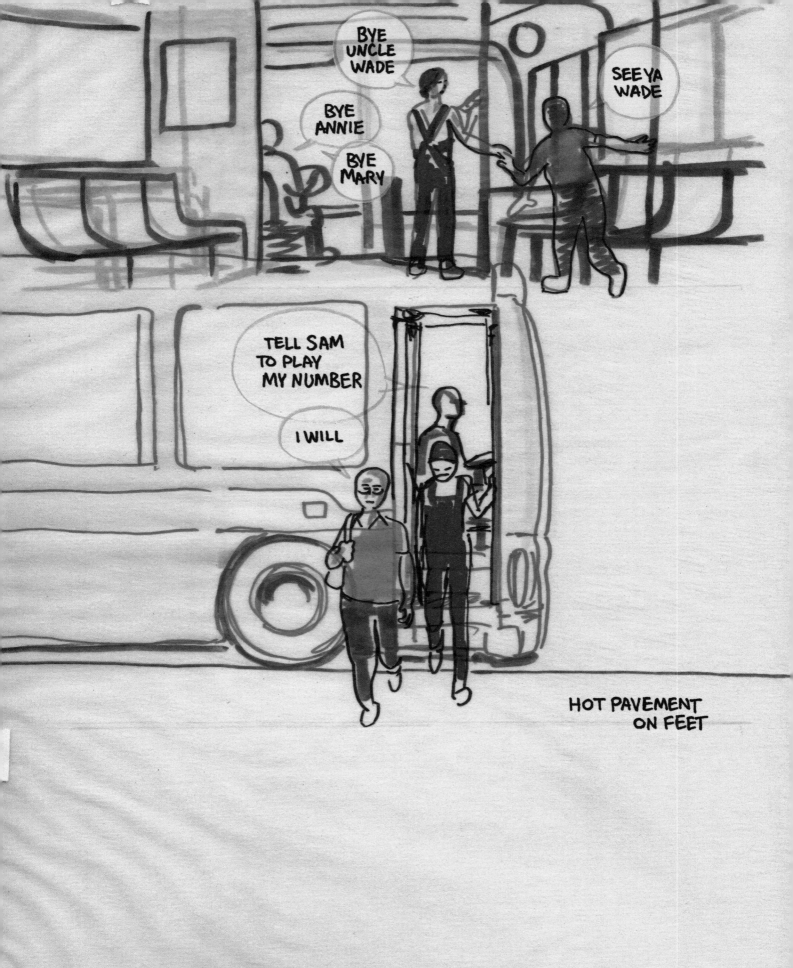

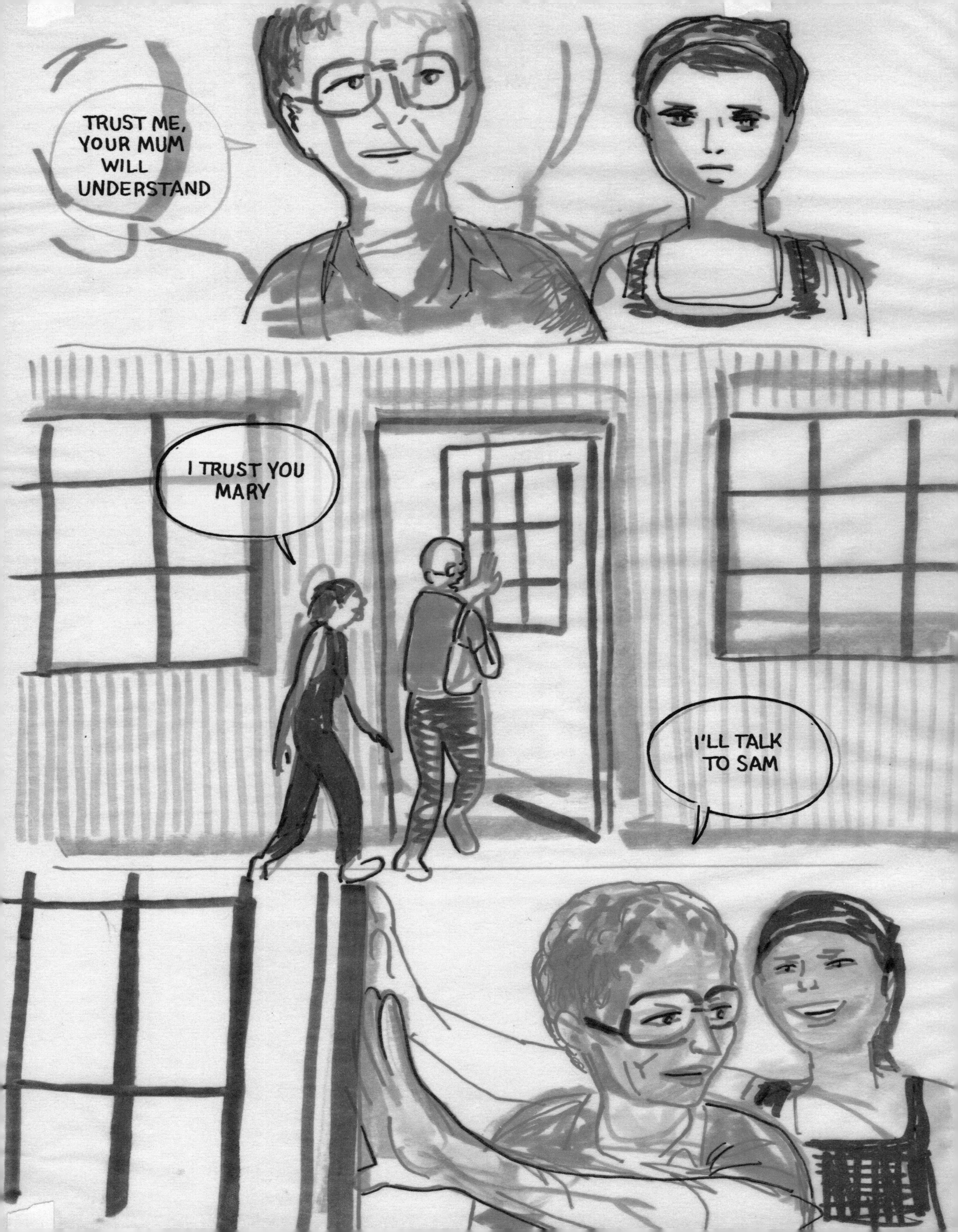
TRUST ME, YOUR MUM WILL UNDERSTAND
I TRUST YOU MARY
I'LL TALK TO SAM

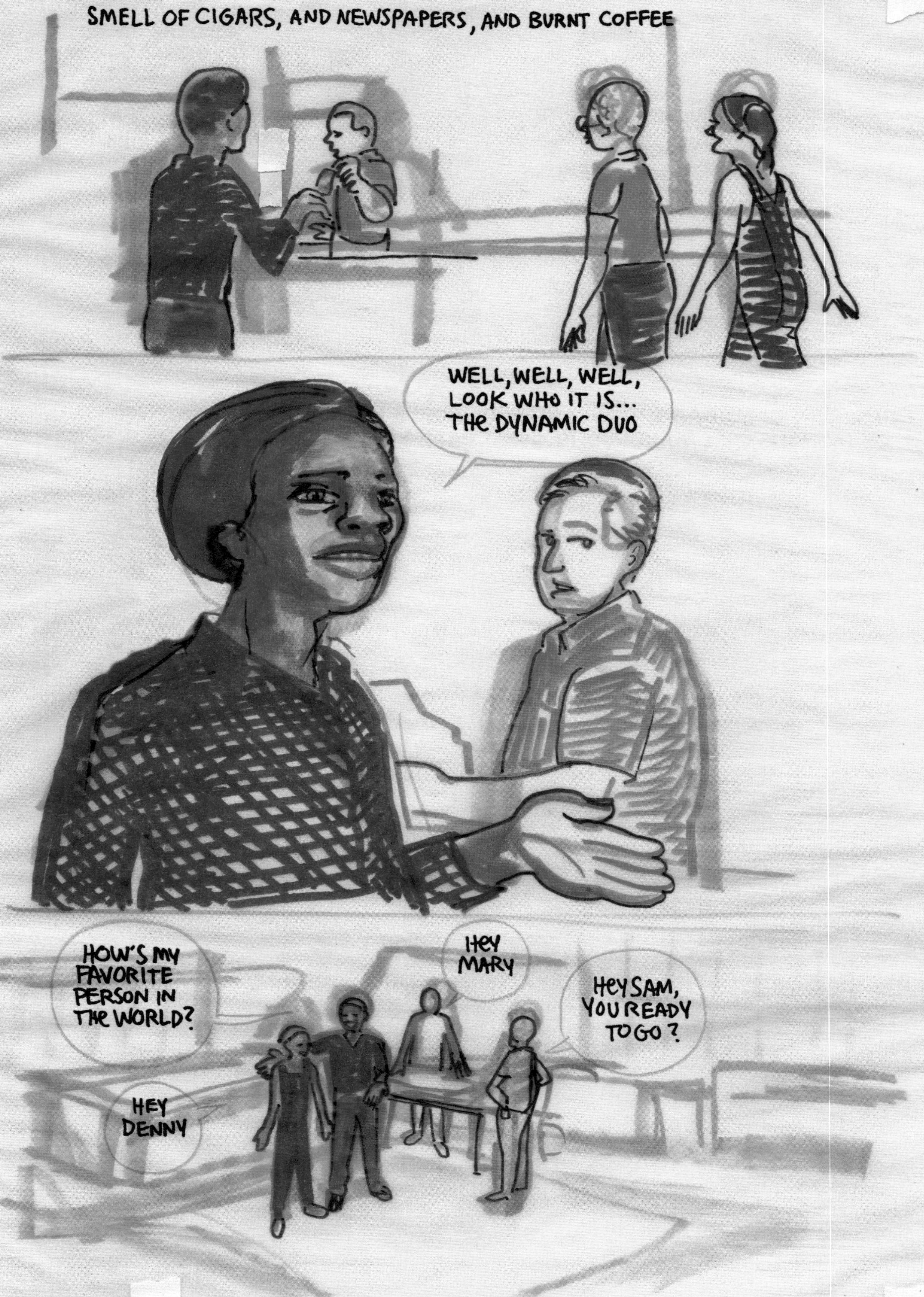
SMELL OF CIGARS, AND NEWSPAPERS, AND BURNT COFFEE
WELL, WELL, WELL, LOOK WHO IT IS... THE DYNAMIC DUO
HOW'S MY FAVORITE PERSON IN THE WORLD?
HEY MARY
HEY SAM, YOU READY TO GO?
HEY DENNY

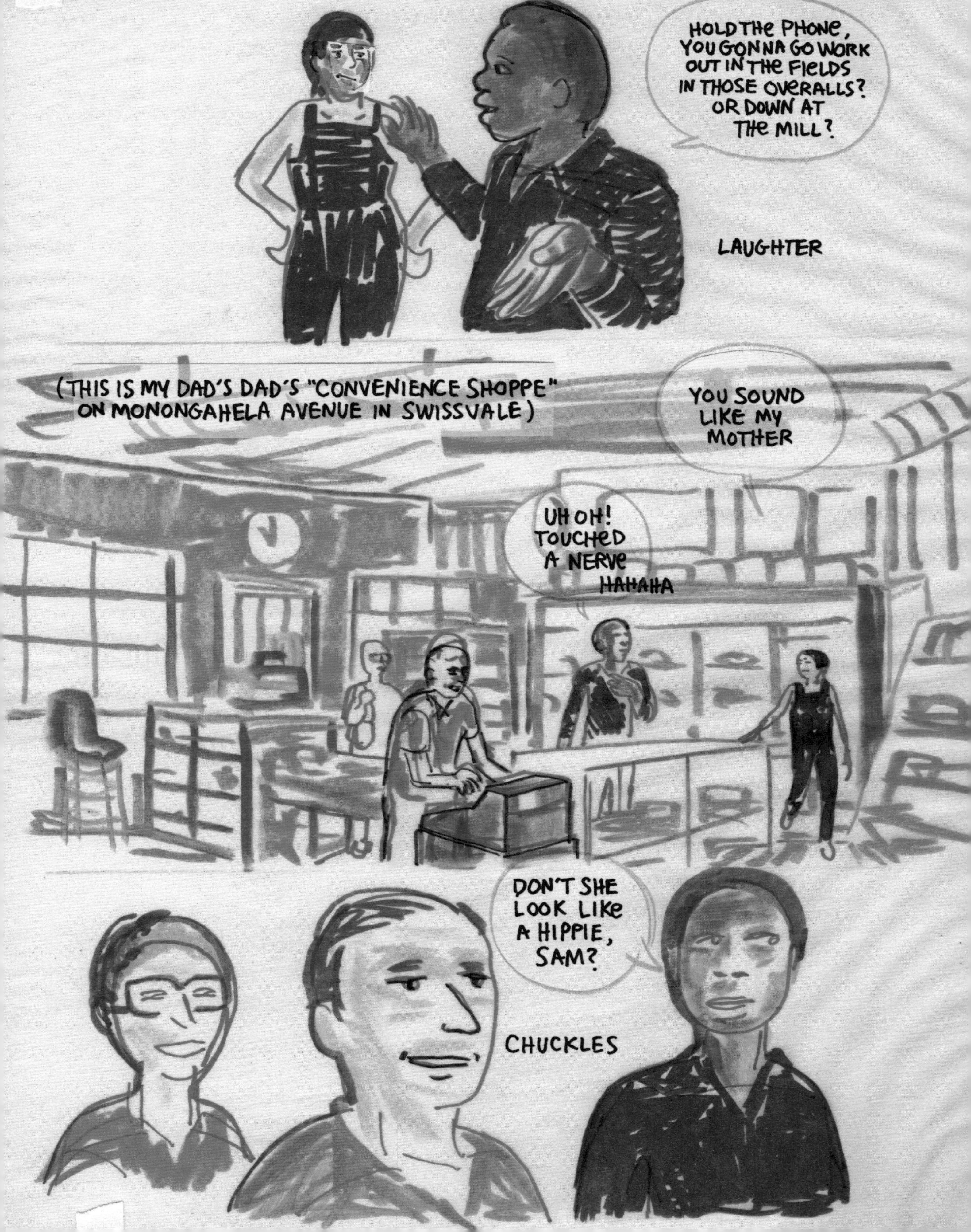
HOLD THE PHONE, YOU GONNA GO WORK OUT IN THE FIELDS IN THOSE OVERALLS? OR DOWN AT THE MILL?
LAUGHTER
(THIS IS MY DAD'S DAD'S "CONVENIENCE SHOPPE" ON MONONGAHELA AVENUE IN SWISSVALE)
YOU SOUND LIKE MY MOTHER
UH OH! TOUCHED A NERVE HAHAHA
DON'T SHE LOOK LIKE A HIPPIE, SAM?
CHUCKLES

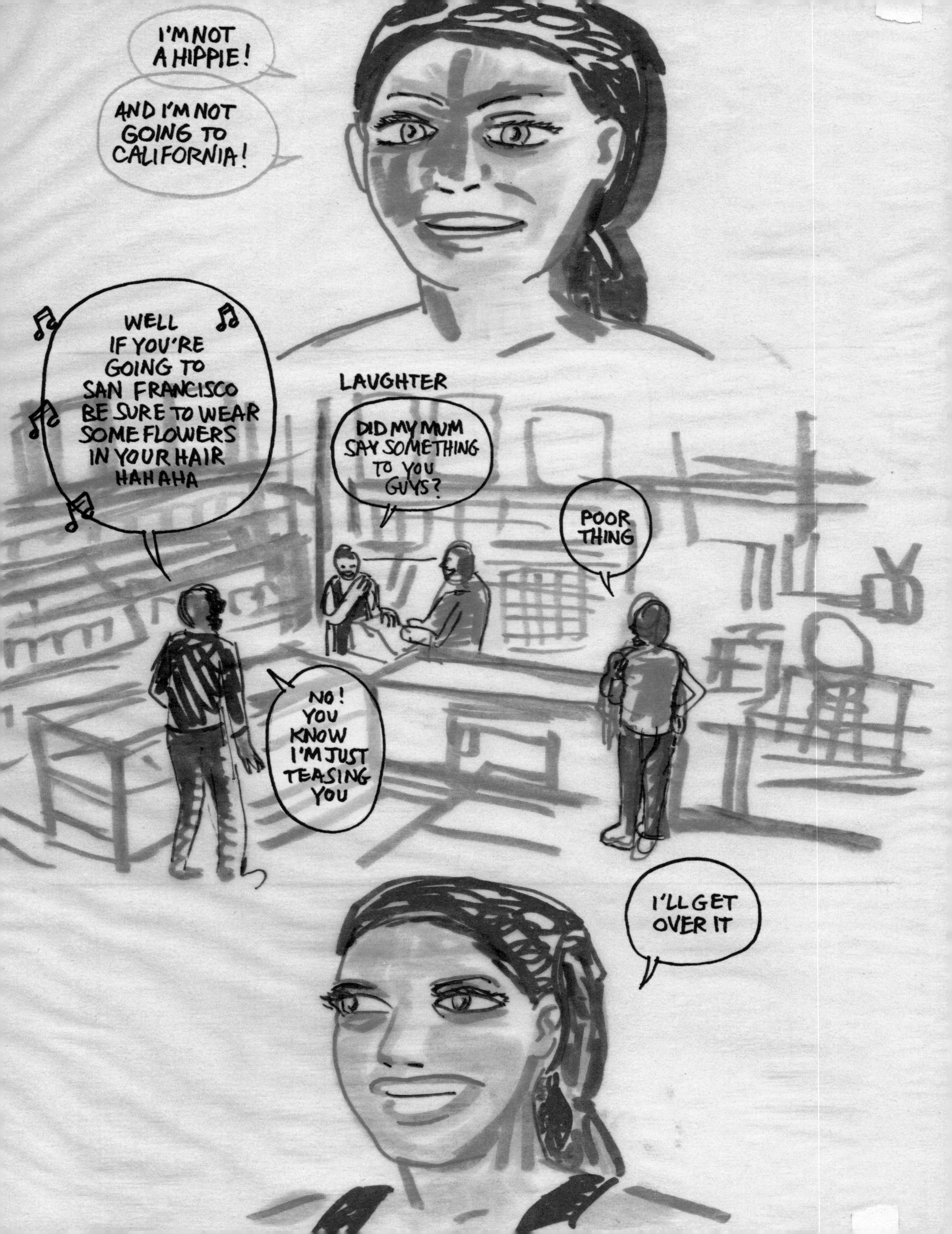
I'M NOT A HIPPIE!
AND I'M NOT GOING TO CALIFORNIA!
WELL IF YOU'RE GOING TO SAN FRANCISCO BE SURE TO WEAR SOME FLOWERS IN YOUR HAIR HAHAHA
LAUGHTER
DID MY MUM SAY SOMETHING TO YOU GUYS?
POOR THING
NO! YOU KNOW I'M JUST TEASING YOU
I'LL GET OVER IT

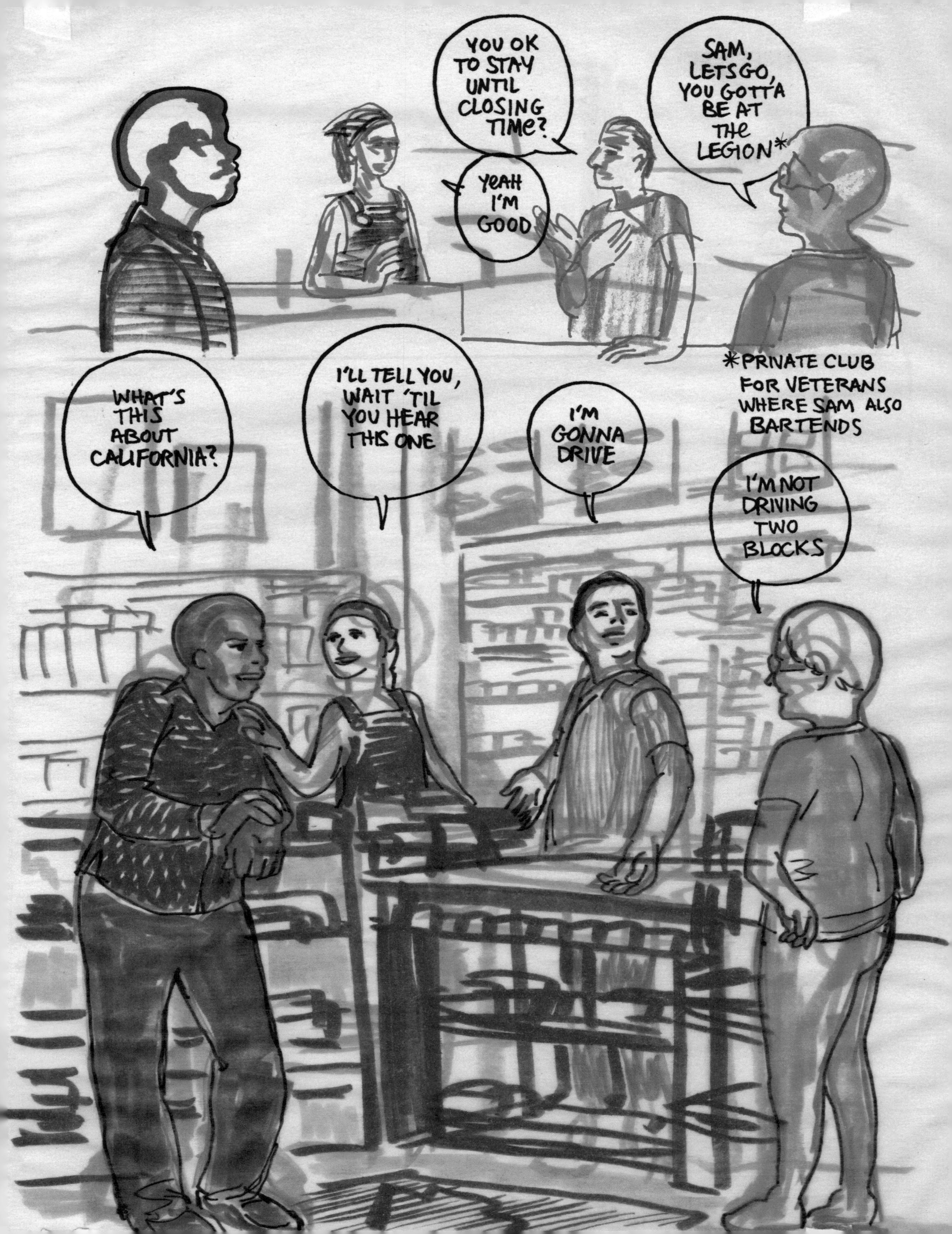
YOU OK TO STAY UNTIL CLOSING TIME?
YeAH I'M GOOD
SAM, LETSGO, YOU GOTT'A BE AT THE LEGION*
*PRIVATE CLUB FOR VETERANS WHERE SAM ALSO BARTENDS
WHAT'S THIS ABOUT CALIFORNIA?
I'LL TELL YOU, WAIT 'TIL YOU HEAR THIS ONE
I'M GONNA DRIVE
I'M NOT DRIVING TWO BLOCKS

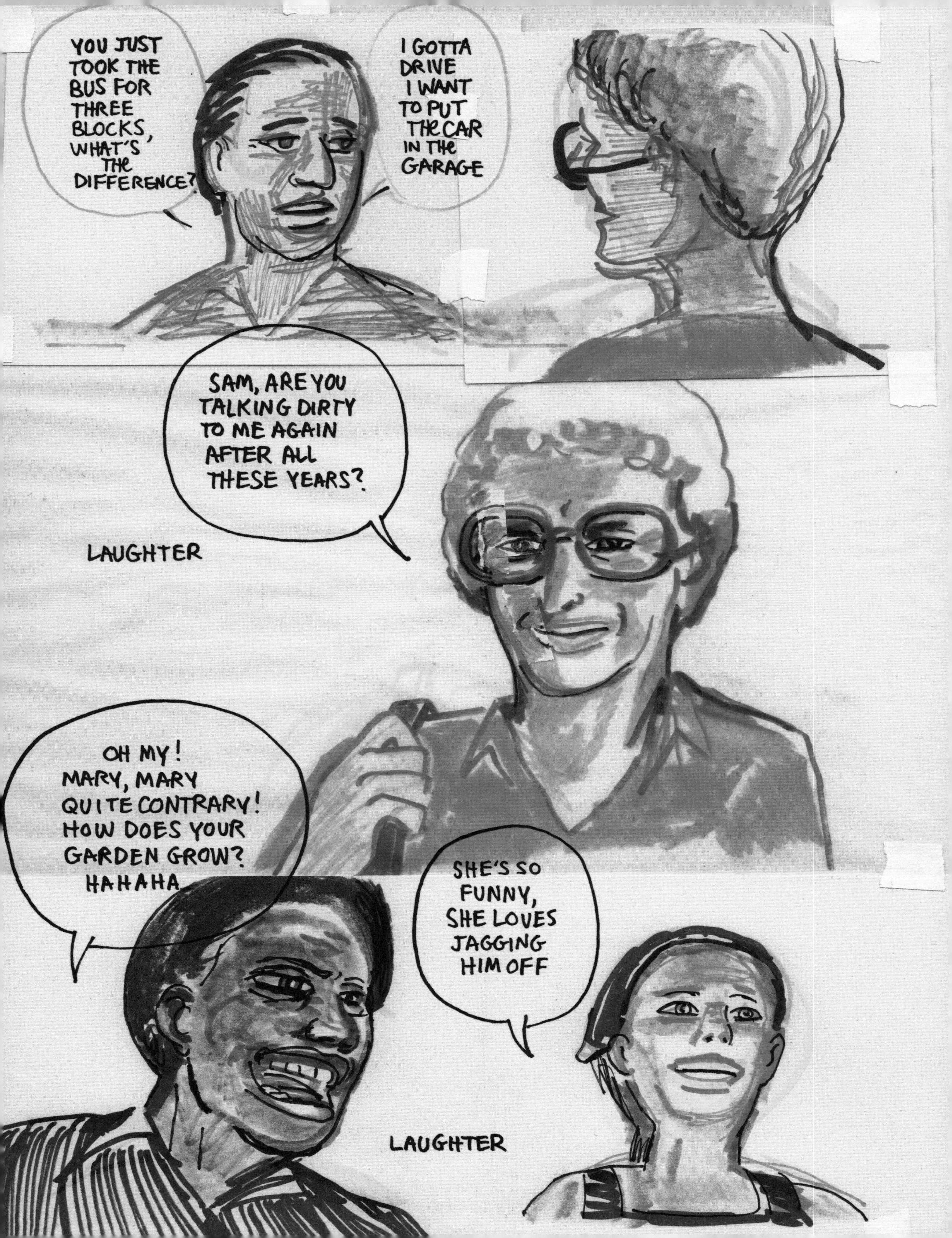
YOU JUST TOOK THE BUS FOR THREE BLOCKS, WHAT'S THE DIFFERENCE?
I GOTTA DRIVE I WANT TO PUT THE CAR IN THE GARAGE
SAM, ARE YOU TALKING DIRTY TO ME AGAIN AFTER ALL THESE YEARS?
LAUGHTER
OH MY! MARY, MARY QUITE CONTRARY! HOW DOES YOUR GARDEN GROW? HAHAHA
SHE'S SO FUNNY, SHE LOVES JAGGING HIM OFF
LAUGHTER

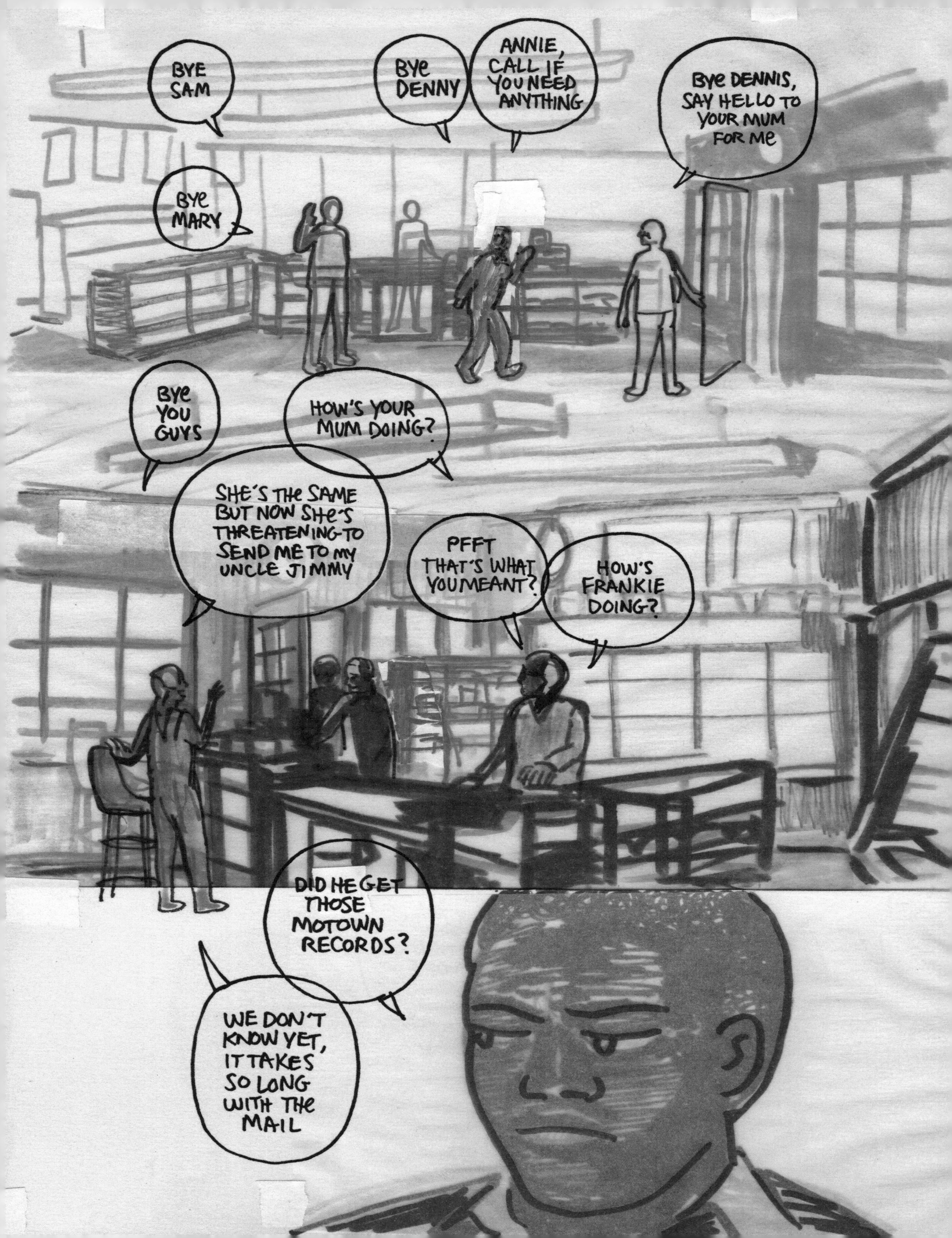
BYE SAM
BYE DENNY
ANNIE, CALL IF YOU NEED ANYTHING
BYE DENNIS, SAY HELLO TO YOUR MUM FOR ME
BYE MARY
BYE YOU GUYS
HOW'S YOUR MUM DOING?
SHE'S THE SAME BUT NOW SHE'S THREATENING TO SEND ME TO MY UNCLE JIMMY
PFFT THAT'S WHAT YOU MEANT?
HOW'S FRANKIE DOING?
DID HE GET THOSE MOTOWN RECORDS?
WE DON'T KNOW YET, IT TAKES SO LONG WITH THE MAIL

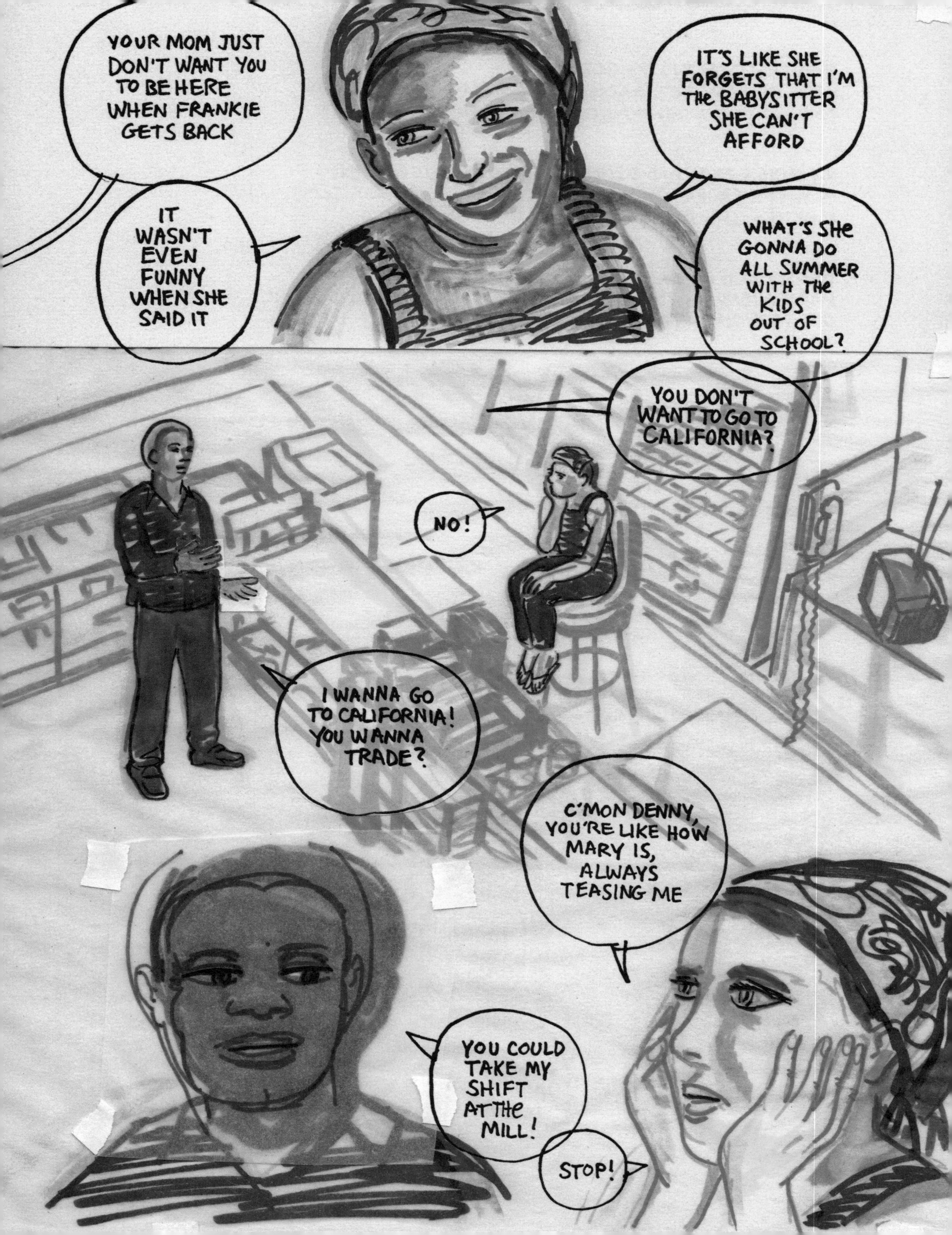
YOUR MOM JUST DON'T WANT YOU TO BE HERE WHEN FRANKIE GETS BACK
IT WASN'T EVEN FUNNY WHEN SHE SAID IT
IT'S LIKE SHE FORGETS THAT I'M THE BABYSITTER SHE CAN'T AFFORD
WHAT'S SHE GONNA DO ALL SUMMER WITH THE KIDS OUT OF SCHOOL?
YOU DON'T WANT TO GO TO CALIFORNIA?
NO!
I WANNA GO TO CALIFORNIA! YOU WANNA TRADE?
C'MON DENNY, YOU'RE LIKE HOW MARY IS, ALWAYS TEASING ME
YOU COULD TAKE MY SHIFT AT THE MILL!
STOP!

DENNY STEWART IS MY GODFATHER
HERE IN 1968, HE'S A COUPLE YEARS OUT OF HIGH SCHOOL
AND WORKING DOWN AT CARRIE FURNACE

MY MUM'S MUM AND DENNY'S MUM WORK TOGETHER
IN WILKINSBURG, OVER AT "MINE SAFETY" ON THE ASSEMBLY LINE
MAKING GAS MASKS FOR COAL MINERS

DENNY AND MY DAD GREW UP ON THE SAME BLOCK,
PARK AVENUE, OVER BY "THE LEGION" AND "THE DAGO CLUB"
OFF MONONGAHELA NEAR "THE TRIANGLE" BAR + GRILL

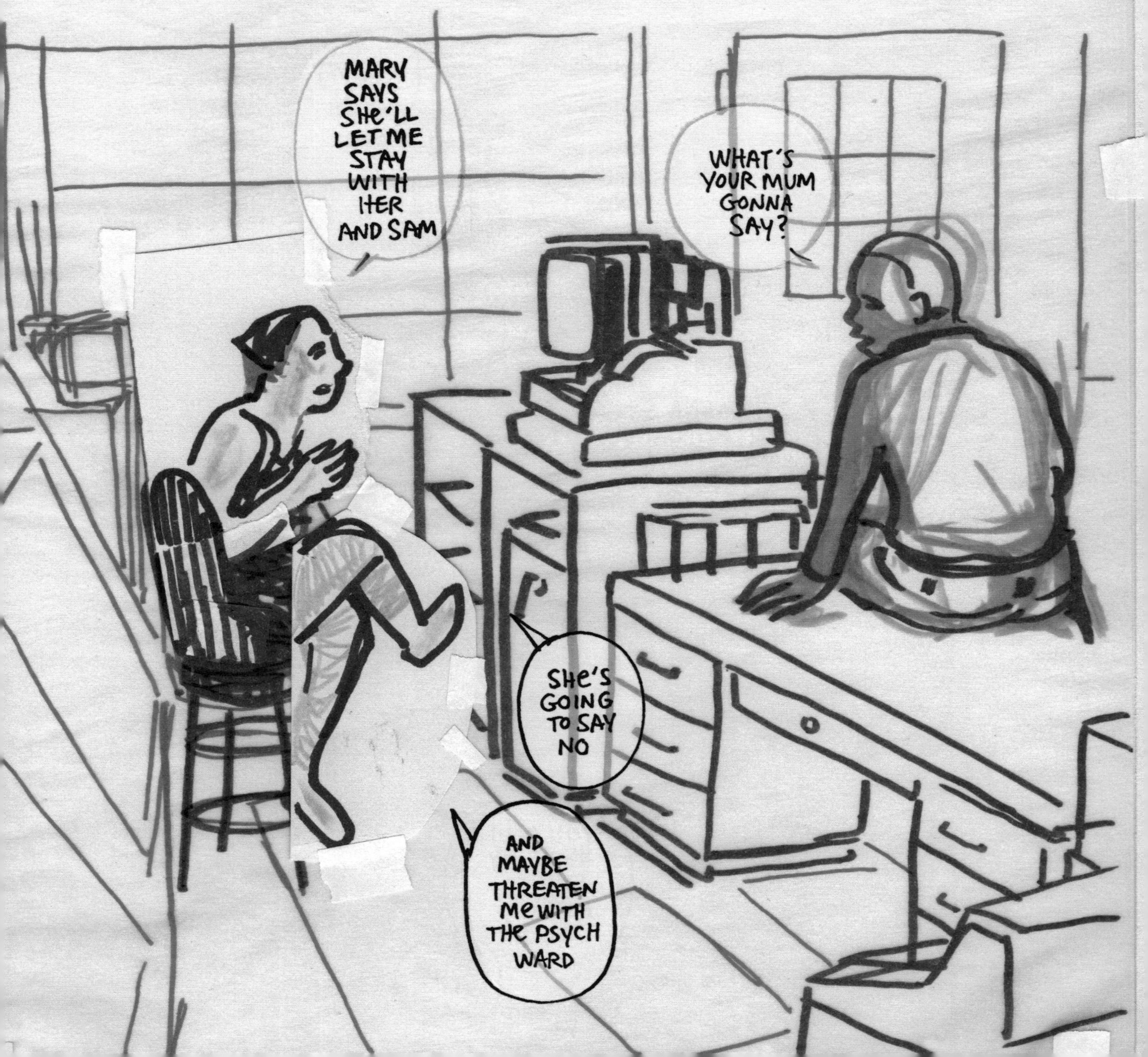
MARY SAYS SHE'LL LET ME STAY WITH HER AND SAM
WHAT'S YOUR MUM GONNA SAY?
SHE'S GOING TO SAY NO
AND MAYBE THREATEN ME WITH THE PSYCH WARD

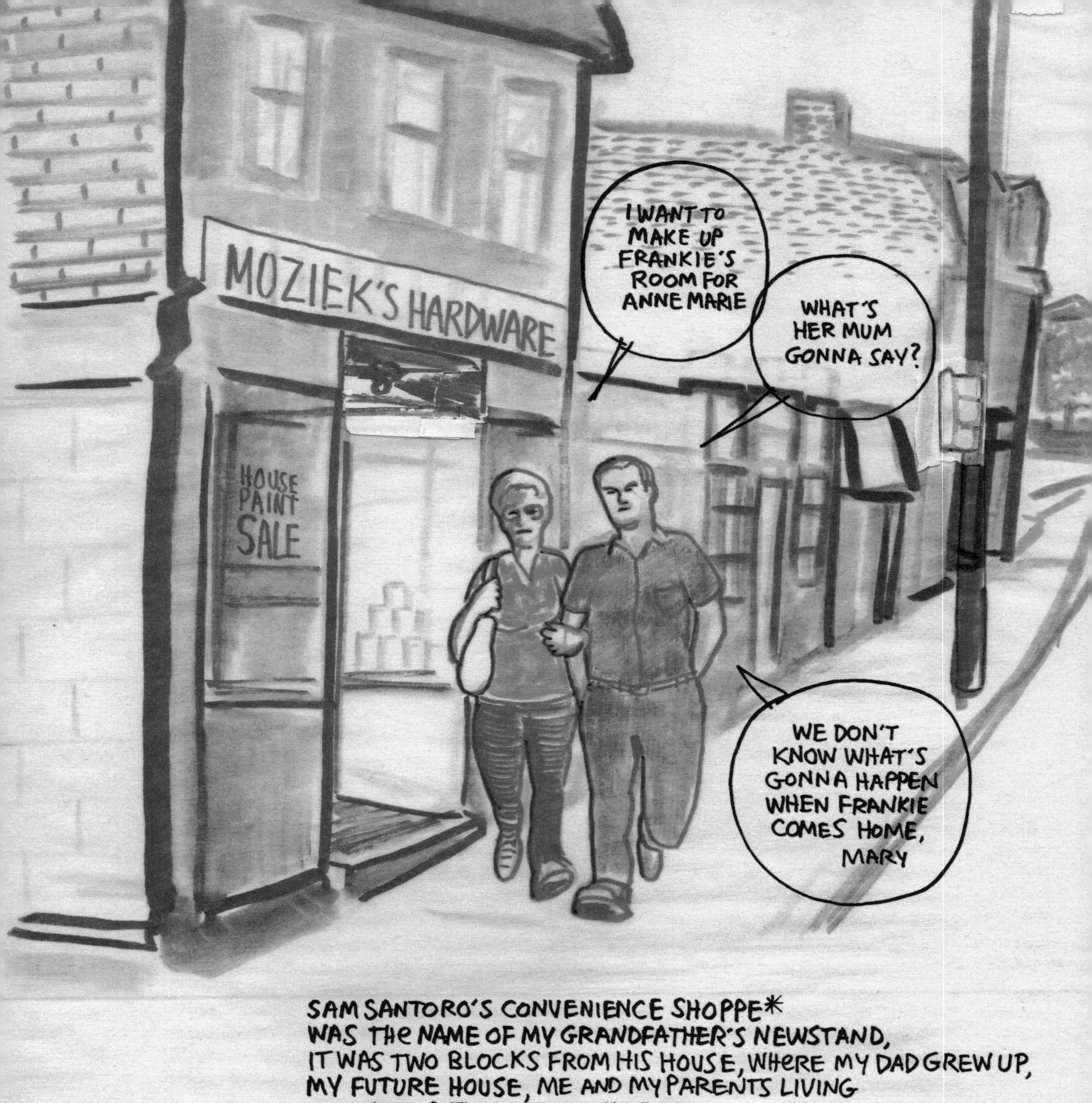
MOZIEK'S HARDWARE
HOUSE PAINT SALE
I WANT TO MAKE UP FRANKIE'S ROOM FOR ANNE MARIE
WHAT'S HER MUM GONNA SAY?
WE DON'T KNOW WHAT'S GONNA HAPPEN WHEN FRANKIE COMES HOME, MARY

SAM SANTORO'S CONVENIENCE SHOPPE*
WAS THE NAME OF MY GRANDFATHER'S NEWSTAND,
IT WAS TWO BLOCKS FROM HIS HOUSE, WHERE MY DAD GREW UP,
MY FUTURE HOUSE, ME AND MY PARENTS LIVING
ON THE TOP FLOOR AND THE ATTIC
AND MY GRANDPARENTS, MARY AND SAM,
LIVING ON THE FIRST FLOOR, ALL IN ONE HOUSE,
AND IF IT WASN'T FOR THIS CONVERSATION,
IT MAY NEVER HAVE HAPPENED...

* MARY INSISTED THE SIGN READ "SHOPPE" WITH YE OLDE TIMEY SPELLING

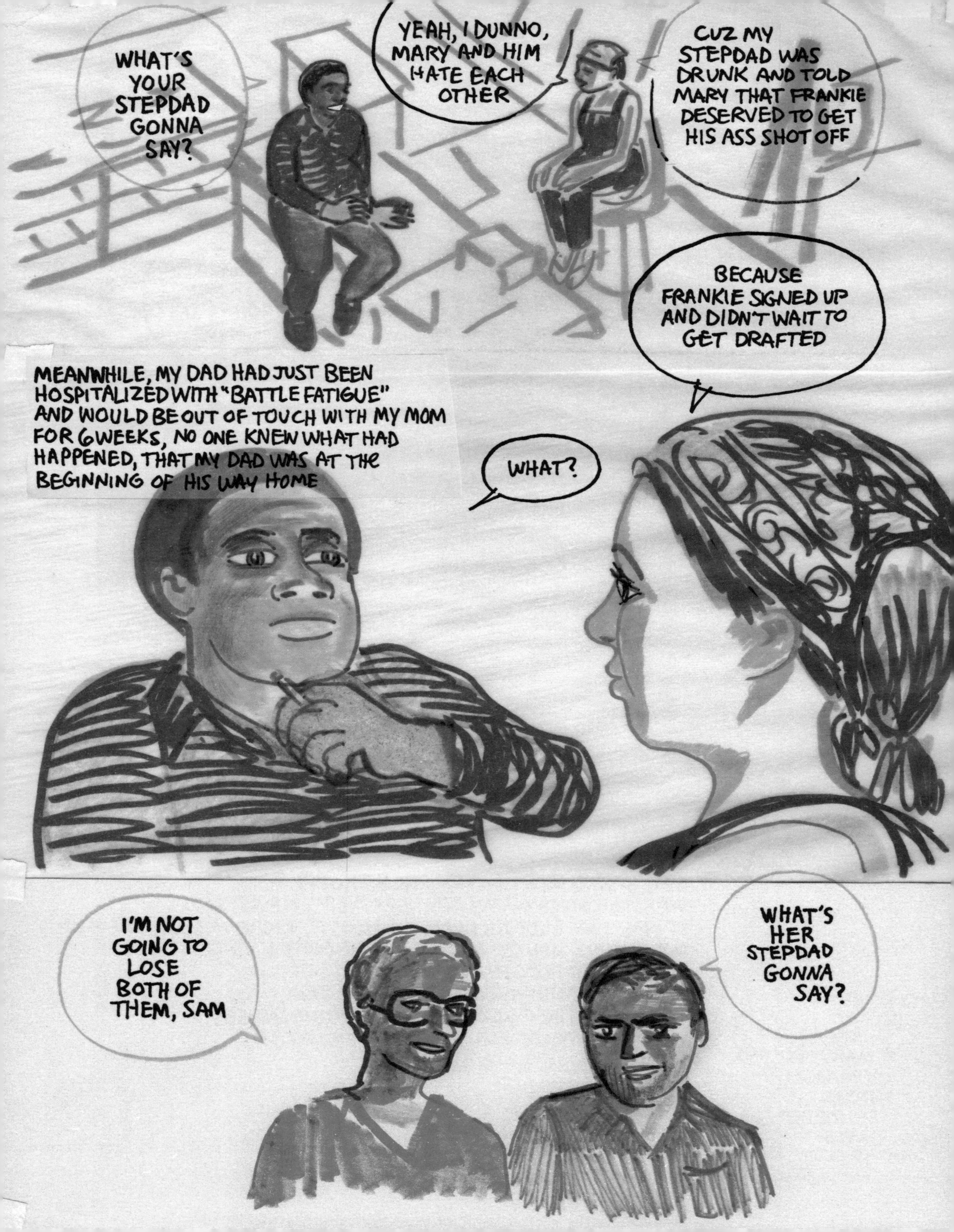
WHAT'S YOUR STEPDAD GONNA SAY?
YEAH, I DUNNO, MARY AND HIM HATE EACH OTHER
CUZ MY STEPDAD WAS DRUNK AND TOLD MARY THAT FRANKIE DESERVED TO GET HIS ASS SHOT OFF
BECAUSE FRANKIE SIGNED UP AND DIDN'T WAIT TO GET DRAFTED
MEANWHILE, MY DAD HAD JUST BEEN HOSPITALIZED WITH "BATTLE FATIGUE" AND WOULD BE OUT OF TOUCH WITH MY MOM FOR 6 WEEKS, NO ONE KNEW WHAT HAD HAPPENED, THAT MY DAD WAS AT THE BEGINNING OF HIS WAY HOME
WHAT?
I'M NOT GOING TO LOSE BOTH OF THEM, SAM
WHAT'S HER STEPDAD GONNA SAY?

WHEN MY DAD MADE IT HOME FROM VIETNAM
LATER THAT SUMMER, THERE WAS AN ENGAGEMENT PARTY
FOR HIM AND MY MOM TO ANNOUNCE THEIR PLANNED WEDDING

NO ONE FROM MY MOTHER'S SIDE SHOWED UP TO THE PARTY,
MY MOM SAID THAT HER AND MY DAD WERE SITTING THERE
UNDER ALL THE PARTY DECORATIONS AT A LONG EMPTY TABLE,
TALKING ABOUT BREAKING UP, THAT MY MUM'S MUM REALLY
WAS AGAINST THEIR MARRIAGE, WHAT ELSE COULD THEY DO?
WHEN MARY SAT DOWN WITH MY PARENTS
AND TOLD THEM THAT THEY WERE GOING TO ELOPE,
GO TO MARYLAND WHERE THE LAWS WERE DIFFERENT,
THAT SAM WAS GOING TO GIVE THEM THE MONEY
AND DRIVE DOWN WITH THEM TO DO IT

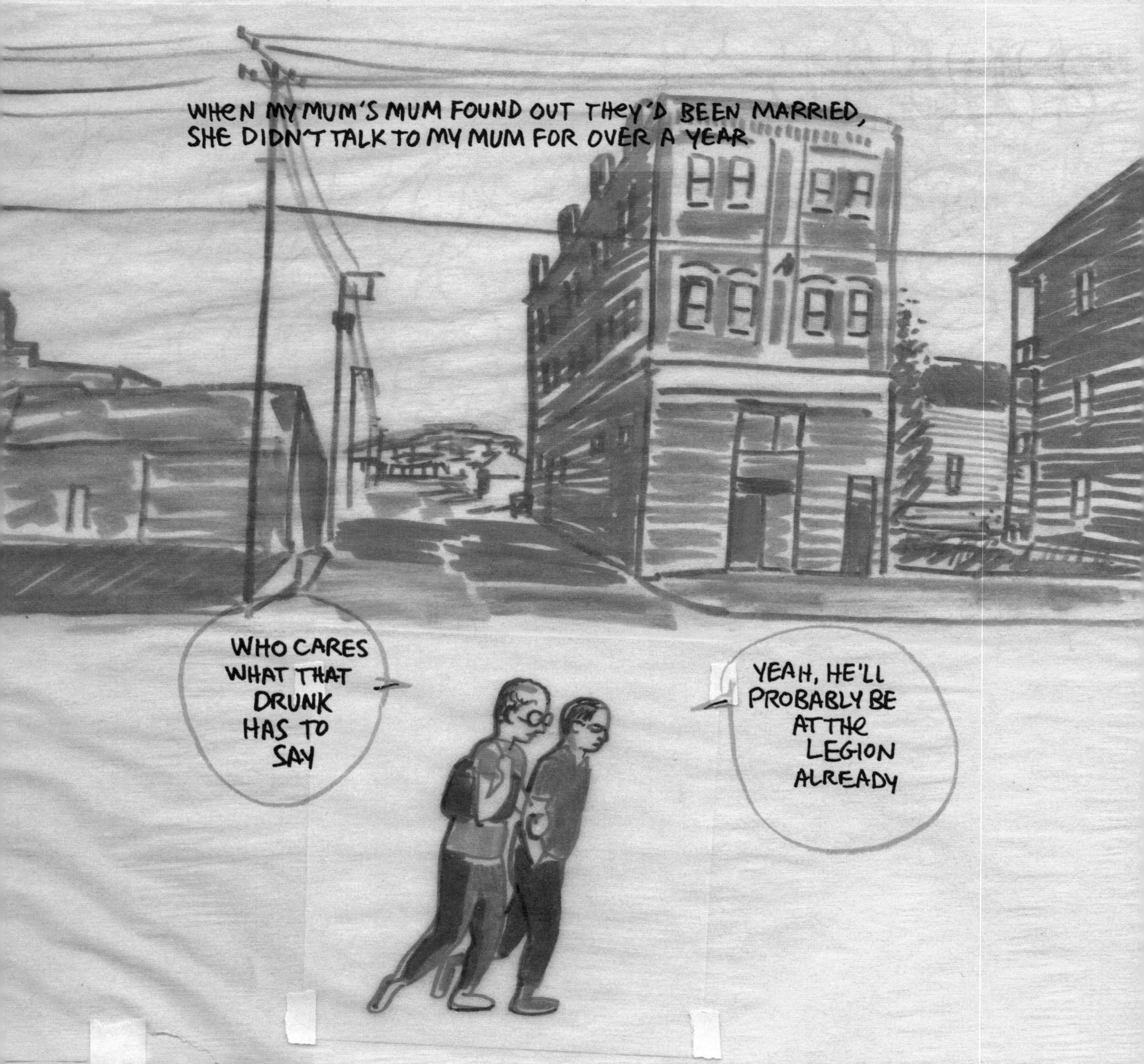
WHEN MY MUM'S MUM FOUND OUT THEY'D BEEN MARRIED,
SHE DIDN'T TALK TO MY MUM FOR OVER A YEAR
WHO CARES WHAT THAT DRUNK HAS TO SAY
YEAH, HE'LL PROBABLY BE AT THE LEGION ALREADY

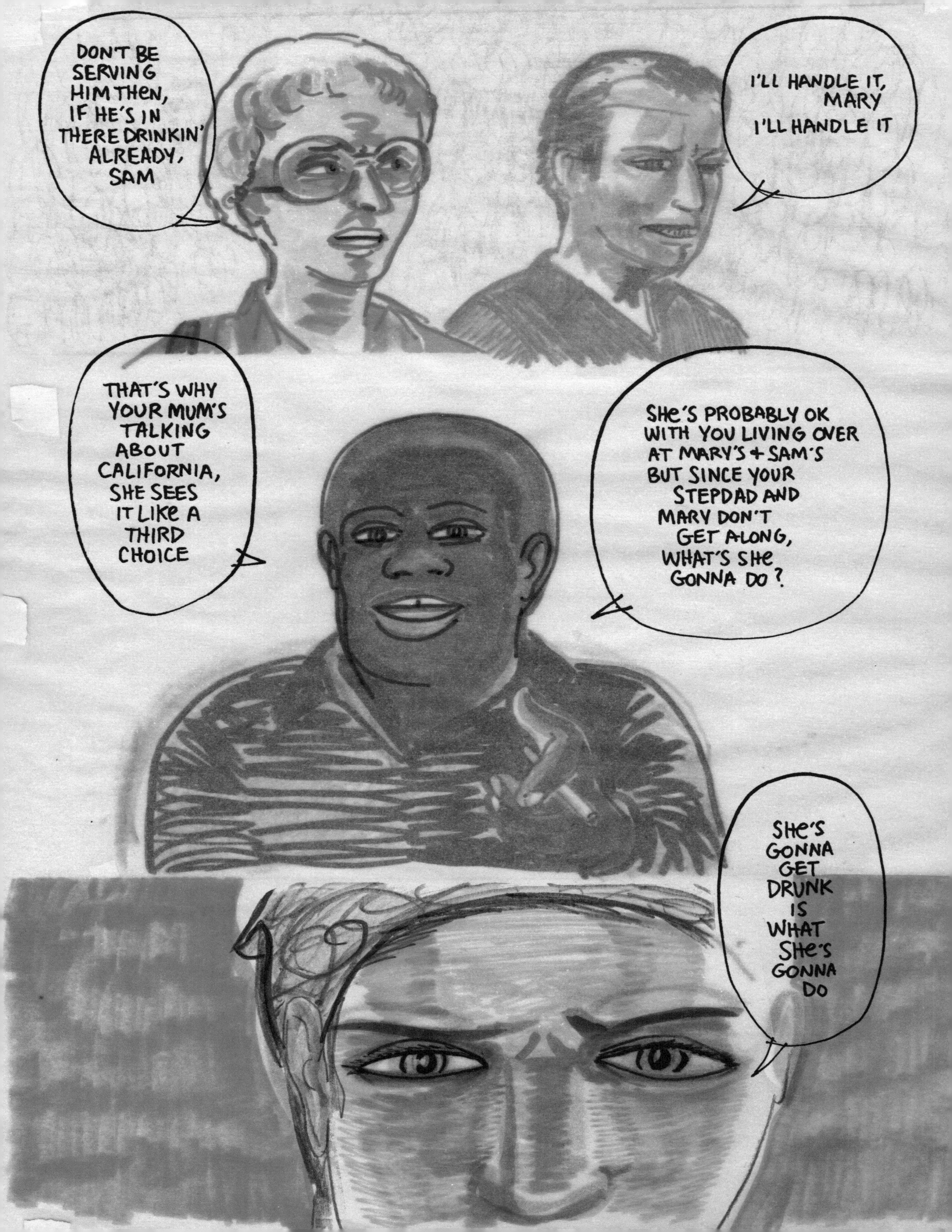
DON'T BE SERVING HIM THEN, IF HE'S IN THERE DRINKIN' ALREADY, SAM
I'LL HANDLE IT, MARY I'LL HANDLE IT
THAT'S WHY YOUR MUM'S TALKING ABOUT CALIFORNIA, SHE SEES IT LIKE A THIRD CHOICE
SHE'S PROBABLY OK WITH YOU LIVING OVER AT MARY'S + SAM'S BUT SINCE YOUR STEPDAD AND MARY DON'T GET ALONG, WHAT'S SHE GONNA DO?
SHE'S GONNA GET DRUNK IS WHAT SHE'S GONNA DO

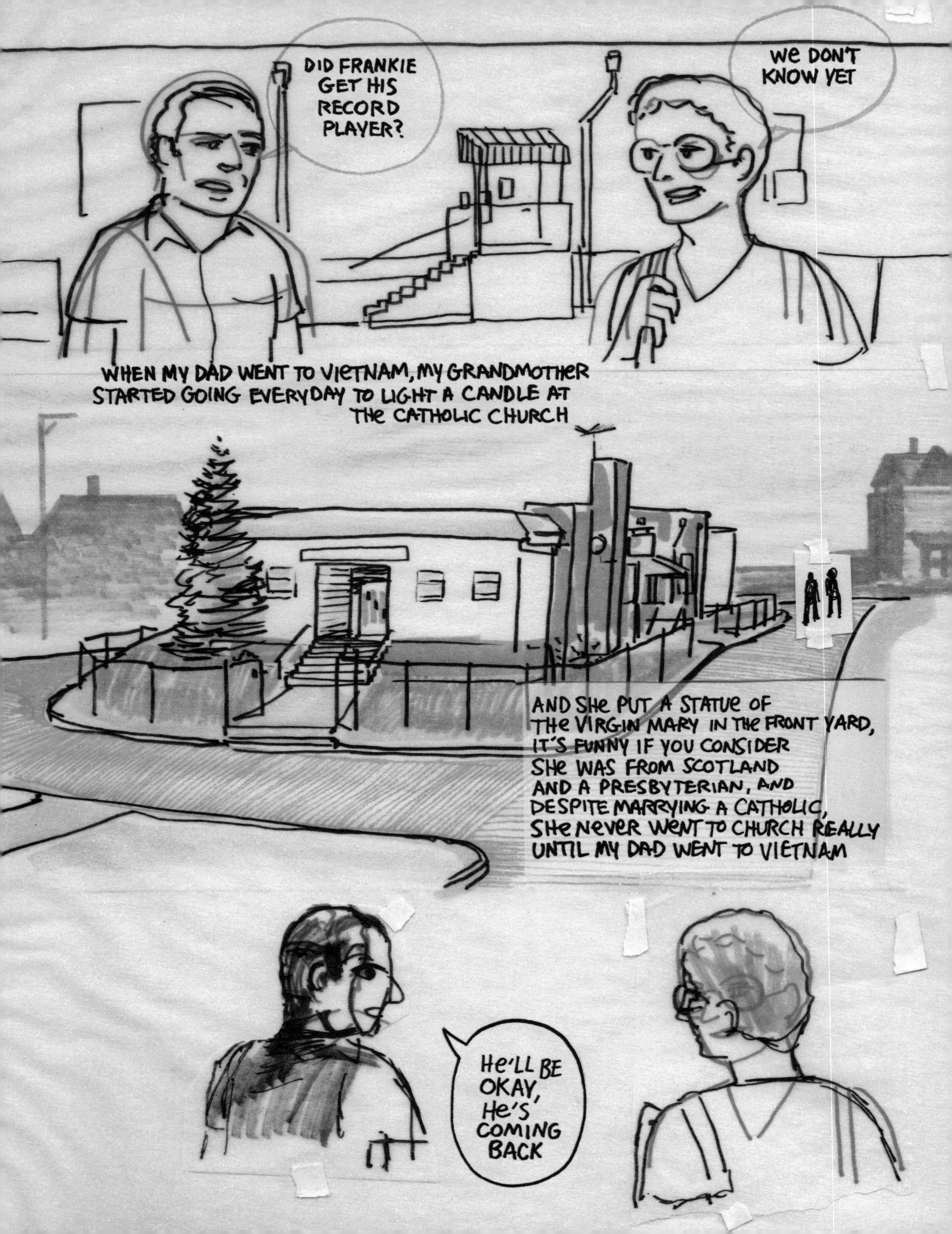
DID FRANKIE GET HIS RECORD PLAYER?
WE DON'T KNOW YET
WHEN MY DAD WENT TO VIETNAM, MY GRANDMOTHER STARTED GOING EVERYDAY TO LIGHT A CANDLE AT THE CATHOLIC CHURCH
AND SHE PUT A STATUE OF THE VIRGIN MARY IN THE FRONT YARD, IT'S FUNNY IF YOU CONSIDER SHE WAS FROM SCOTLAND AND A PRESBYTERIAN, AND DESPITE MARRYING A CATHOLIC, SHE NEVER WENT TO CHURCH REALLY UNTIL MY DAD WENT TO VIETNAM
HE'LL BE OKAY, HE'S COMING BACK

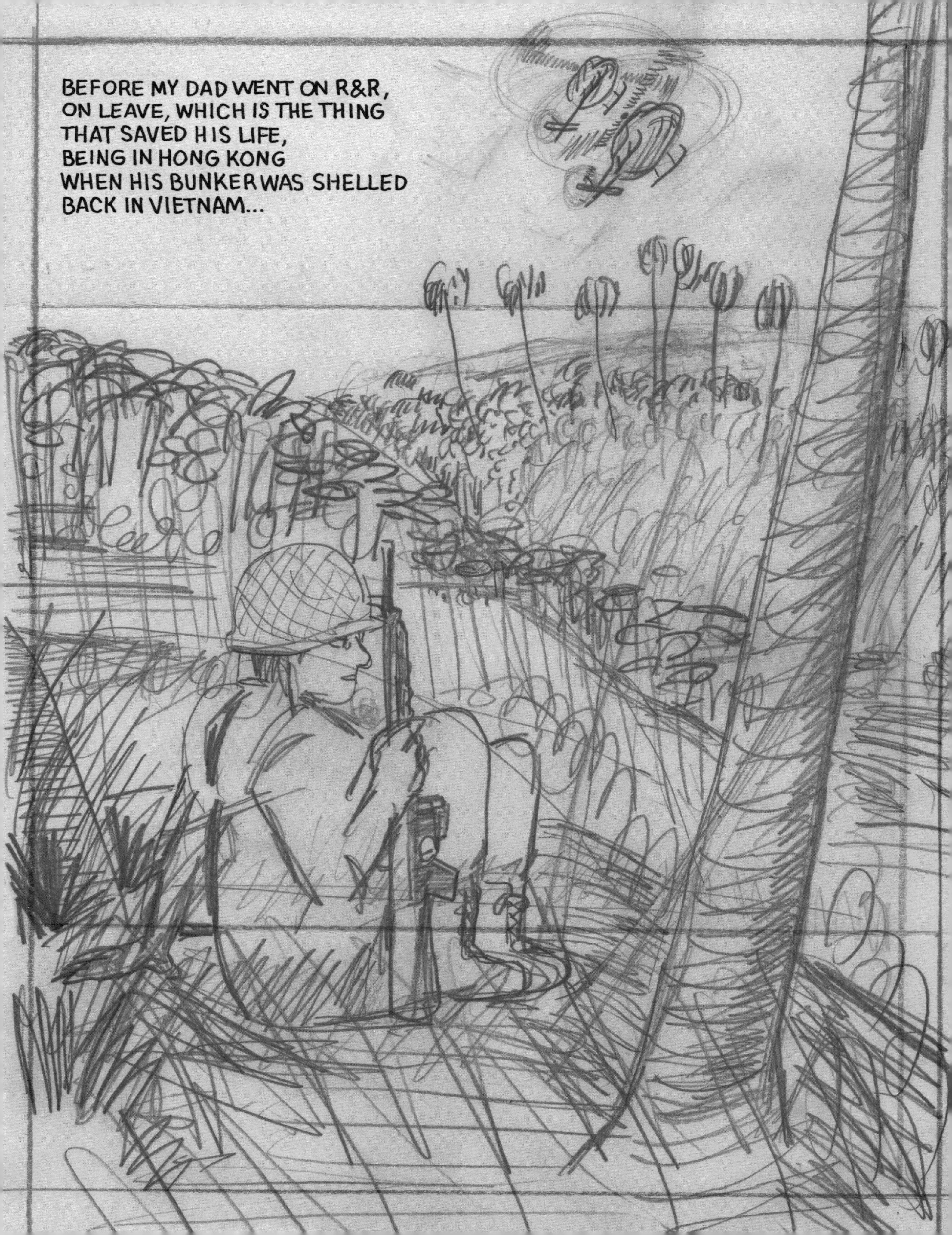
BEFORE MY DAD WENT ON R&R,
ON LEAVE, WHICH IS THE THING
THAT SAVED HIS LIFE,
BEING IN HONG KONG
WHEN HIS BUNKER WAS SHELLED
BACK IN VIETNAM...

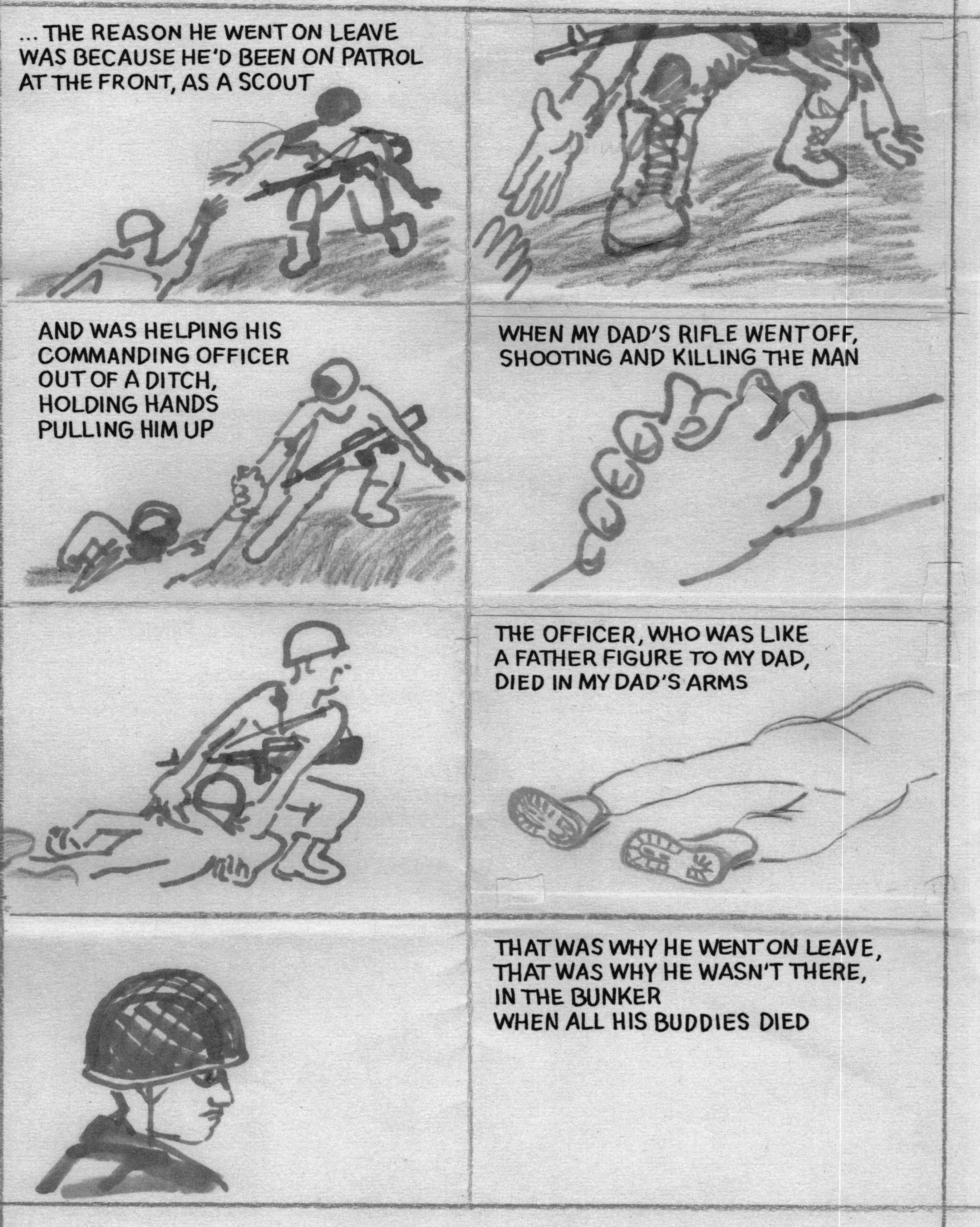
... THE REASON HE WENT ON LEAVE WAS BECAUSE HE'D BEEN ON PATROL AT THE FRONT, AS A SCOUT
AND WAS HELPING HIS COMMANDING OFFICER OUT OF A DITCH, HOLDING HANDS PULLING HIM UP
WHEN MY DAD'S RIFLE WENT OFF, SHOOTING AND KILLING THE MAN
THE OFFICER, WHO WAS LIKE A FATHER FIGURE TO MY DAD, DIED IN MY DAD'S ARMS
THAT WAS WHY HE WENT ON LEAVE, THAT WAS WHY HE WASN'T THERE, IN THE BUNKER WHEN ALL HIS BUDDIES DIED

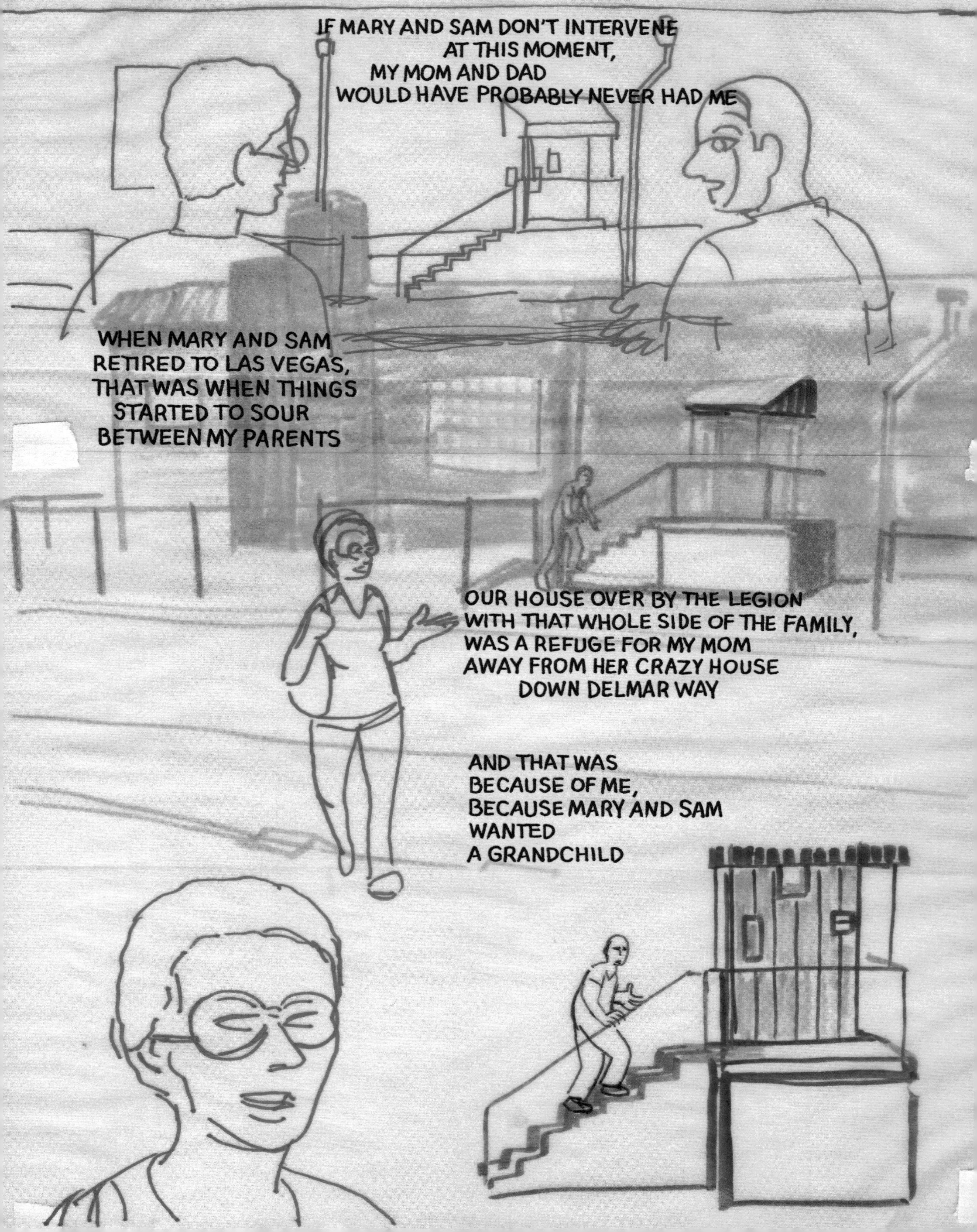
IF MARY AND SAM DON'T INTERVENE AT THIS MOMENT, MY MOM AND DAD WOULD HAVE PROBABLY NEVER HAD ME
WHEN MARY AND SAM RETIRED TO LAS VEGAS, THAT WAS WHEN THINGS STARTED TO SOUR BETWEEN MY PARENTS
OUR HOUSE OVER BY THE LEGION WITH THAT WHOLE SIDE OF THE FAMILY, WAS A REFUGE FOR MY MOM AWAY FROM HER CRAZY HOUSE DOWN DELMAR WAY
AND THAT WAS BECAUSE OF ME, BECAUSE MARY AND SAM WANTED A GRANDCHILD

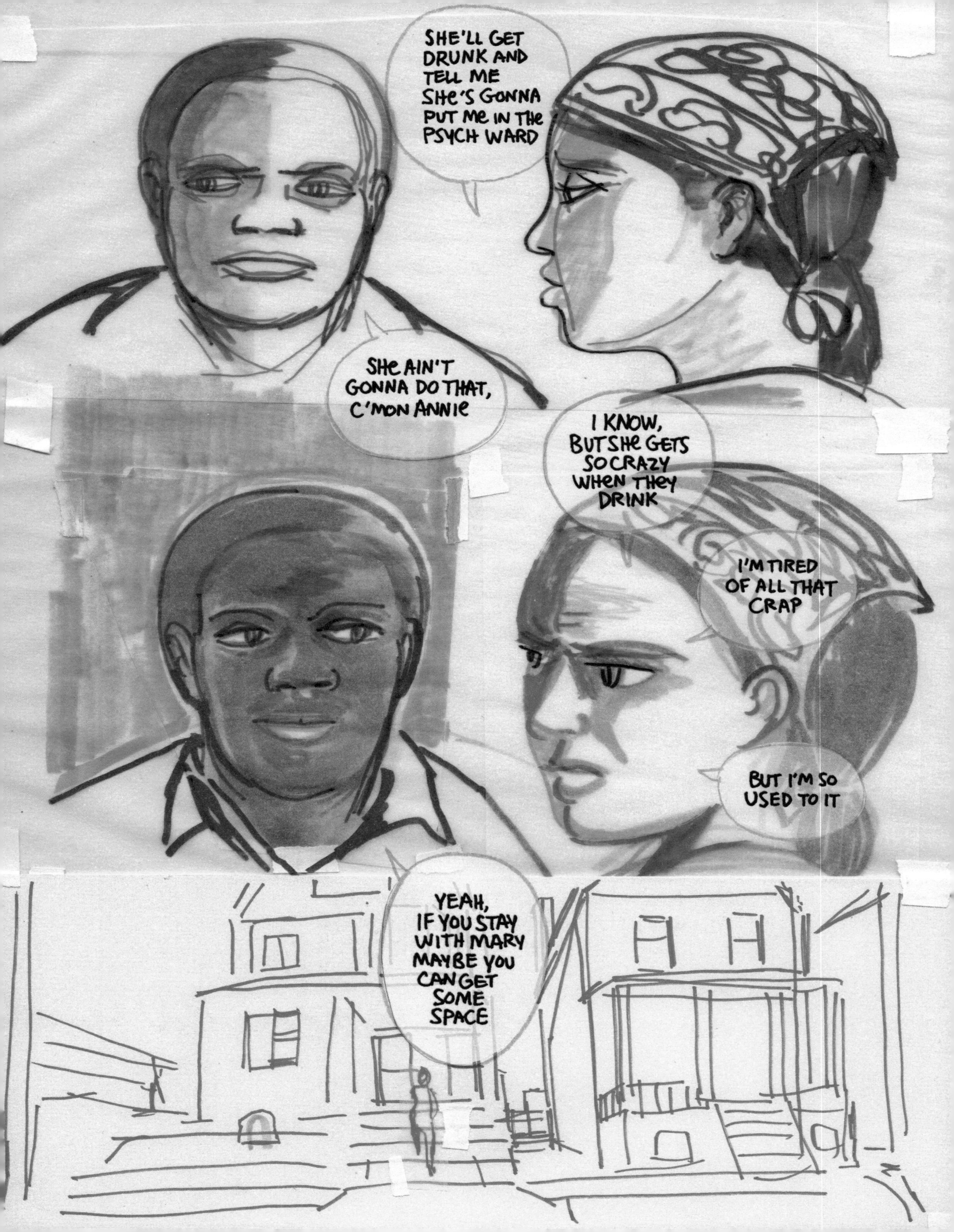
SHE'LL GET DRUNK AND TELL ME SHE'S GONNA PUT ME IN THE PSYCH WARD
SHE AIN'T GONNA DO THAT, C'MON ANNIE
I KNOW, BUT SHE GETS SO CRAZY WHEN THEY DRINK
I'M TIRED OF ALL THAT CRAP
BUT I'M SO USED TO IT
YEAH, IF YOU STAY WITH MARY MAYBE YOU CAN GET SOME SPACE

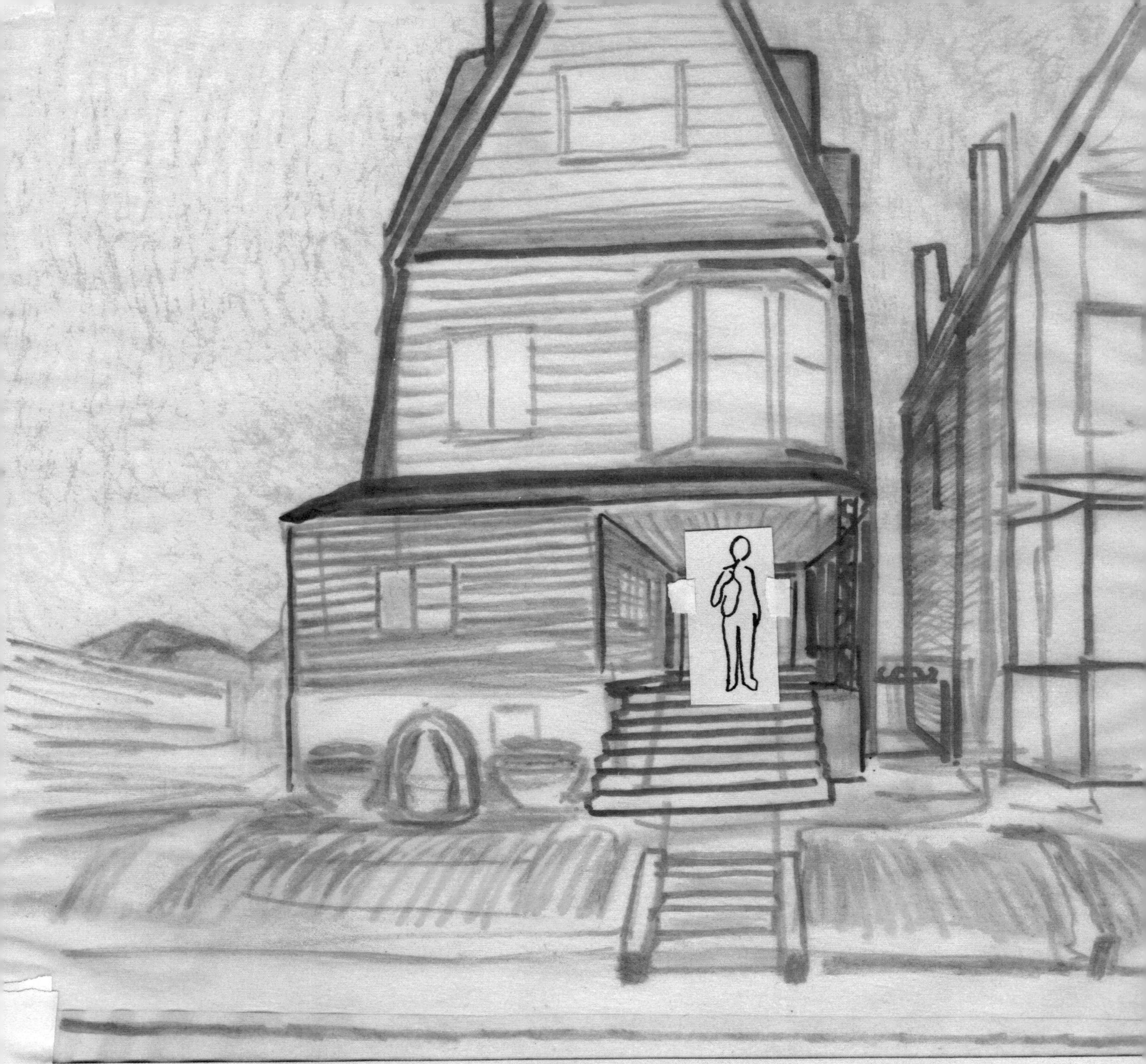

I DIDN'T KNOW MOST OF THESE STORIES
UNTIL I WAS ALMOST 30 YEARS OLD,
IT ALL CAME OUT LONG AFTER THE DIVORCE

♫ *the way you d*

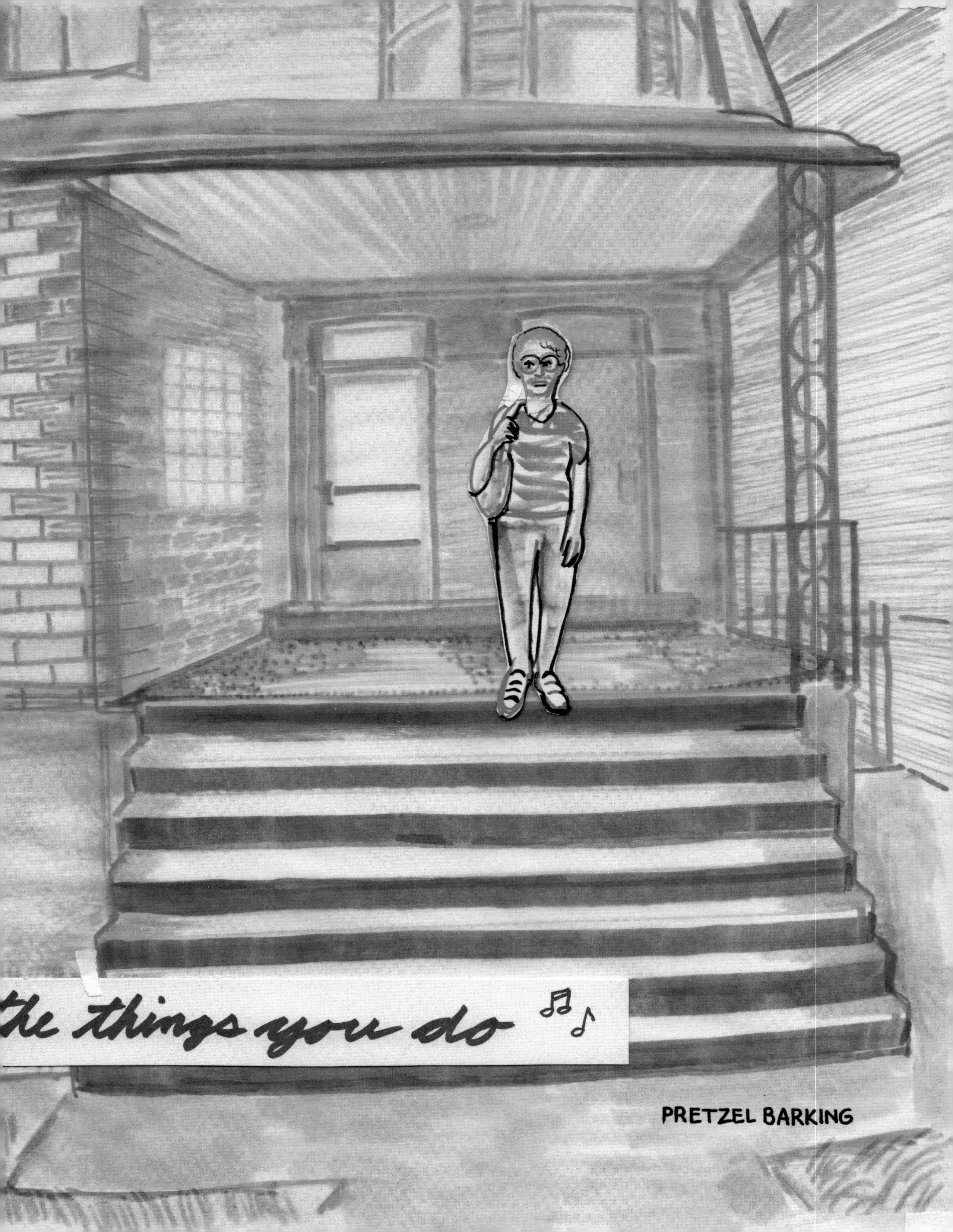
the things you do
PRETZEL BARKING

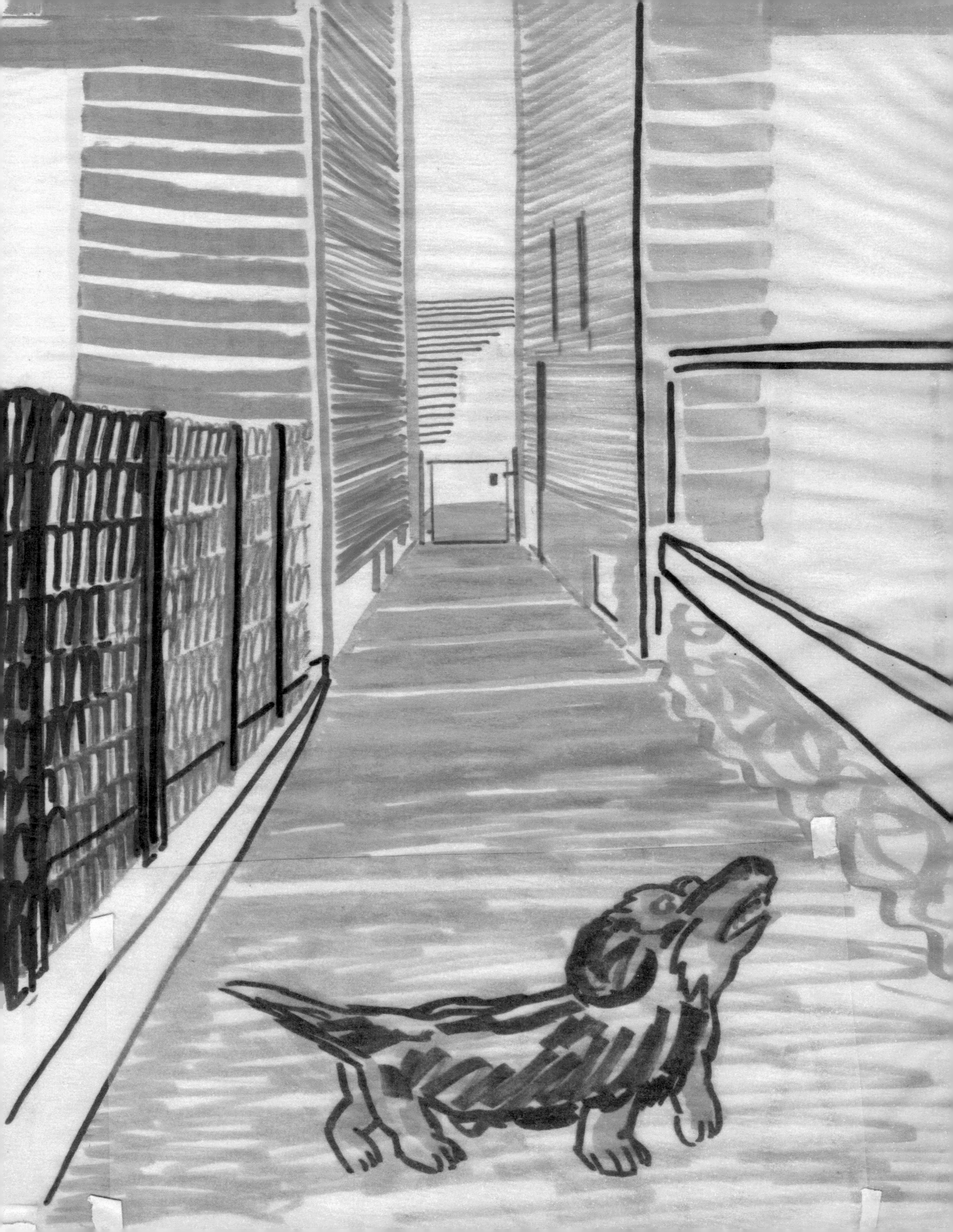

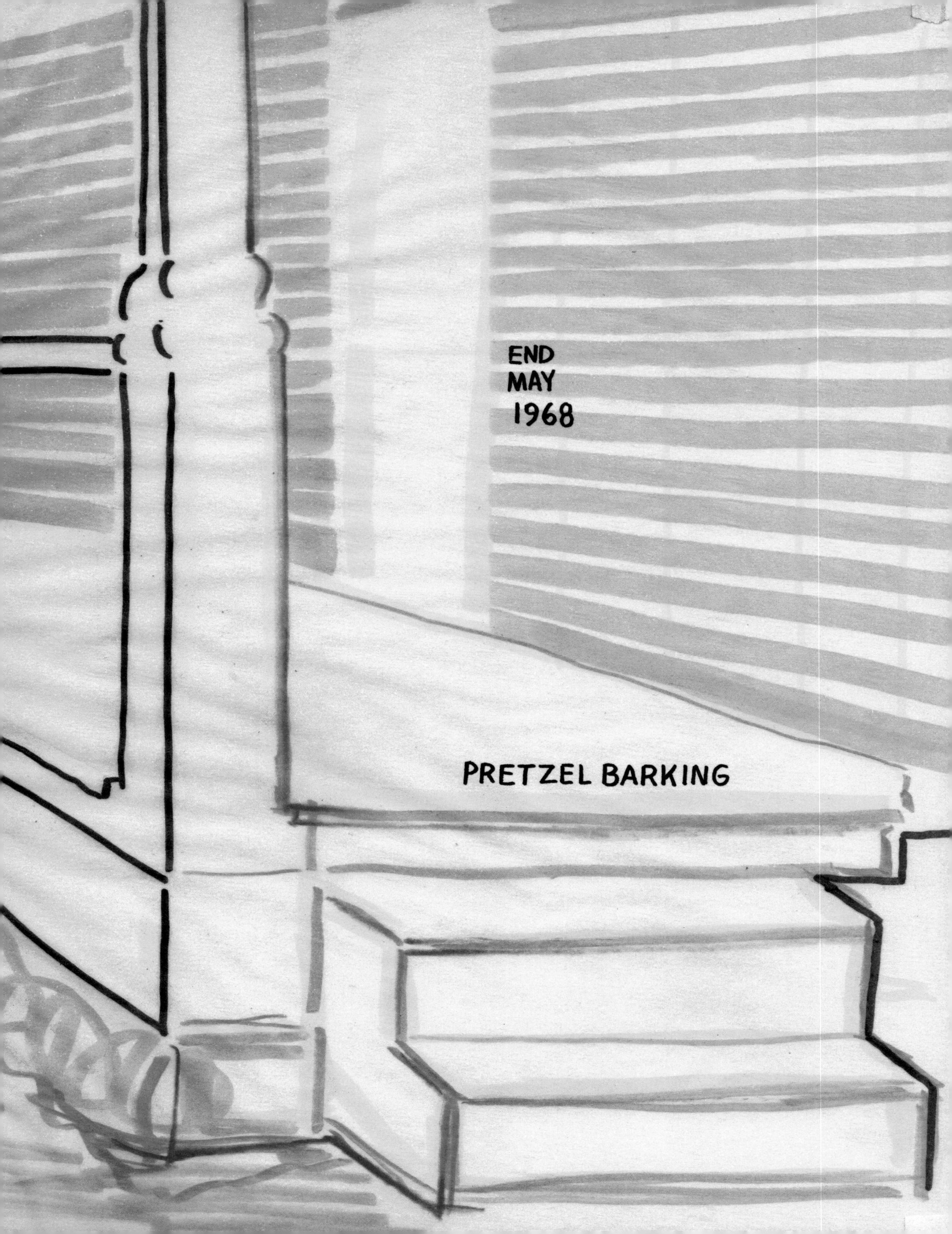
END
MAY
1968
PRETZEL BARKING

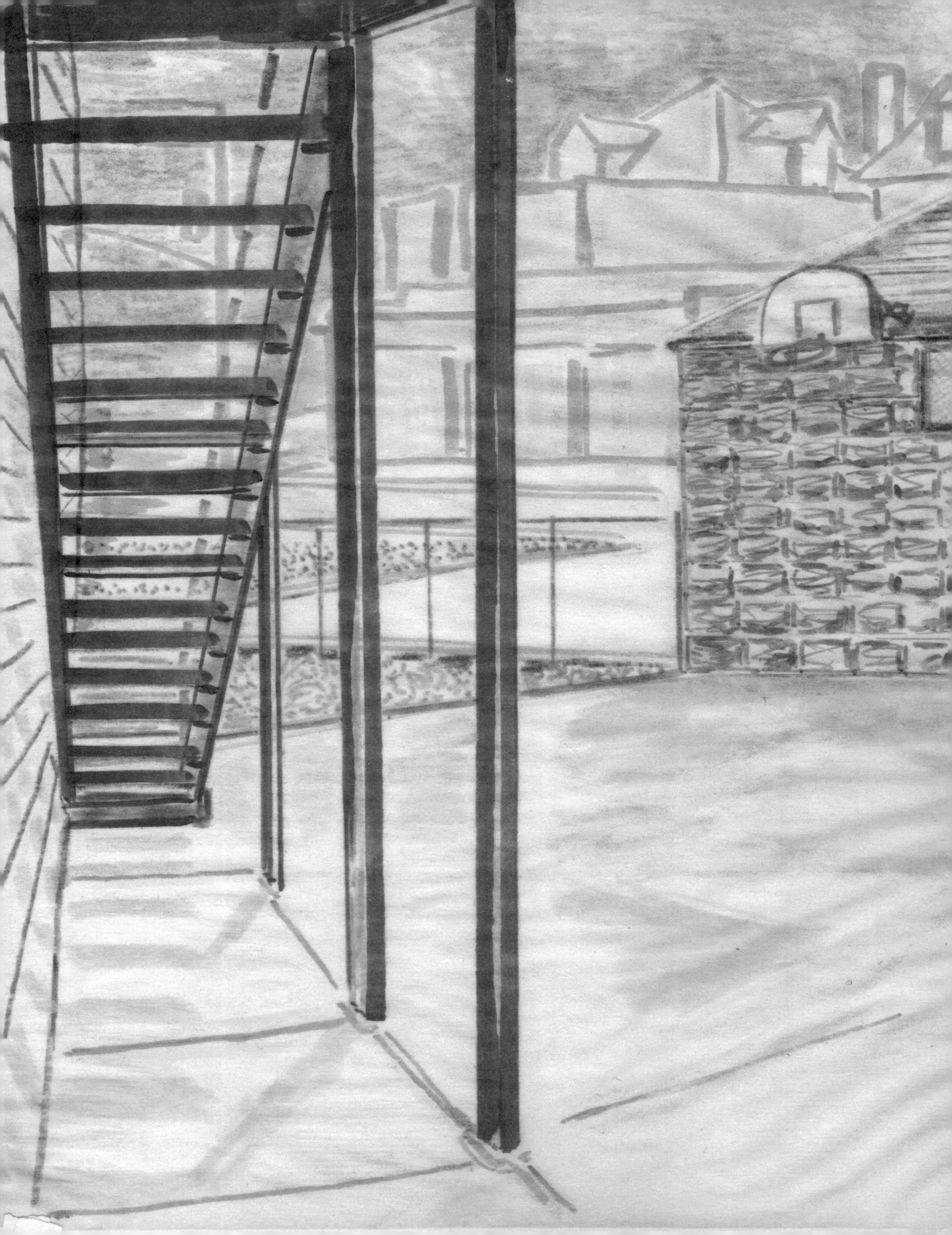

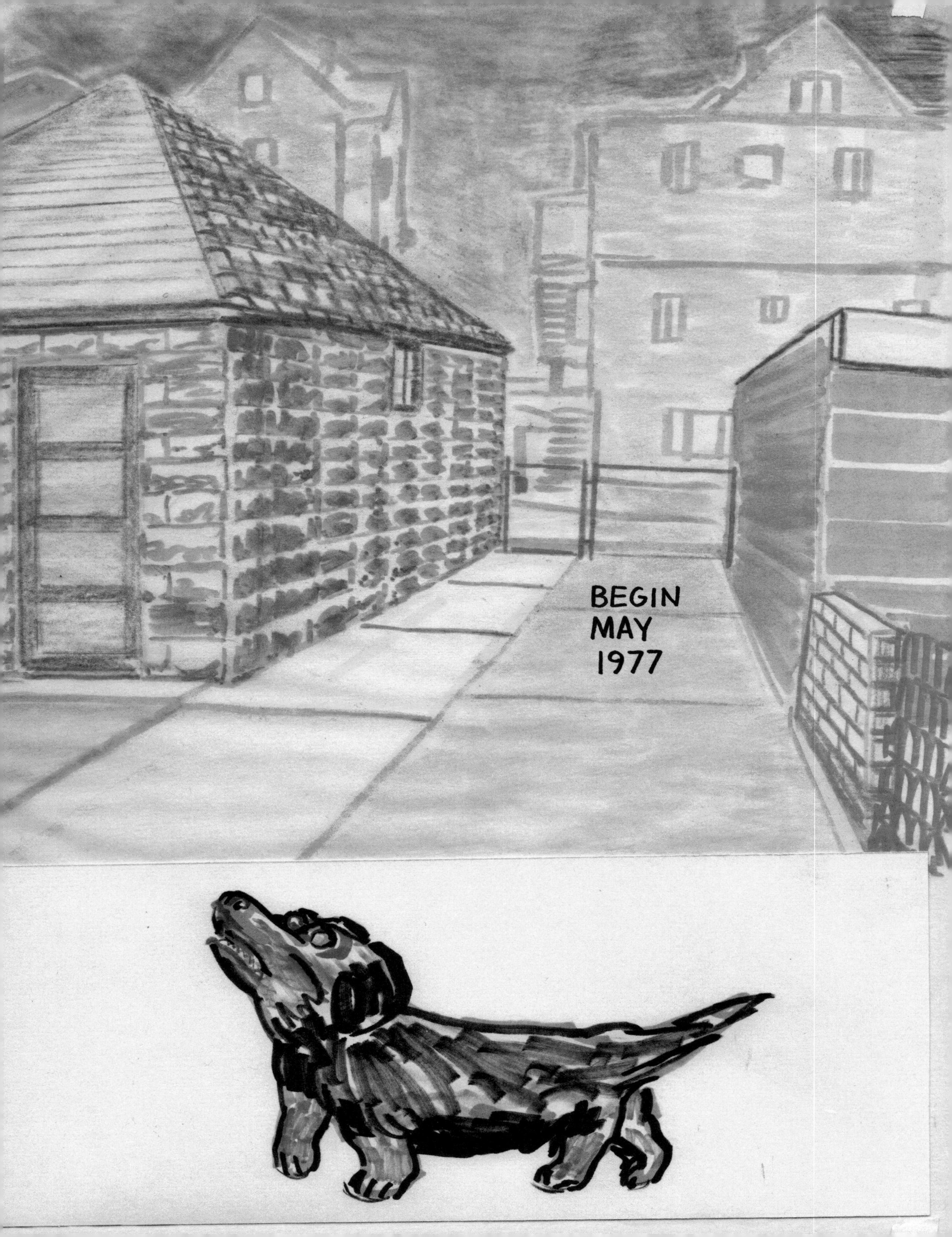
BEGIN
MAY
1977

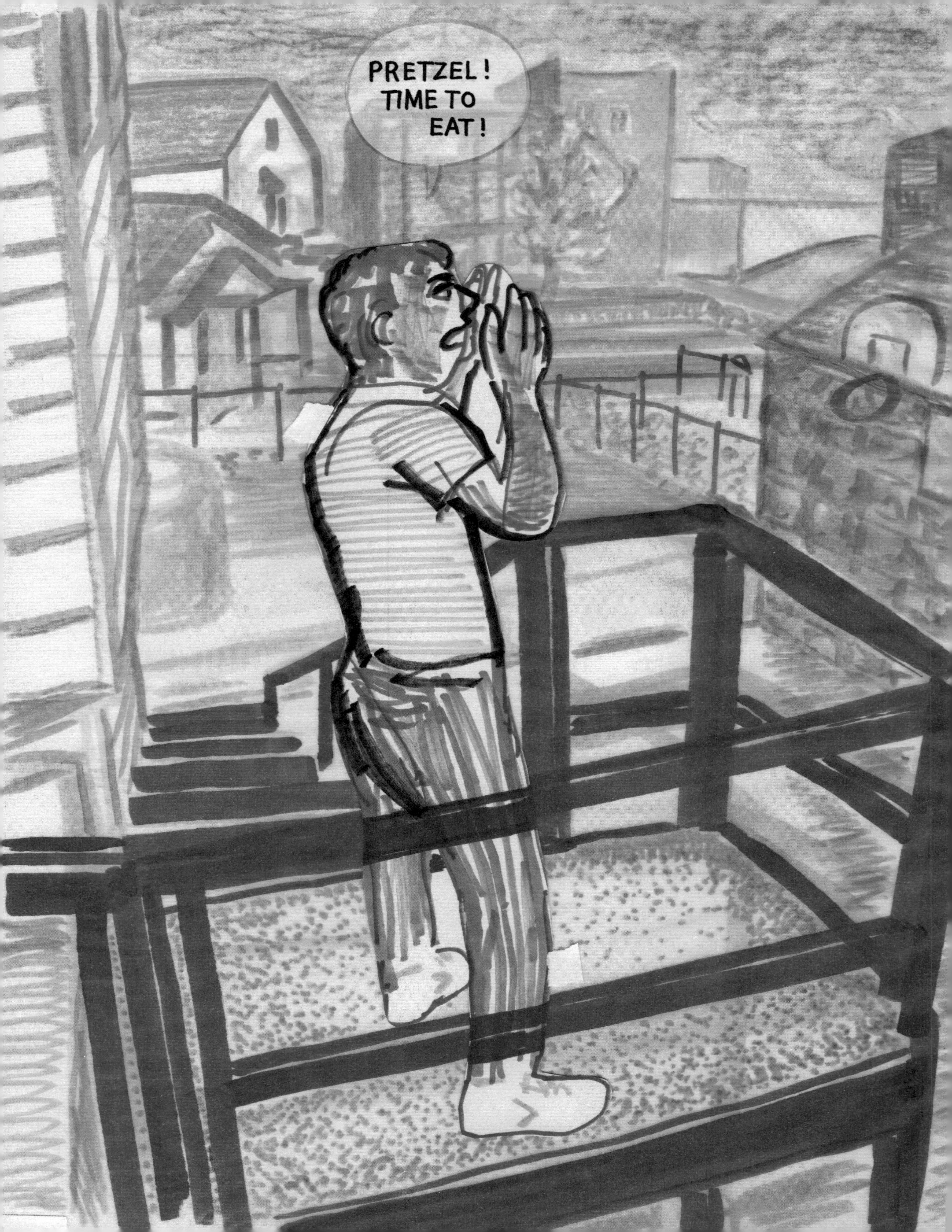
PRETZEL! TIME TO EAT!

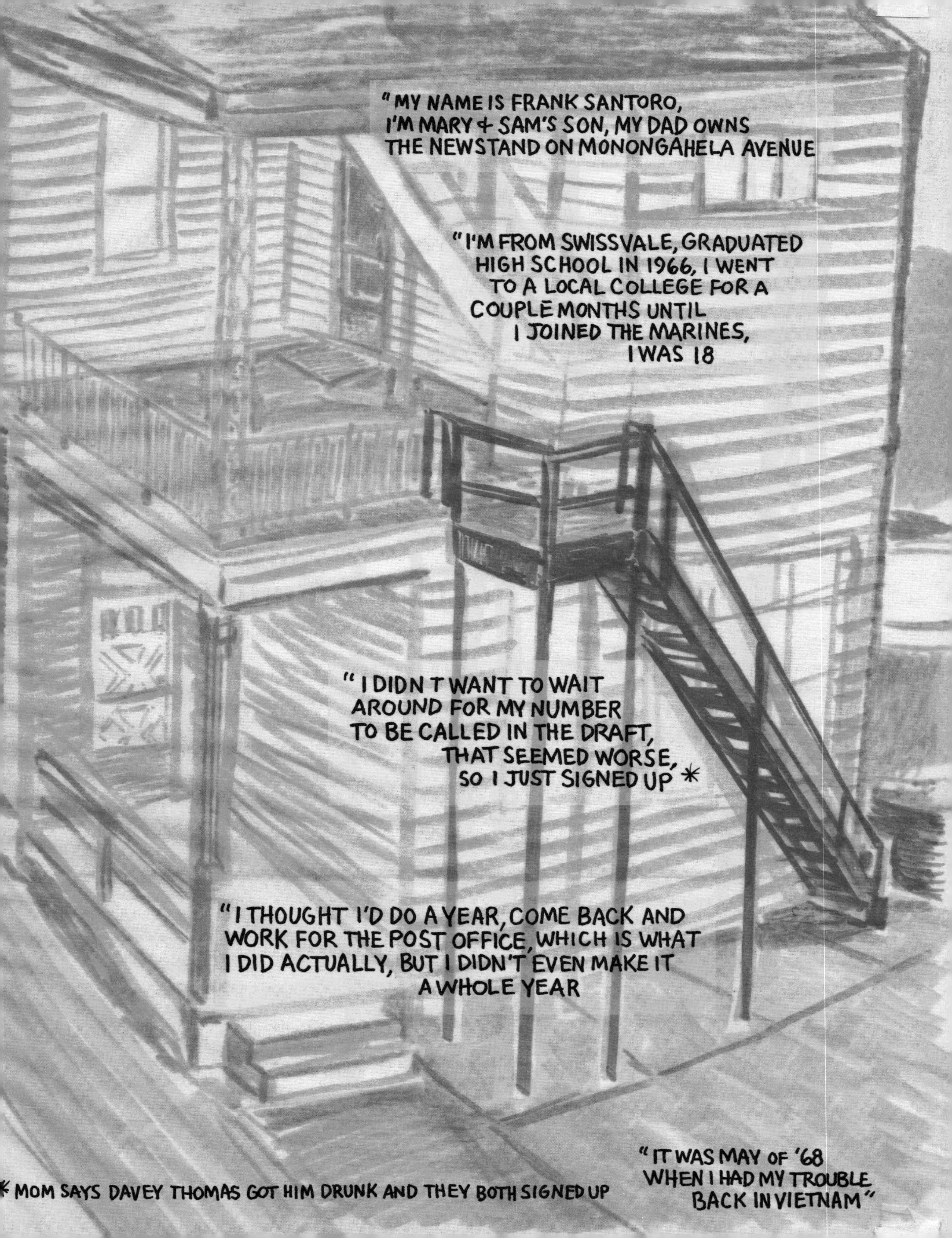
"MY NAME IS FRANK SANTORO, I'M MARY + SAM'S SON, MY DAD OWNS THE NEWSTAND ON MONONGAHELA AVENUE
"I'M FROM SWISSVALE, GRADUATED HIGH SCHOOL IN 1966, I WENT TO A LOCAL COLLEGE FOR A COUPLE MONTHS UNTIL I JOINED THE MARINES, I WAS 18
" I DIDN T WANT TO WAIT AROUND FOR MY NUMBER TO BE CALLED IN THE DRAFT, THAT SEEMED WORSE, SO I JUST SIGNED UP *
"I THOUGHT I'D DO A YEAR, COME BACK AND WORK FOR THE POST OFFICE, WHICH IS WHAT I DID ACTUALLY, BUT I DIDN'T EVEN MAKE IT A WHOLE YEAR
* MOM SAYS DAVEY THOMAS GOT HIM DRUNK AND THEY BOTH SIGNED UP
"IT WAS MAY OF '68 WHEN I HAD MY TROUBLE BACK IN VIETNAM"

" MY WHOLE SQUAD GOT WIPED OUT WHILE I WAS
ON R+R
OUR LITTLE BUNKER WHERE WE LIVED FOR 76 DAYS
GOT SHELLED
MY BUDDIES, MY THREE REALLY CLOSE BUDDIES, ALL DIED
AND I WOULD'VE DIED TOO BUT I WAS
ON R+R
ON LEAVE, SO I GOT REAL BAD
SURVIVOR'S GUILT "

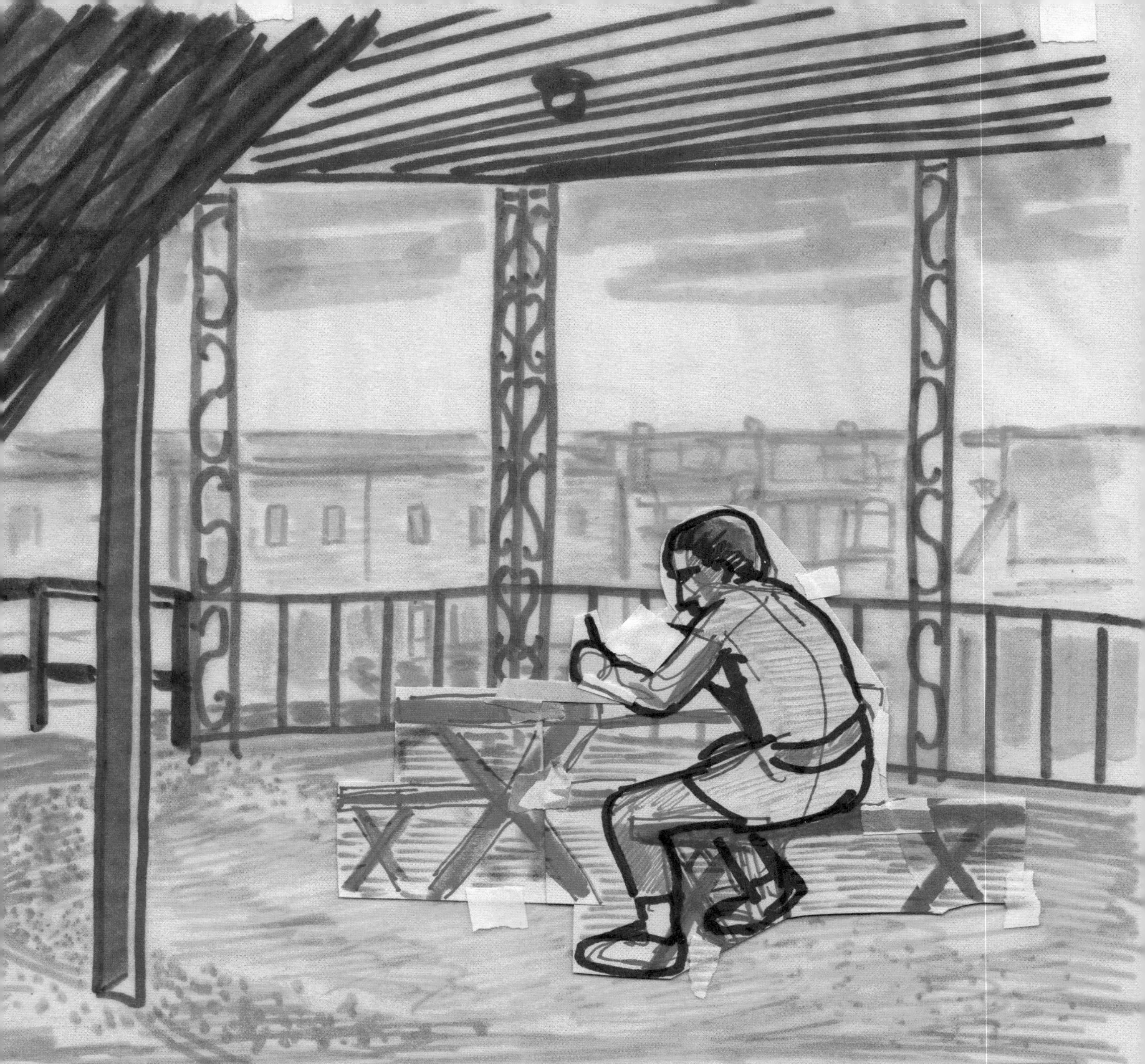

"HERE, I'M 28 YEARS OLD, AND I JUST HAD THIS REALLY BAD NIGHTMARE ABOUT VIETNAM, SO I'M WRITING EVERYTHING DOWN THAT I CAN REMEMBER"

("THE WAY YOU DO THE THINGS YOU DO" BY "THE TEMPTATIONS", 1964, CAN BE HEARD PLAYING ON THE STEREO INSIDE THE HOUSE THROUGH THE OPEN WINDOW)

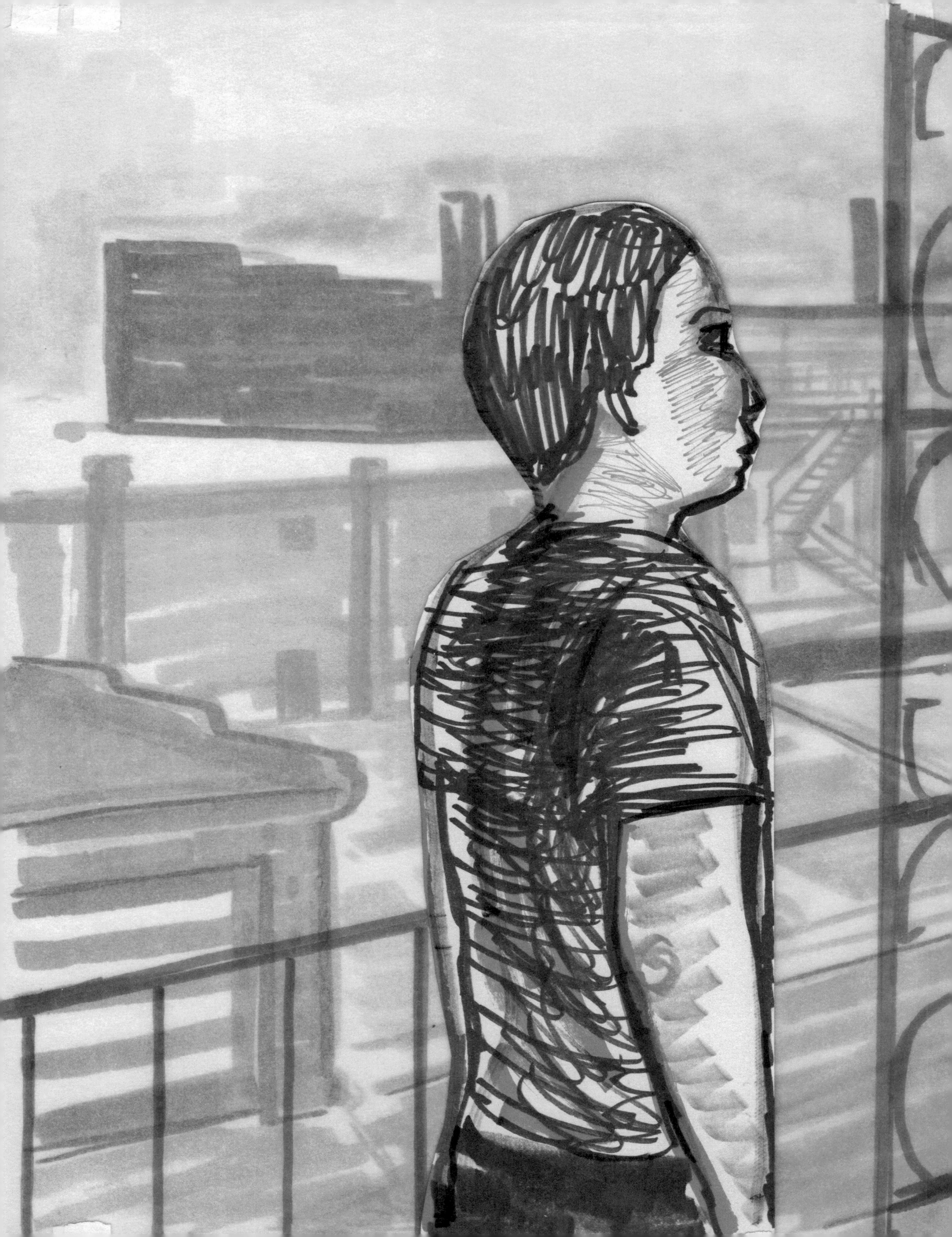

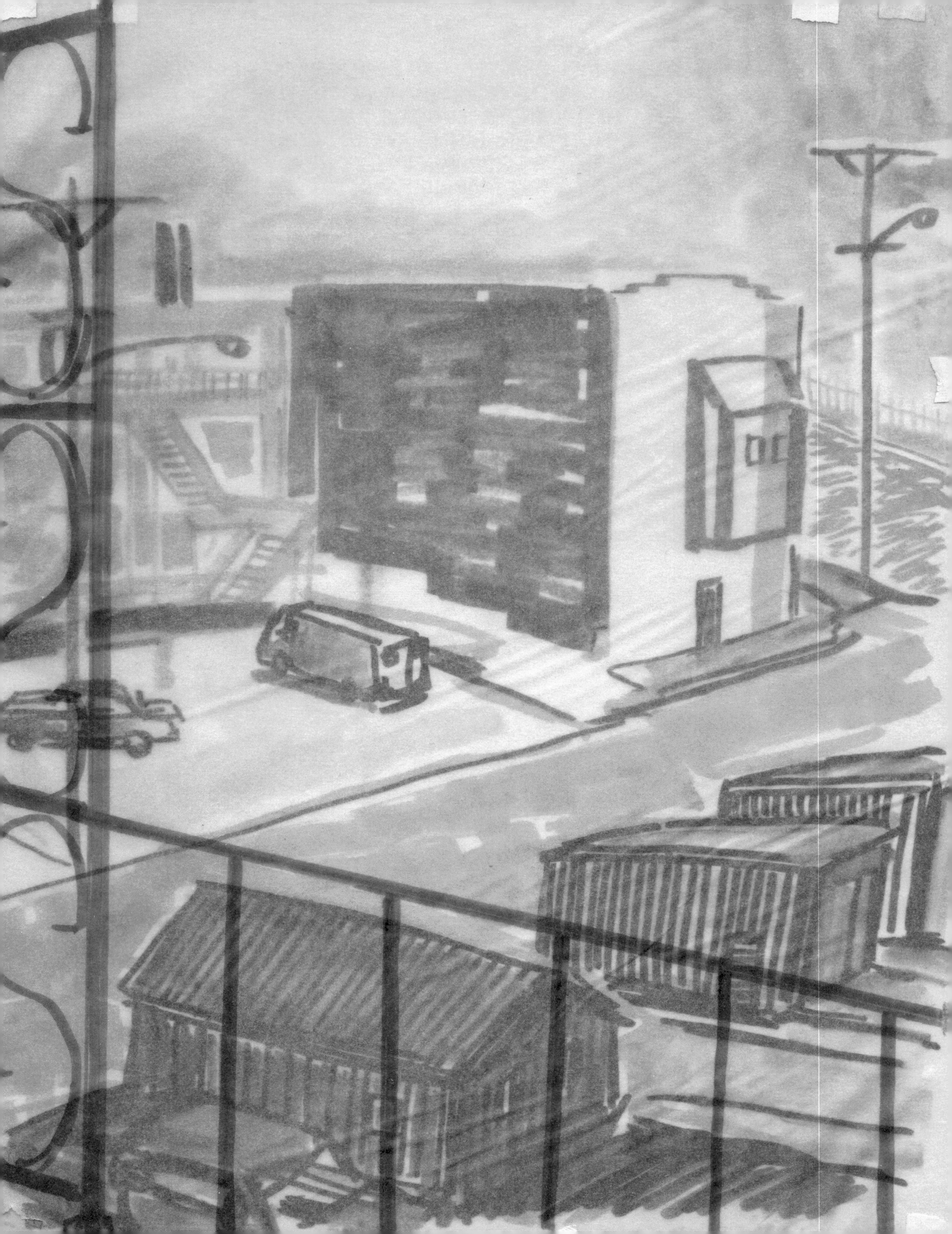

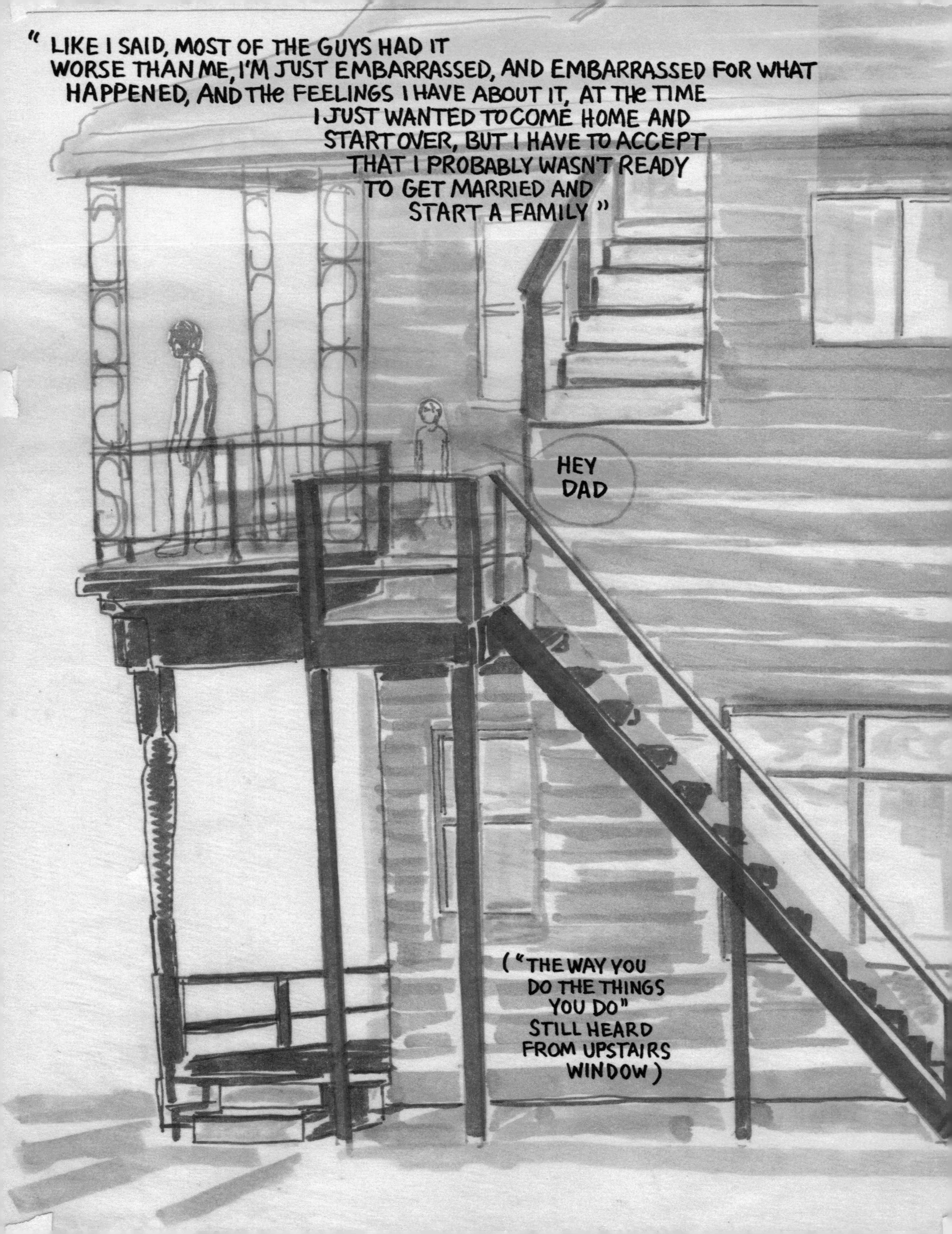
" LIKE I SAID, MOST OF THE GUYS HAD IT WORSE THAN ME, I'M JUST EMBARRASSED, AND EMBARRASSED FOR WHAT HAPPENED, AND THE FEELINGS I HAVE ABOUT IT, AT THE TIME I JUST WANTED TO COME HOME AND START OVER, BUT I HAVE TO ACCEPT THAT I PROBABLY WASN'T READY TO GET MARRIED AND START A FAMILY "
HEY DAD
("THE WAY YOU DO THE THINGS YOU DO" STILL HEARD FROM UPSTAIRS WINDOW)

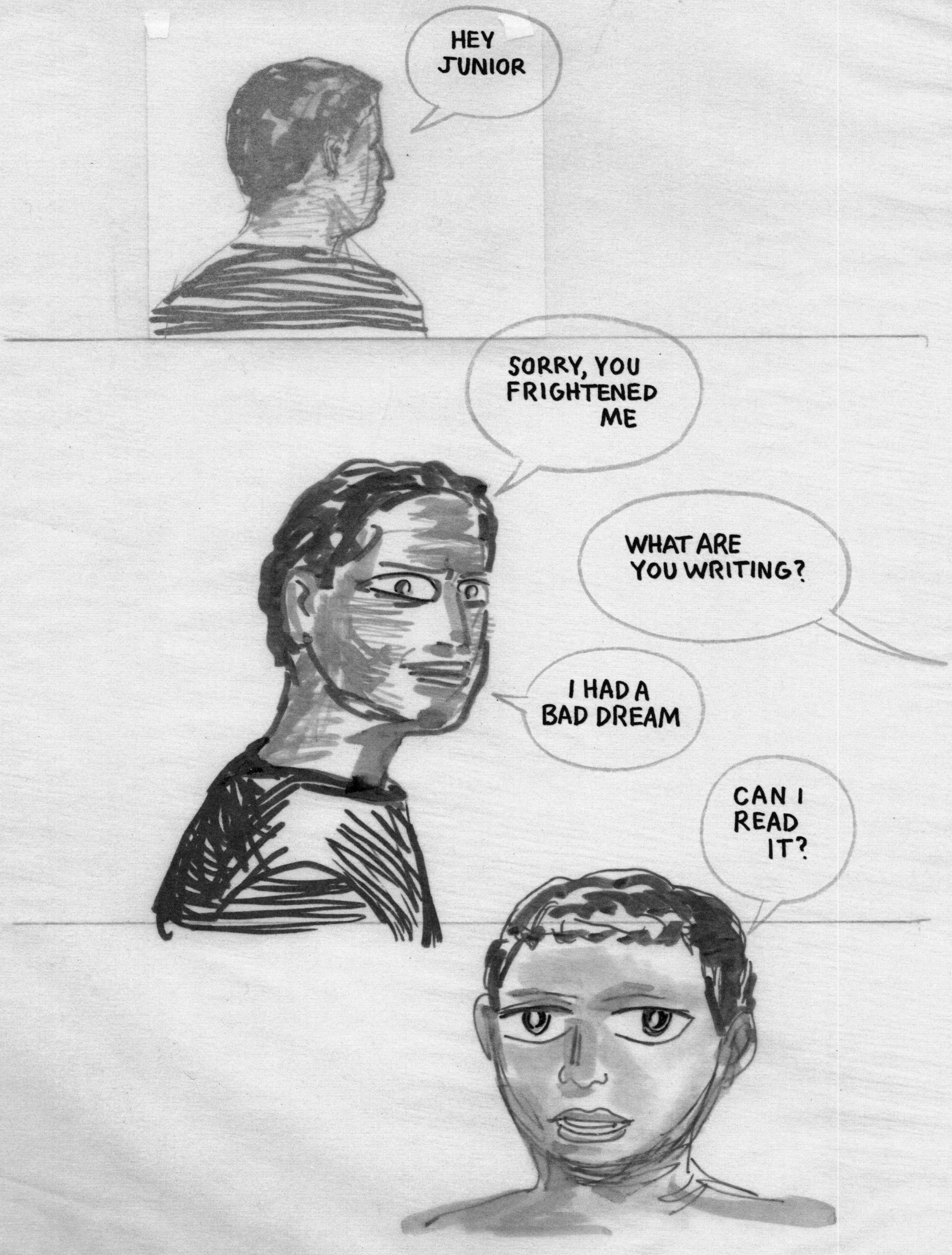
HEY JUNIOR
SORRY, YOU FRIGHTENED ME
WHAT ARE YOU WRITING?
I HAD A BAD DREAM
CAN I READ IT?

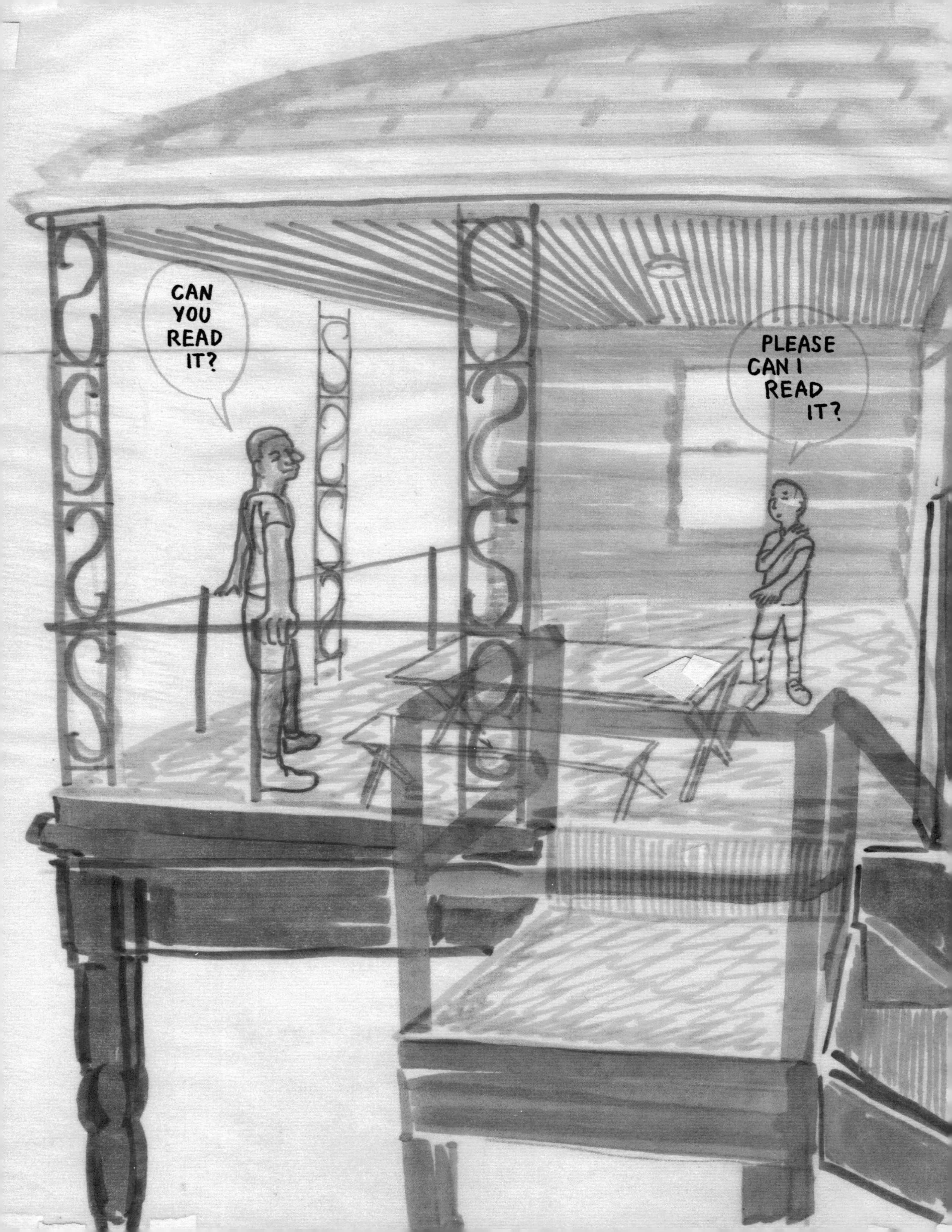
CAN YOU READ IT?
PLEASE CAN I READ IT?

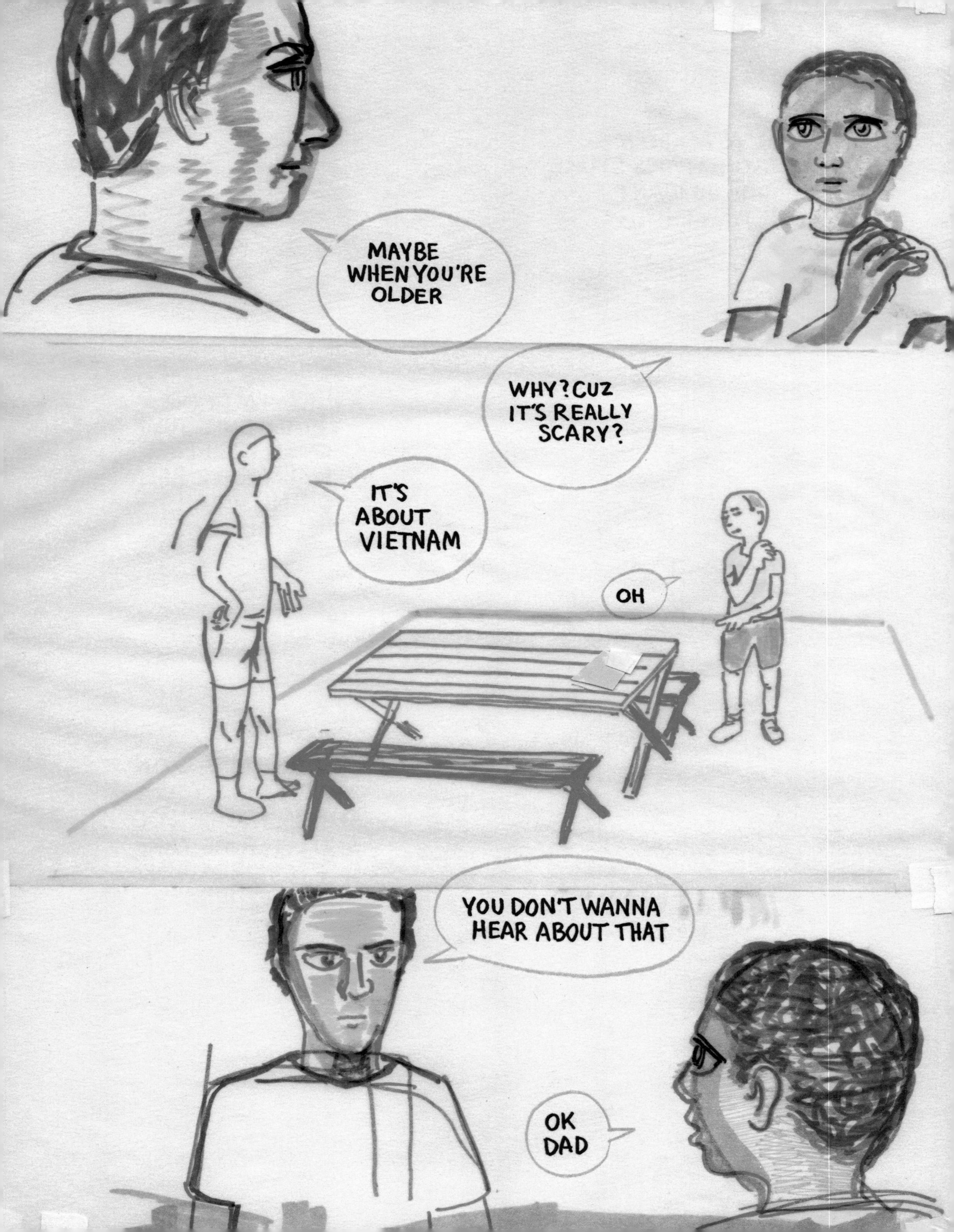
MAYBE WHEN YOU'RE OLDER
WHY? CUZ IT'S REALLY SCARY?
IT'S ABOUT VIETNAM
OH
YOU DON'T WANNA HEAR ABOUT THAT
OK DAD

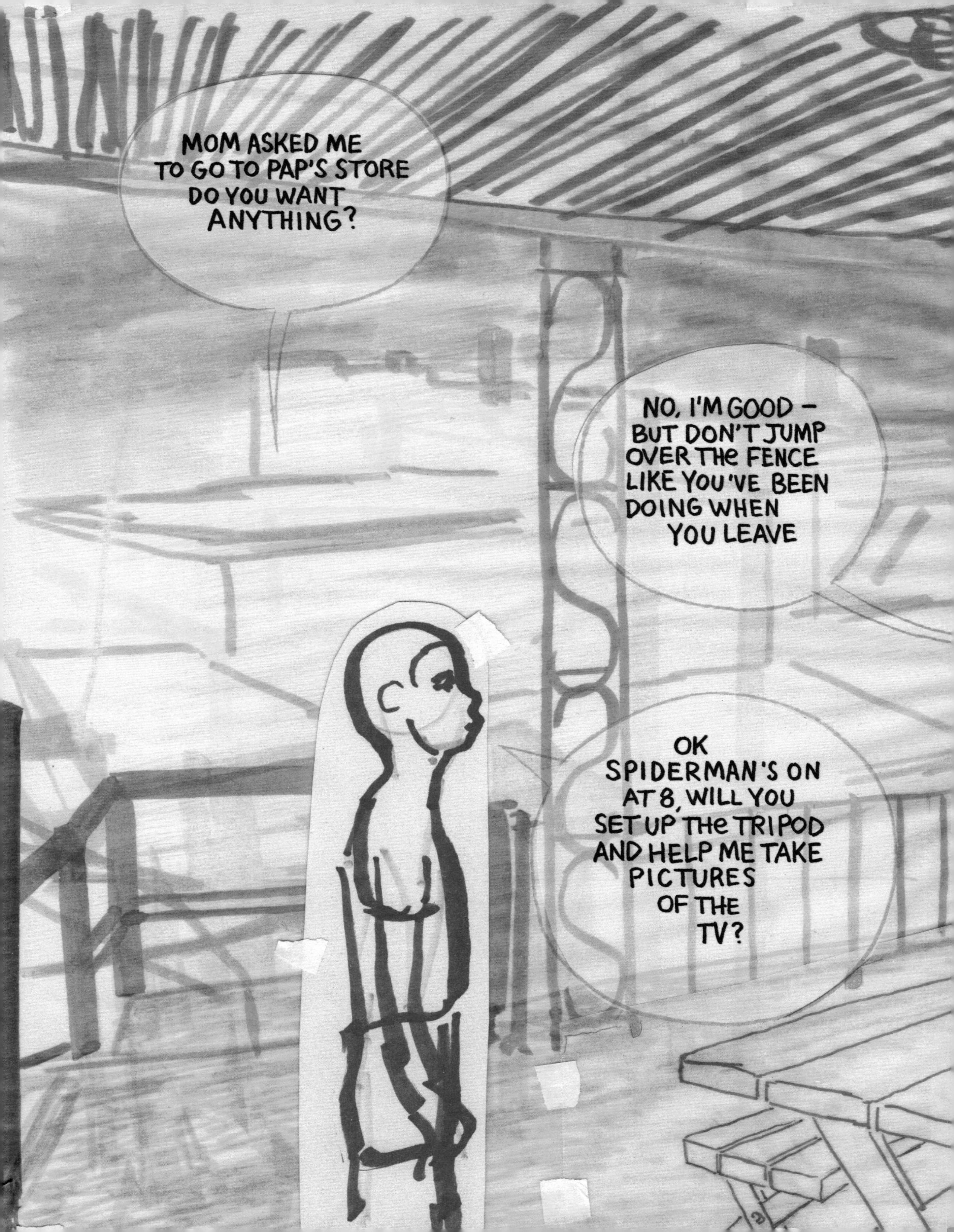
MOM ASKED ME TO GO TO PAP'S STORE DO YOU WANT ANYTHING?
NO, I'M GOOD - BUT DON'T JUMP OVER THE FENCE LIKE YOU'VE BEEN DOING WHEN YOU LEAVE
OK SPIDERMAN'S ON AT 8, WILL YOU SET UP THE TRIPOD AND HELP ME TAKE PICTURES OF THE TV?

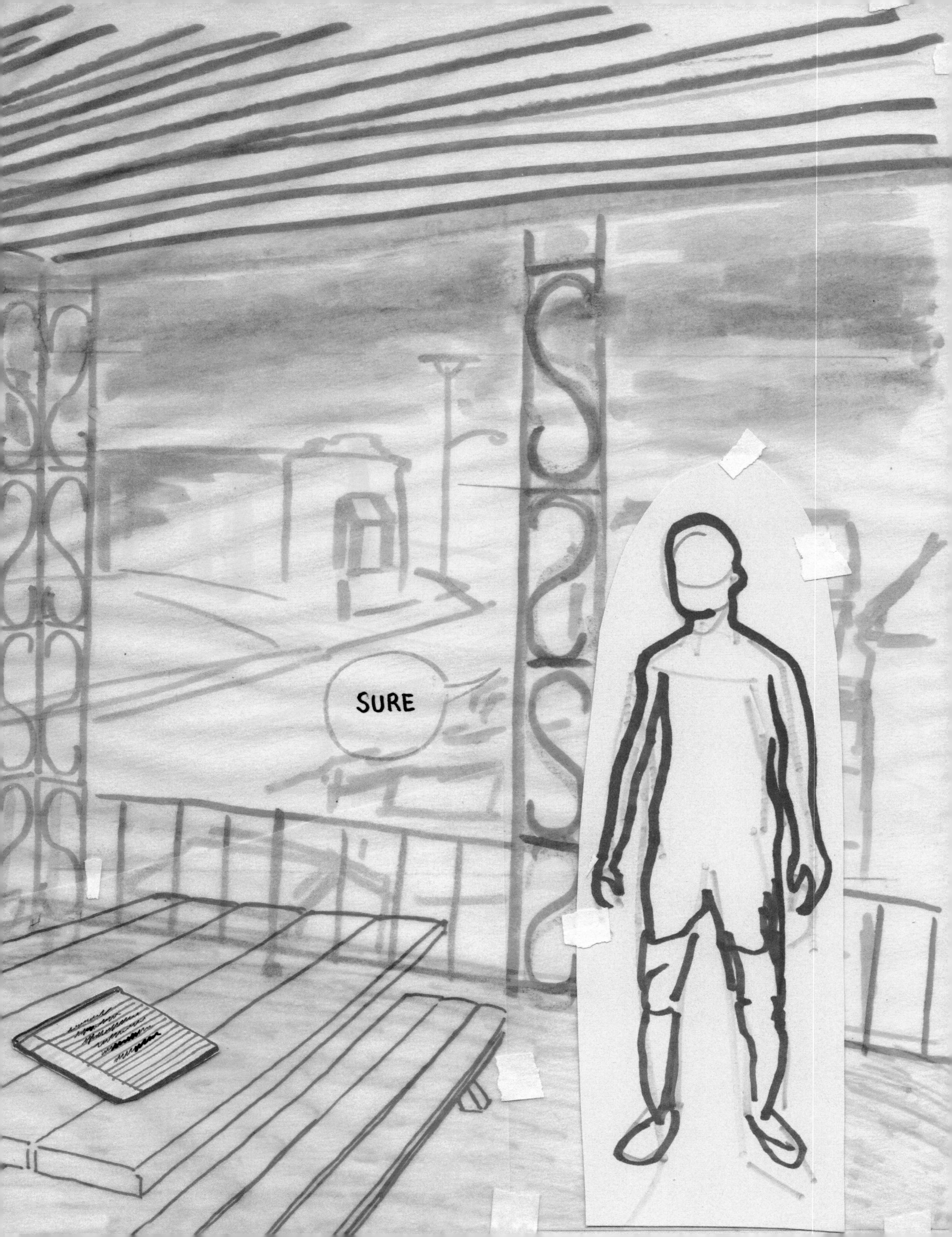
SURE

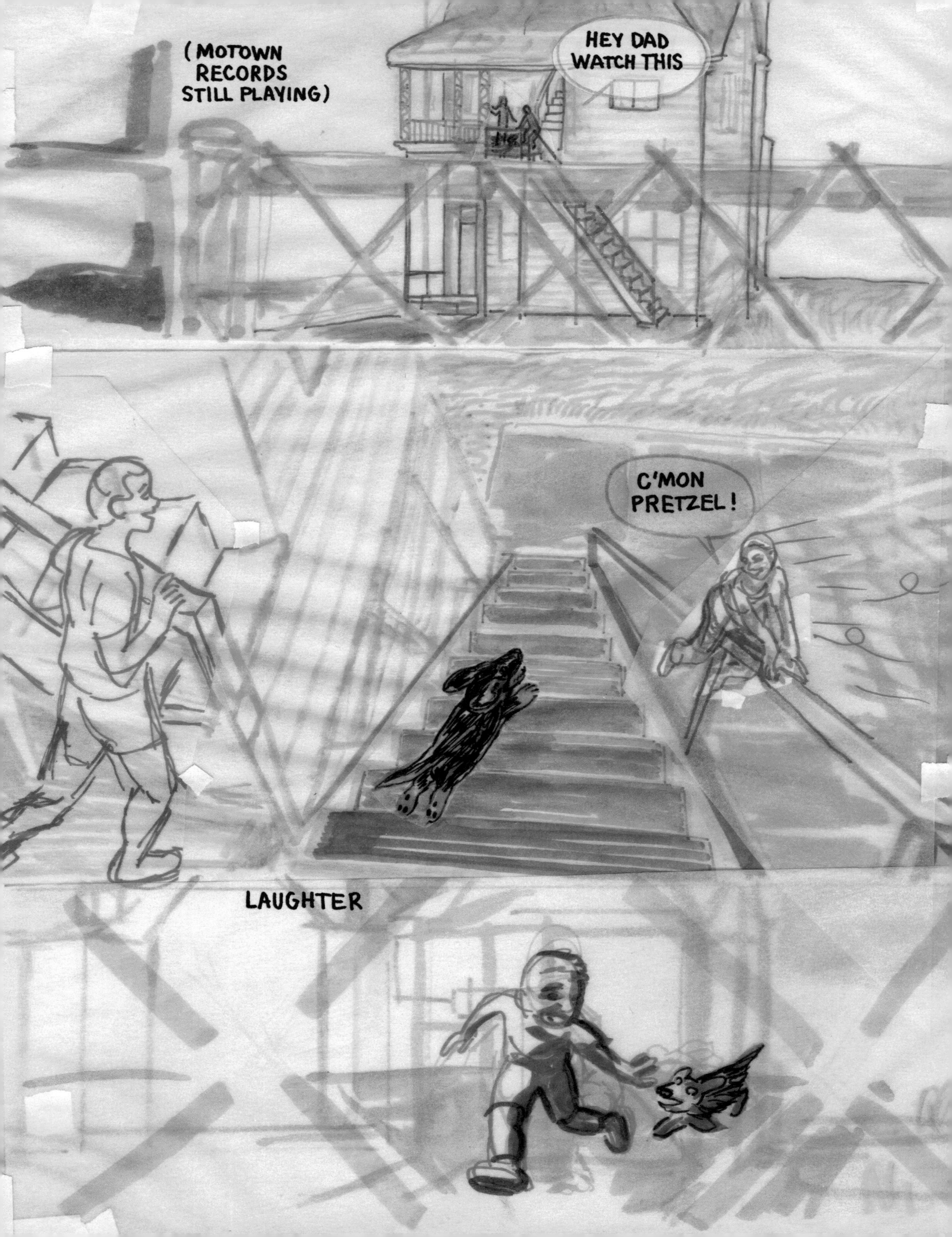
(MOTOWN RECORDS STILL PLAYING)
HEY DAD WATCH THIS
C'MON PRETZEL!
LAUGHTER

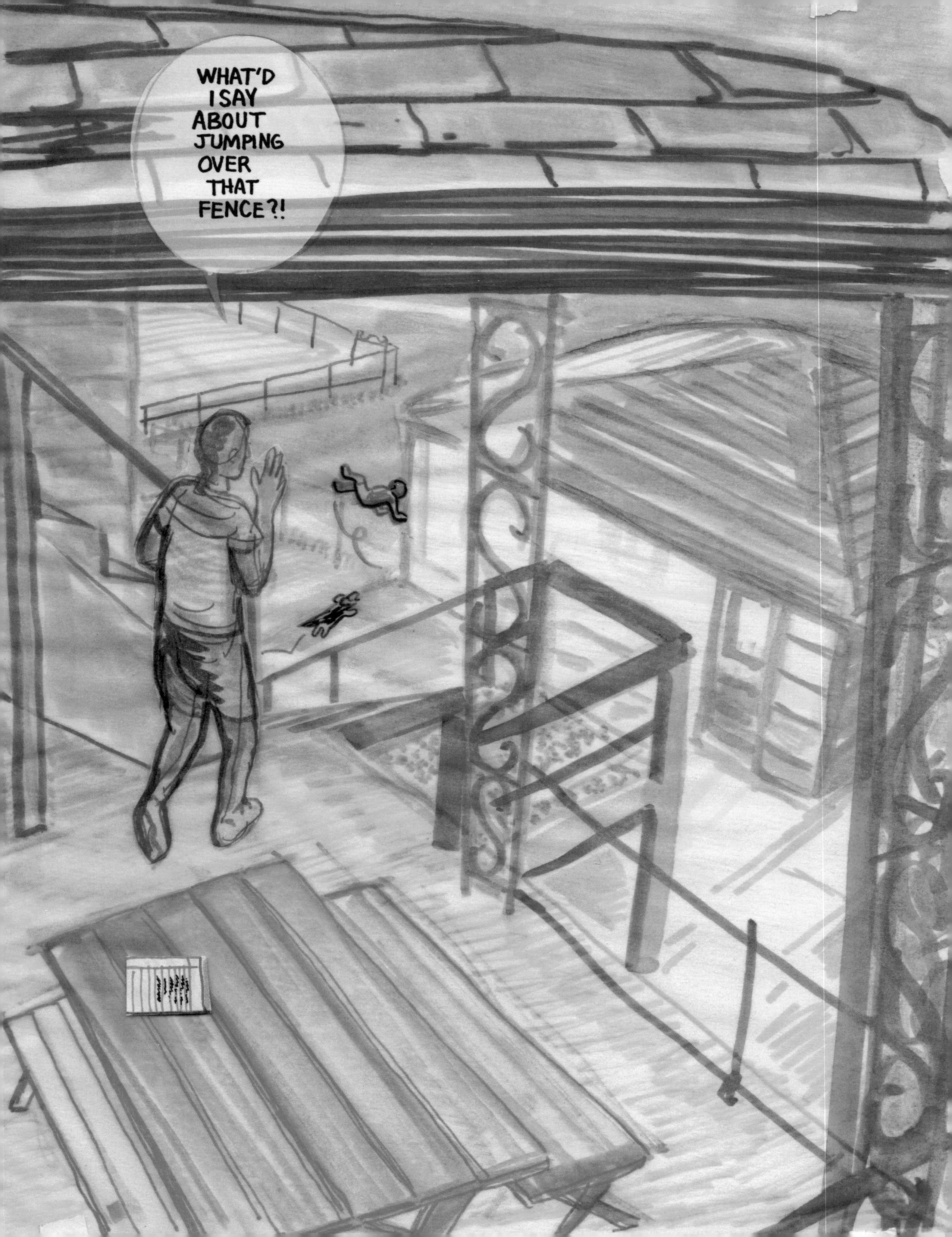
WHAT'D I SAY ABOUT JUMPING OVER THAT FENCE?!

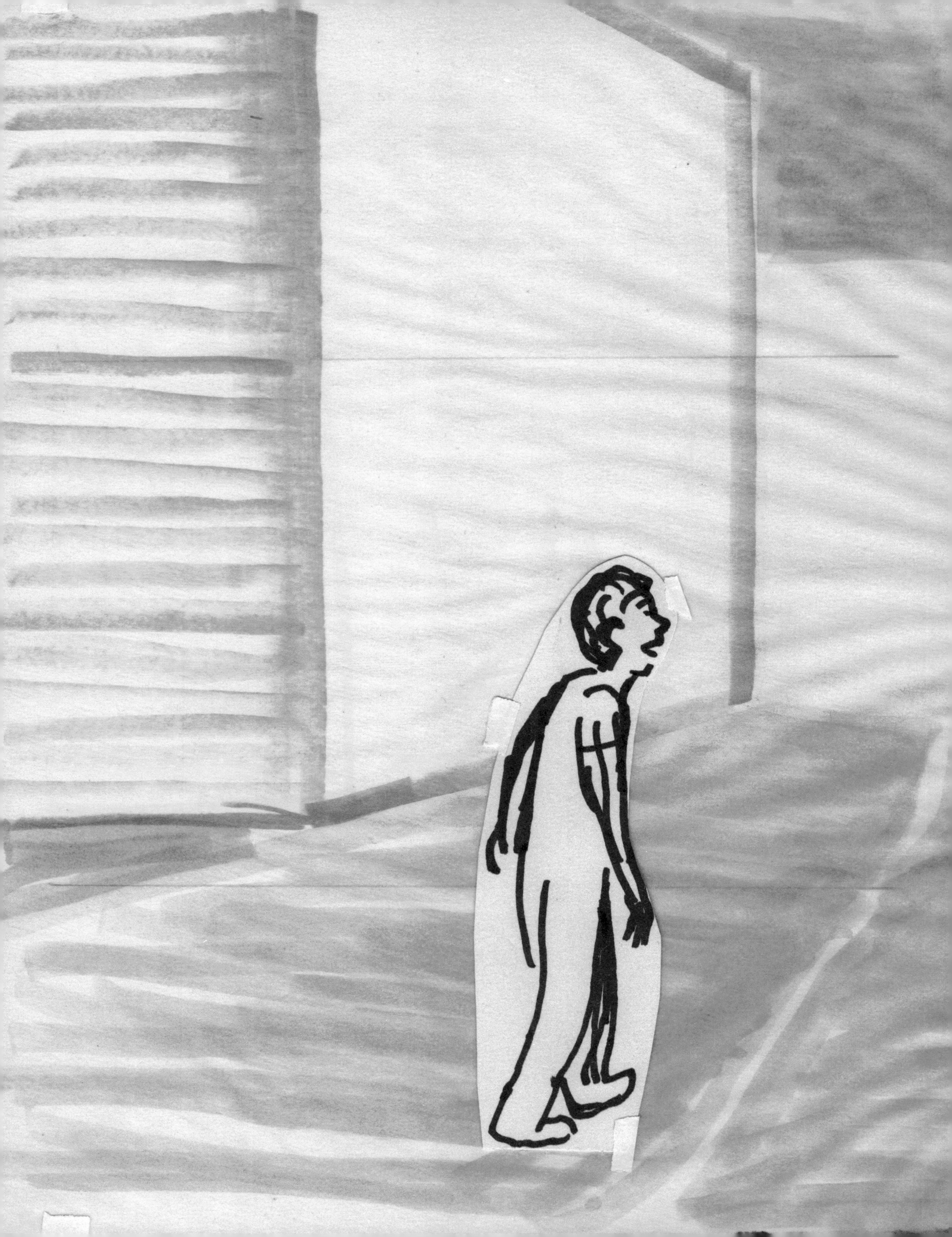

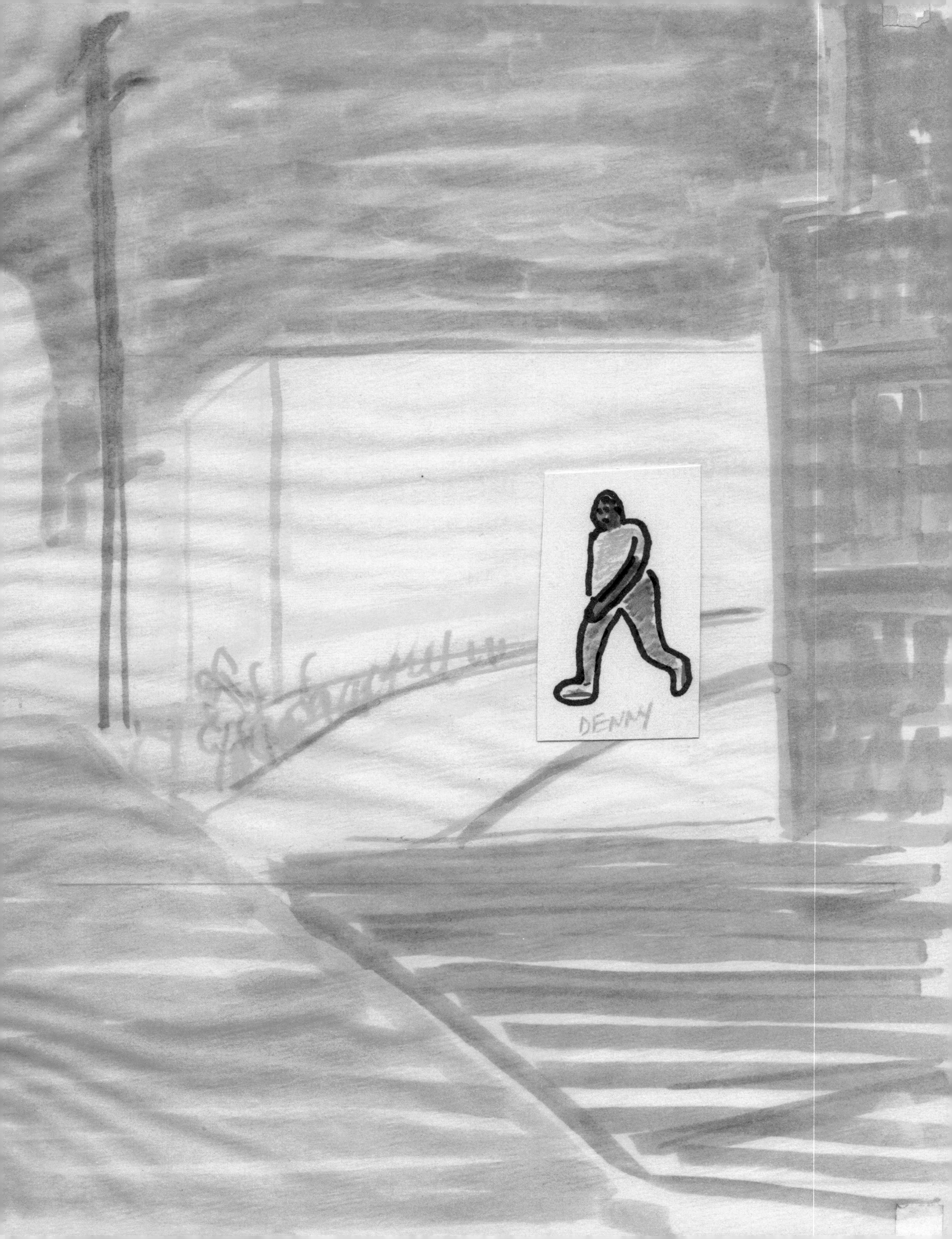
DENNY

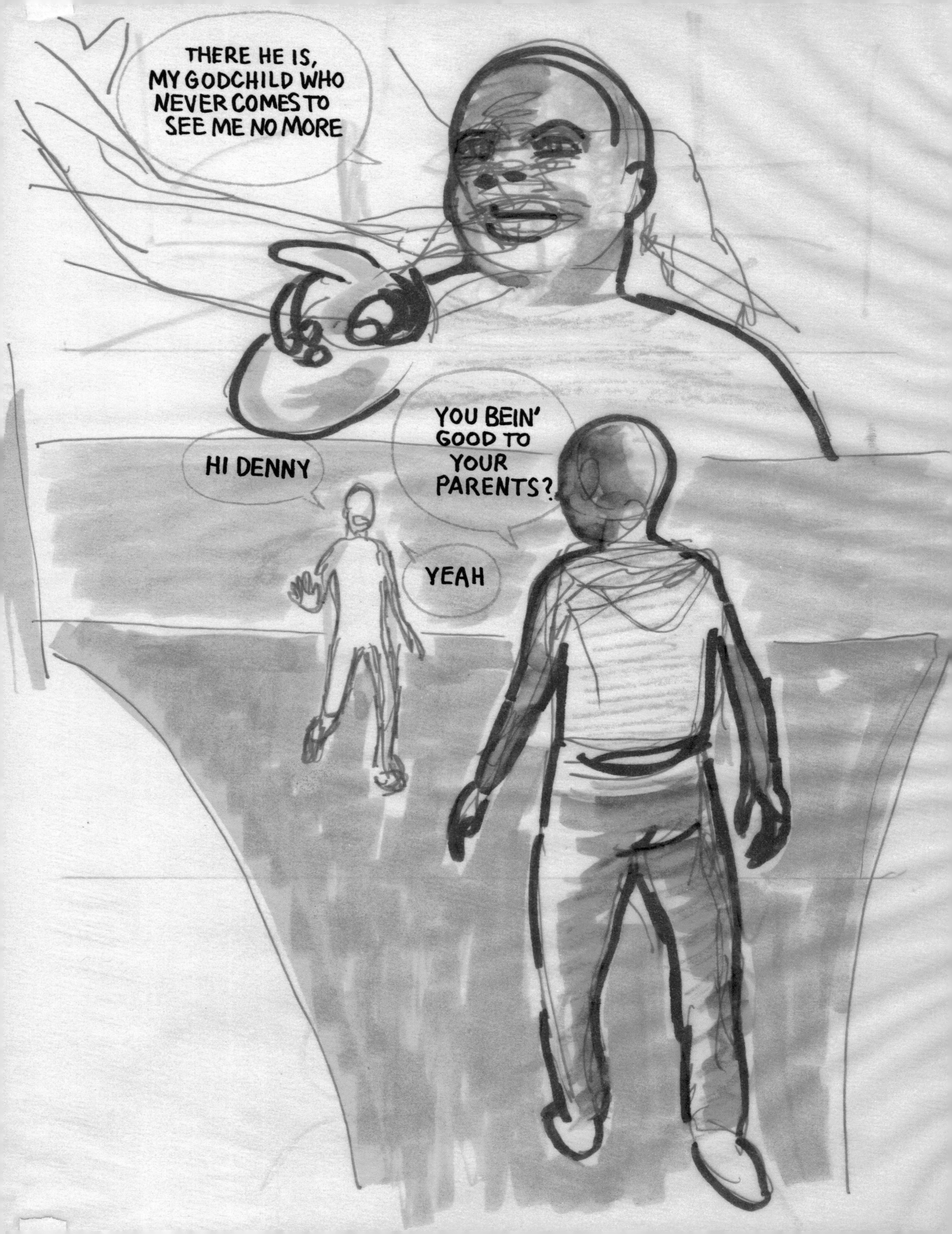
THERE HE IS, MY GODCHILD WHO NEVER COMES TO SEE ME NO MORE
HI DENNY
YOU BEIN' GOOD TO YOUR PARENTS?
YEAH

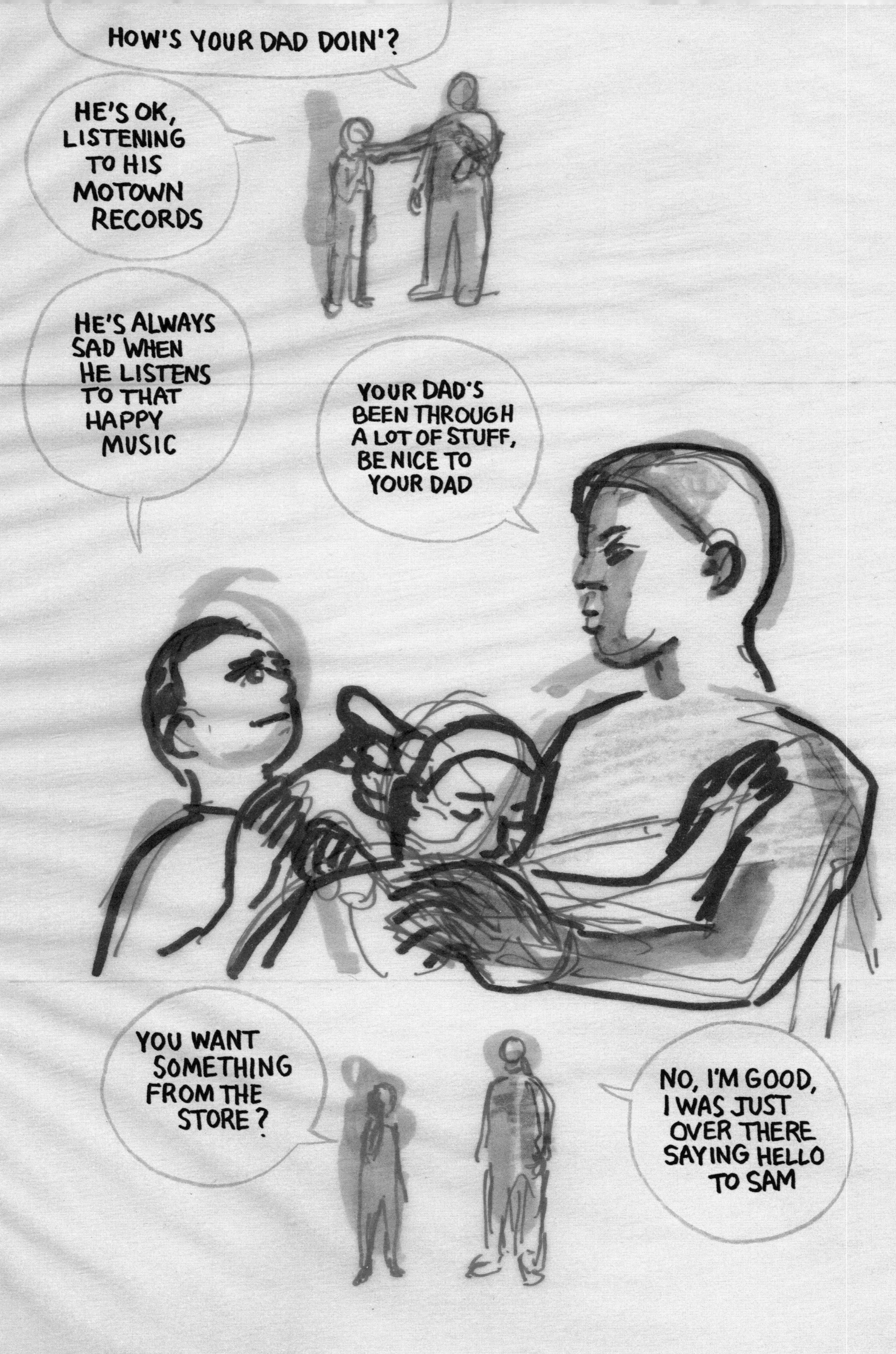
HOW'S YOUR DAD DOIN'?
HE'S OK, LISTENING TO HIS MOTOWN RECORDS
HE'S ALWAYS SAD WHEN HE LISTENS TO THAT HAPPY MUSIC
YOUR DAD'S BEEN THROUGH A LOT OF STUFF, BE NICE TO YOUR DAD
YOU WANT SOMETHING FROM THE STORE?
NO, I'M GOOD, I WAS JUST OVER THERE SAYING HELLO TO SAM

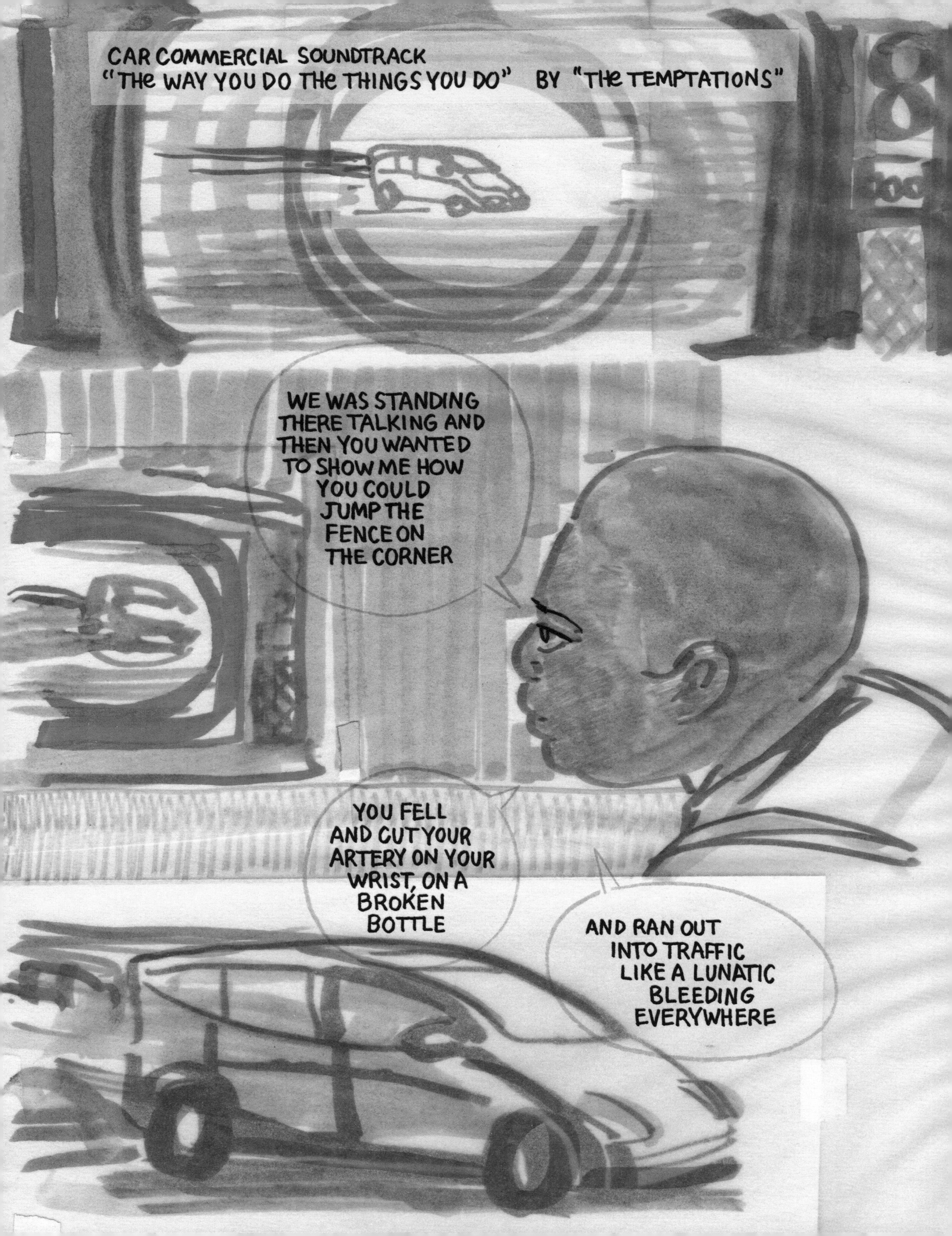
CAR COMMERCIAL SOUNDTRACK
"THE WAY YOU DO THE THINGS YOU DO" BY "THE TEMPTATIONS"
WE WAS STANDING THERE TALKING AND THEN YOU WANTED TO SHOW ME HOW YOU COULD JUMP THE FENCE ON THE CORNER
YOU FELL AND CUT YOUR ARTERY ON YOUR WRIST, ON A BROKEN BOTTLE
AND RAN OUT INTO TRAFFIC LIKE A LUNATIC BLEEDING EVERYWHERE

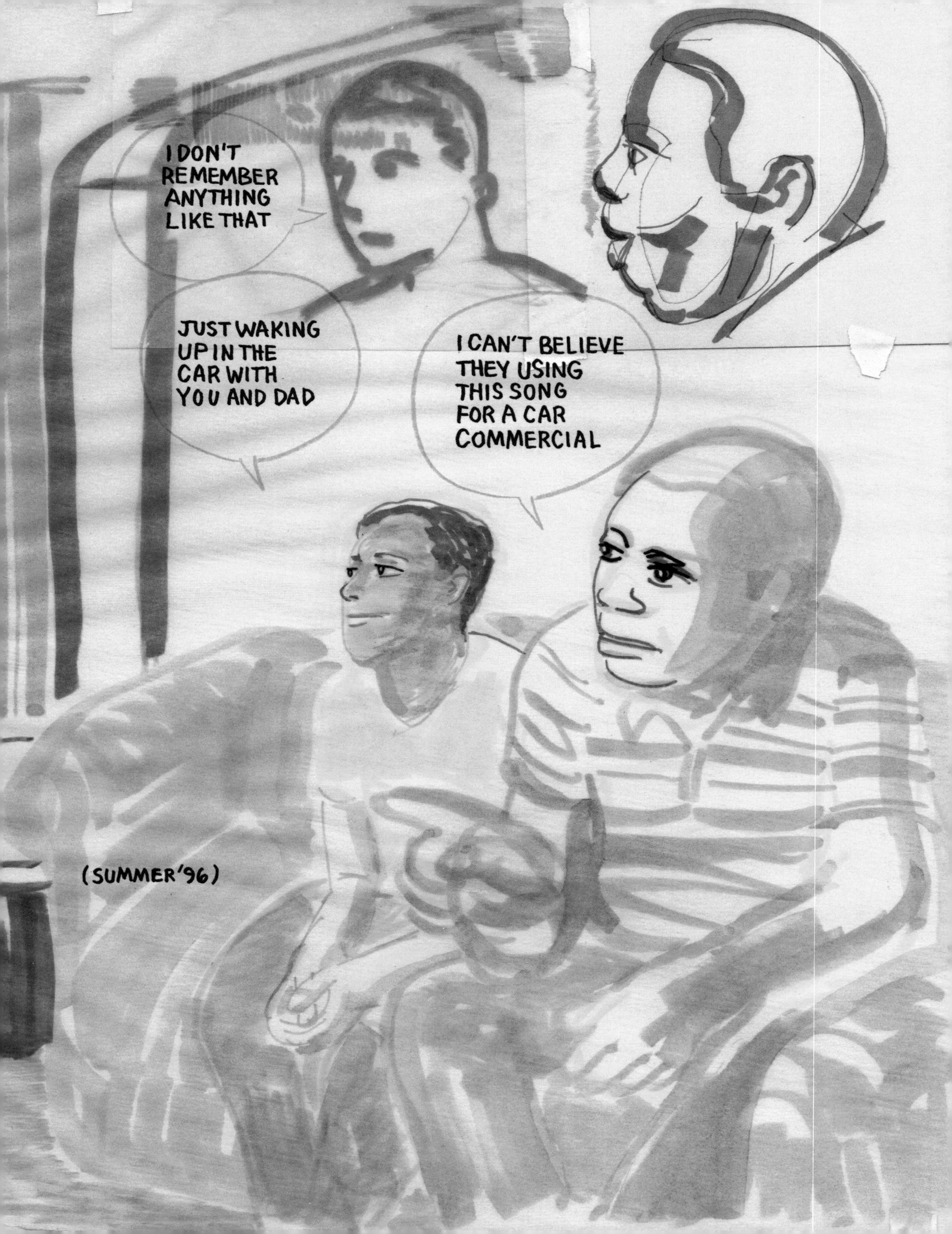
I DON'T REMEMBER ANYTHING LIKE THAT
JUST WAKING UP IN THE CAR WITH YOU AND DAD
I CAN'T BELIEVE THEY USING THIS SONG FOR A CAR COMMERCIAL
(SUMMER '96)

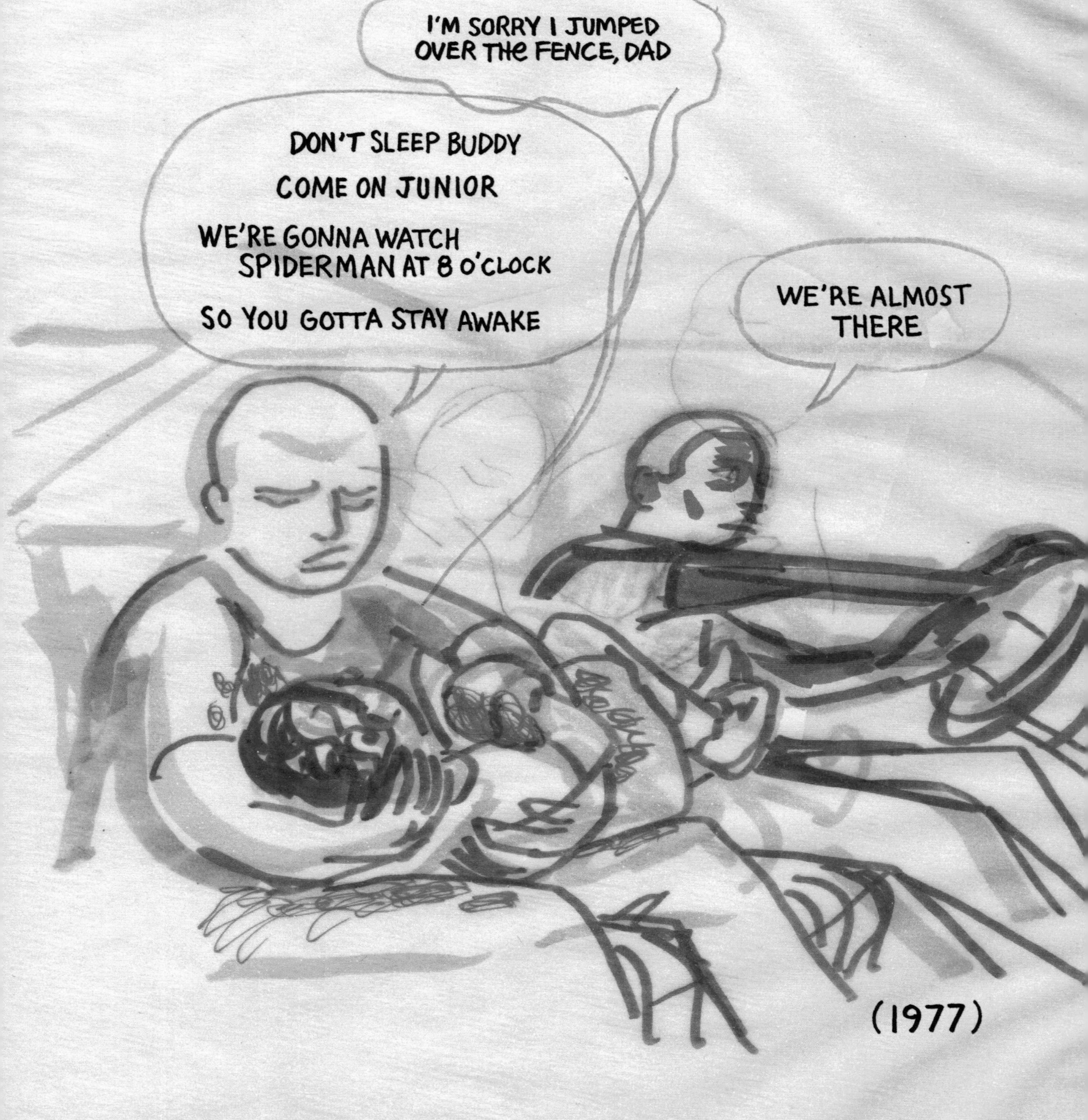
I'M SORRY I JUMPED OVER THE FENCE, DAD
DON'T SLEEP BUDDY
COME ON JUNIOR
WE'RE GONNA WATCH SPIDERMAN AT 8 O'CLOCK
SO YOU GOTTA STAY AWAKE
WE'RE ALMOST THERE
(1977)

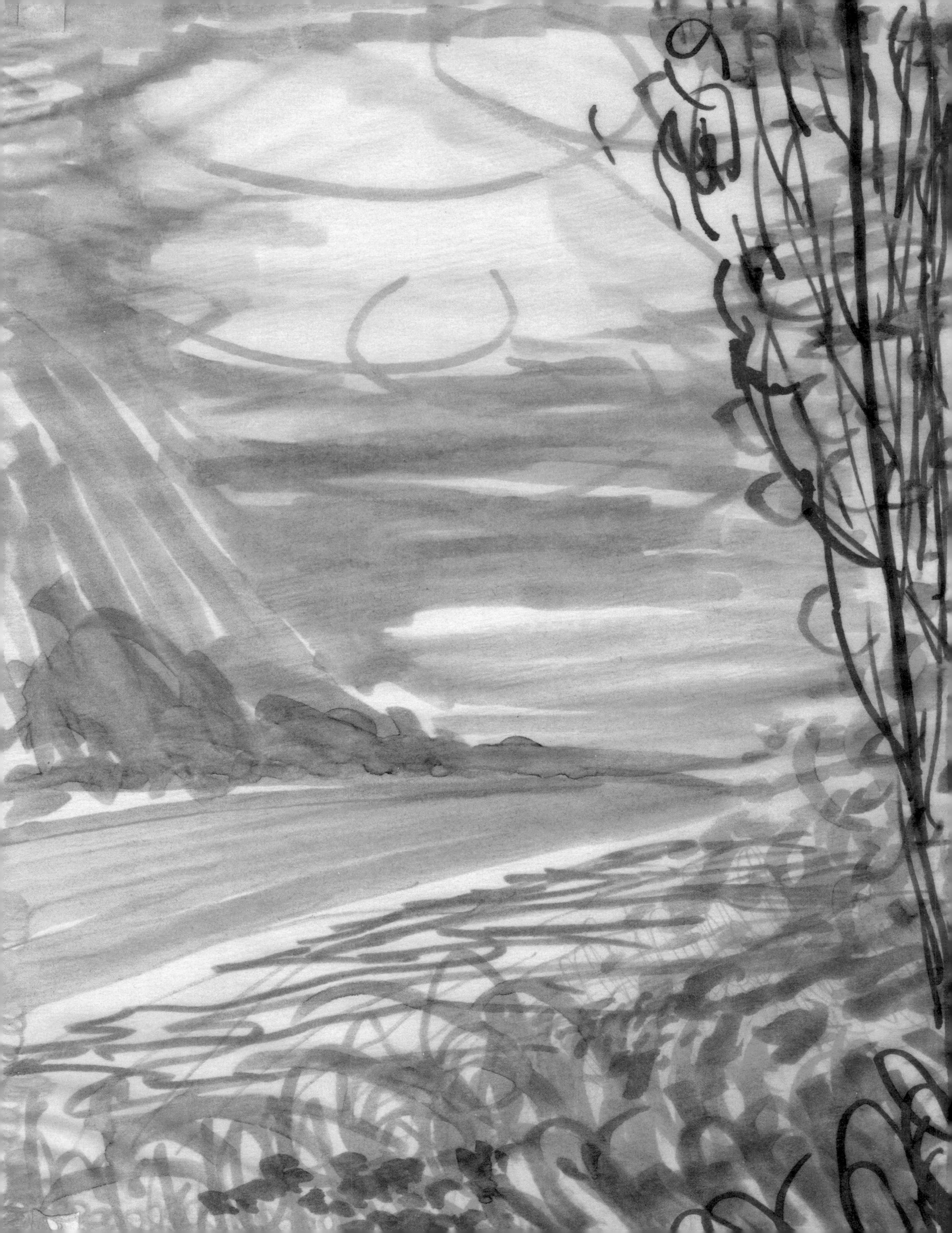

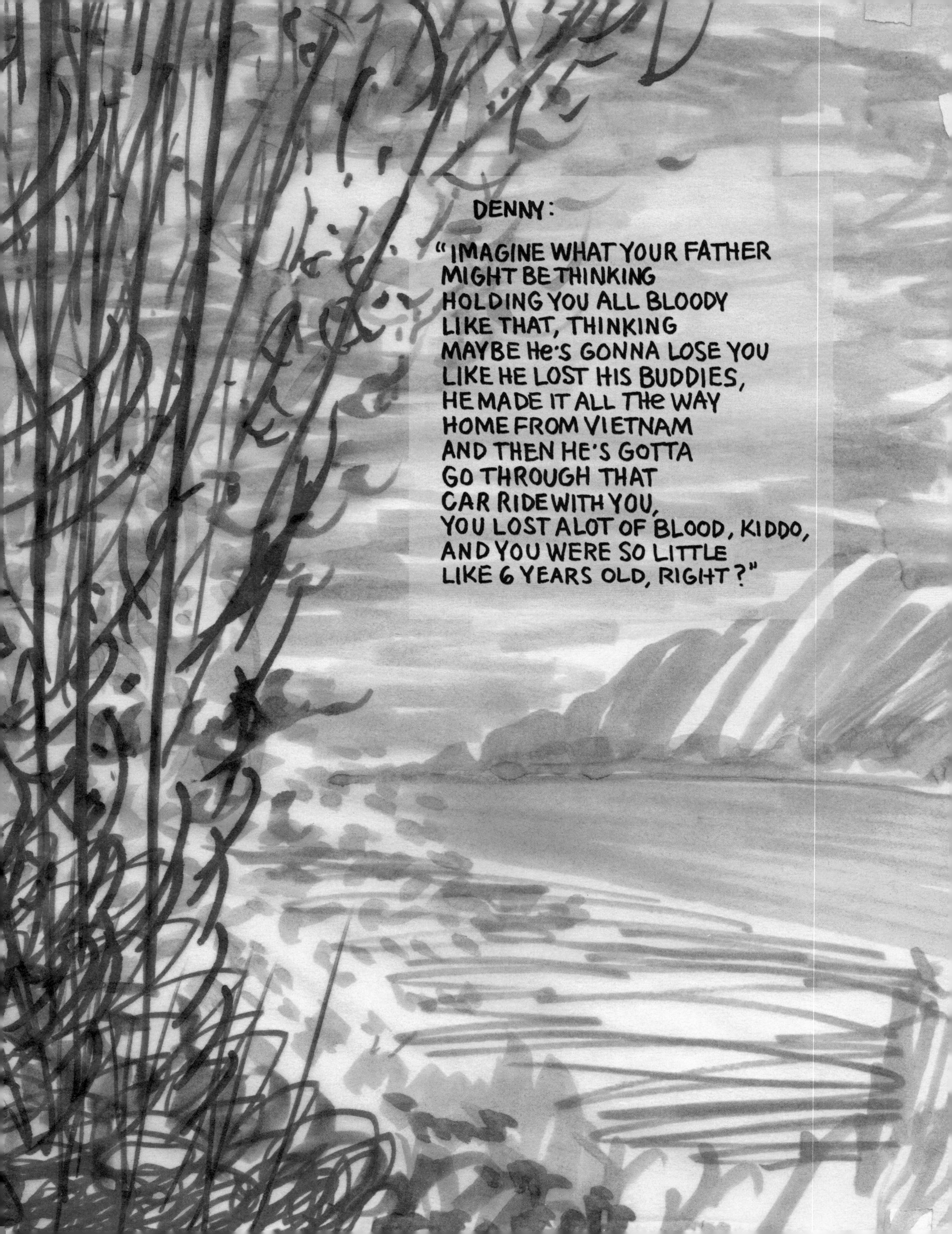
DENNY:
"IMAGINE WHAT YOUR FATHER MIGHT BE THINKING HOLDING YOU ALL BLOODY LIKE THAT, THINKING MAYBE HE'S GONNA LOSE YOU LIKE HE LOST HIS BUDDIES, HE MADE IT ALL THE WAY HOME FROM VIETNAM AND THEN HE'S GOTTA GO THROUGH THAT CAR RIDE WITH YOU, YOU LOST ALOT OF BLOOD, KIDDO, AND YOU WERE SO LITTLE LIKE 6 YEARS OLD, RIGHT?"

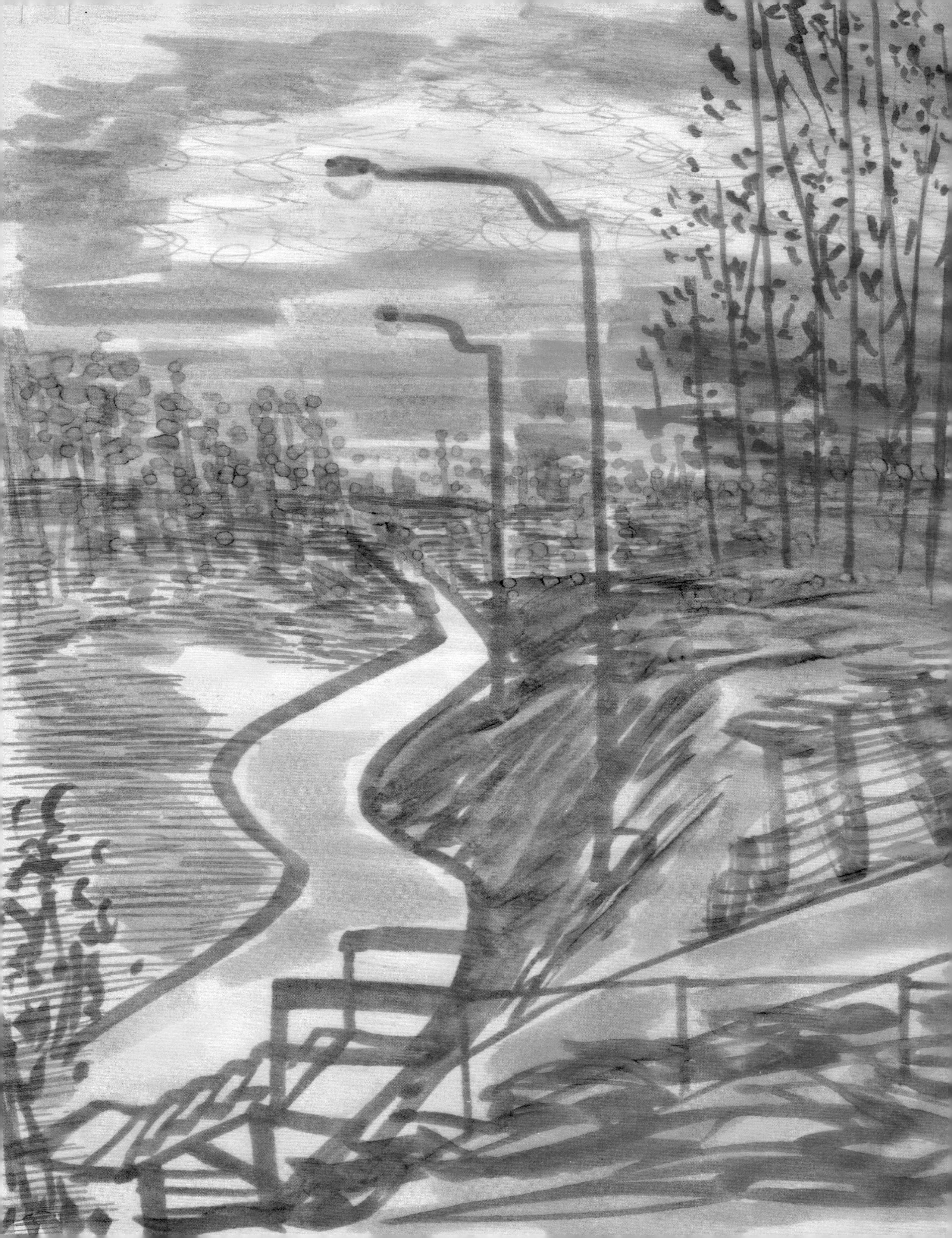

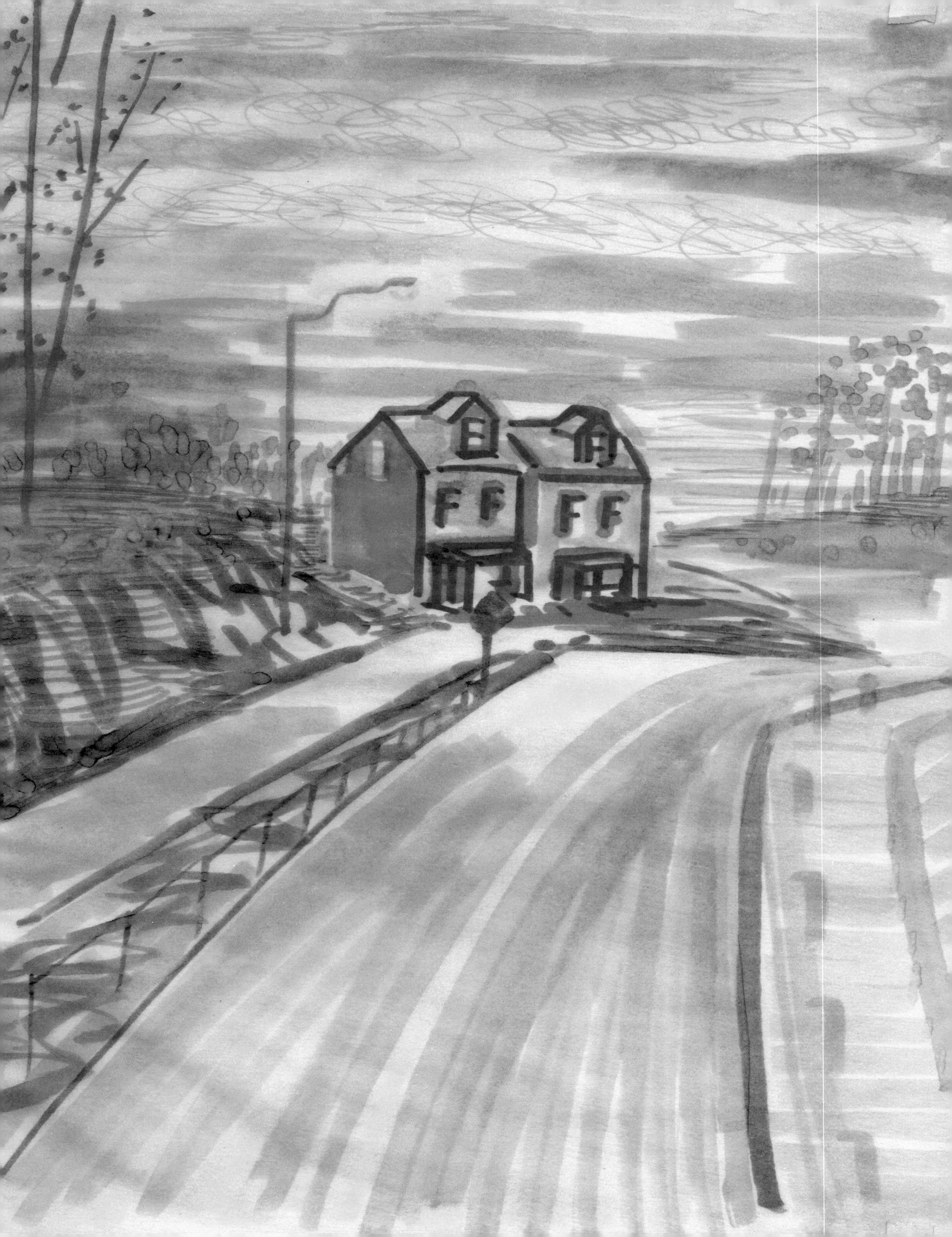

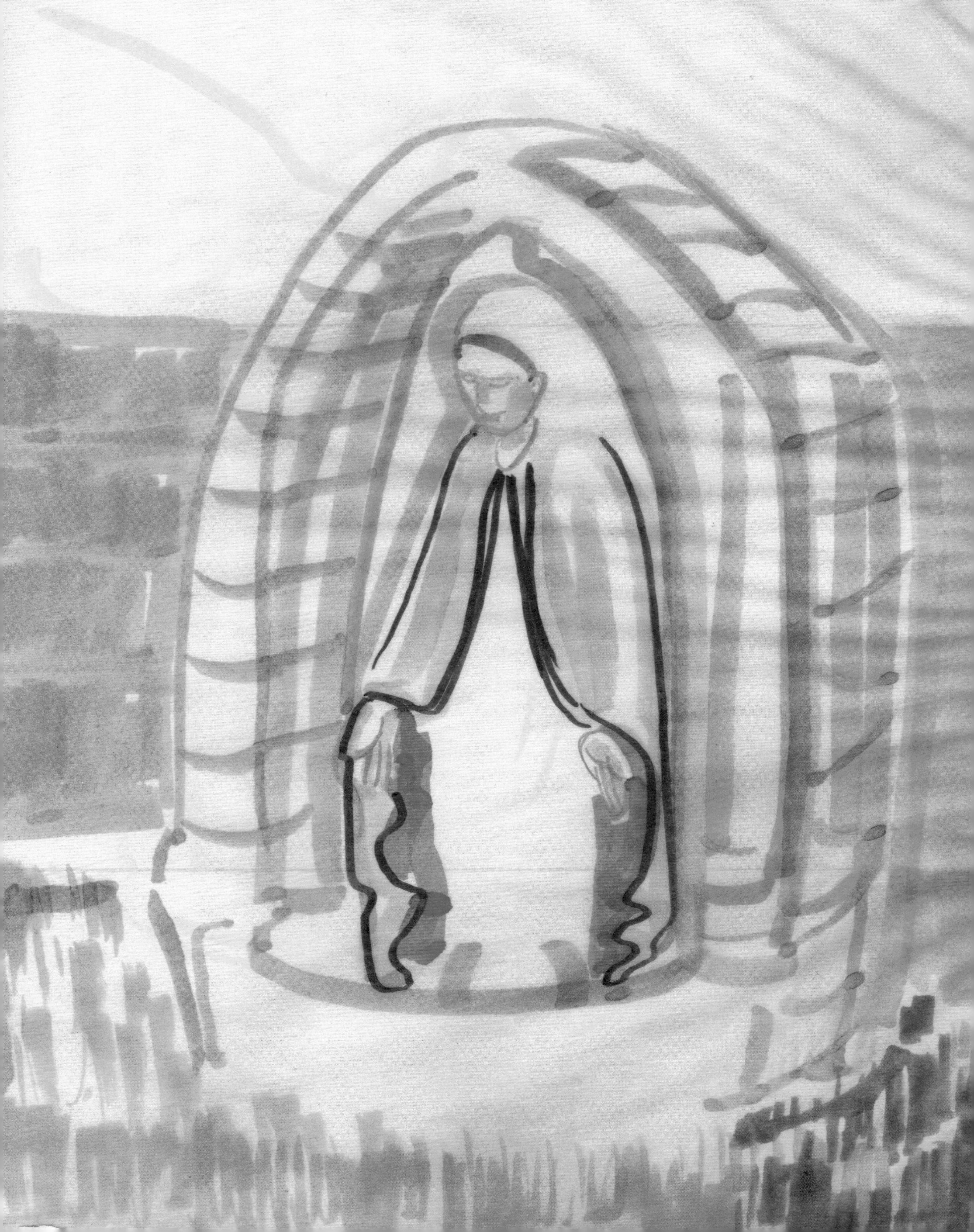

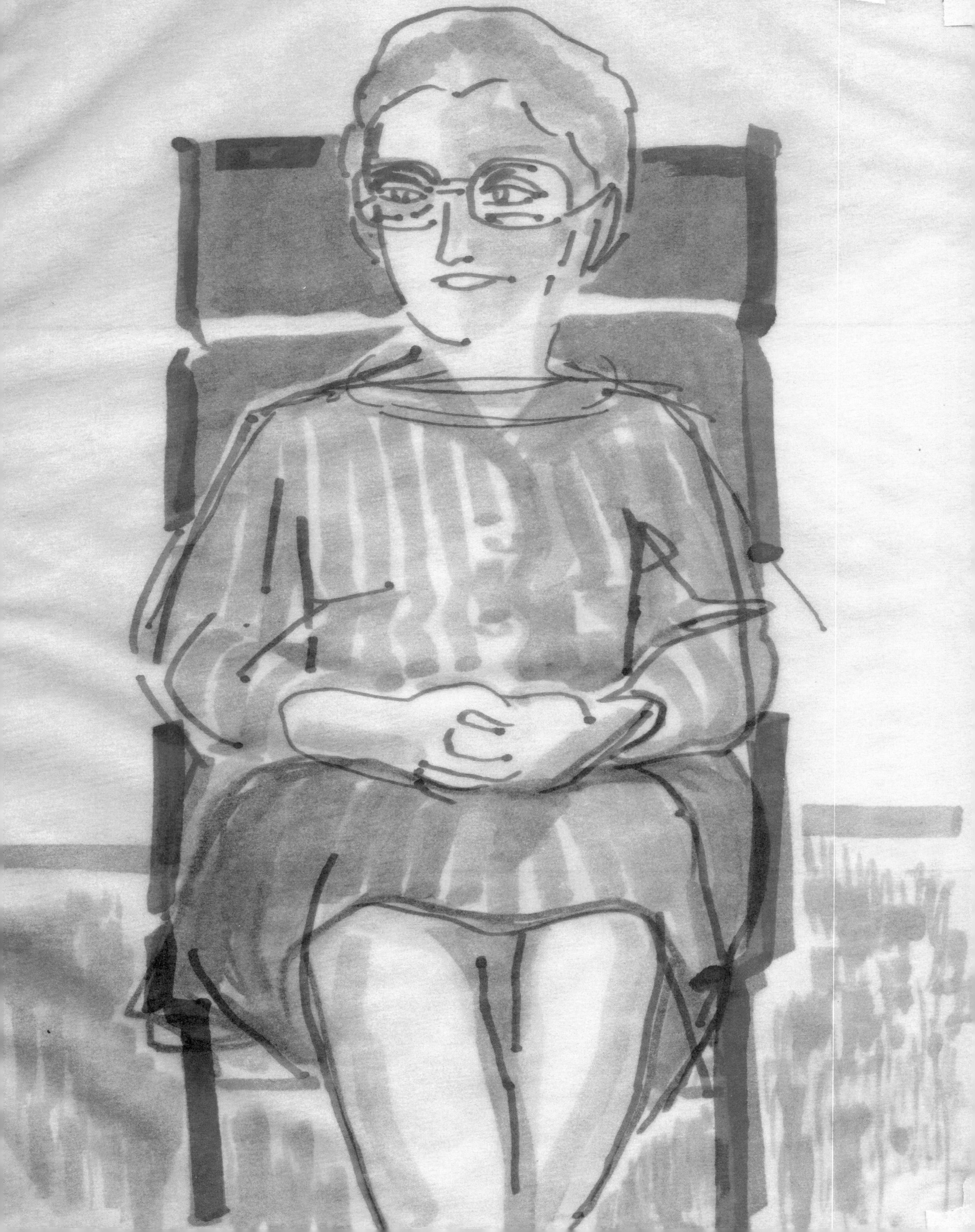

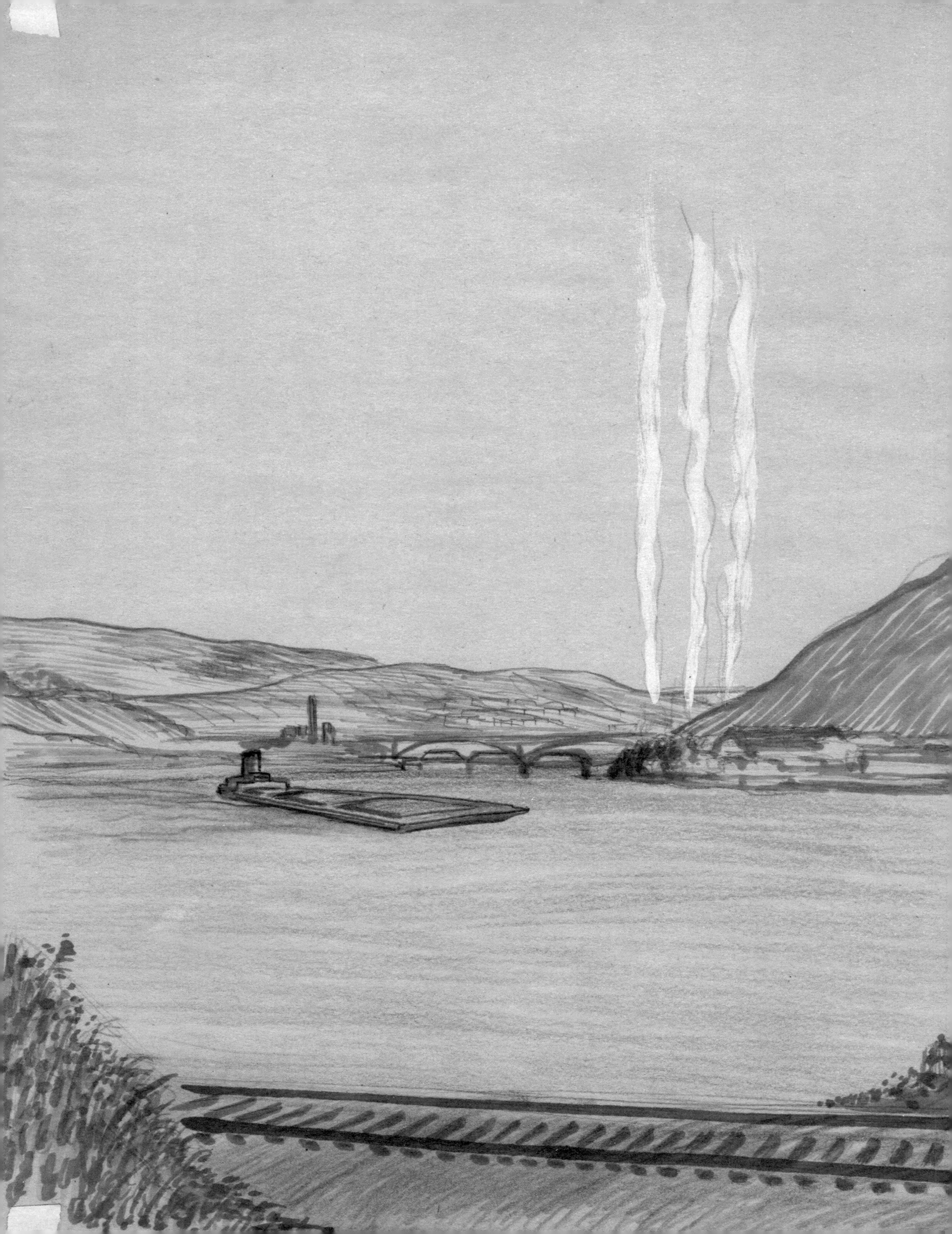

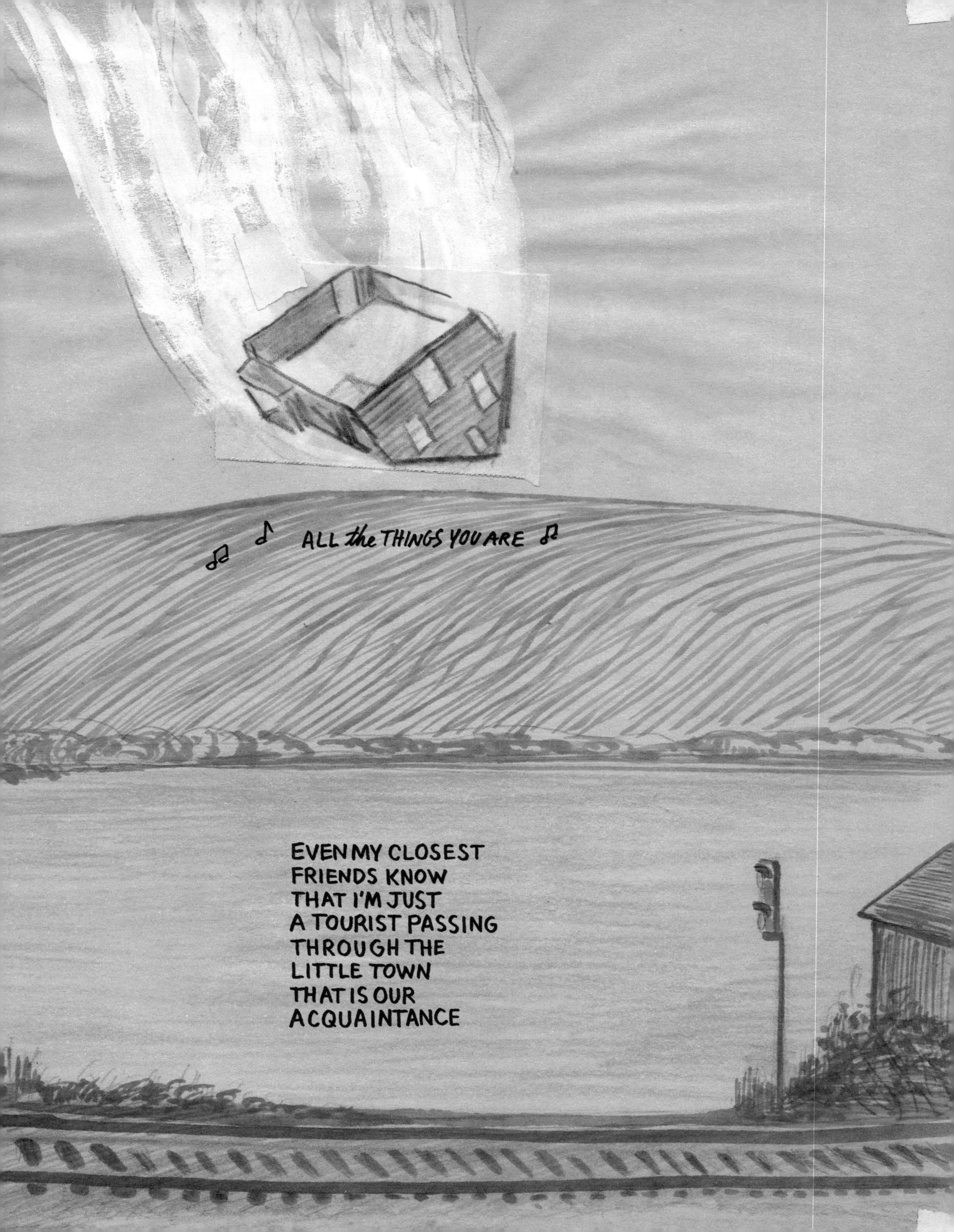
ALL the THINGS YOU ARE
EVEN MY CLOSEST FRIENDS KNOW THAT I'M JUST A TOURIST PASSING THROUGH THE LITTLE TOWN THAT IS OUR ACQUAINTANCE

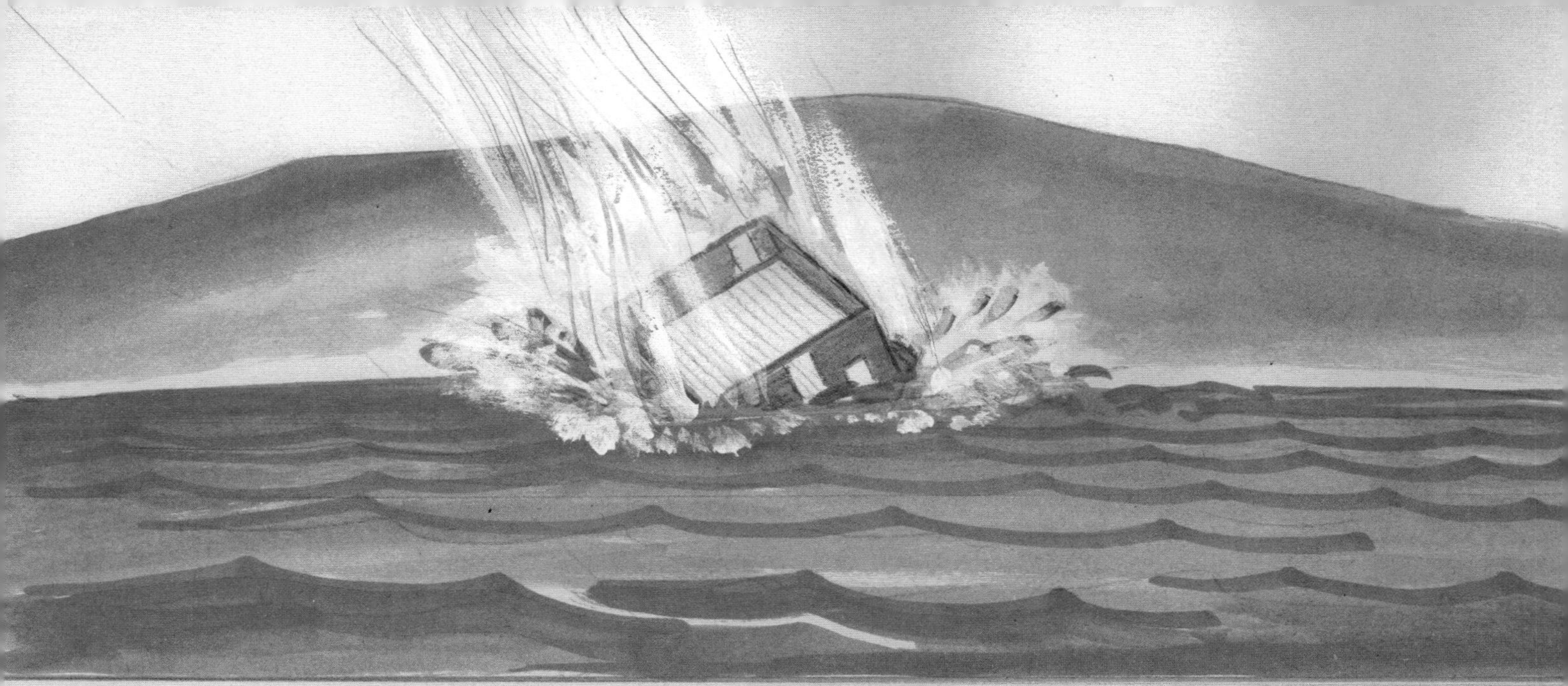

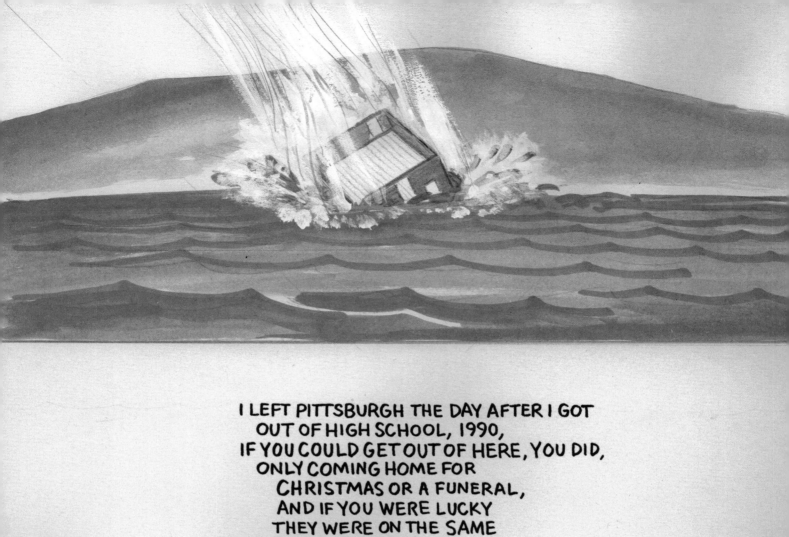

I LEFT PITTSBURGH THE DAY AFTER I GOT
OUT OF HIGH SCHOOL, 1990,
IF YOU COULD GET OUT OF HERE, YOU DID,
ONLY COMING HOME FOR
CHRISTMAS OR A FUNERAL,
AND IF YOU WERE LUCKY
THEY WERE ON THE SAME
WEEKEND

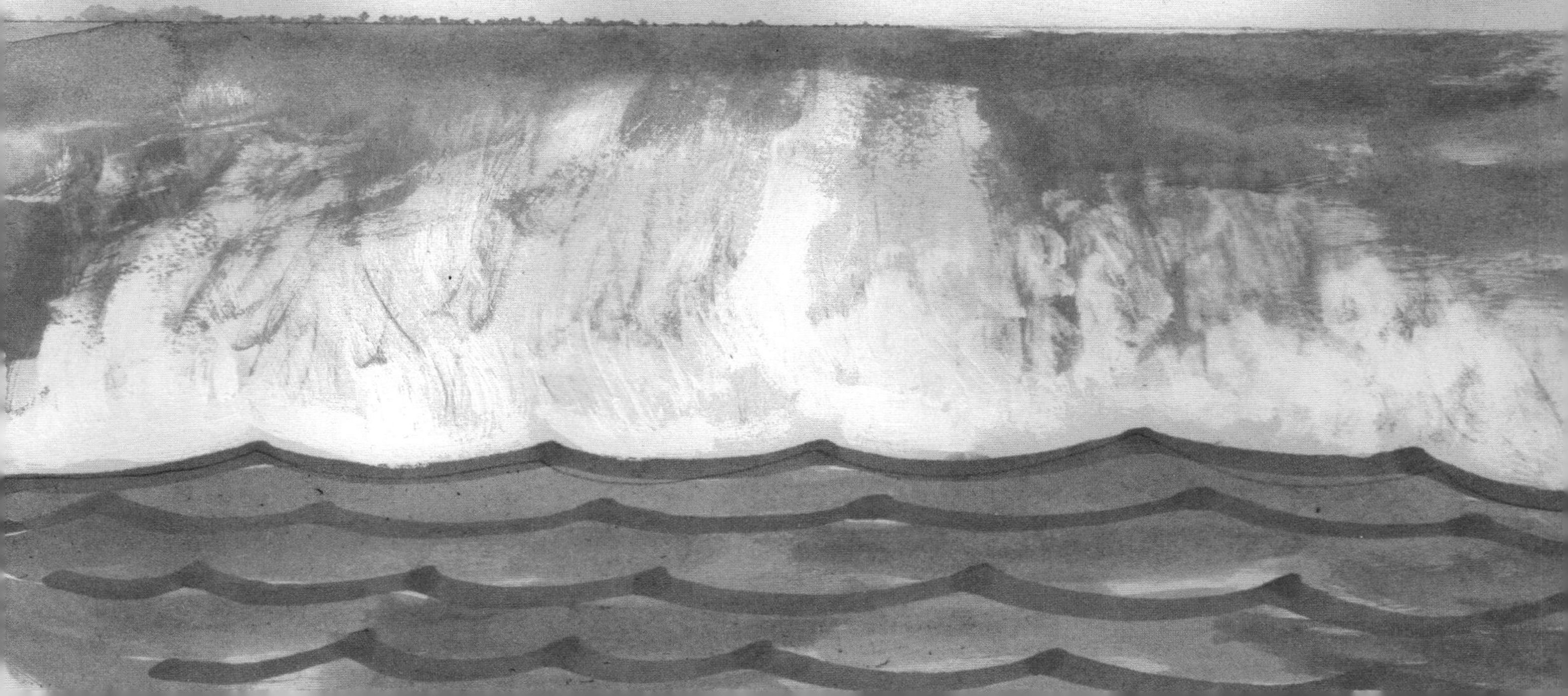

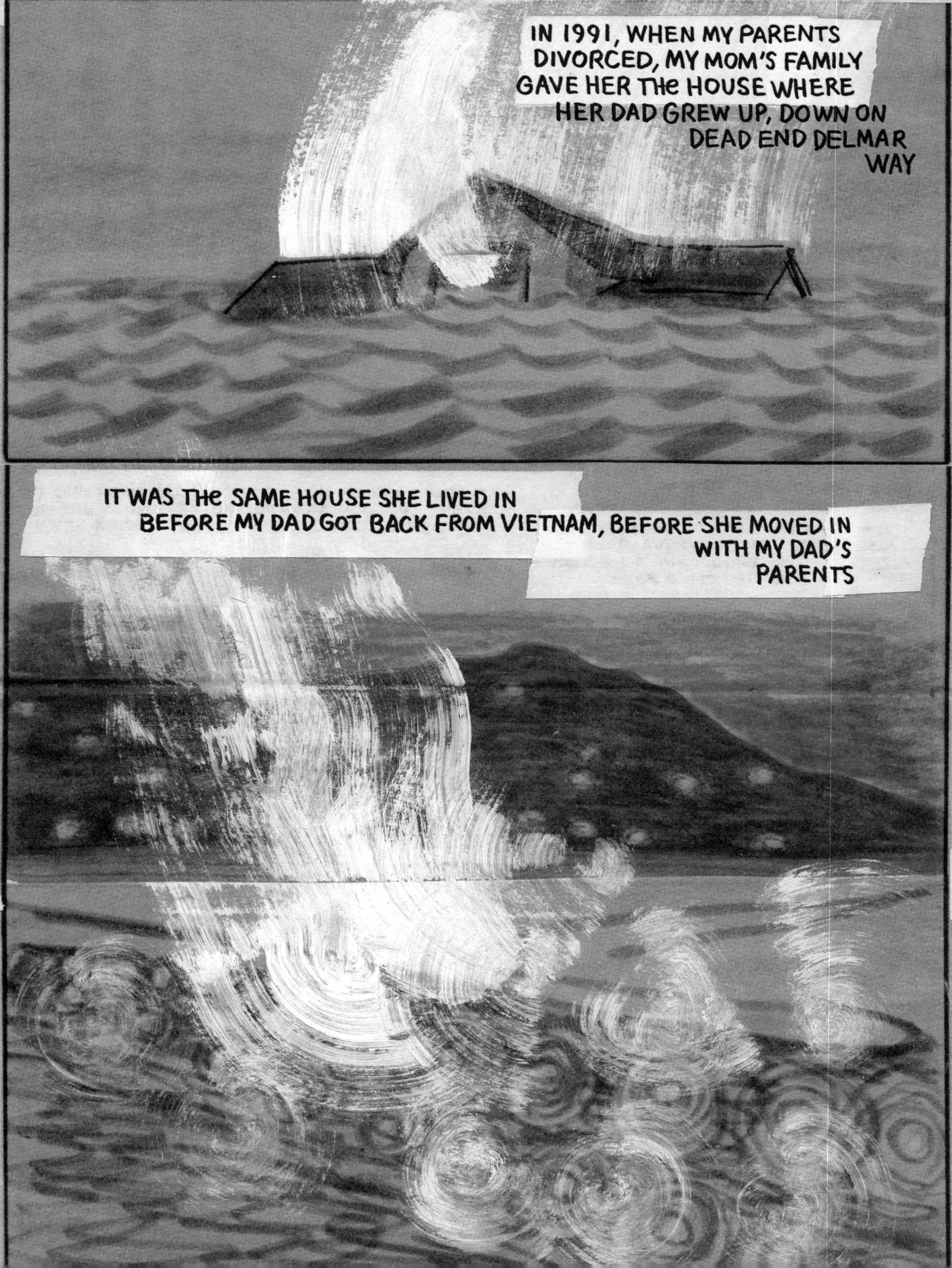
IN 1991, WHEN MY PARENTS DIVORCED, MY MOM'S FAMILY GAVE HER THE HOUSE WHERE HER DAD GREW UP, DOWN ON DEAD END DELMAR WAY
IT WAS THE SAME HOUSE SHE LIVED IN BEFORE MY DAD GOT BACK FROM VIETNAM, BEFORE SHE MOVED IN WITH MY DAD'S PARENTS

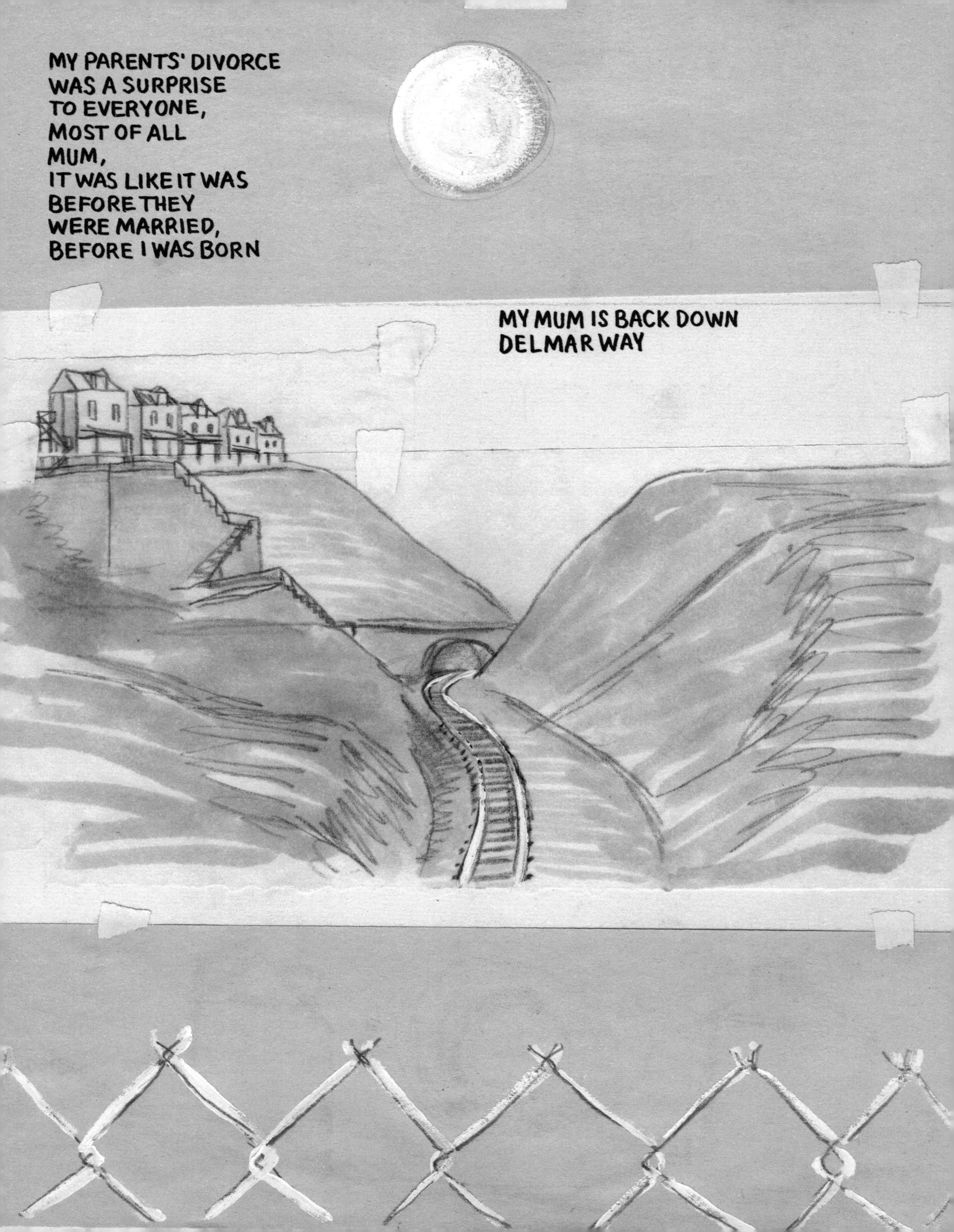
MY PARENTS' DIVORCE WAS A SURPRISE TO EVERYONE, MOST OF ALL MUM, IT WAS LIKE IT WAS BEFORE THEY WERE MARRIED, BEFORE I WAS BORN
MY MUM IS BACK DOWN DELMAR WAY

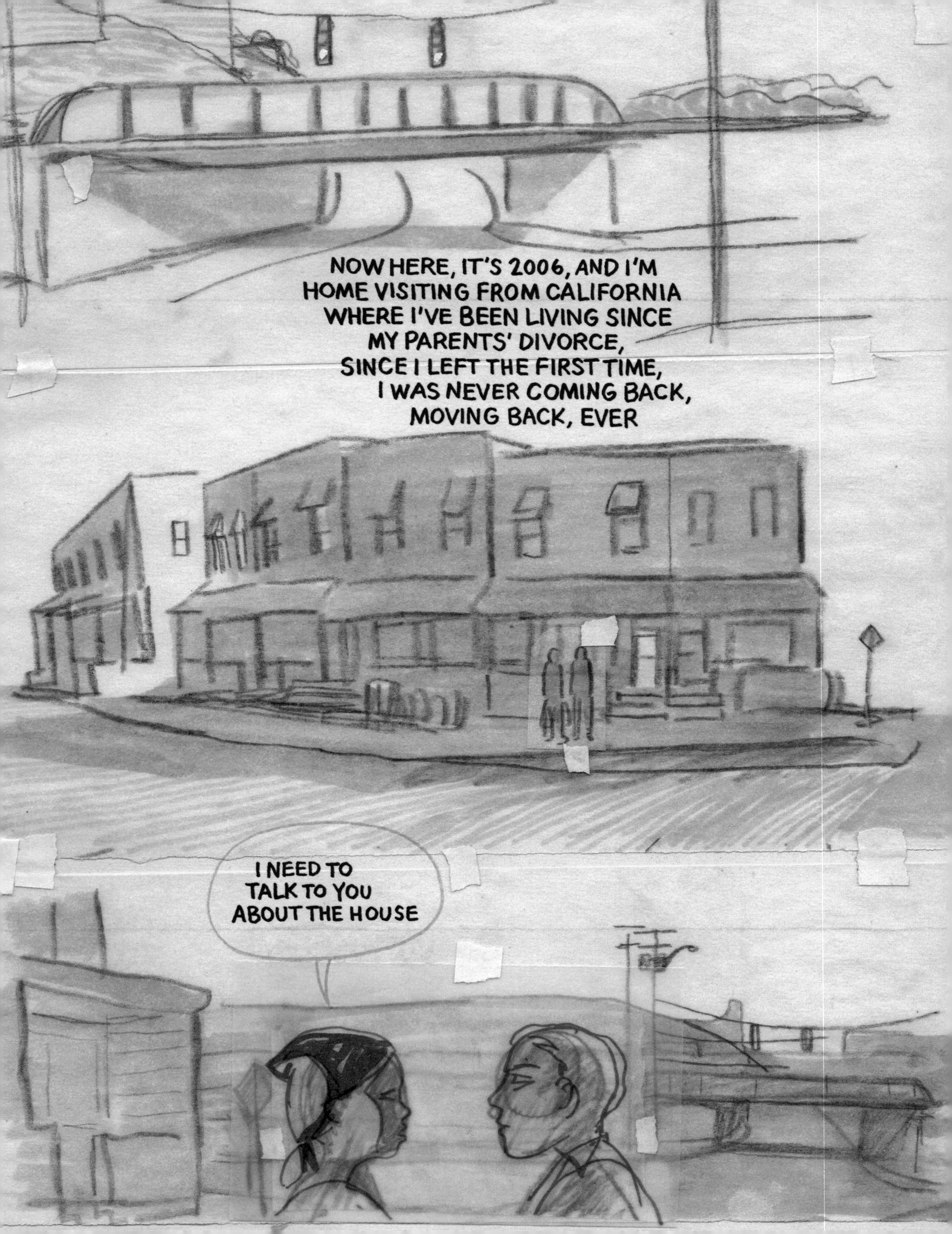
NOW HERE, IT'S 2006, AND I'M HOME VISITING FROM CALIFORNIA WHERE I'VE BEEN LIVING SINCE MY PARENTS' DIVORCE, SINCE I LEFT THE FIRST TIME, I WAS NEVER COMING BACK, MOVING BACK, EVER
I NEED TO TALK TO YOU ABOUT THE HOUSE

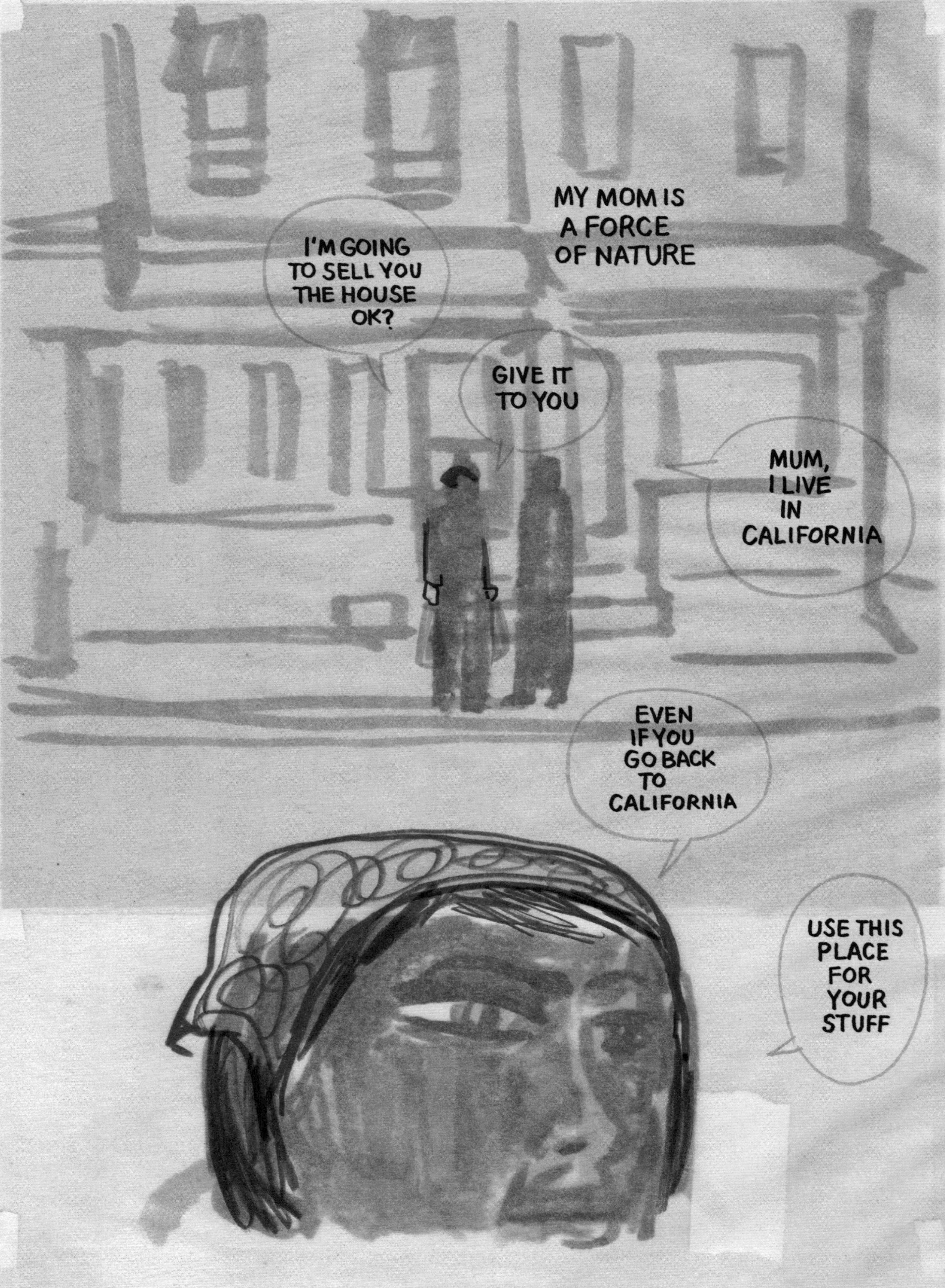
MY MOM IS A FORCE OF NATURE
I'M GOING TO SELL YOU THE HOUSE OK?
GIVE IT TO YOU
MUM, I LIVE IN CALIFORNIA
EVEN IF YOU GO BACK TO CALIFORNIA
USE THIS PLACE FOR YOUR STUFF

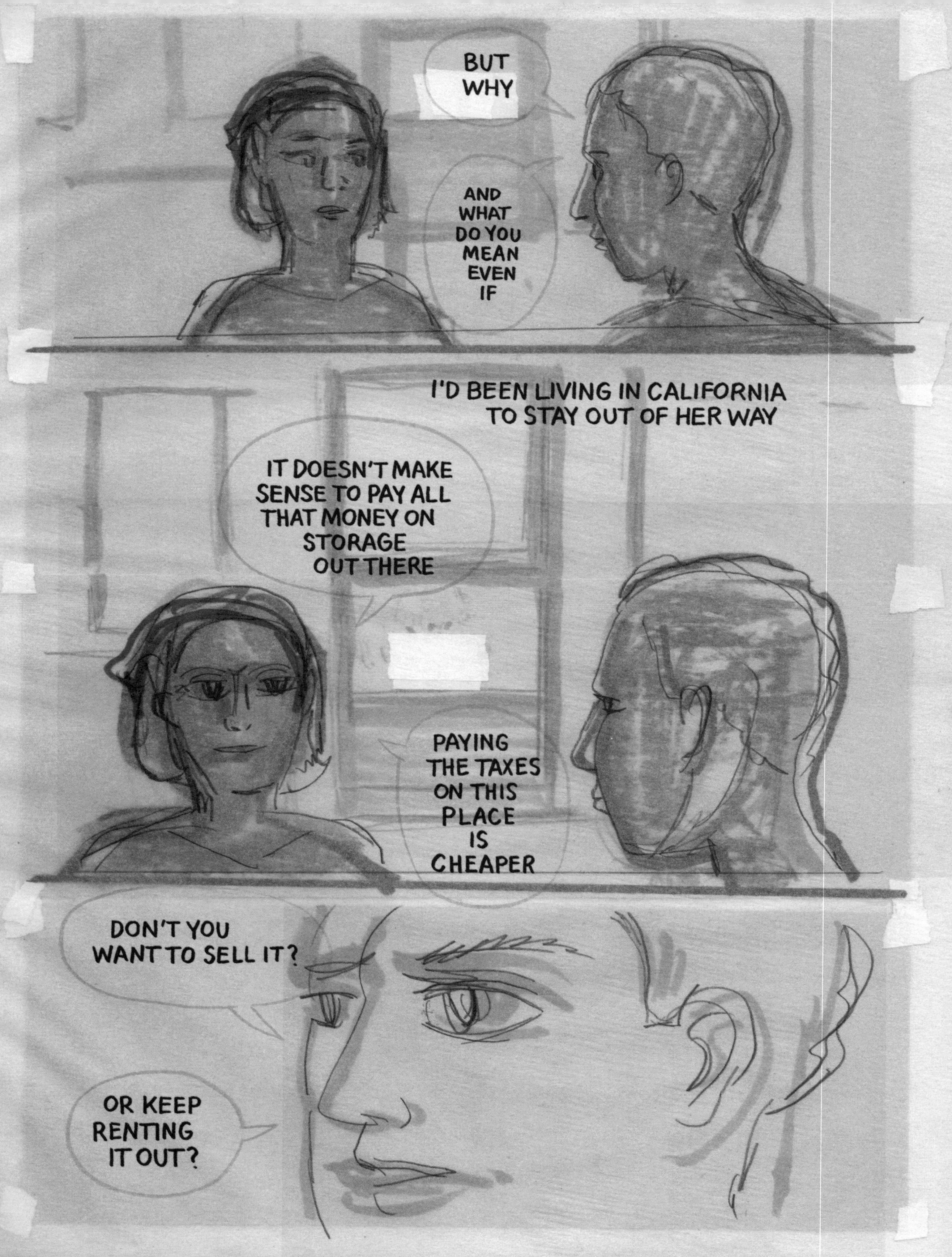
BUT WHY
AND WHAT DO YOU MEAN EVEN IF
I'D BEEN LIVING IN CALIFORNIA TO STAY OUT OF HER WAY
IT DOESN'T MAKE SENSE TO PAY ALL THAT MONEY ON STORAGE OUT THERE
PAYING THE TAXES ON THIS PLACE IS CHEAPER
DON'T YOU WANT TO SELL IT?
OR KEEP RENTING IT OUT?

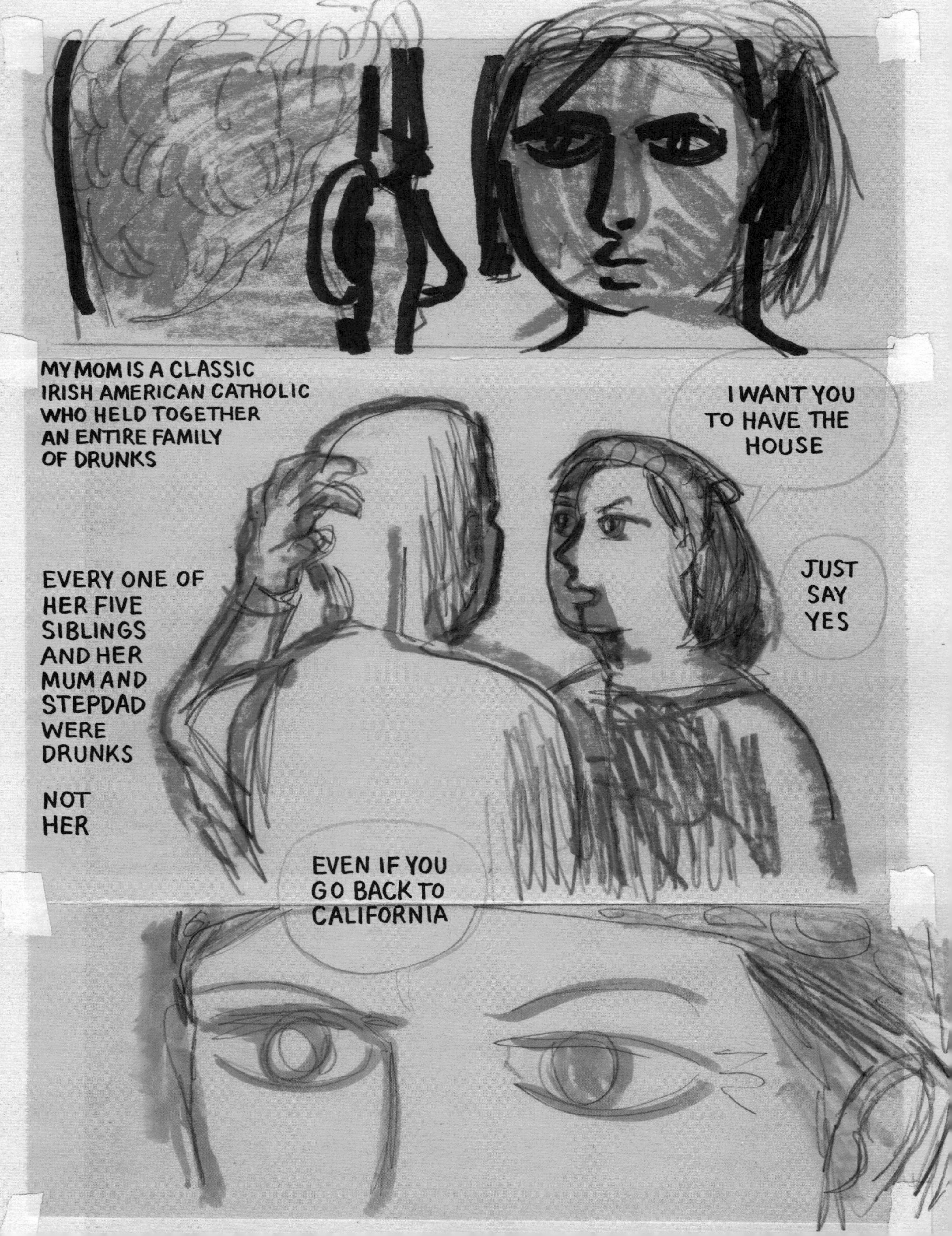
MY MOM IS A CLASSIC IRISH AMERICAN CATHOLIC WHO HELD TOGETHER AN ENTIRE FAMILY OF DRUNKS
I WANT YOU TO HAVE THE HOUSE
EVERY ONE OF HER FIVE SIBLINGS AND HER MUM AND STEPDAD WERE DRUNKS
JUST SAY YES
NOT HER
EVEN IF YOU GO BACK TO CALIFORNIA

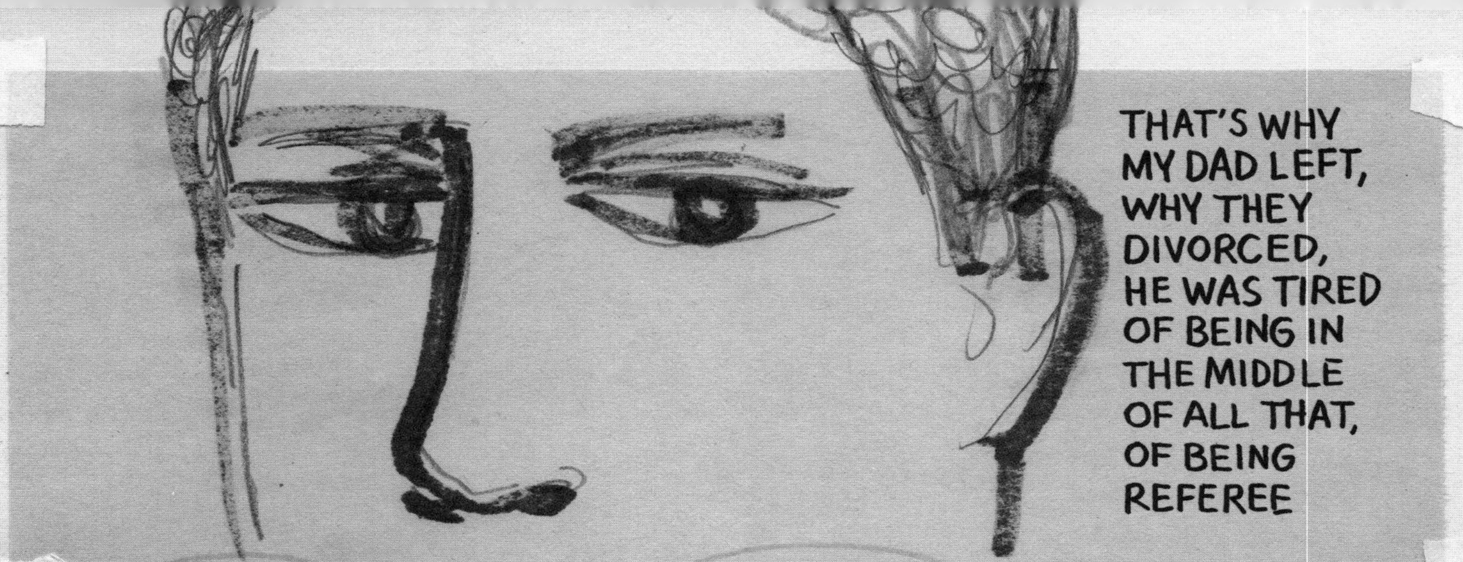
THAT'S WHY MY DAD LEFT, WHY THEY DIVORCED, HE WAS TIRED OF BEING IN THE MIDDLE OF ALL THAT, OF BEING REFEREE

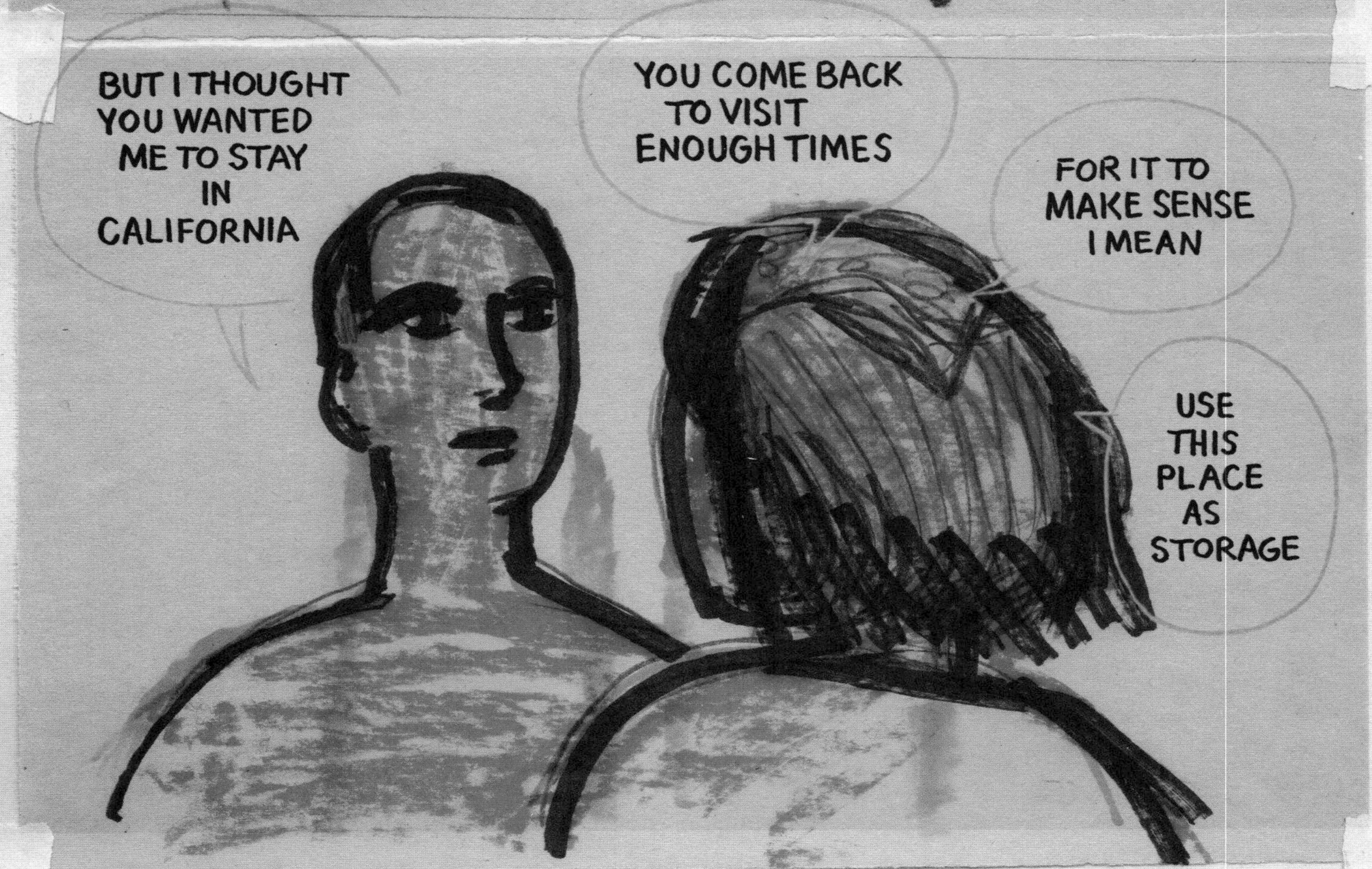
BUT I THOUGHT YOU WANTED ME TO STAY IN CALIFORNIA
YOU COME BACK TO VISIT ENOUGH TIMES
FOR IT TO MAKE SENSE I MEAN
USE THIS PLACE AS STORAGE

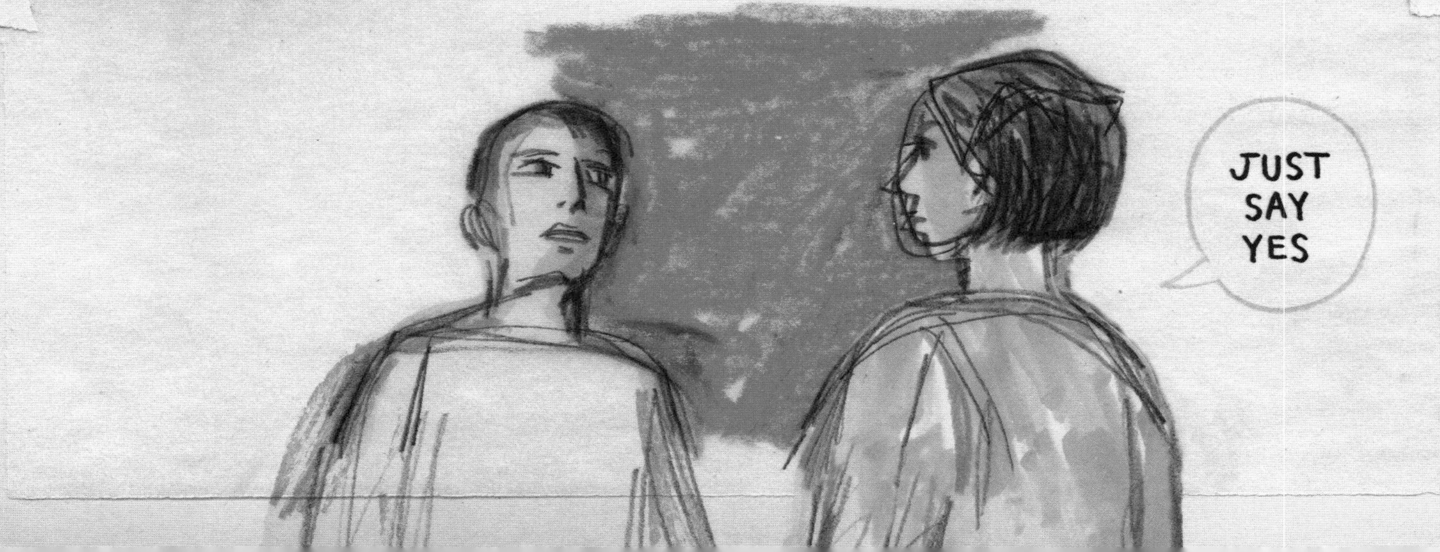
JUST SAY YES

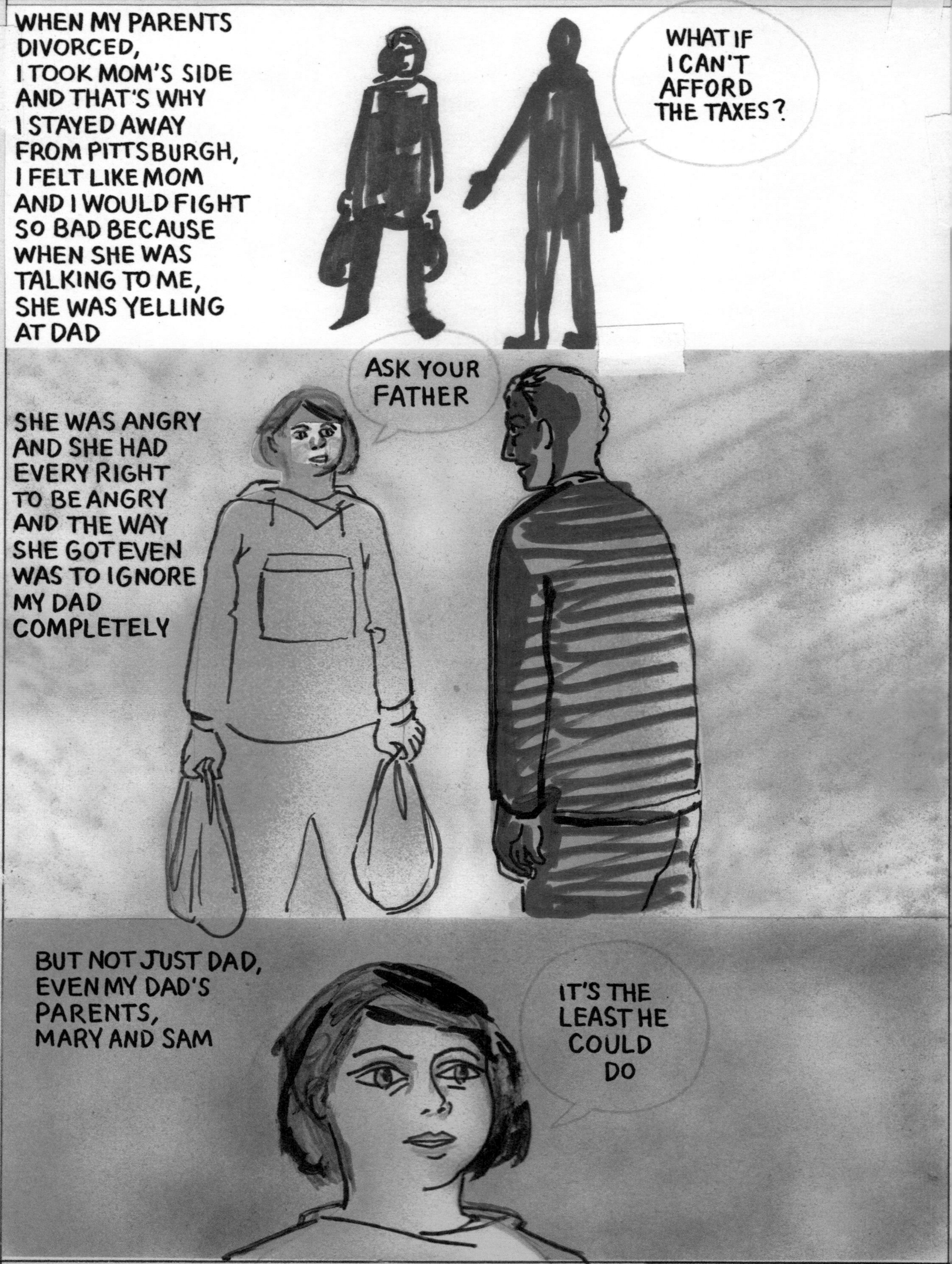

WHEN MY PARENTS DIVORCED, I TOOK MOM'S SIDE AND THAT'S WHY I STAYED AWAY FROM PITTSBURGH, I FELT LIKE MOM AND I WOULD FIGHT SO BAD BECAUSE WHEN SHE WAS TALKING TO ME, SHE WAS YELLING AT DAD

WHAT IF I CAN'T AFFORD THE TAXES?

SHE WAS ANGRY AND SHE HAD EVERY RIGHT TO BE ANGRY AND THE WAY SHE GOT EVEN WAS TO IGNORE MY DAD COMPLETELY

ASK YOUR FATHER

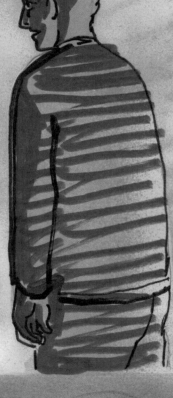

BUT NOT JUST DAD, EVEN MY DAD'S PARENTS, MARY AND SAM

IT'S THE LEAST HE COULD DO

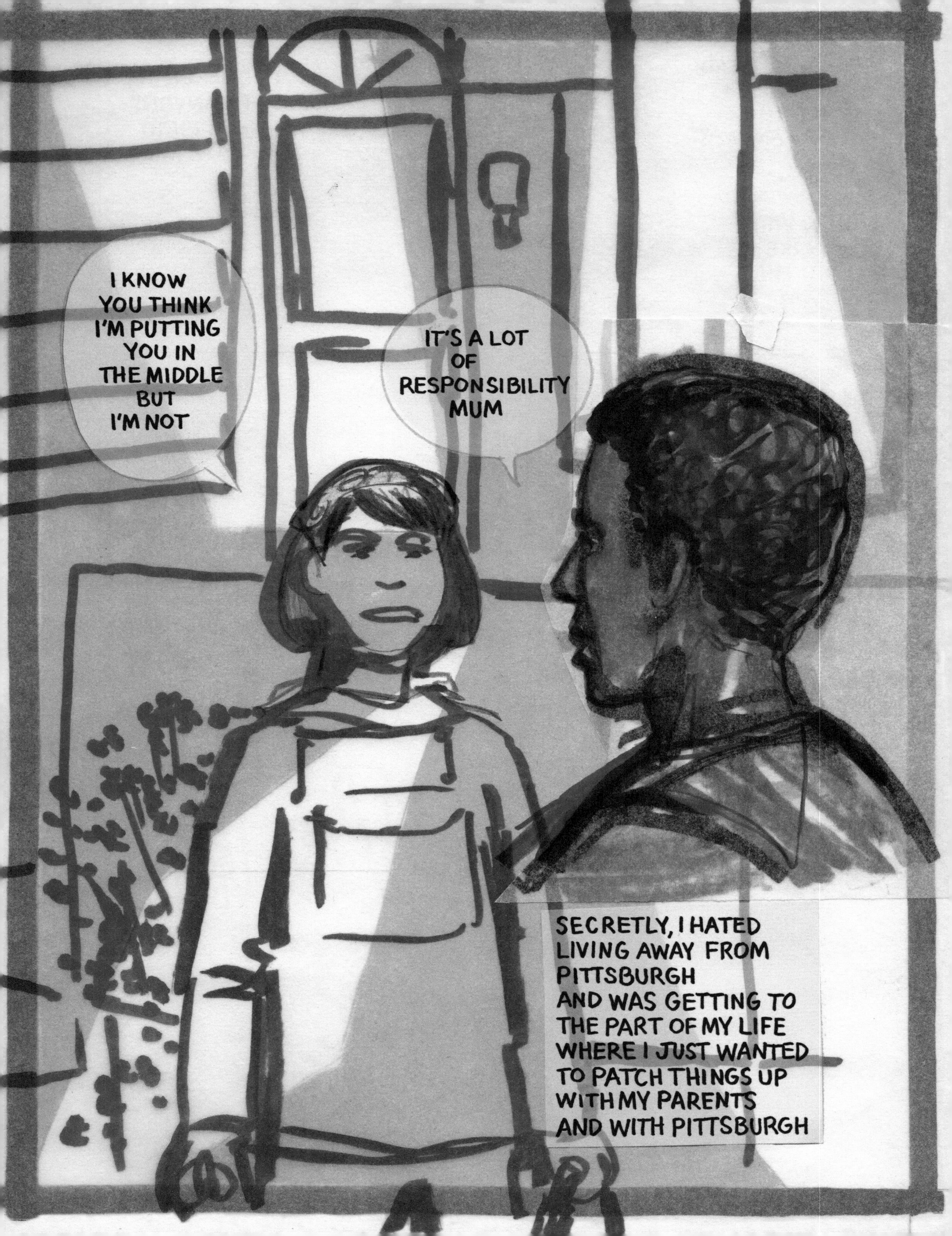
I KNOW YOU THINK I'M PUTTING YOU IN THE MIDDLE BUT I'M NOT
IT'S A LOT OF RESPONSIBILITY MUM
SECRETLY, I HATED LIVING AWAY FROM PITTSBURGH AND WAS GETTING TO THE PART OF MY LIFE WHERE I JUST WANTED TO PATCH THINGS UP WITH MY PARENTS AND WITH PITTSBURGH

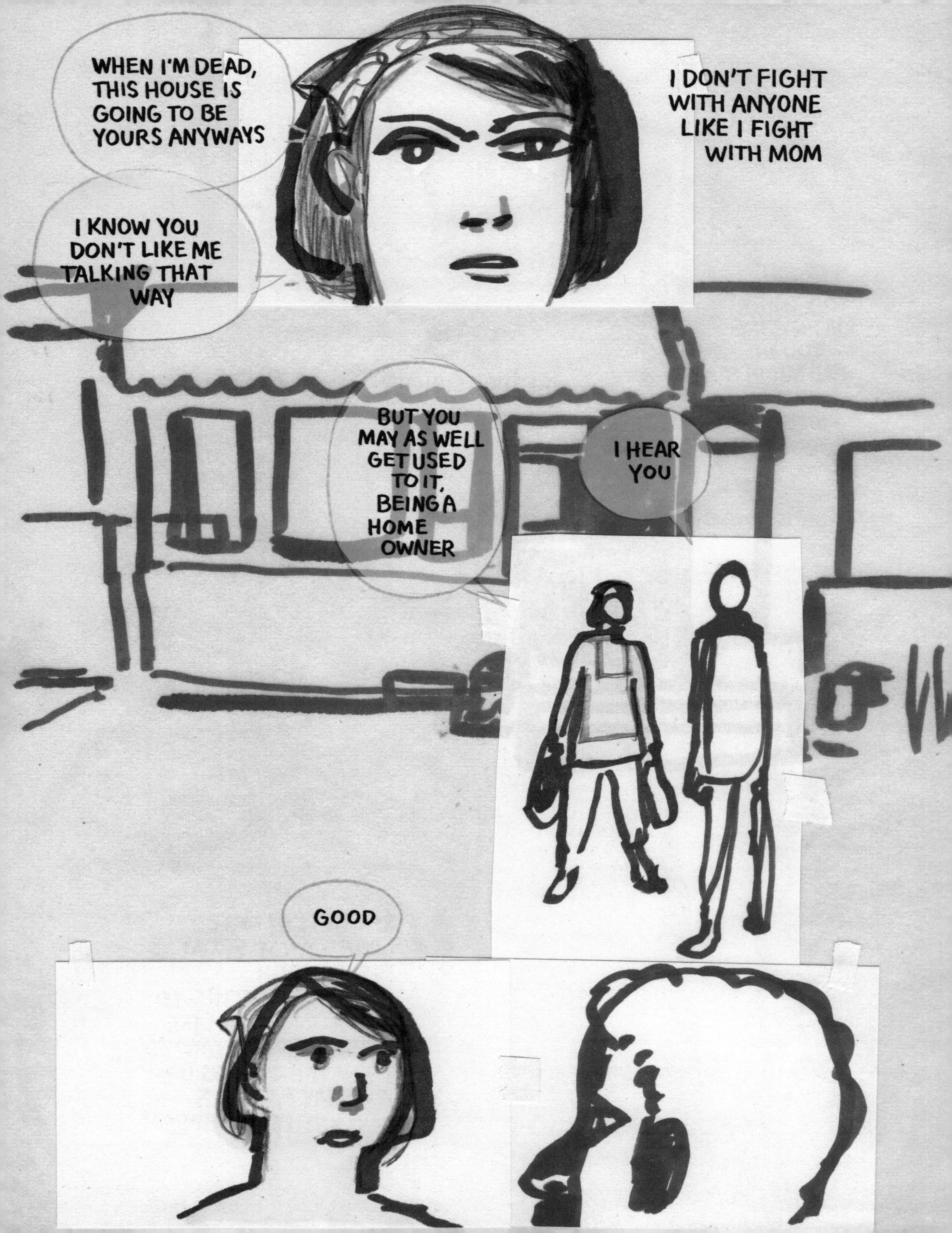
WHEN I'M DEAD, THIS HOUSE IS GOING TO BE YOURS ANYWAYS
I DON'T FIGHT WITH ANYONE LIKE I FIGHT WITH MOM
I KNOW YOU DON'T LIKE ME TALKING THAT WAY
BUT YOU MAY AS WELL GET USED TO IT, BEING A HOME OWNER
I HEAR YOU
GOOD

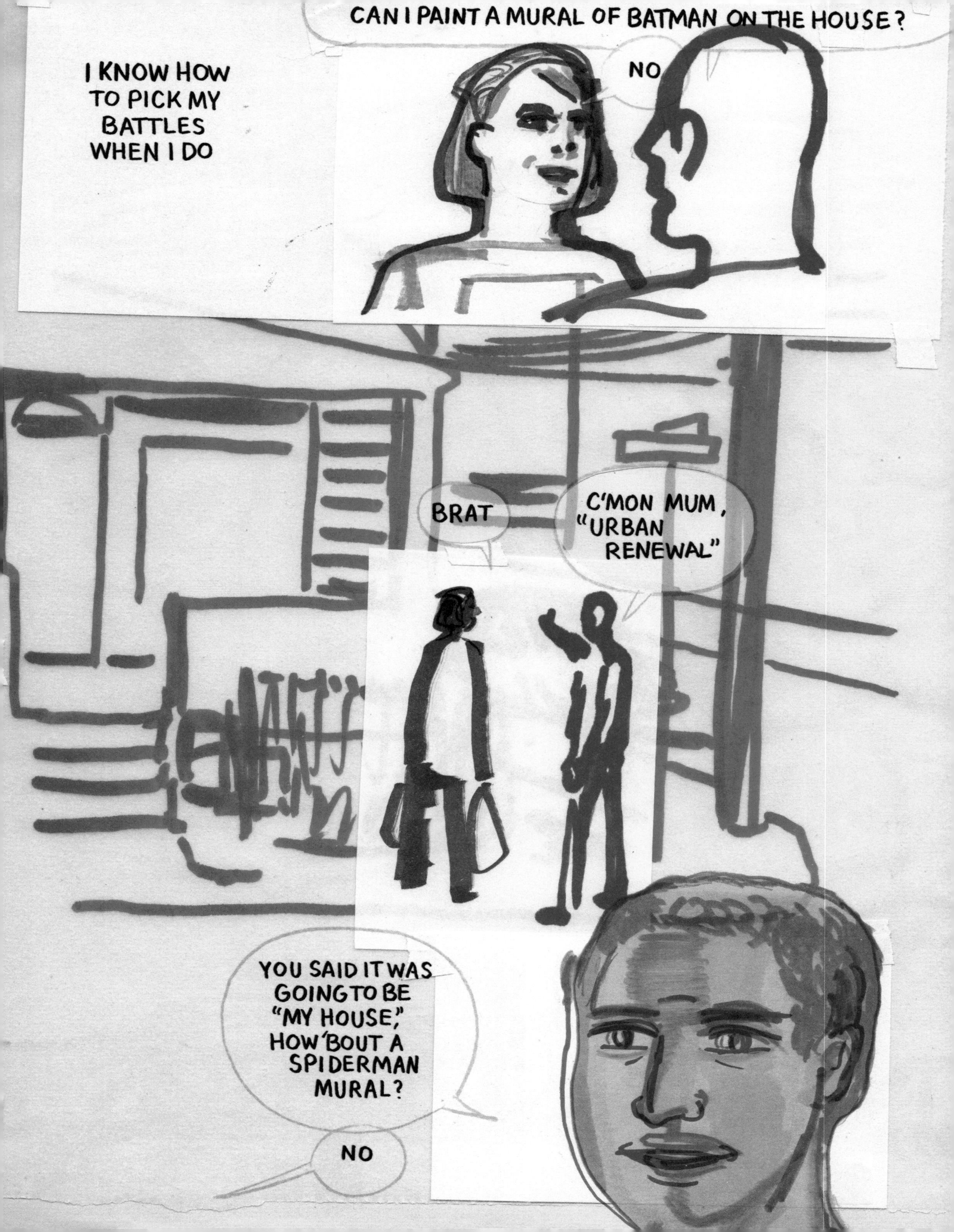
CAN I PAINT A MURAL OF BATMAN ON THE HOUSE?
I KNOW HOW TO PICK MY BATTLES WHEN I DO
NO
BRAT
C'MON MUM, "URBAN RENEWAL"
YOU SAID IT WAS GOING TO BE "MY HOUSE," HOW'BOUT A SPIDERMAN MURAL?
NO

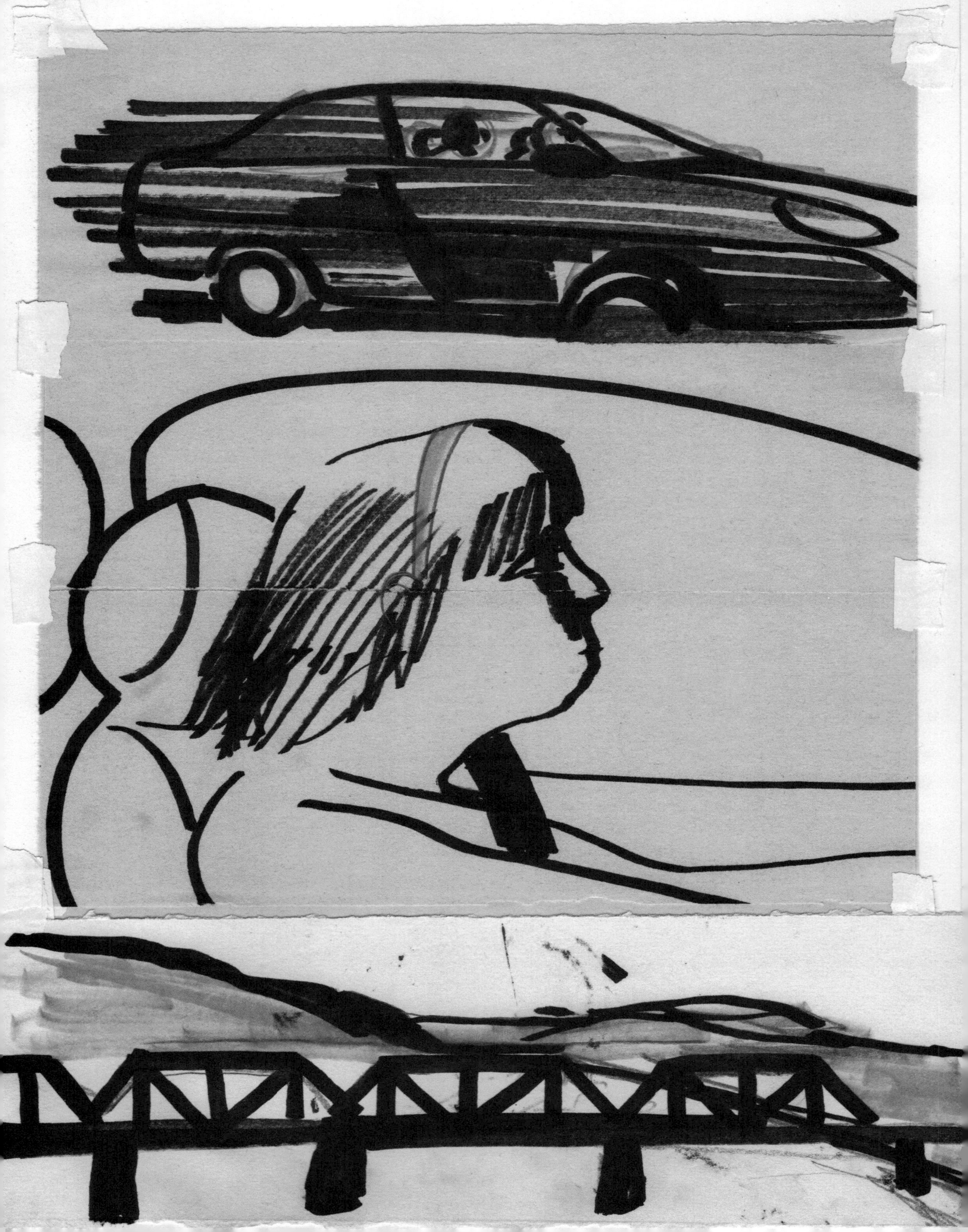

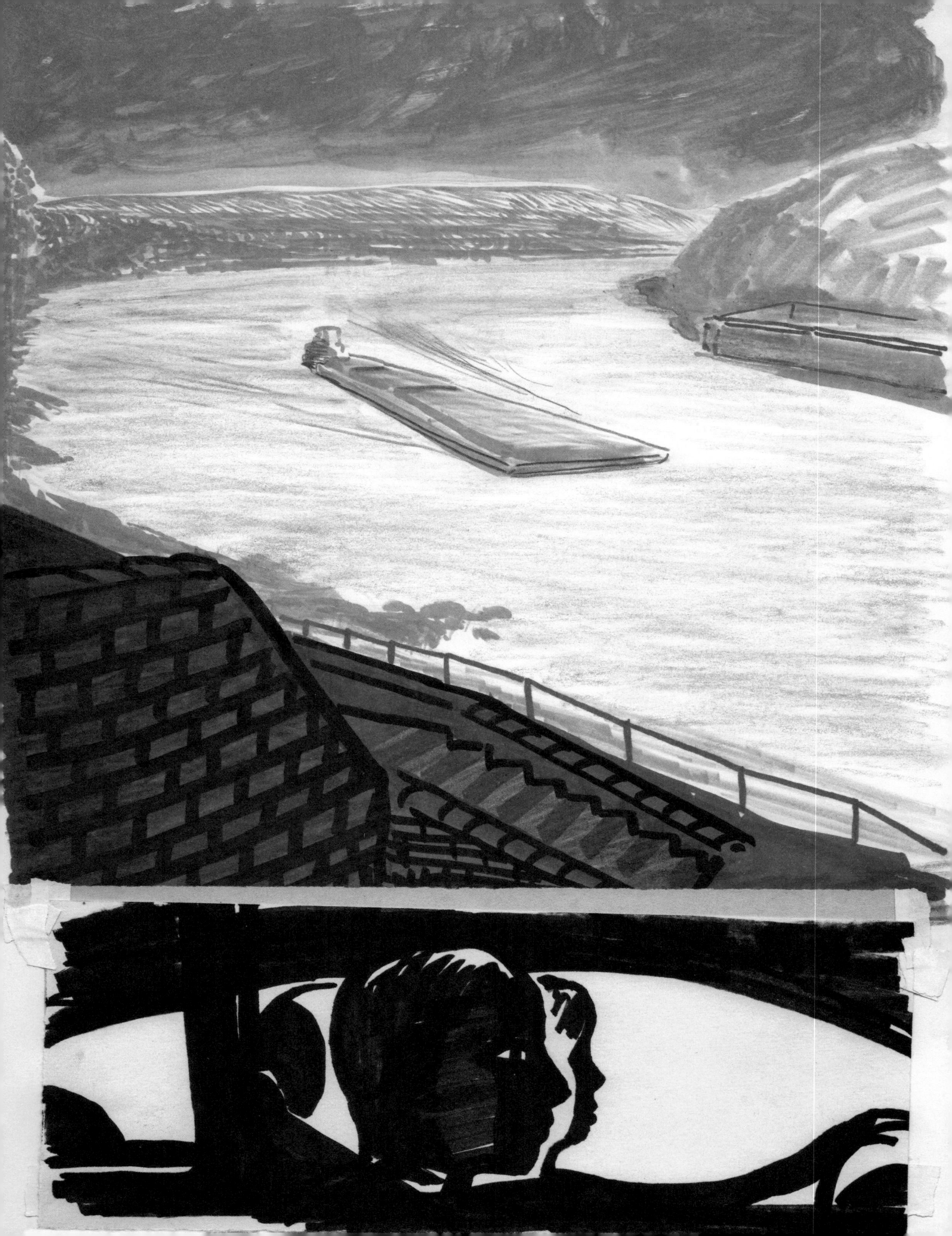

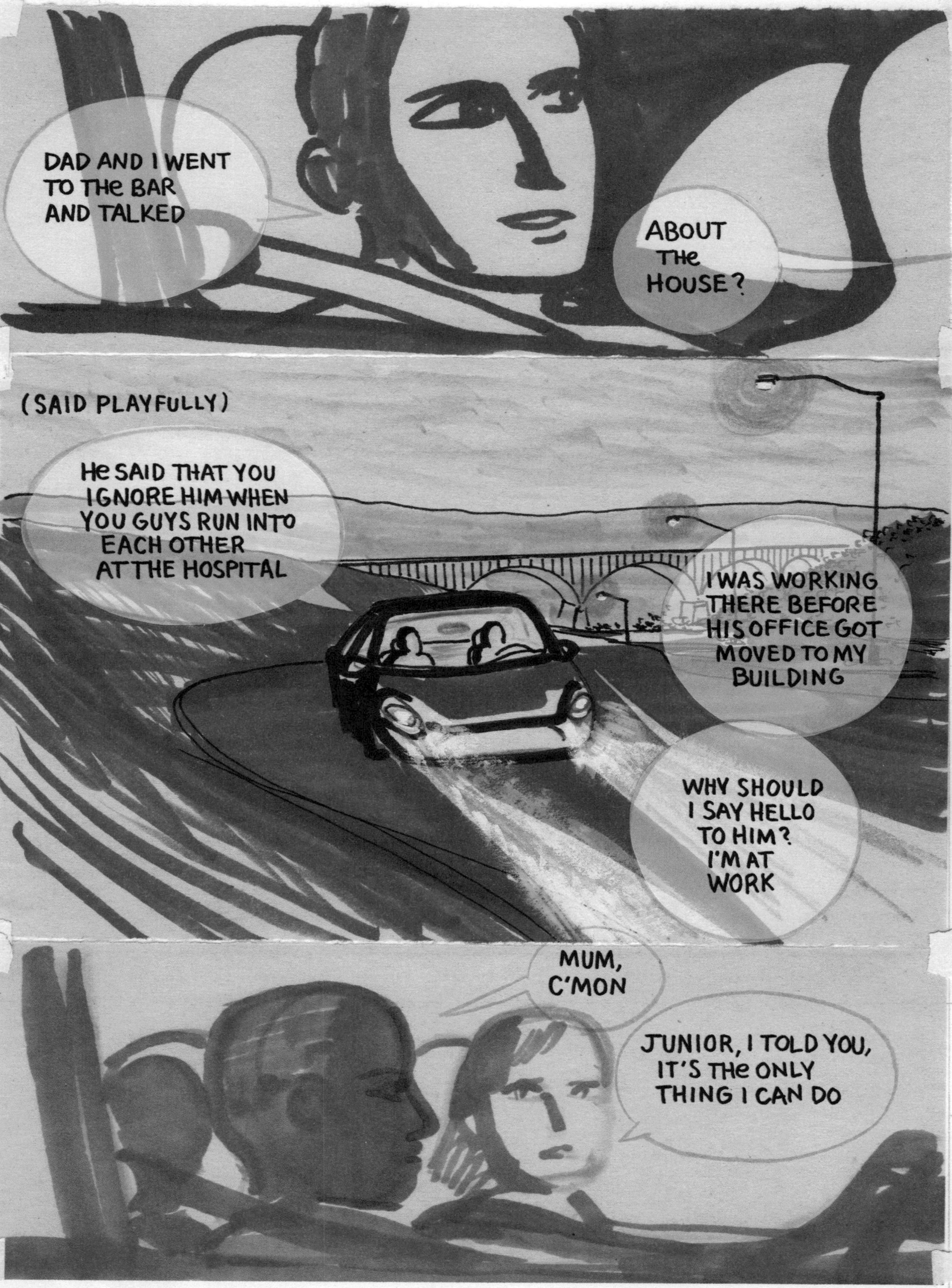
DAD AND I WENT TO THE BAR AND TALKED
ABOUT THE HOUSE?
(SAID PLAYFULLY)
HE SAID THAT YOU IGNORE HIM WHEN YOU GUYS RUN INTO EACH OTHER AT THE HOSPITAL
I WAS WORKING THERE BEFORE HIS OFFICE GOT MOVED TO MY BUILDING
WHY SHOULD I SAY HELLO TO HIM? I'M AT WORK
MUM, C'MON
JUNIOR, I TOLD YOU, IT'S THE ONLY THING I CAN DO

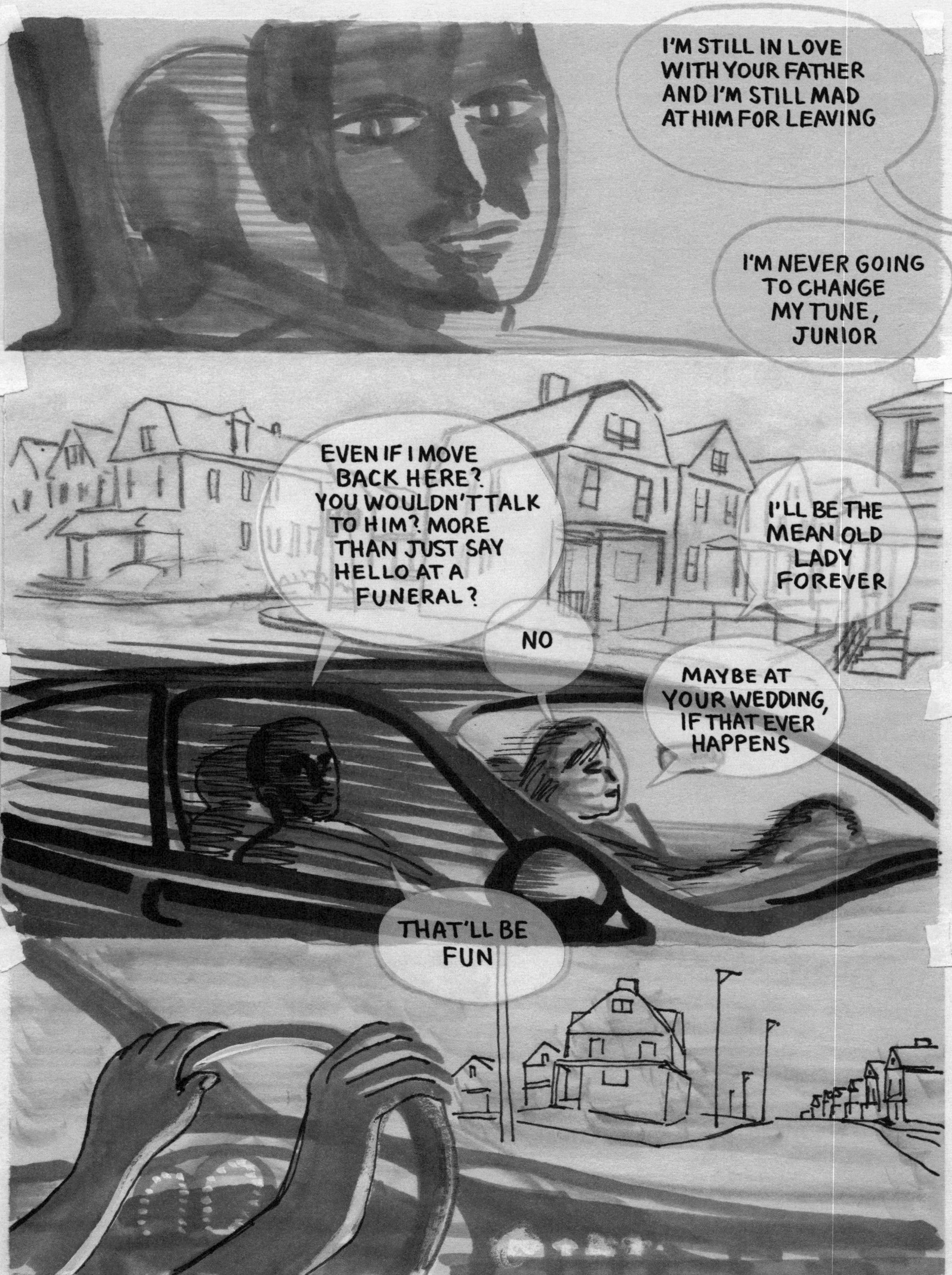
I'M STILL IN LOVE WITH YOUR FATHER AND I'M STILL MAD AT HIM FOR LEAVING
I'M NEVER GOING TO CHANGE MY TUNE, JUNIOR
EVEN IF I MOVE BACK HERE? YOU WOULDN'T TALK TO HIM? MORE THAN JUST SAY HELLO AT A FUNERAL?
I'LL BE THE MEAN OLD LADY FOREVER
NO
MAYBE AT YOUR WEDDING, IF THAT EVER HAPPENS
THAT'LL BE FUN

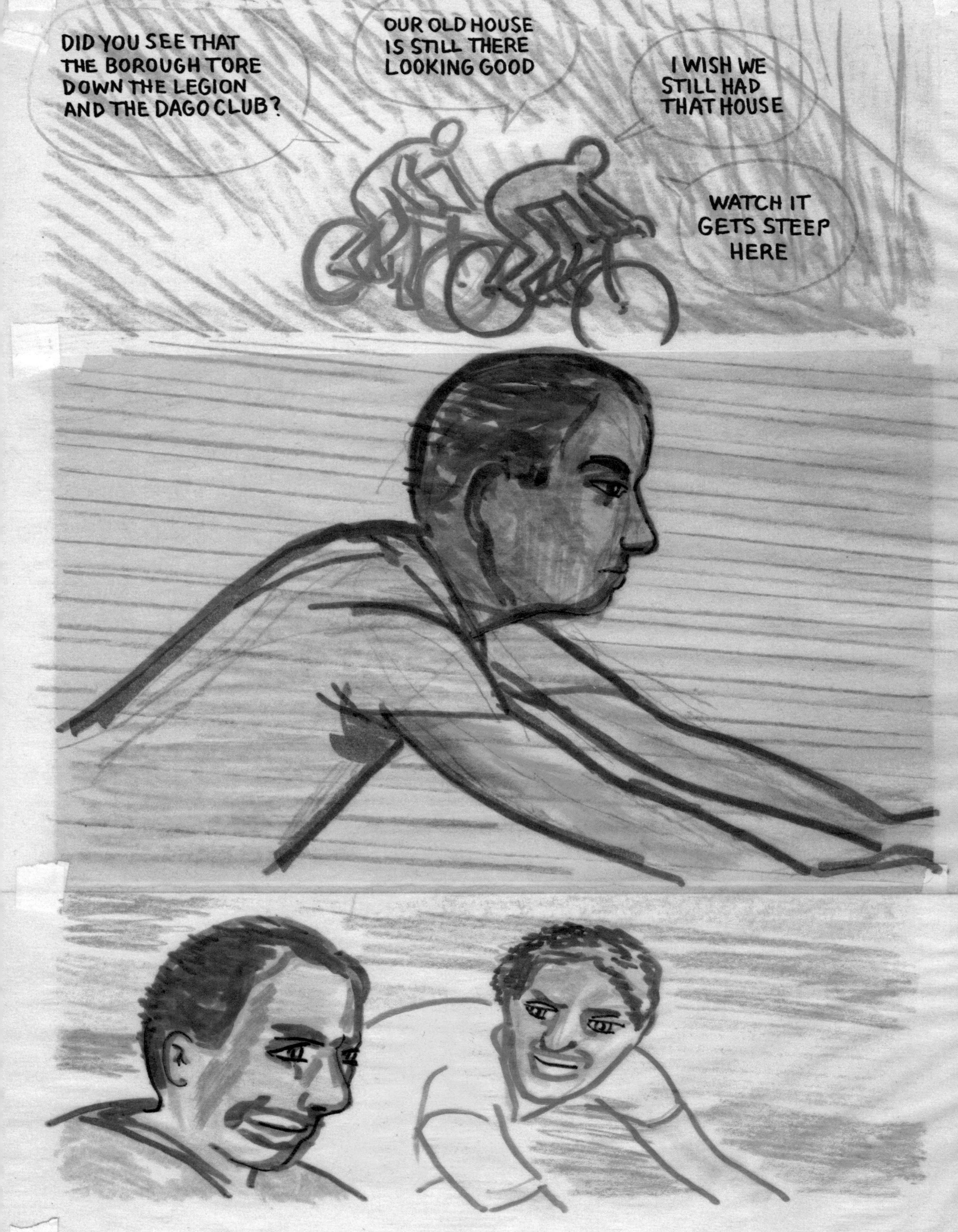
DID YOU SEE THAT THE BOROUGH TORE DOWN THE LEGION AND THE DAGO CLUB?
OUR OLD HOUSE IS STILL THERE LOOKING GOOD
I WISH WE STILL HAD THAT HOUSE
WATCH IT GETS STEEP HERE

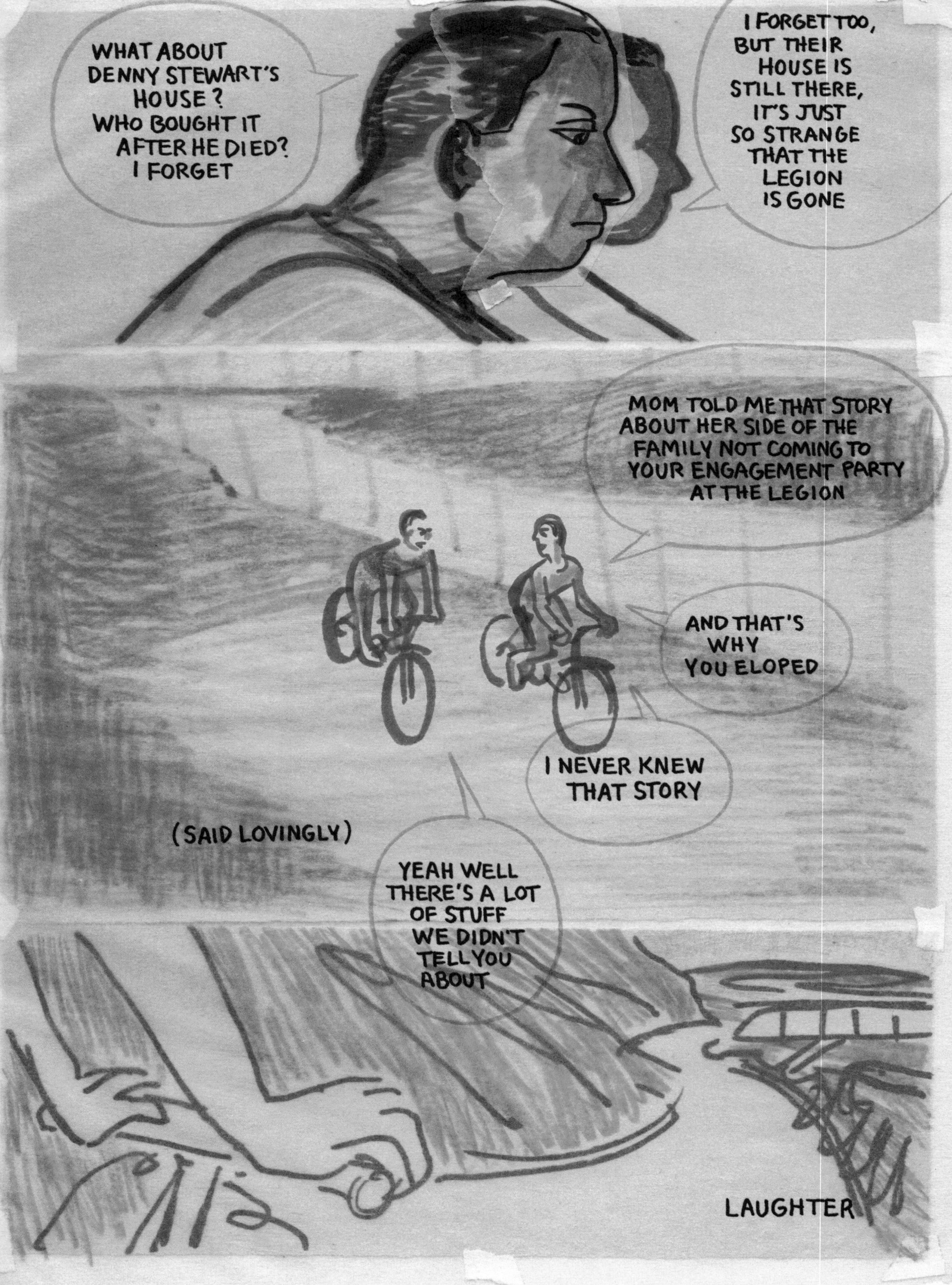
WHAT ABOUT DENNY STEWART'S HOUSE? WHO BOUGHT IT AFTER HE DIED? I FORGET
I FORGET TOO, BUT THEIR HOUSE IS STILL THERE, IT'S JUST SO STRANGE THAT THE LEGION IS GONE
MOM TOLD ME THAT STORY ABOUT HER SIDE OF THE FAMILY NOT COMING TO YOUR ENGAGEMENT PARTY AT THE LEGION
AND THAT'S WHY YOU ELOPED
I NEVER KNEW THAT STORY
(SAID LOVINGLY)
YEAH WELL THERE'S A LOT OF STUFF WE DIDN'T TELL YOU ABOUT
LAUGHTER

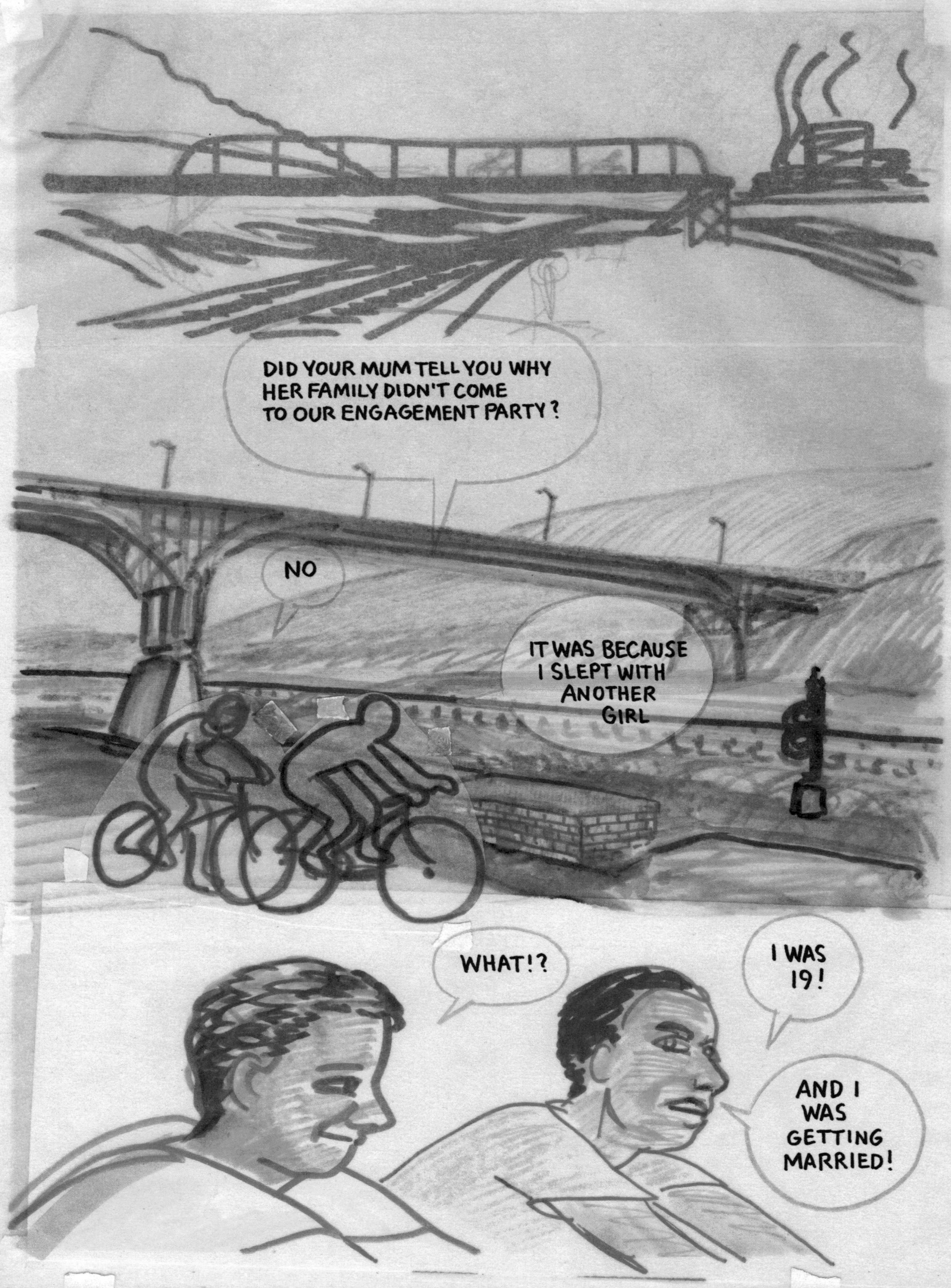
DID YOUR MUM TELL YOU WHY HER FAMILY DIDN'T COME TO OUR ENGAGEMENT PARTY?
NO
IT WAS BECAUSE I SLEPT WITH ANOTHER GIRL
WHAT!?
I WAS 19!
AND I WAS GETTING MARRIED!

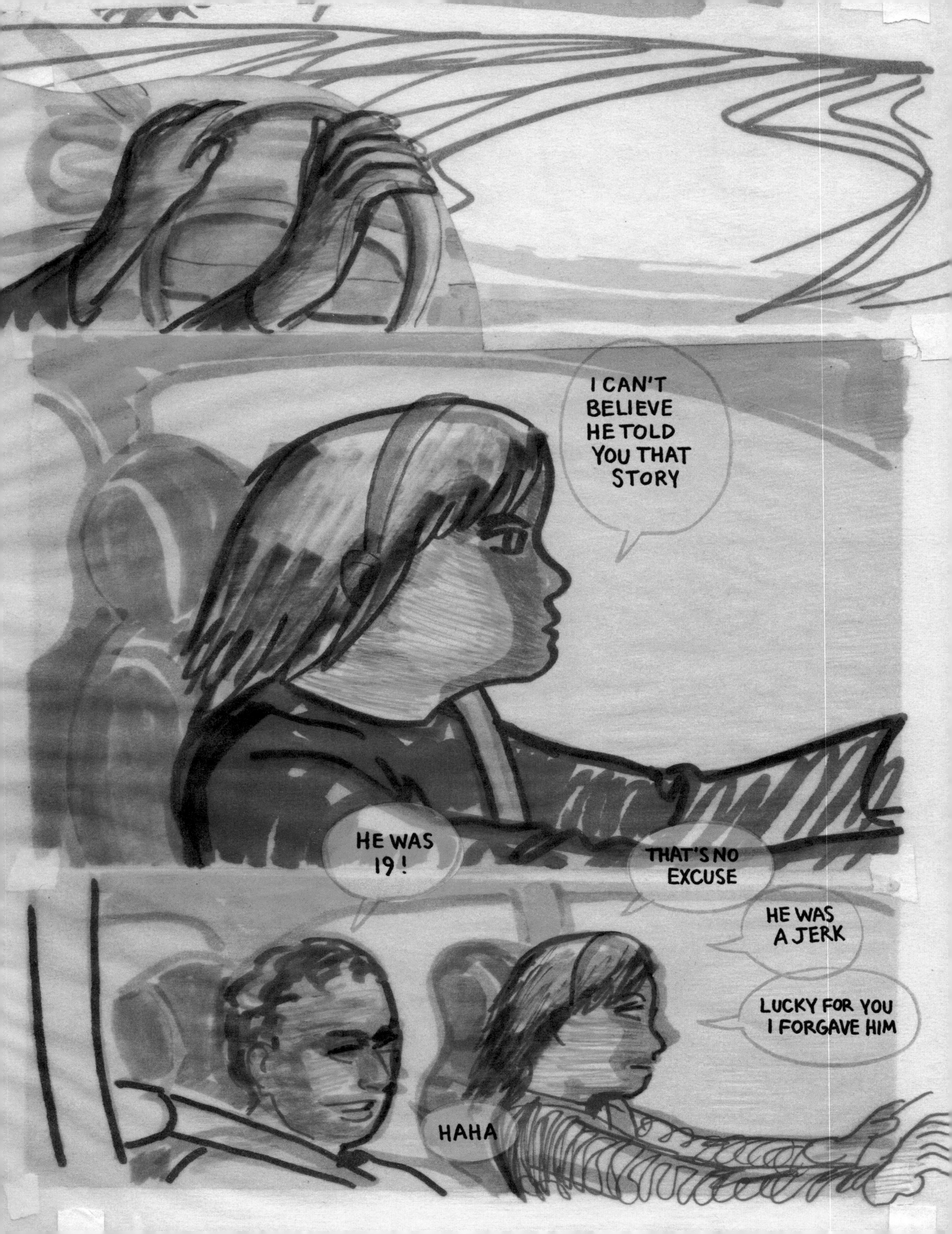
I CAN'T BELIEVE HE TOLD YOU THAT STORY
HE WAS 19!
THAT'S NO EXCUSE
HE WAS A JERK
LUCKY FOR YOU I FORGAVE HIM
HAHA

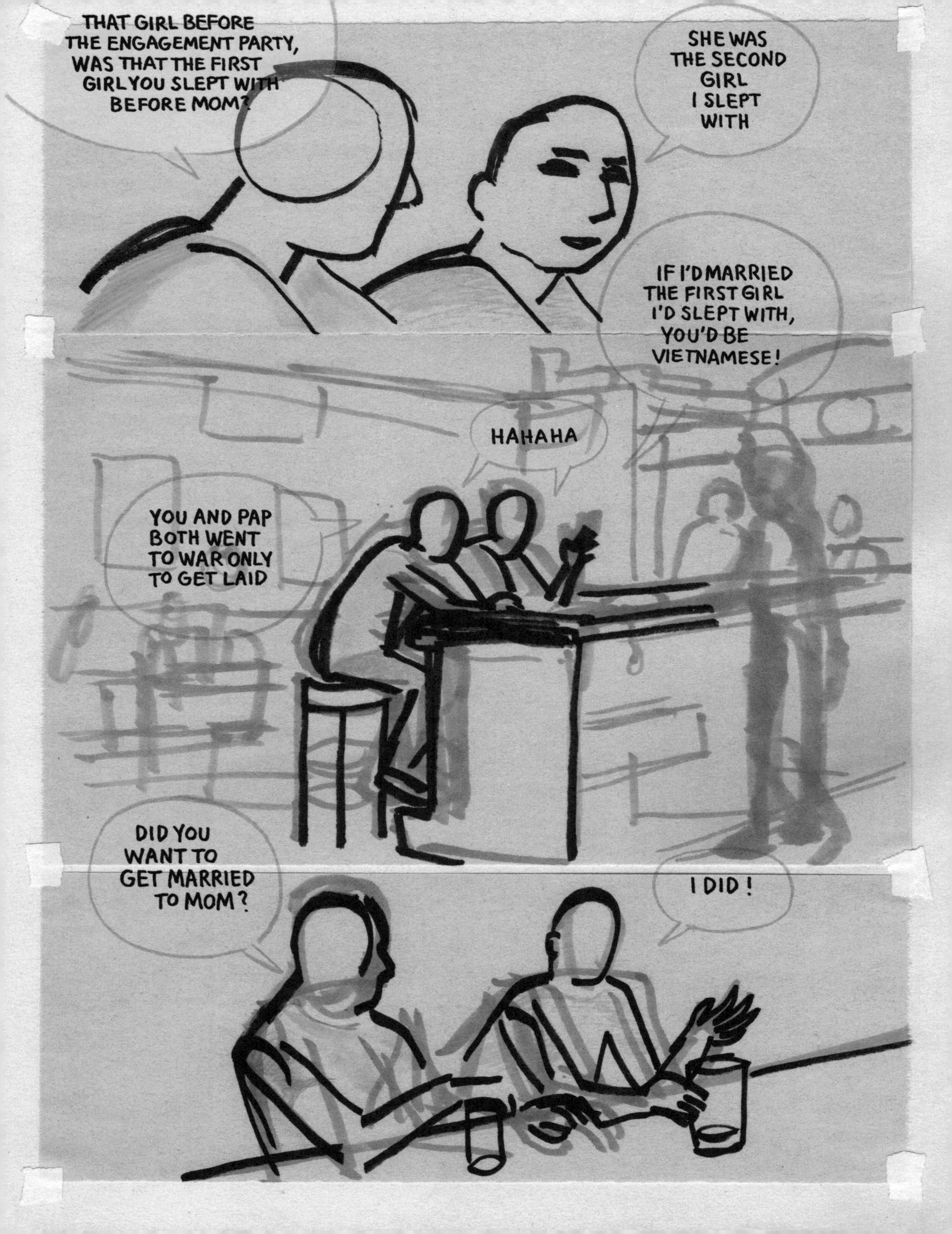
THAT GIRL BEFORE THE ENGAGEMENT PARTY, WAS THAT THE FIRST GIRL YOU SLEPT WITH BEFORE MOM?
SHE WAS THE SECOND GIRL I SLEPT WITH
IF I'D MARRIED THE FIRST GIRL I'D SLEPT WITH, YOU'D BE VIETNAMESE!
HAHAHA
YOU AND PAP BOTH WENT TO WAR ONLY TO GET LAID
DID YOU WANT TO GET MARRIED TO MOM?
I DID!

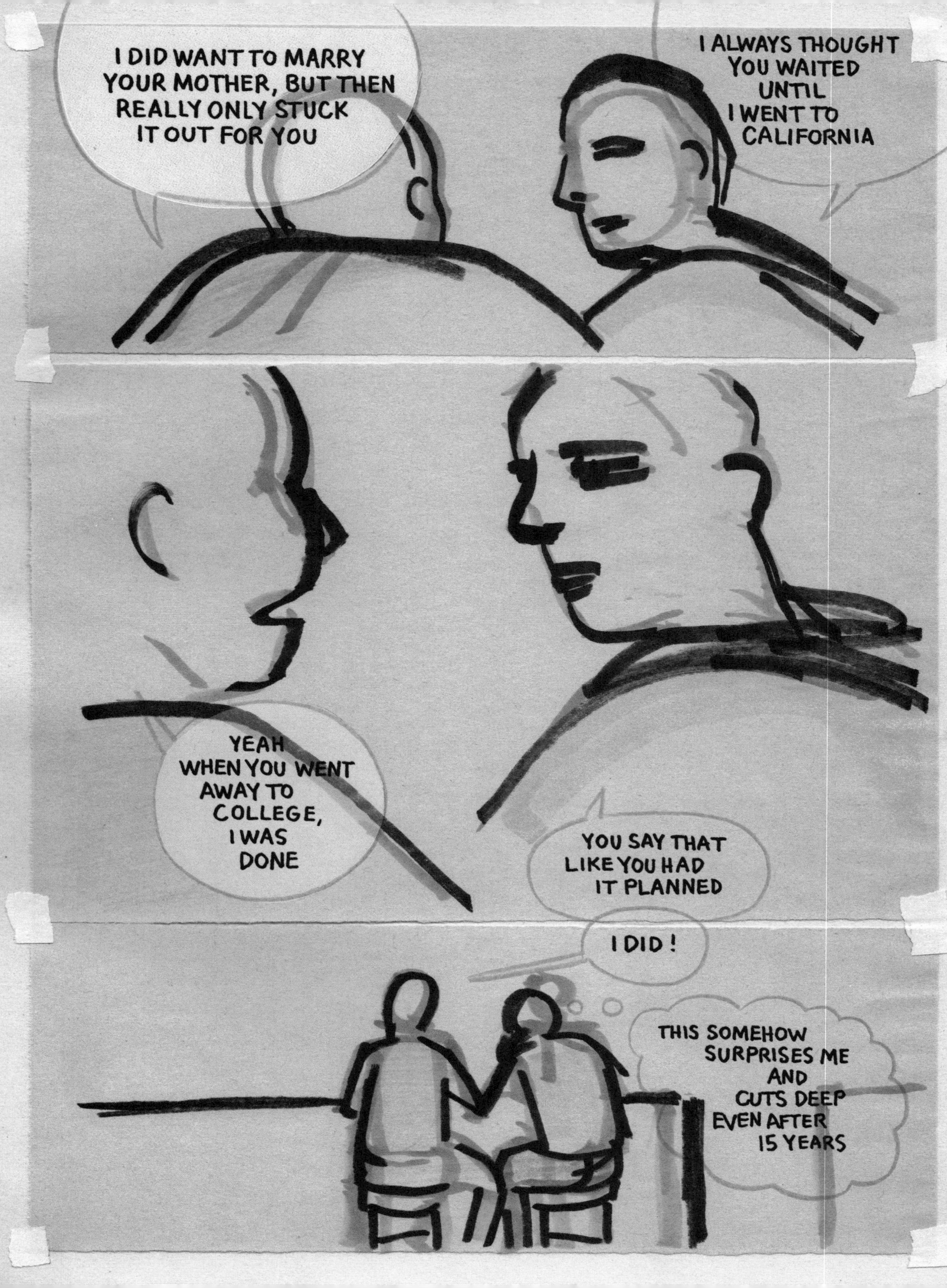
I DID WANT TO MARRY YOUR MOTHER, BUT THEN REALLY ONLY STUCK IT OUT FOR YOU
I ALWAYS THOUGHT YOU WAITED UNTIL I WENT TO CALIFORNIA
YEAH WHEN YOU WENT AWAY TO COLLEGE, I WAS DONE
YOU SAY THAT LIKE YOU HAD IT PLANNED
I DID!
THIS SOMEHOW SURPRISES ME AND CUTS DEEP EVEN AFTER 15 YEARS

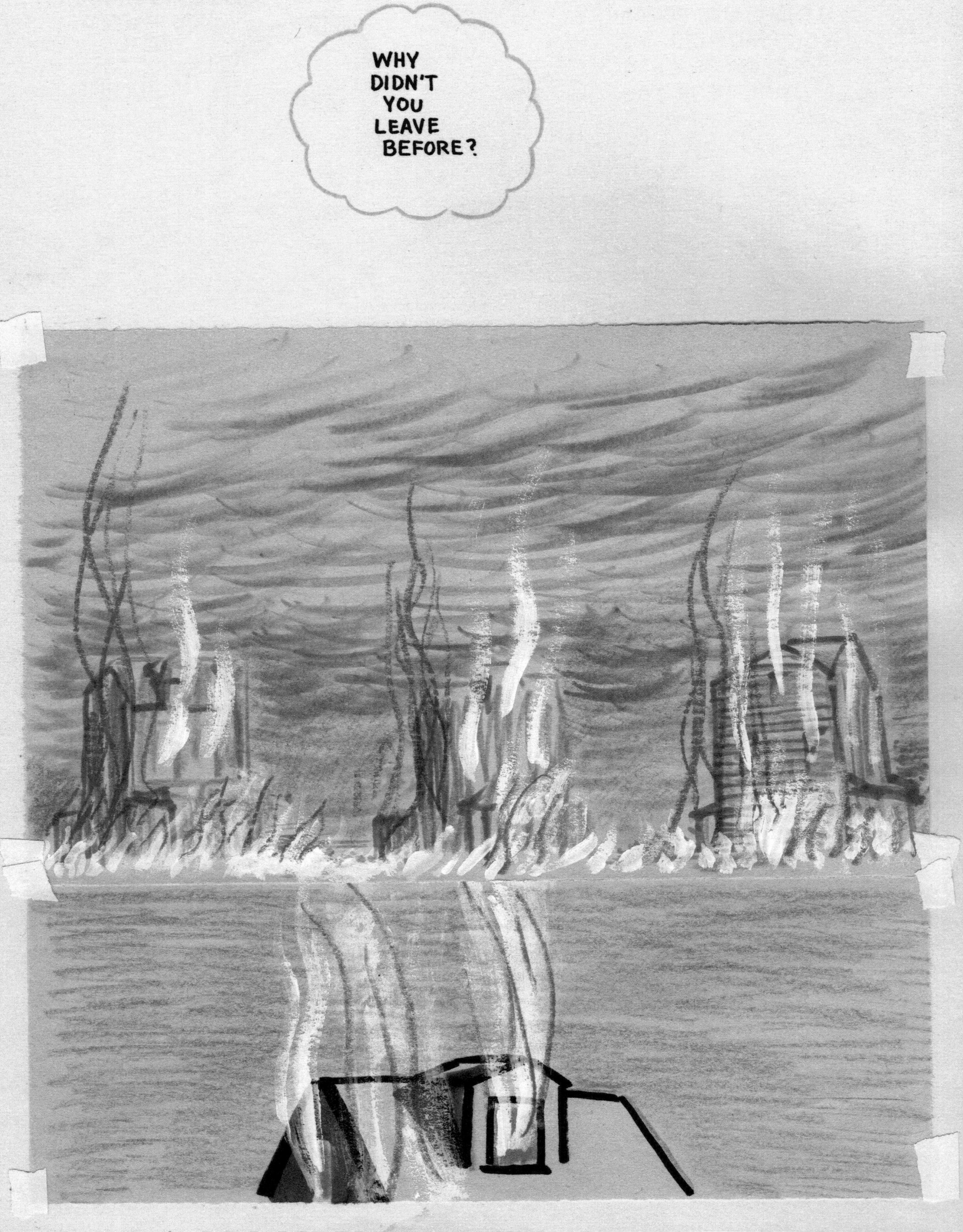
WHY DIDN'T YOU LEAVE BEFORE?

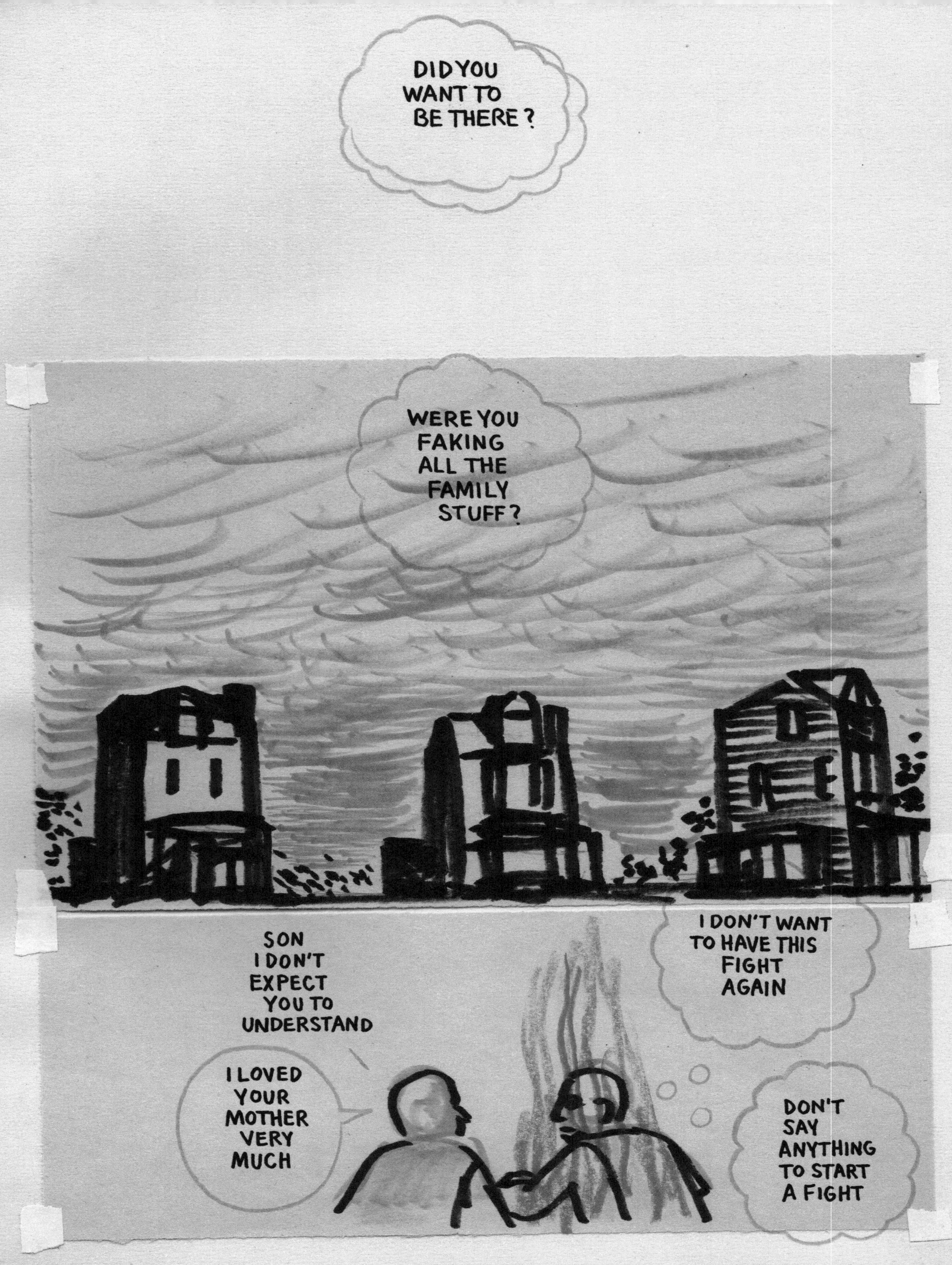
DID YOU WANT TO BE THERE?
WERE YOU FAKING ALL THE FAMILY STUFF?
SON I DON'T EXPECT YOU TO UNDERSTAND
I DON'T WANT TO HAVE THIS FIGHT AGAIN
I LOVED YOUR MOTHER VERY MUCH
DON'T SAY ANYTHING TO START A FIGHT

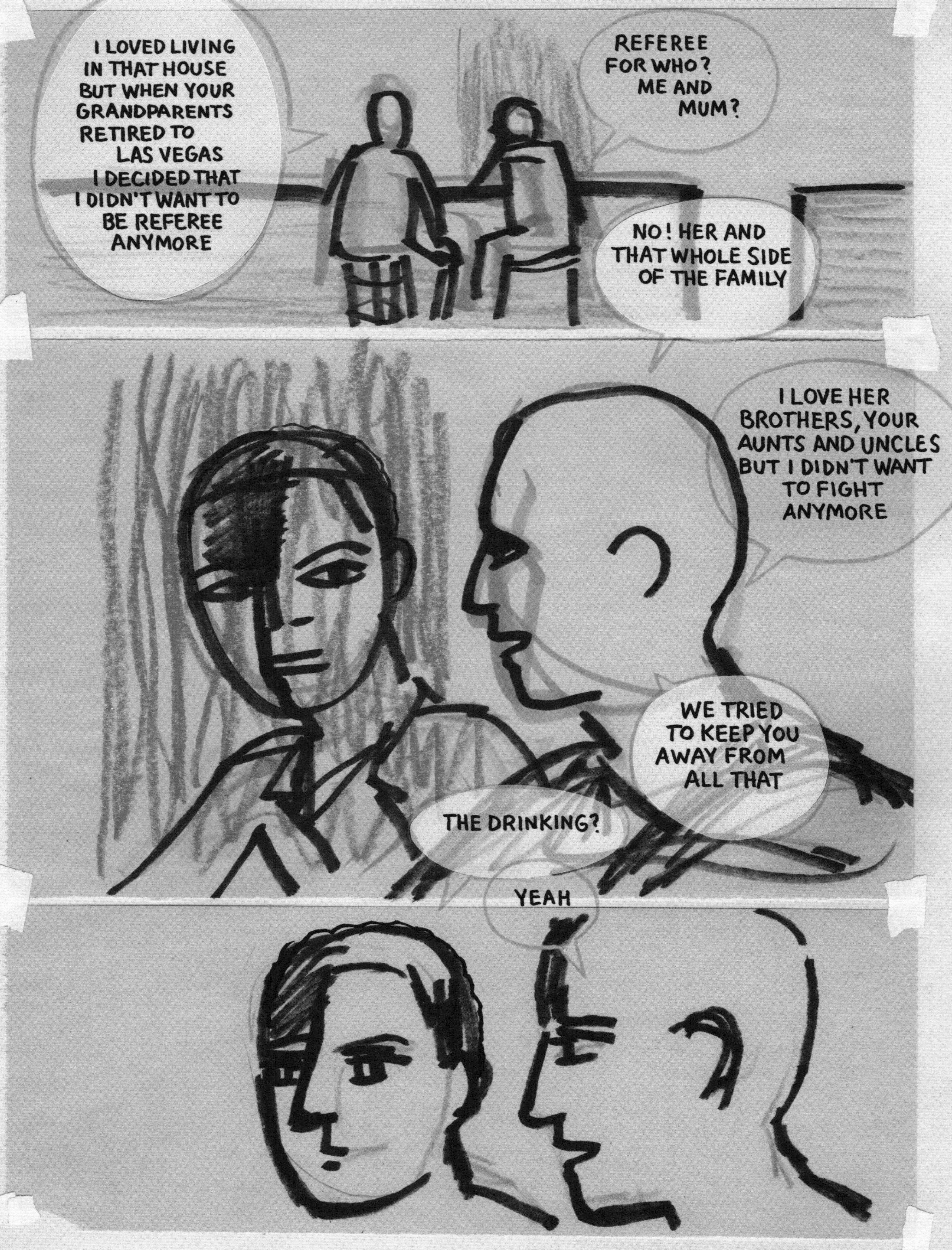
I LOVED LIVING IN THAT HOUSE BUT WHEN YOUR GRANDPARENTS RETIRED TO LAS VEGAS I DECIDED THAT I DIDN'T WANT TO BE REFEREE ANYMORE
REFEREE FOR WHO? ME AND MUM?
NO! HER AND THAT WHOLE SIDE OF THE FAMILY
I LOVE HER BROTHERS, YOUR AUNTS AND UNCLES BUT I DIDN'T WANT TO FIGHT ANYMORE
WE TRIED TO KEEP YOU AWAY FROM ALL THAT
THE DRINKING?
YEAH

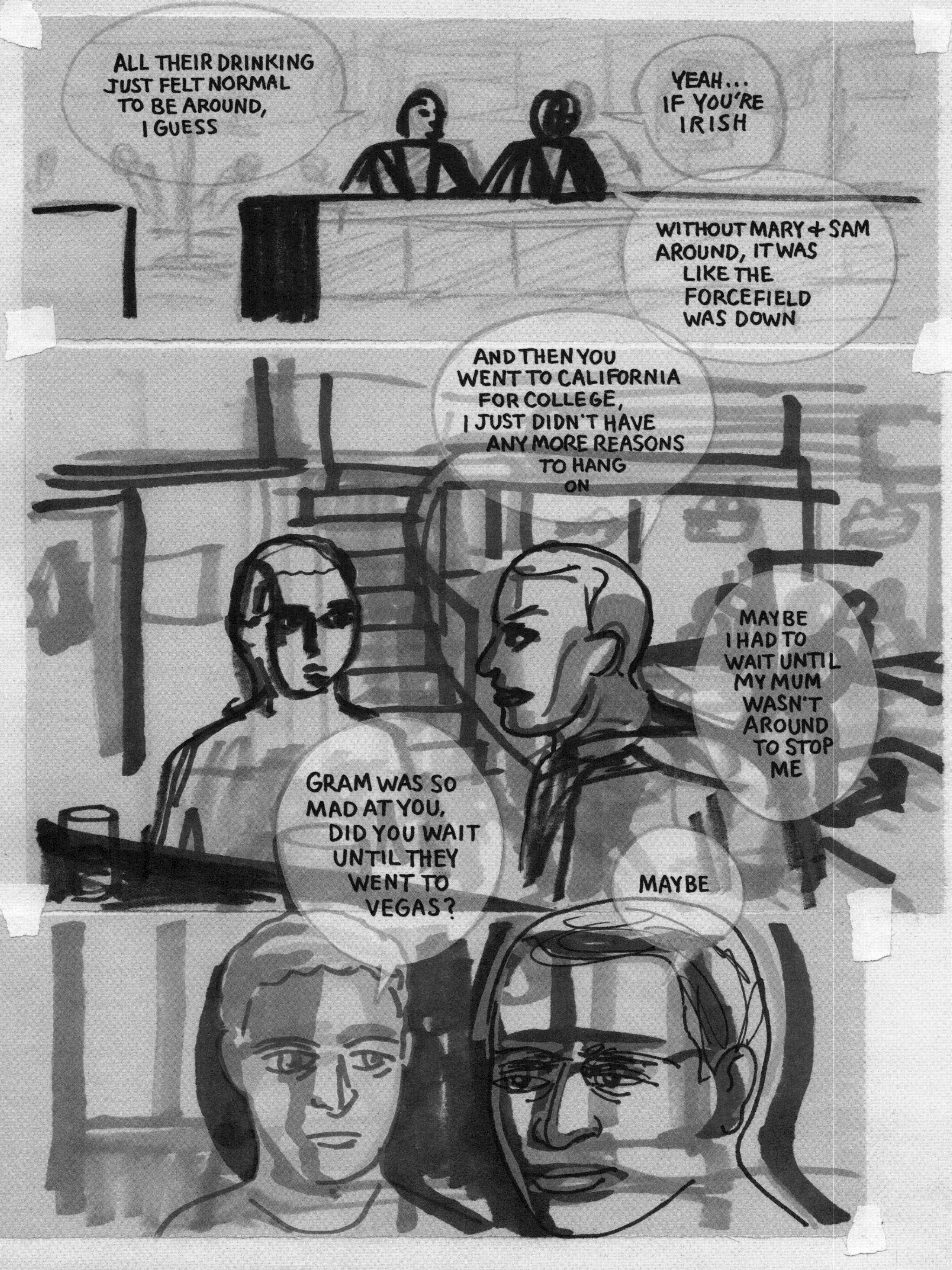
ALL THEIR DRINKING JUST FELT NORMAL TO BE AROUND, I GUESS
YEAH... IF YOU'RE IRISH
WITHOUT MARY & SAM AROUND, IT WAS LIKE THE FORCEFIELD WAS DOWN
AND THEN YOU WENT TO CALIFORNIA FOR COLLEGE, I JUST DIDN'T HAVE ANY MORE REASONS TO HANG ON
MAYBE I HAD TO WAIT UNTIL MY MUM WASN'T AROUND TO STOP ME
GRAM WAS SO MAD AT YOU, DID YOU WAIT UNTIL THEY WENT TO VEGAS?
MAYBE

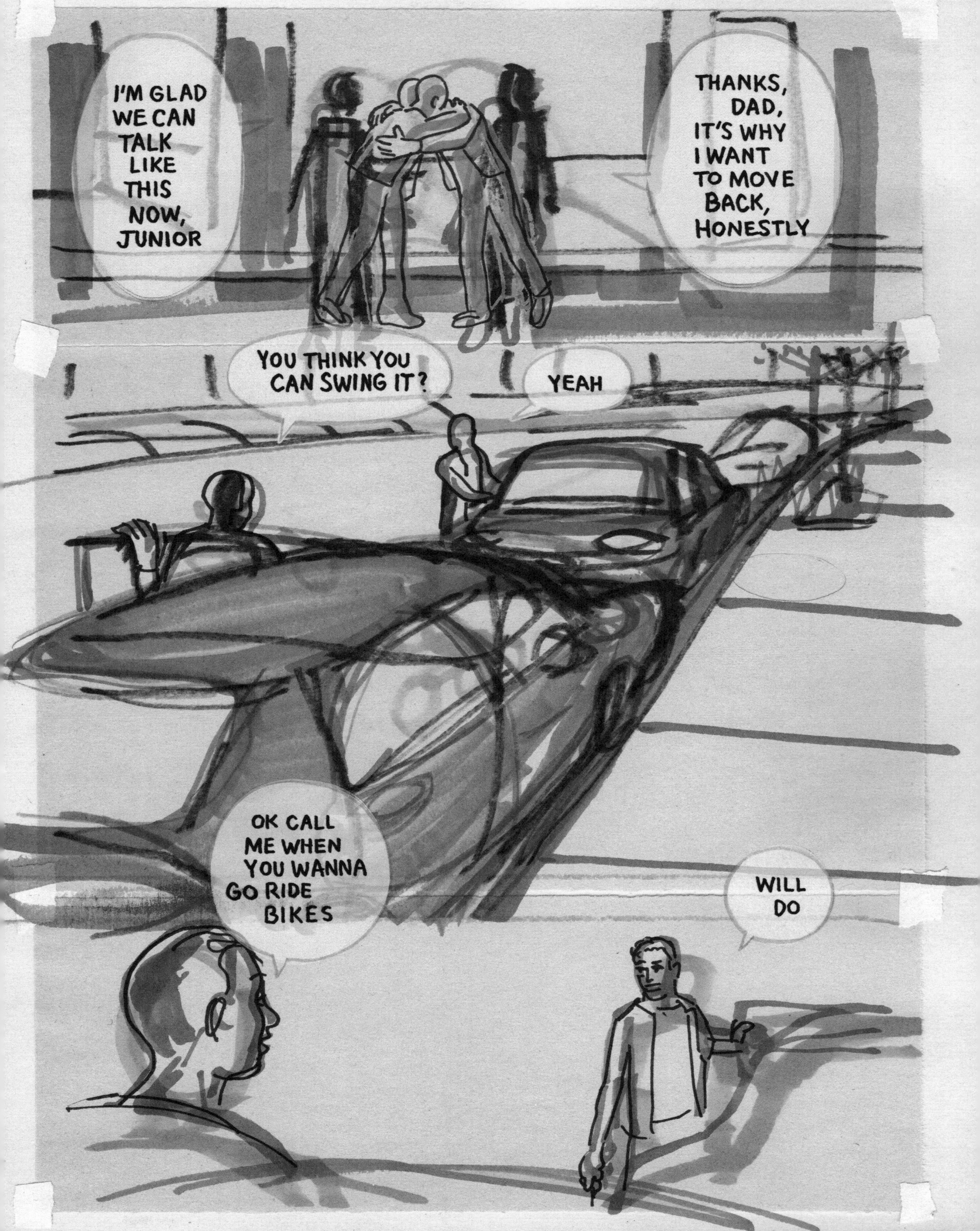
I'M GLAD WE CAN TALK LIKE THIS NOW, JUNIOR
THANKS, DAD, IT'S WHY I WANT TO MOVE BACK, HONESTLY
YOU THINK YOU CAN SWING IT?
YEAH
OK CALL ME WHEN YOU WANNA GO RIDE BIKES
WILL DO

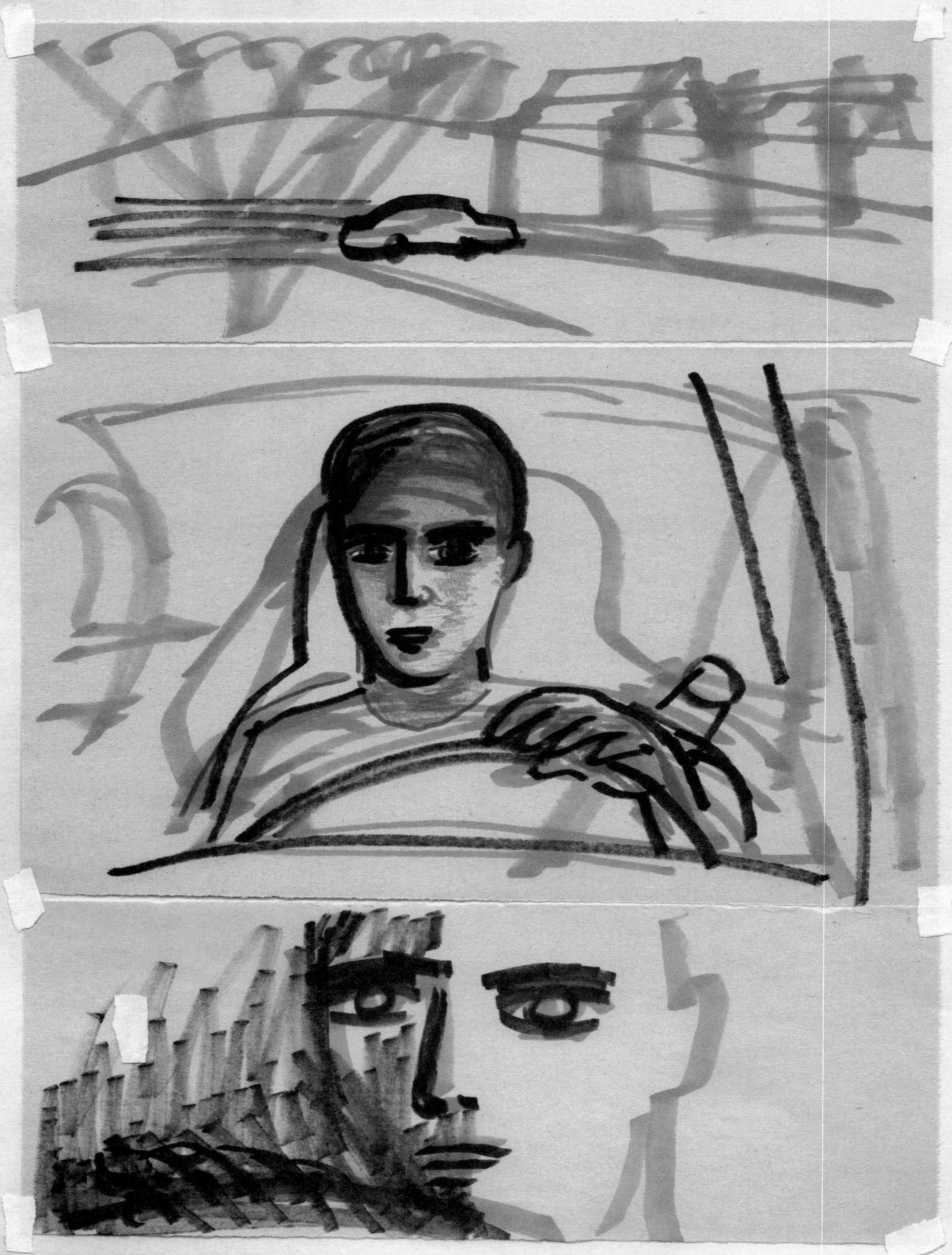

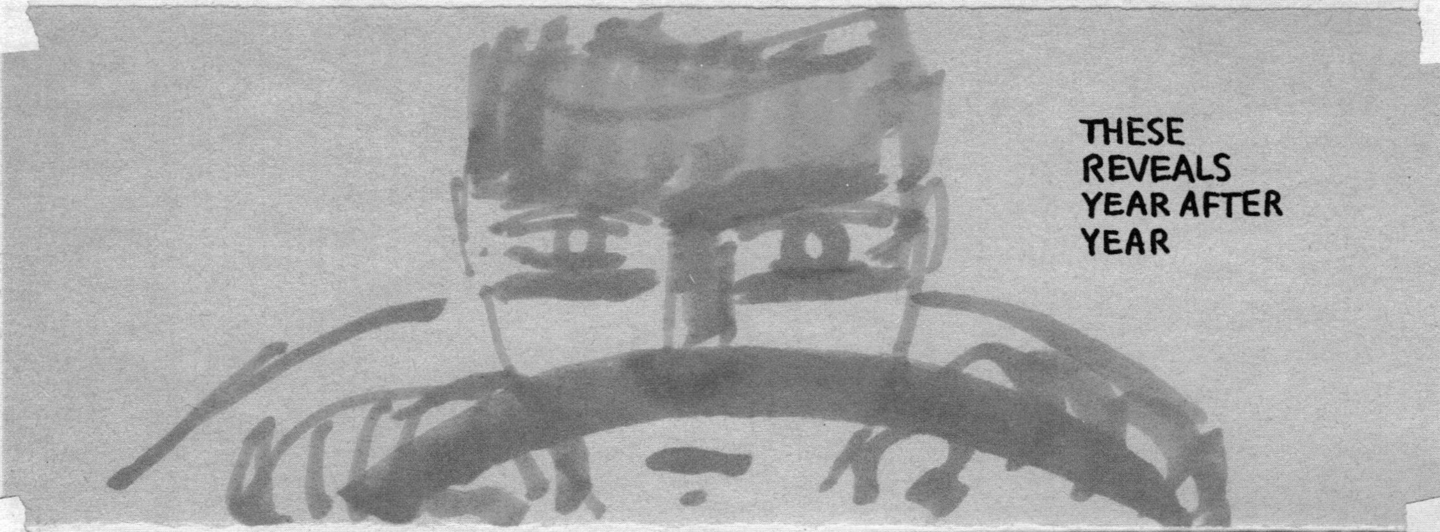
THESE
REVEALS
YEAR AFTER
YEAR

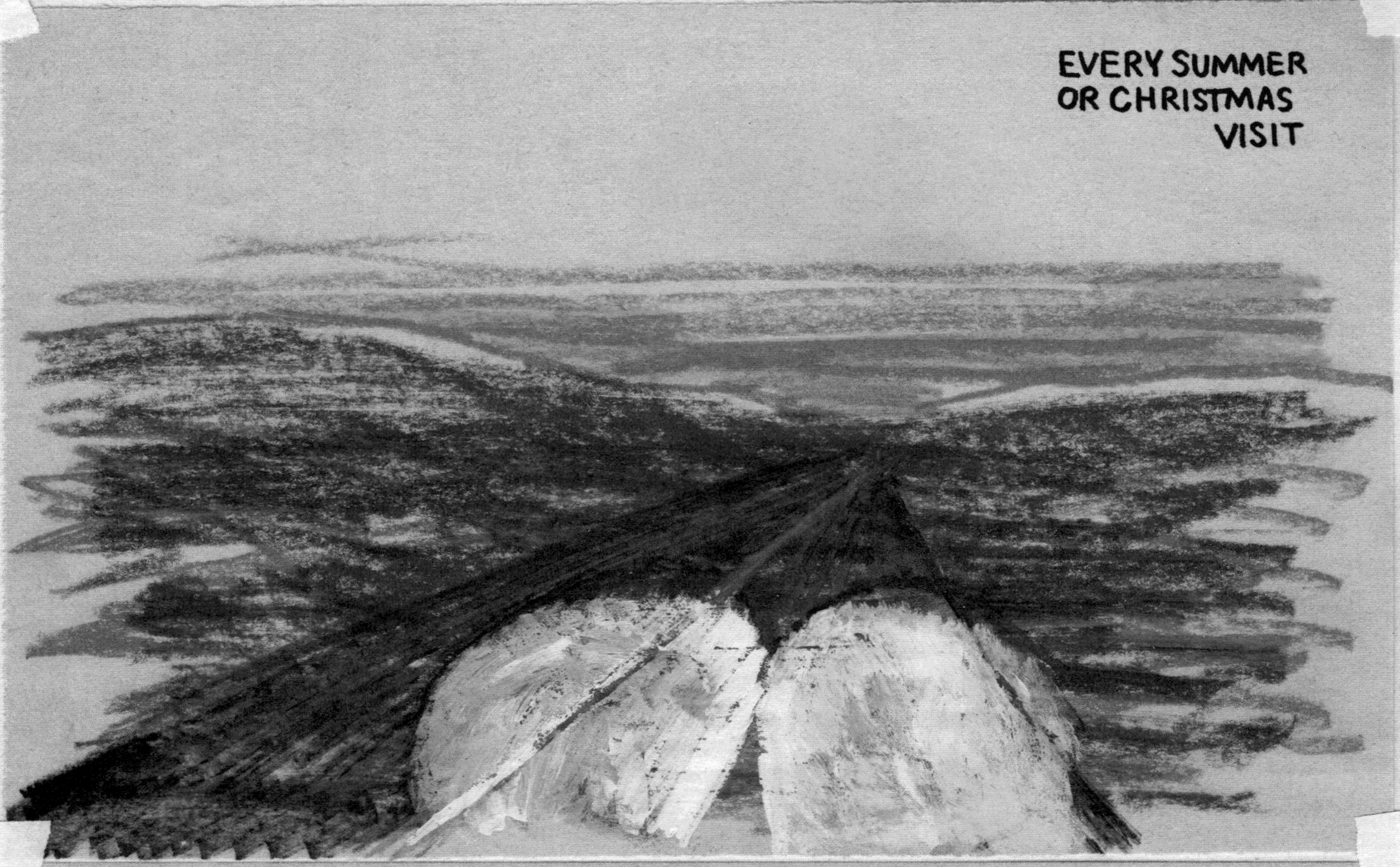
EVERY SUMMER
OR CHRISTMAS
VISIT

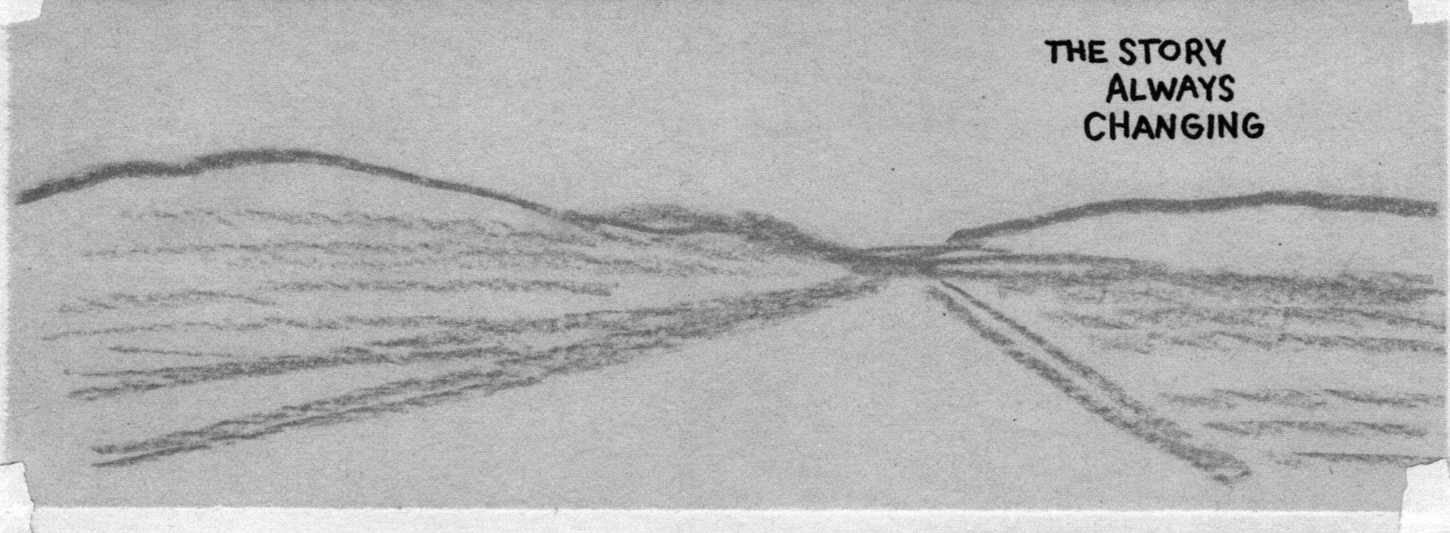
THE STORY
ALWAYS
CHANGING

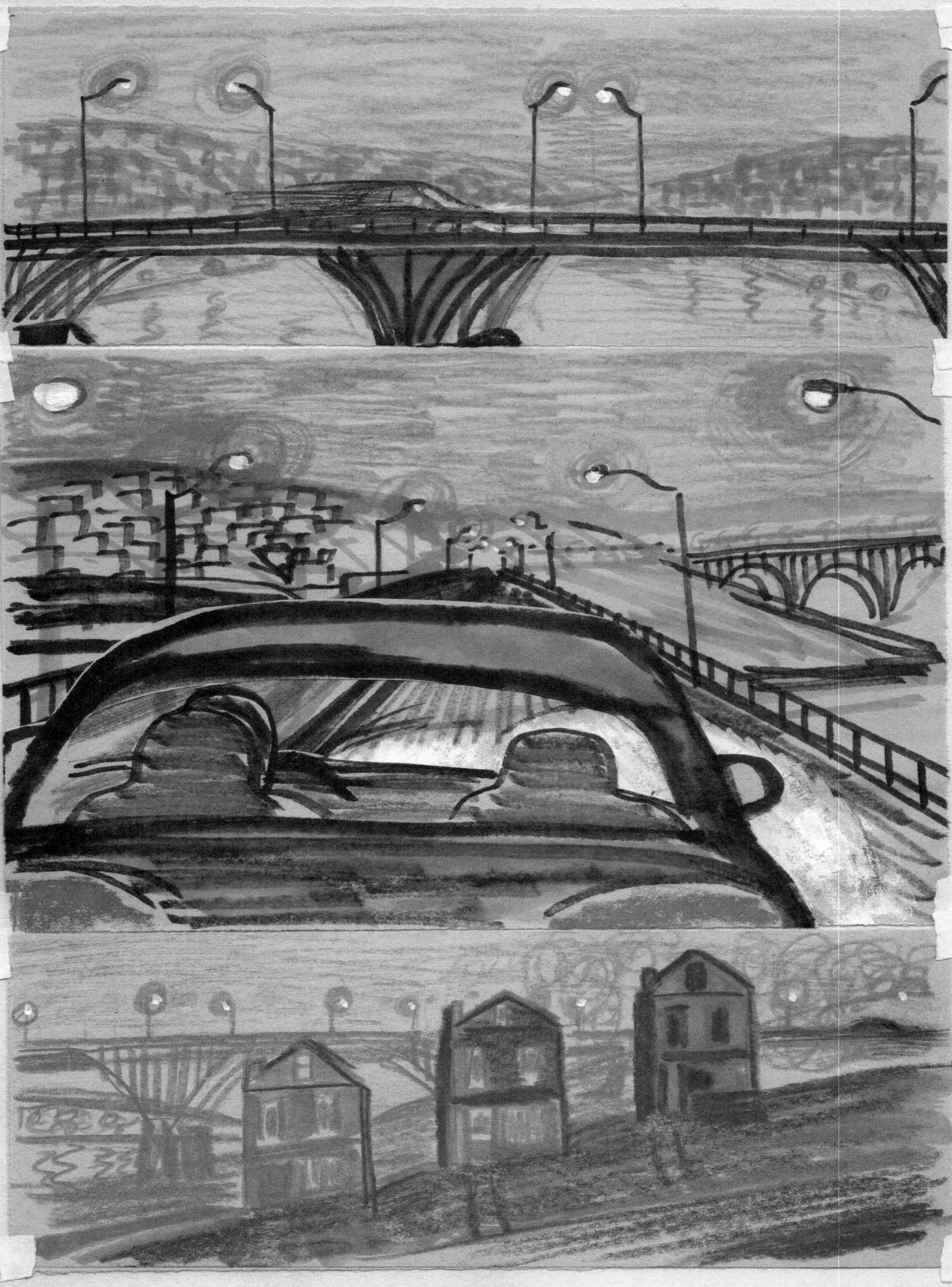

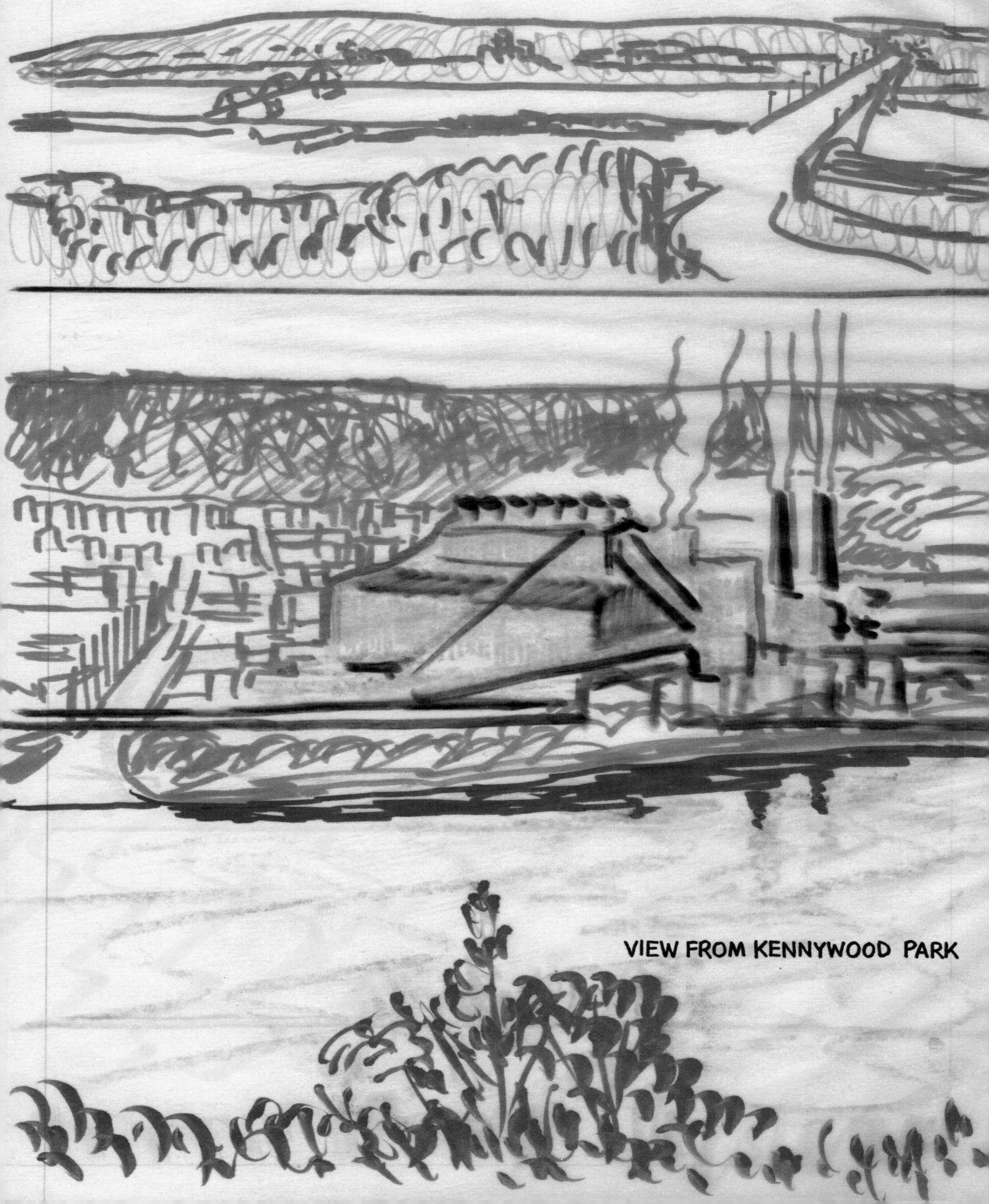

VIEW FROM KENNYWOOD PARK

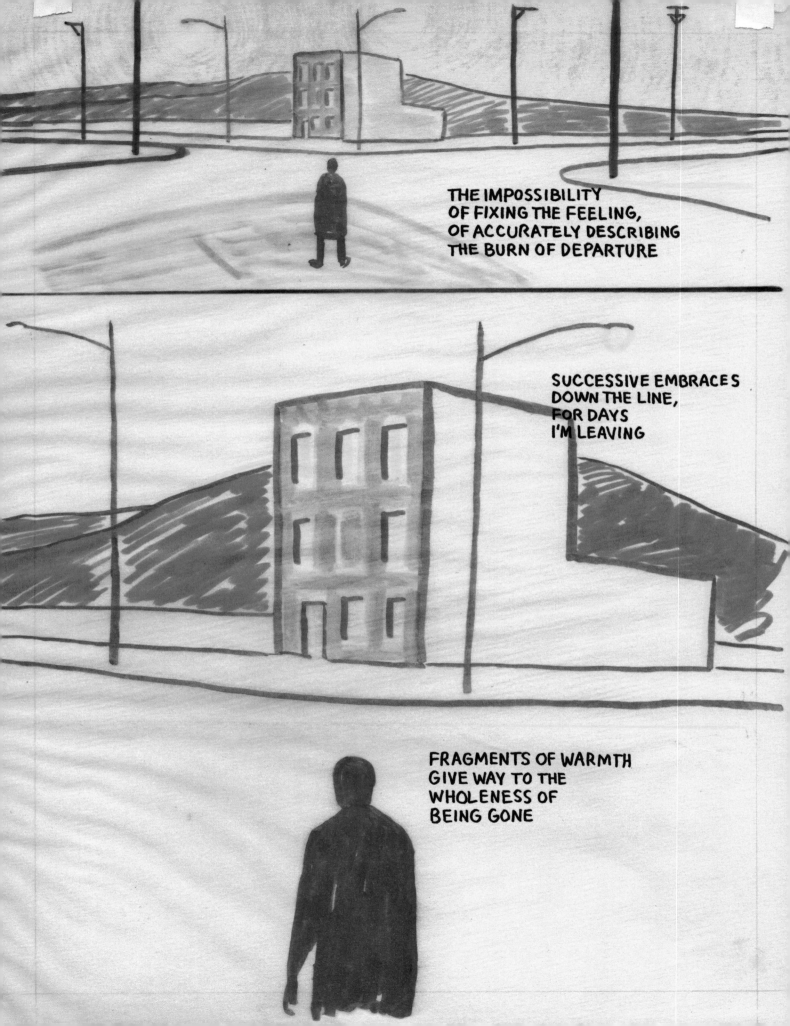

THE IMPOSSIBILITY
OF FIXING THE FEELING,
OF ACCURATELY DESCRIBING
THE BURN OF DEPARTURE

SUCCESSIVE EMBRACES
DOWN THE LINE,
FOR DAYS
I'M LEAVING

FRAGMENTS OF WARMTH
GIVE WAY TO THE
WHOLENESS OF
BEING GONE

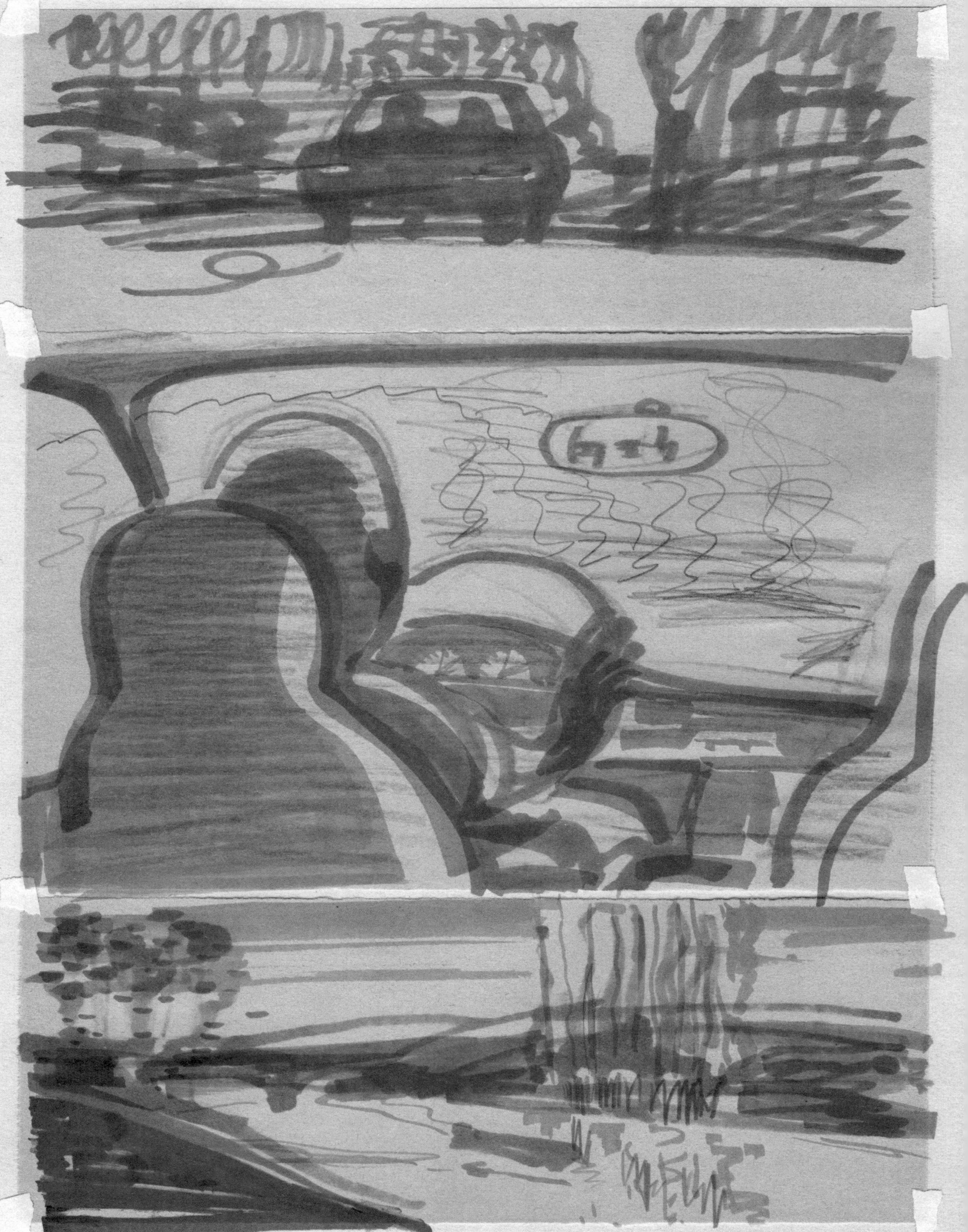

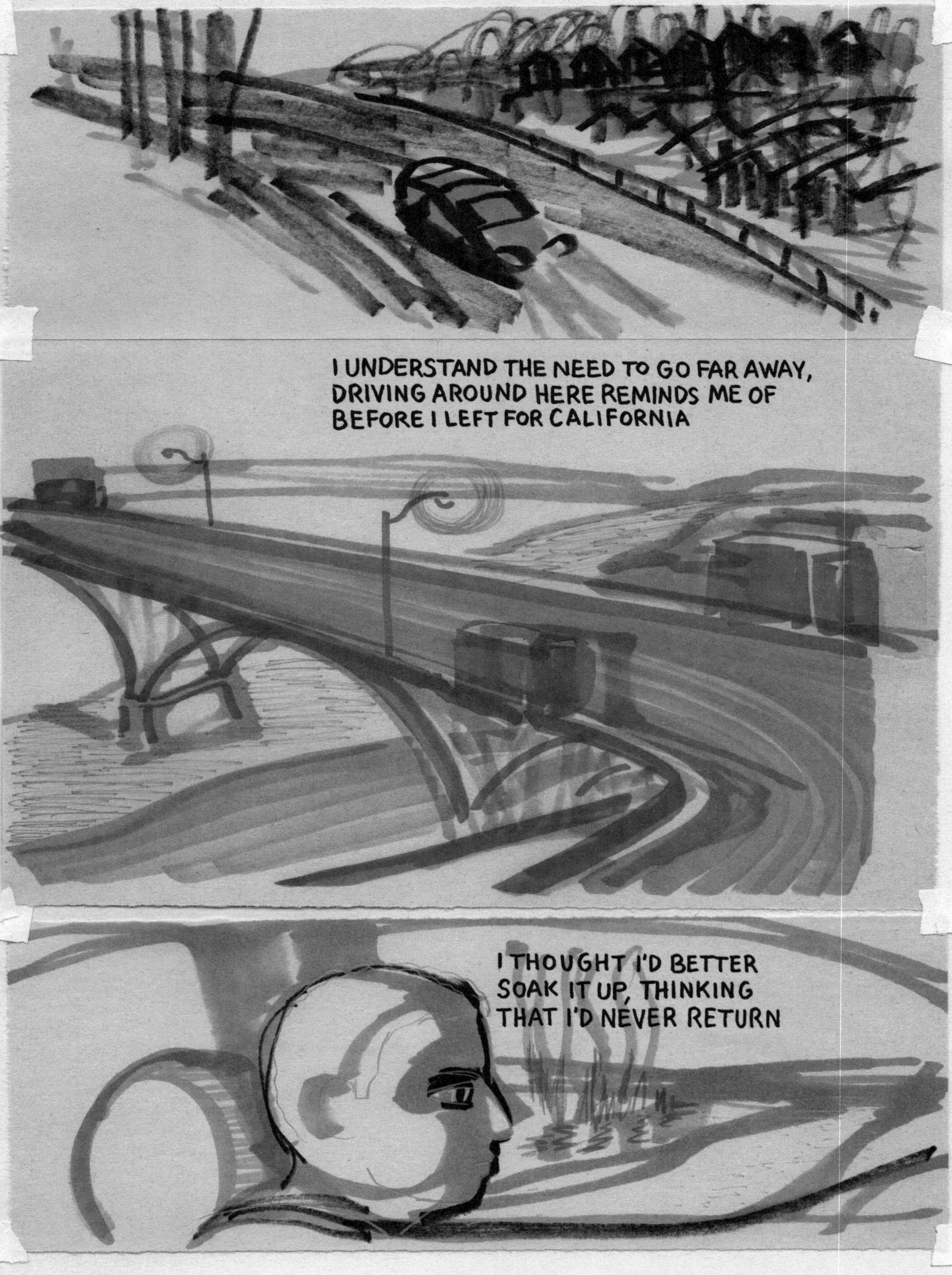
I UNDERSTAND THE NEED TO GO FAR AWAY, DRIVING AROUND HERE REMINDS ME OF BEFORE I LEFT FOR CALIFORNIA
I THOUGHT I'D BETTER SOAK IT UP, THINKING THAT I'D NEVER RETURN

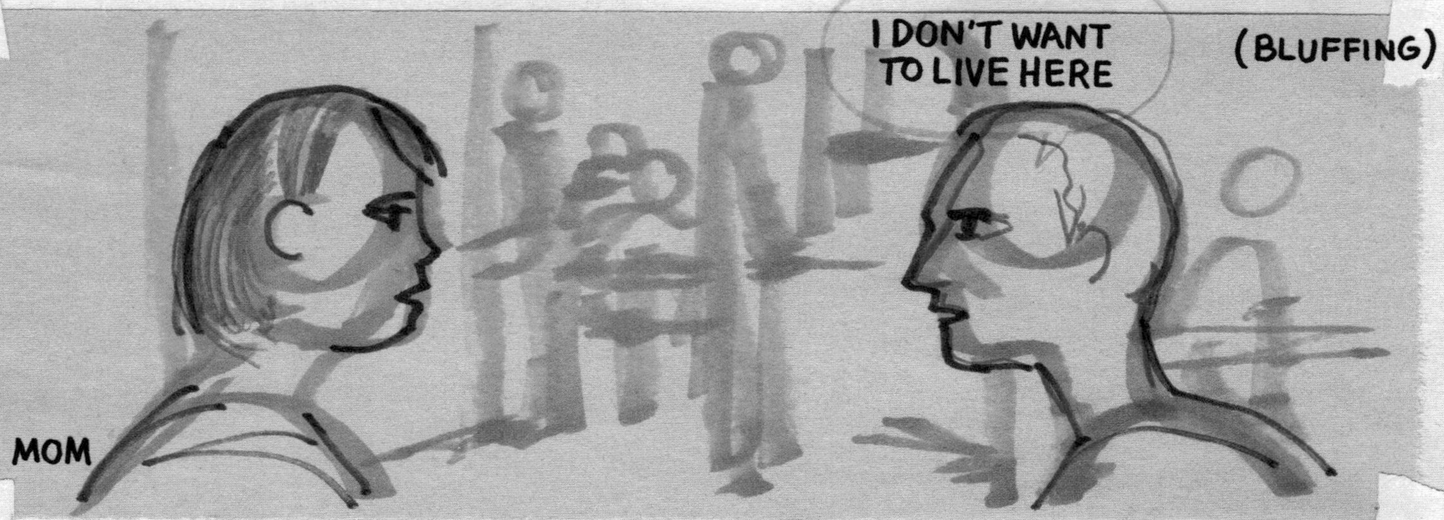
I DON'T WANT TO LIVE HERE
(BLUFFING)
MOM

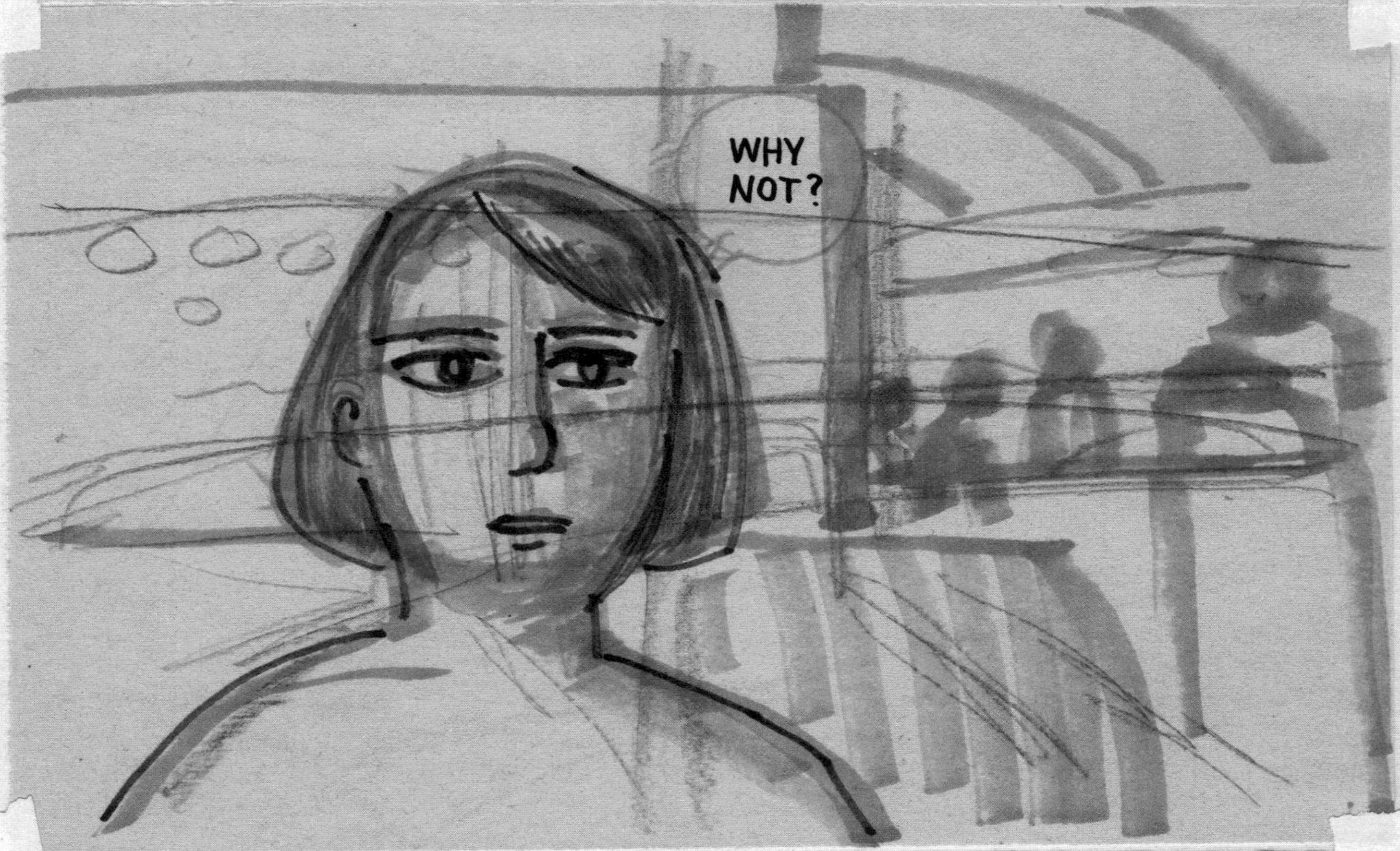
WHY NOT?

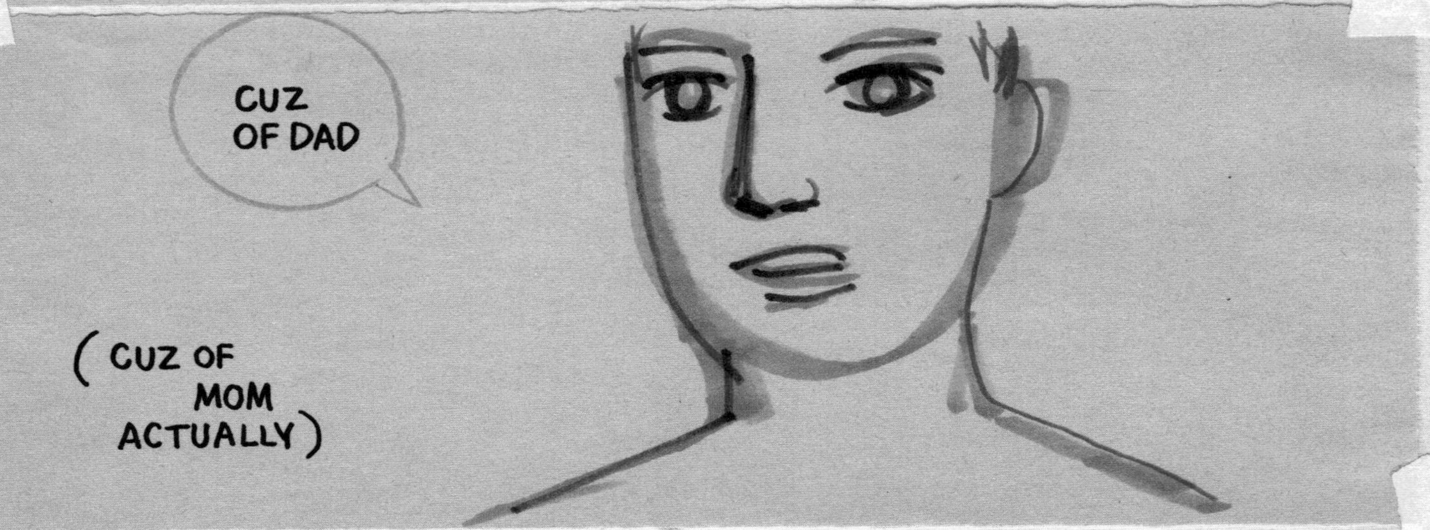
CUZ OF DAD
(CUZ OF MOM ACTUALLY)

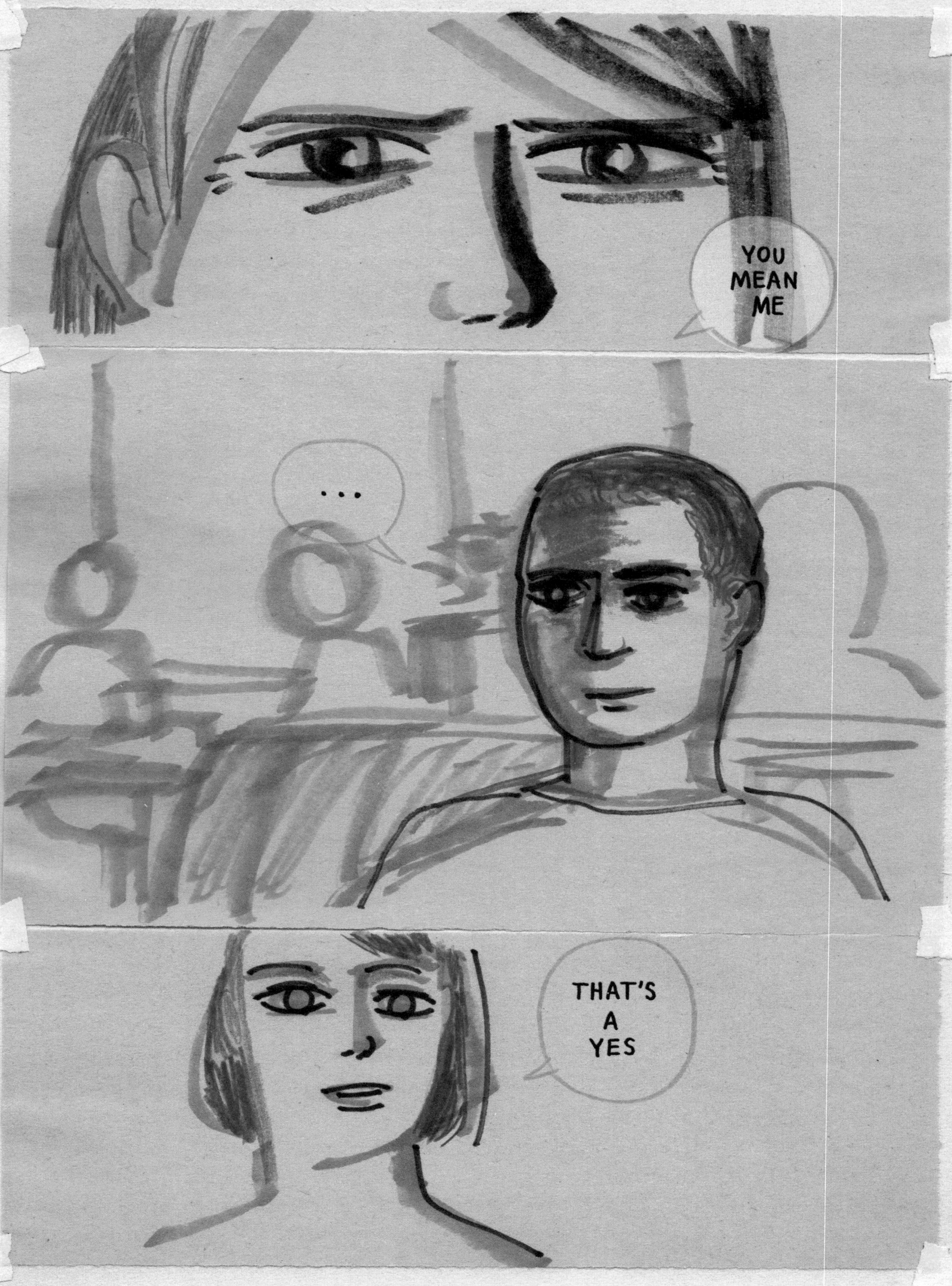
YOU MEAN ME
...
THAT'S A YES

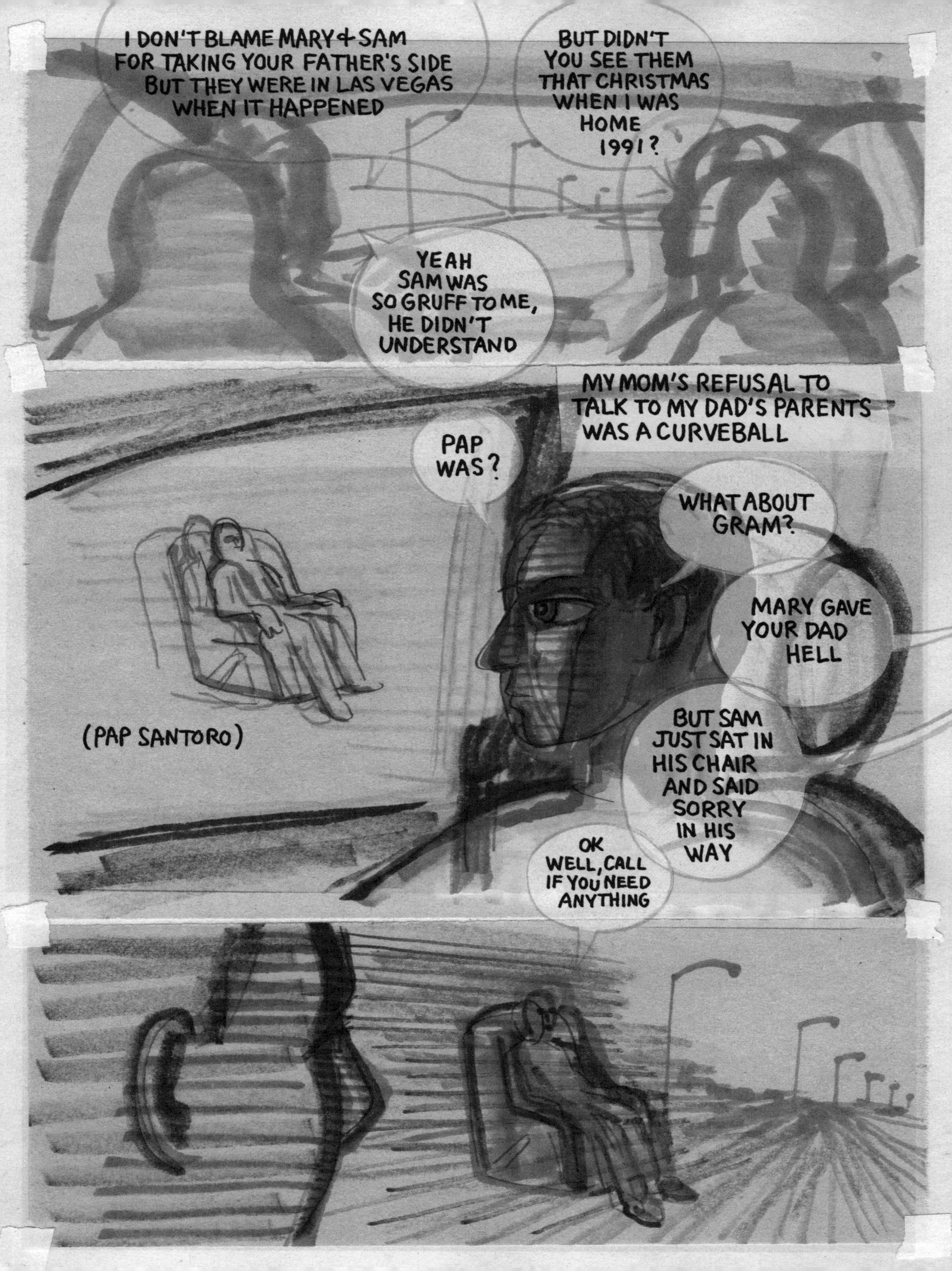
I DON'T BLAME MARY & SAM FOR TAKING YOUR FATHER'S SIDE BUT THEY WERE IN LAS VEGAS WHEN IT HAPPENED
BUT DIDN'T YOU SEE THEM THAT CHRISTMAS WHEN I WAS HOME 1991?
YEAH SAM WAS SO GRUFF TO ME, HE DIDN'T UNDERSTAND
MY MOM'S REFUSAL TO TALK TO MY DAD'S PARENTS WAS A CURVEBALL
PAP WAS?
WHAT ABOUT GRAM?
MARY GAVE YOUR DAD HELL
(PAP SANTORO)
BUT SAM JUST SAT IN HIS CHAIR AND SAID SORRY IN HIS WAY
OK WELL, CALL IF YOU NEED ANYTHING

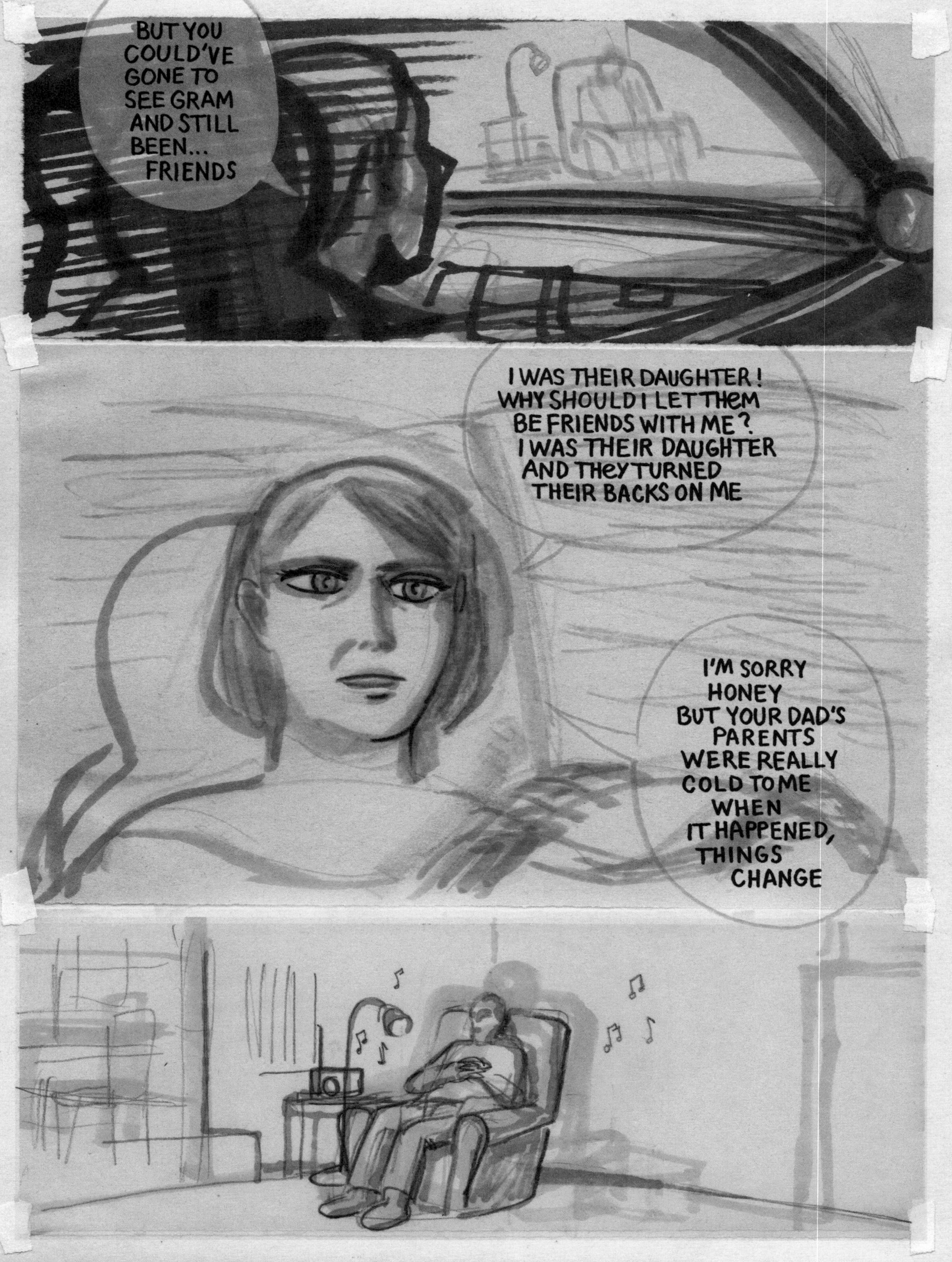
BUT YOU COULD'VE GONE TO SEE GRAM AND STILL BEEN... FRIENDS
I WAS THEIR DAUGHTER! WHY SHOULD I LET THEM BE FRIENDS WITH ME? I WAS THEIR DAUGHTER AND THEY TURNED THEIR BACKS ON ME
I'M SORRY HONEY BUT YOUR DAD'S PARENTS WERE REALLY COLD TO ME WHEN IT HAPPENED, THINGS CHANGE

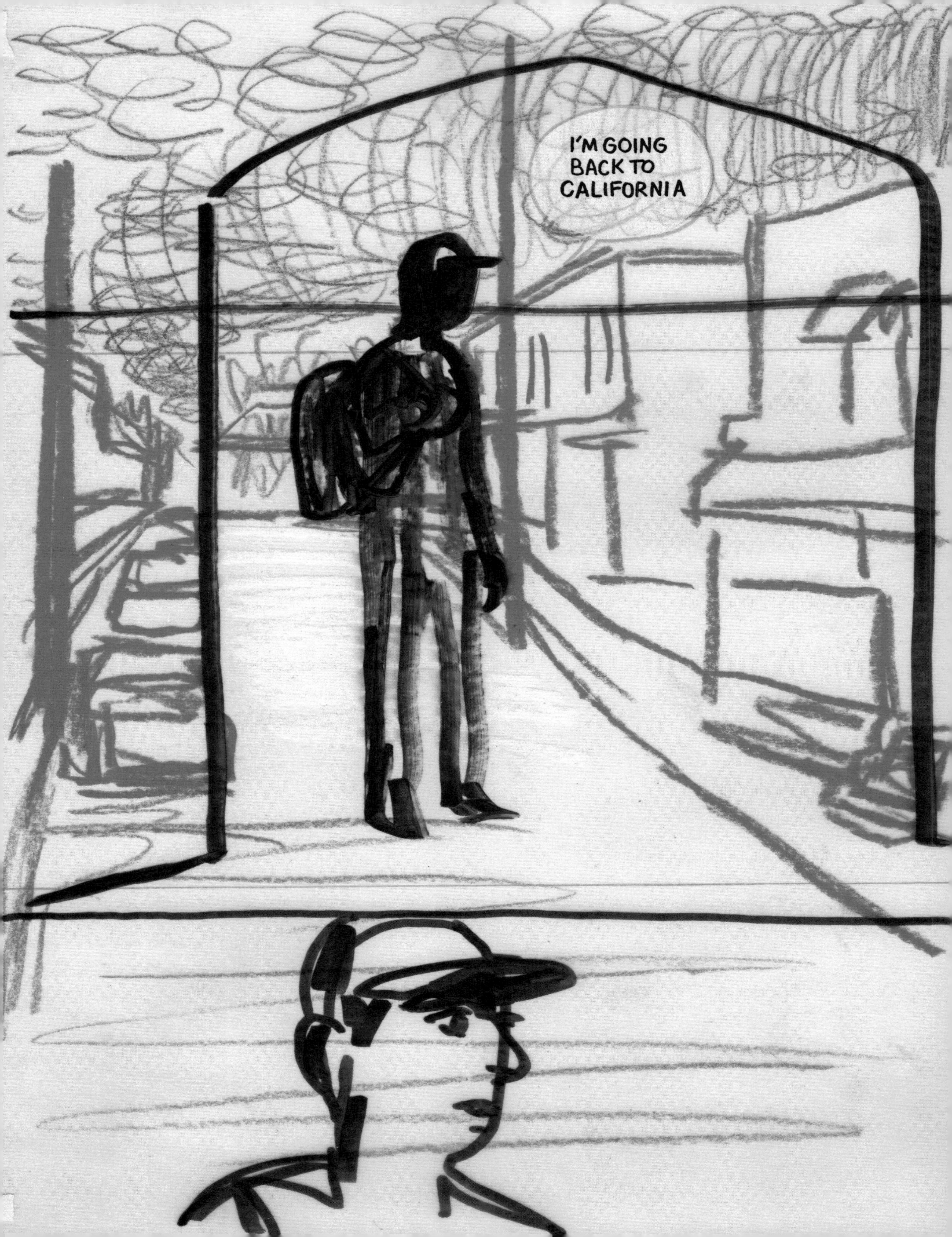
I'M GOING BACK TO CALIFORNIA

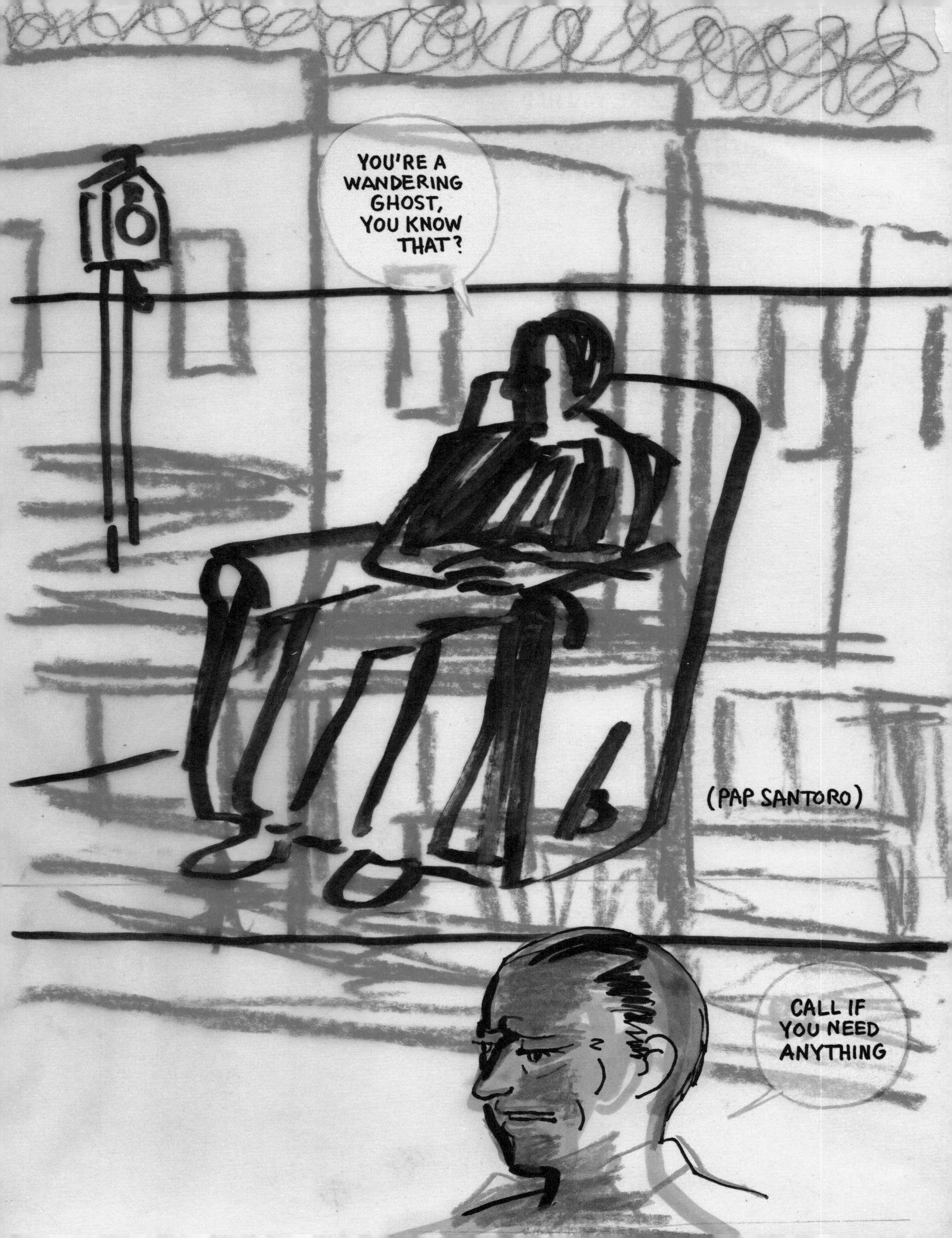
YOU'RE A WANDERING GHOST, YOU KNOW THAT?
(PAP SANTORO)
CALL IF YOU NEED ANYTHING

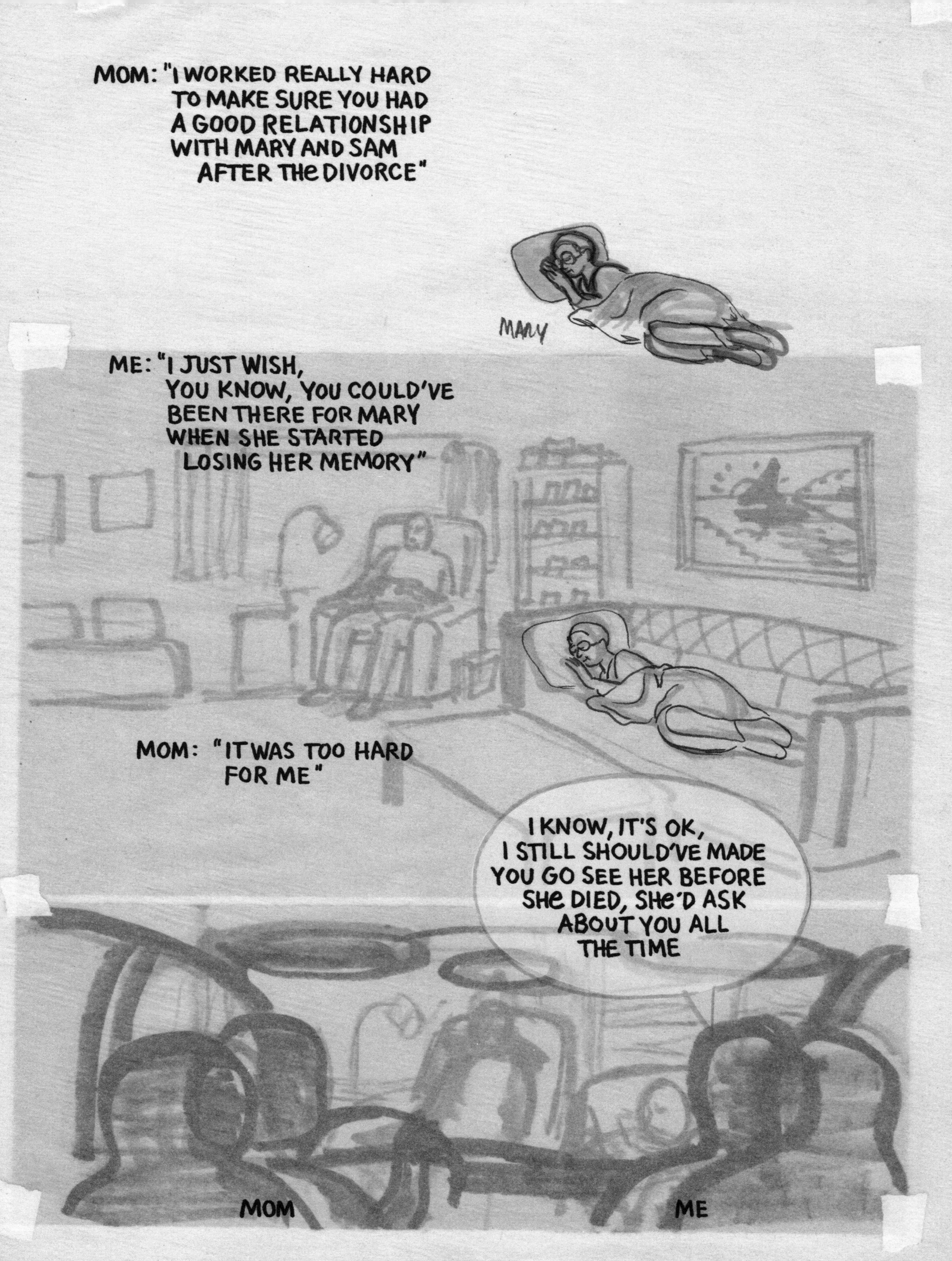

MOM: "I WORKED REALLY HARD TO MAKE SURE YOU HAD A GOOD RELATIONSHIP WITH MARY AND SAM AFTER THE DIVORCE"

MARY

ME: "I JUST WISH, YOU KNOW, YOU COULD'VE BEEN THERE FOR MARY WHEN SHE STARTED LOSING HER MEMORY"

MOM: "IT WAS TOO HARD FOR ME"

I KNOW, IT'S OK, I STILL SHOULD'VE MADE YOU GO SEE HER BEFORE SHE DIED, SHE'D ASK ABOUT YOU ALL THE TIME

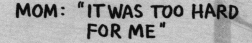

MOM   ME

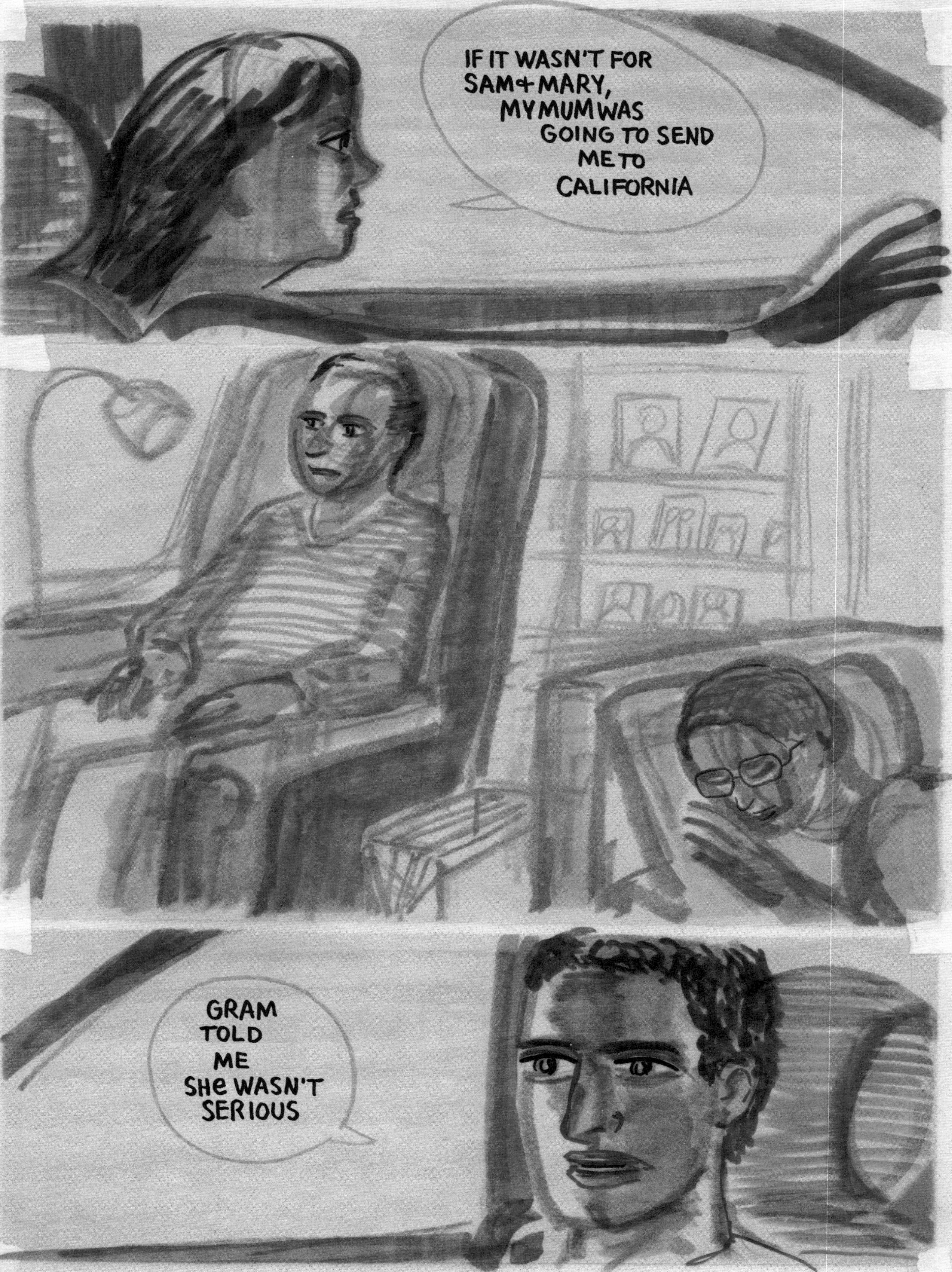
IF IT WASN'T FOR SAM + MARY, MY MUM WAS GOING TO SEND ME TO CALIFORNIA
GRAM TOLD ME SHE WASN'T SERIOUS

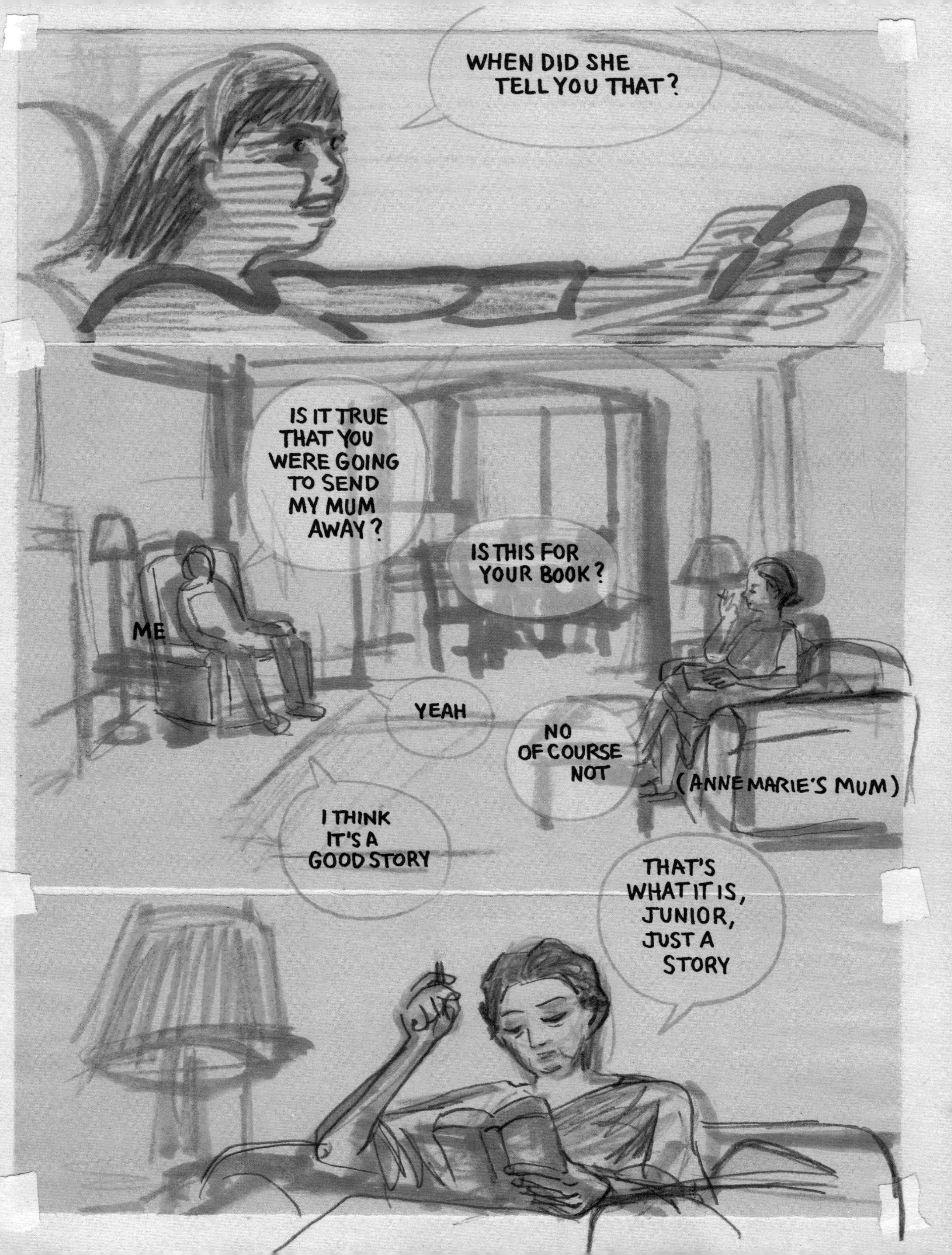
WHEN DID SHE TELL YOU THAT?
IS IT TRUE THAT YOU WERE GOING TO SEND MY MUM AWAY?
IS THIS FOR YOUR BOOK?
ME
YEAH
NO OF COURSE NOT
(ANNE MARIE'S MUM)
I THINK IT'S A GOOD STORY
THAT'S WHAT IT IS, JUNIOR, JUST A STORY

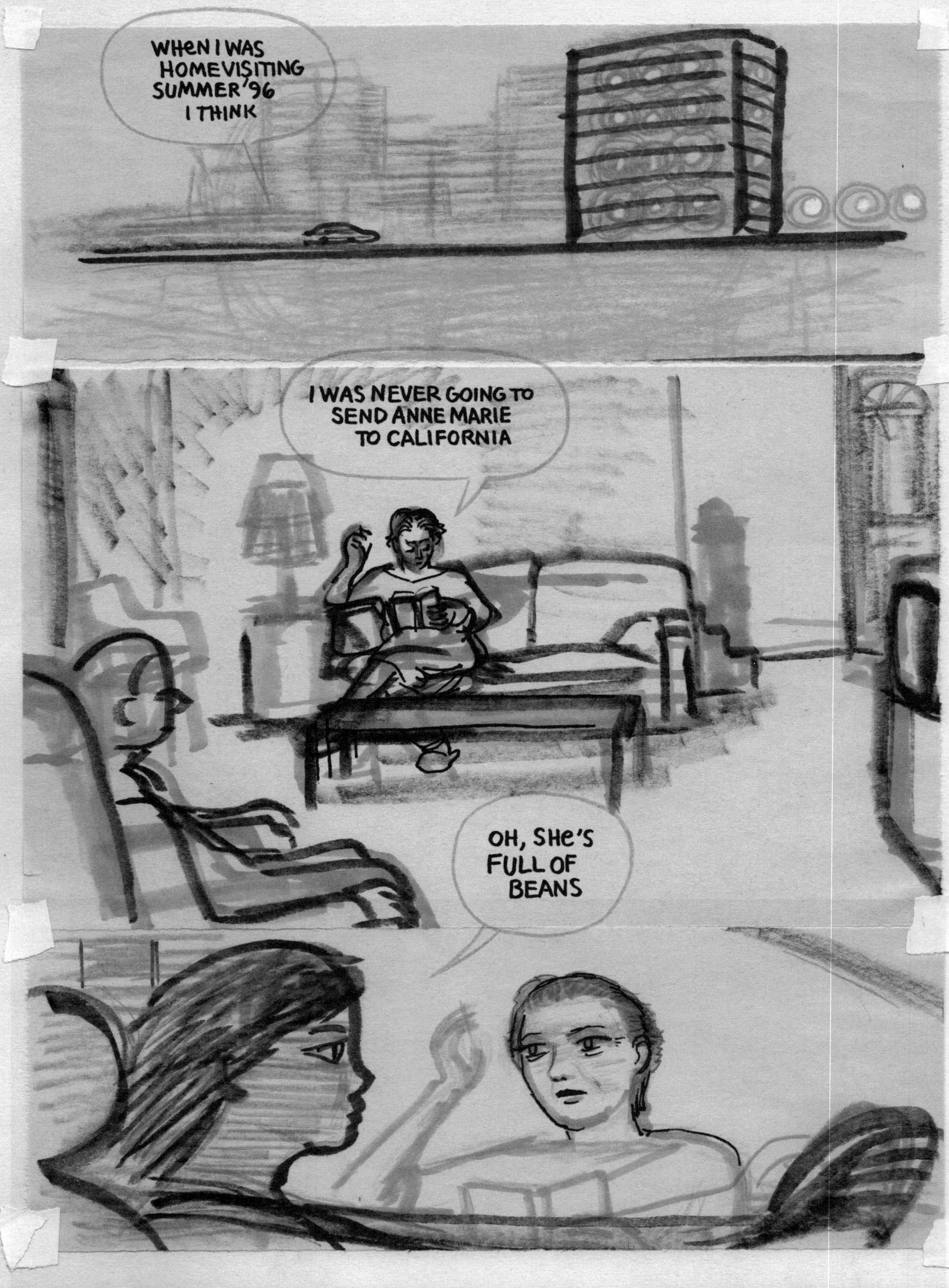
WHEN I WAS HOMEVISITING SUMMER '96 I THINK
I WAS NEVER GOING TO SEND ANNE MARIE TO CALIFORNIA
OH, SHE'S FULL OF BEANS

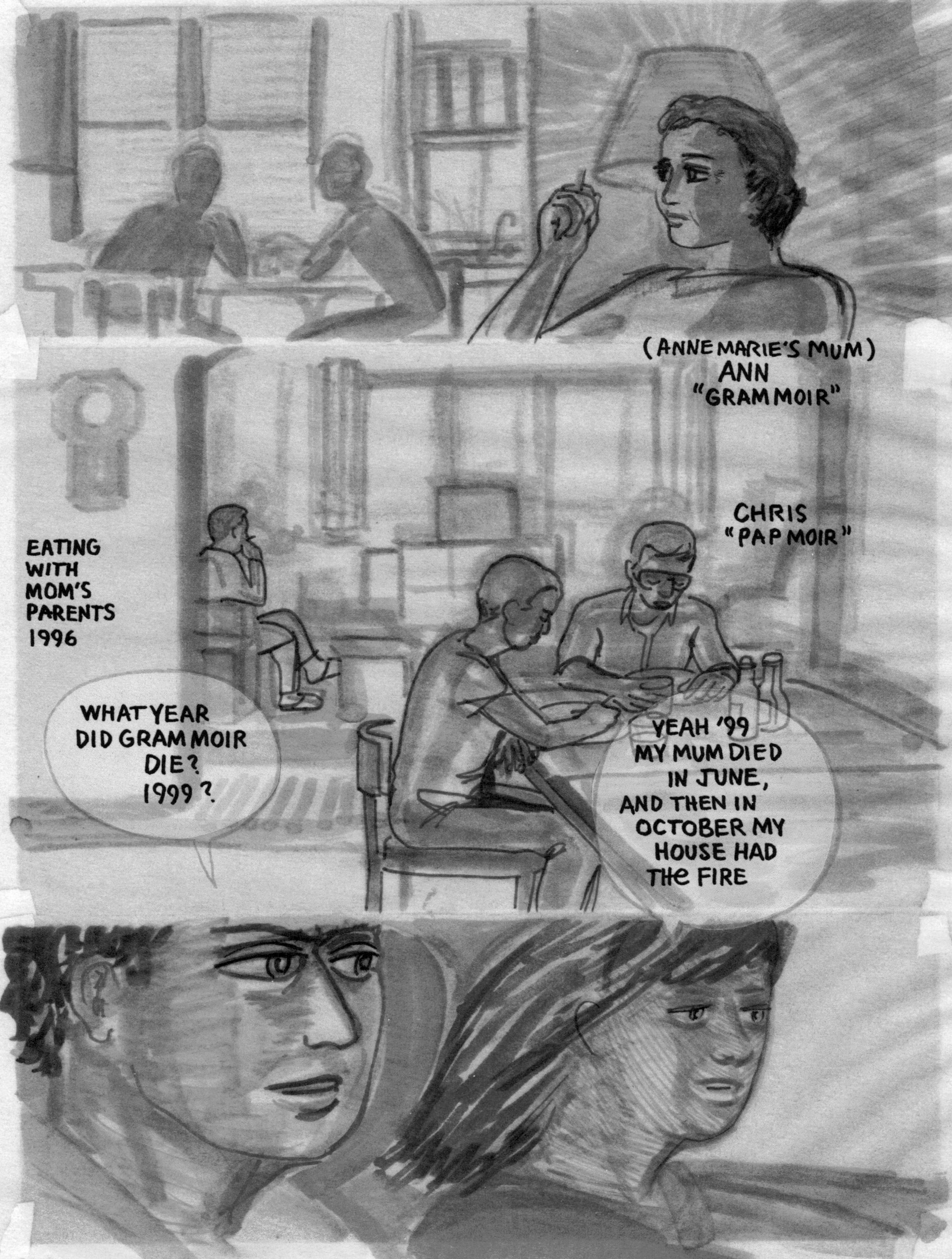
(ANNE MARIE'S MUM)
ANN
"GRAMMOIR"
CHRIS
"PAP MOIR"
EATING WITH MOM'S PARENTS 1996
WHAT YEAR DID GRAMMOIR DIE? 1999?
YEAH '99 MY MUM DIED IN JUNE, AND THEN IN OCTOBER MY HOUSE HAD THE FIRE

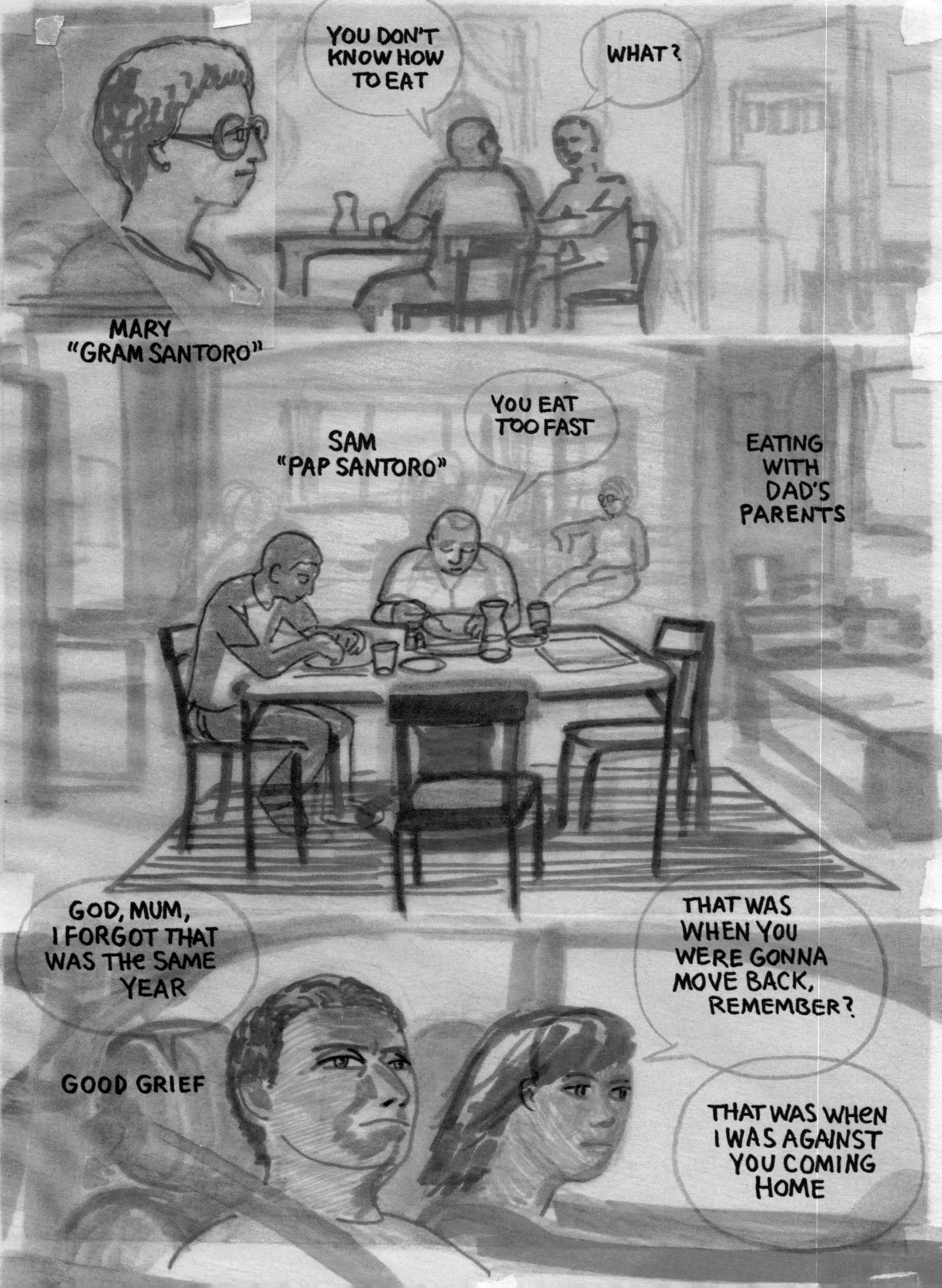
YOU DON'T KNOW HOW TO EAT
WHAT?
MARY "GRAM SANTORO"
SAM "PAP SANTORO"
YOU EAT TOO FAST
EATING WITH DAD'S PARENTS
GOD, MUM, I FORGOT THAT WAS THE SAME YEAR
THAT WAS WHEN YOU WERE GONNA MOVE BACK, REMEMBER?
GOOD GRIEF
THAT WAS WHEN I WAS AGAINST YOU COMING HOME

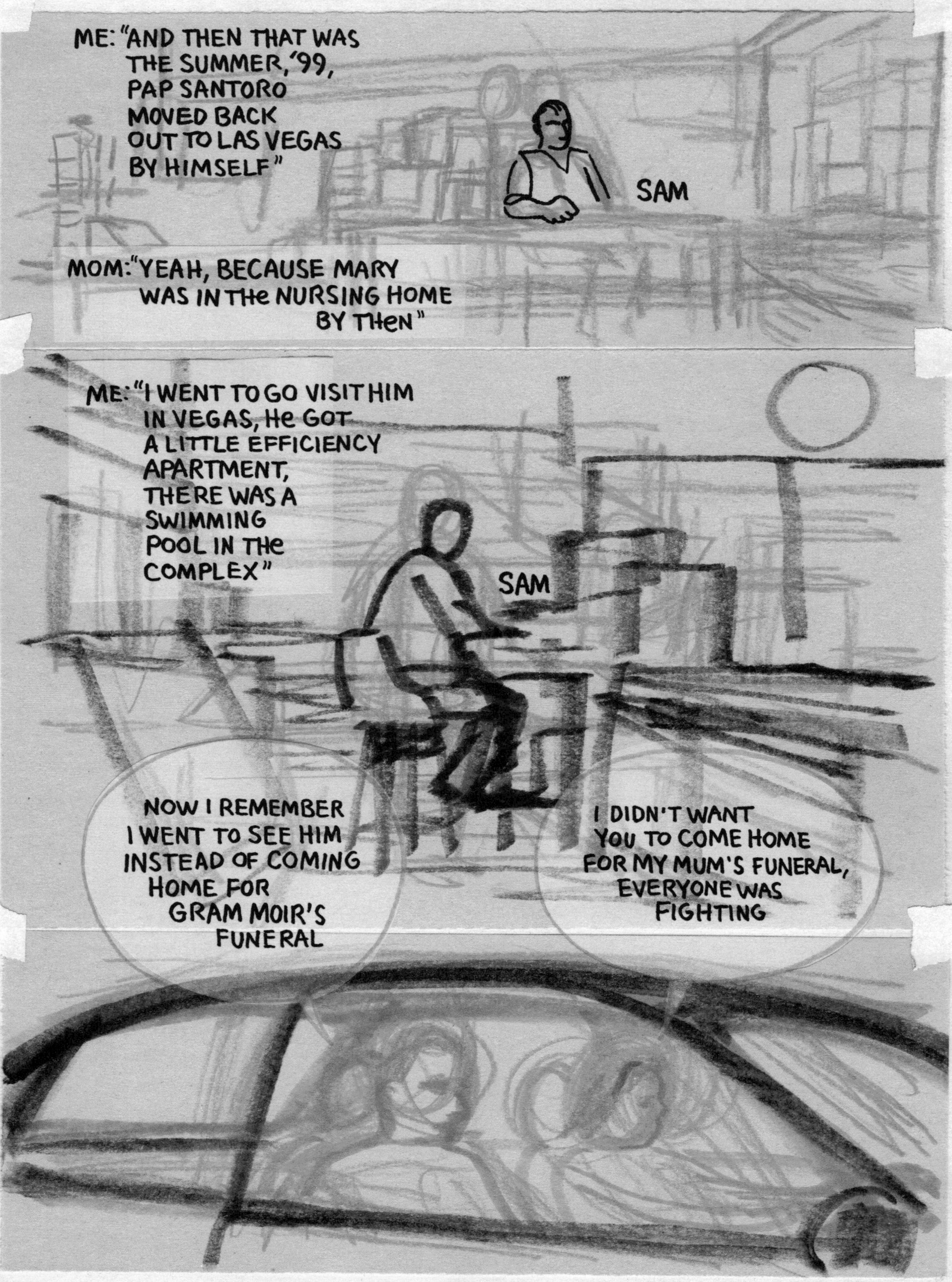
ME: "AND THEN THAT WAS THE SUMMER, '99, PAP SANTORO MOVED BACK OUT TO LAS VEGAS BY HIMSELF"
SAM
MOM: "YEAH, BECAUSE MARY WAS IN THE NURSING HOME BY THEN"
ME: "I WENT TO GO VISIT HIM IN VEGAS, HE GOT A LITTLE EFFICIENCY APARTMENT, THERE WAS A SWIMMING POOL IN THE COMPLEX"
SAM
NOW I REMEMBER I WENT TO SEE HIM INSTEAD OF COMING HOME FOR GRAM MOIR'S FUNERAL
I DIDN'T WANT YOU TO COME HOME FOR MY MUM'S FUNERAL, EVERYONE WAS FIGHTING

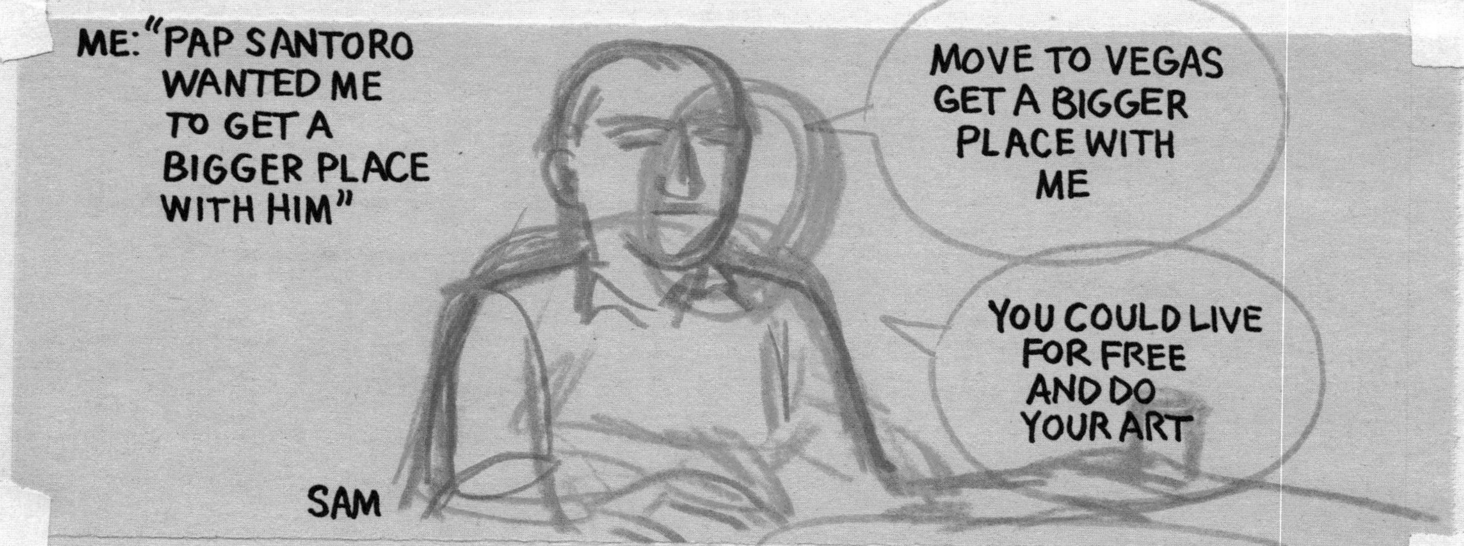
ME: "PAP SANTORO WANTED ME TO GET A BIGGER PLACE WITH HIM"
MOVE TO VEGAS GET A BIGGER PLACE WITH ME
YOU COULD LIVE FOR FREE AND DO YOUR ART
SAM

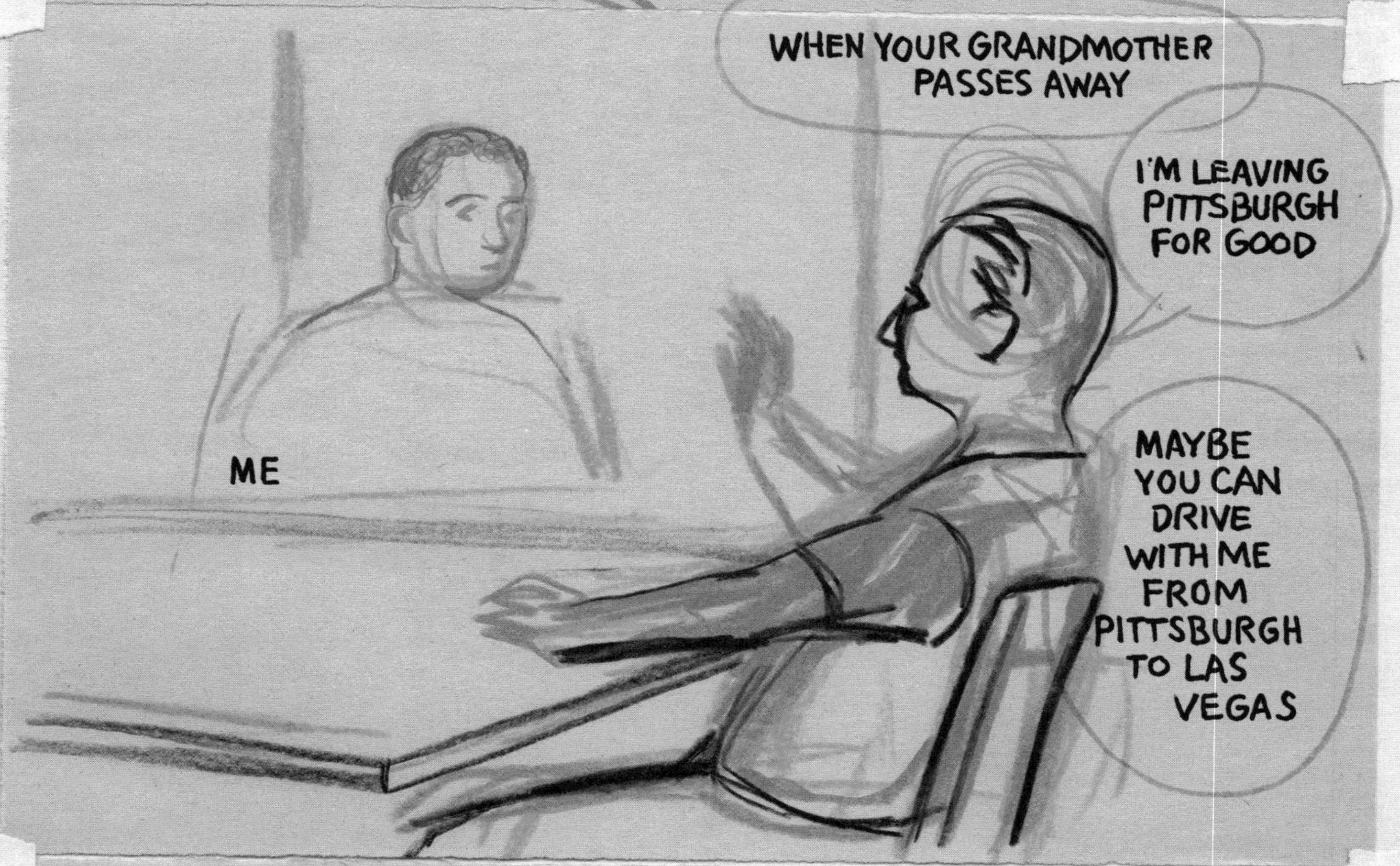
WHEN YOUR GRANDMOTHER PASSES AWAY
I'M LEAVING PITTSBURGH FOR GOOD
MAYBE YOU CAN DRIVE WITH ME FROM PITTSBURGH TO LAS VEGAS
ME

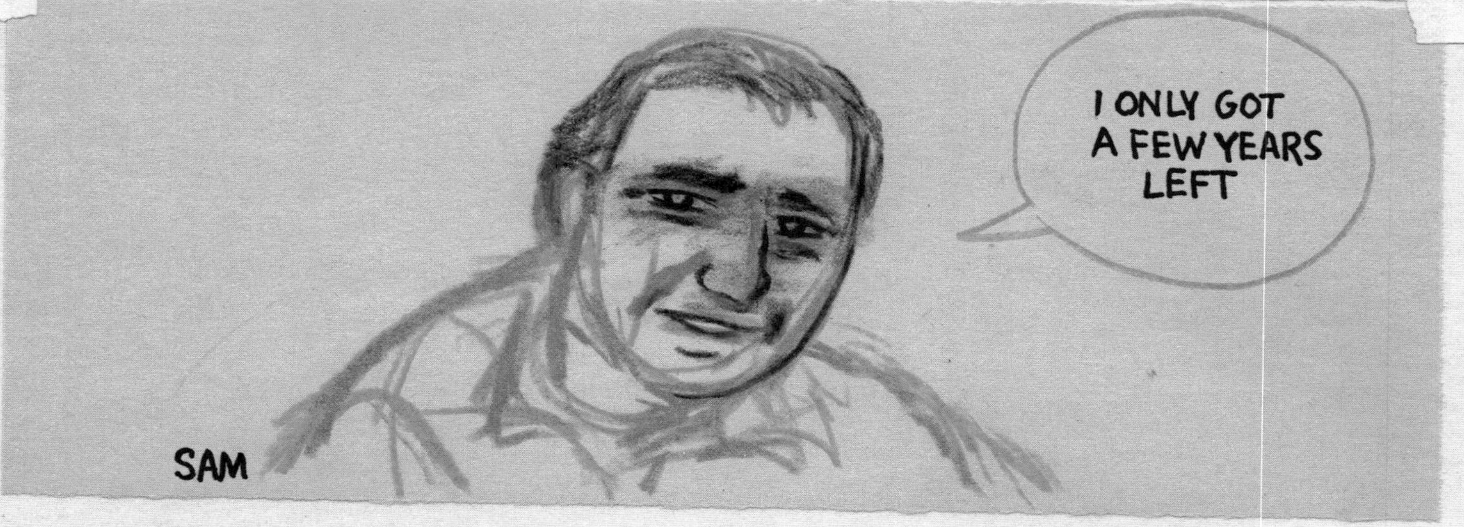
I ONLY GOT A FEW YEARS LEFT
SAM

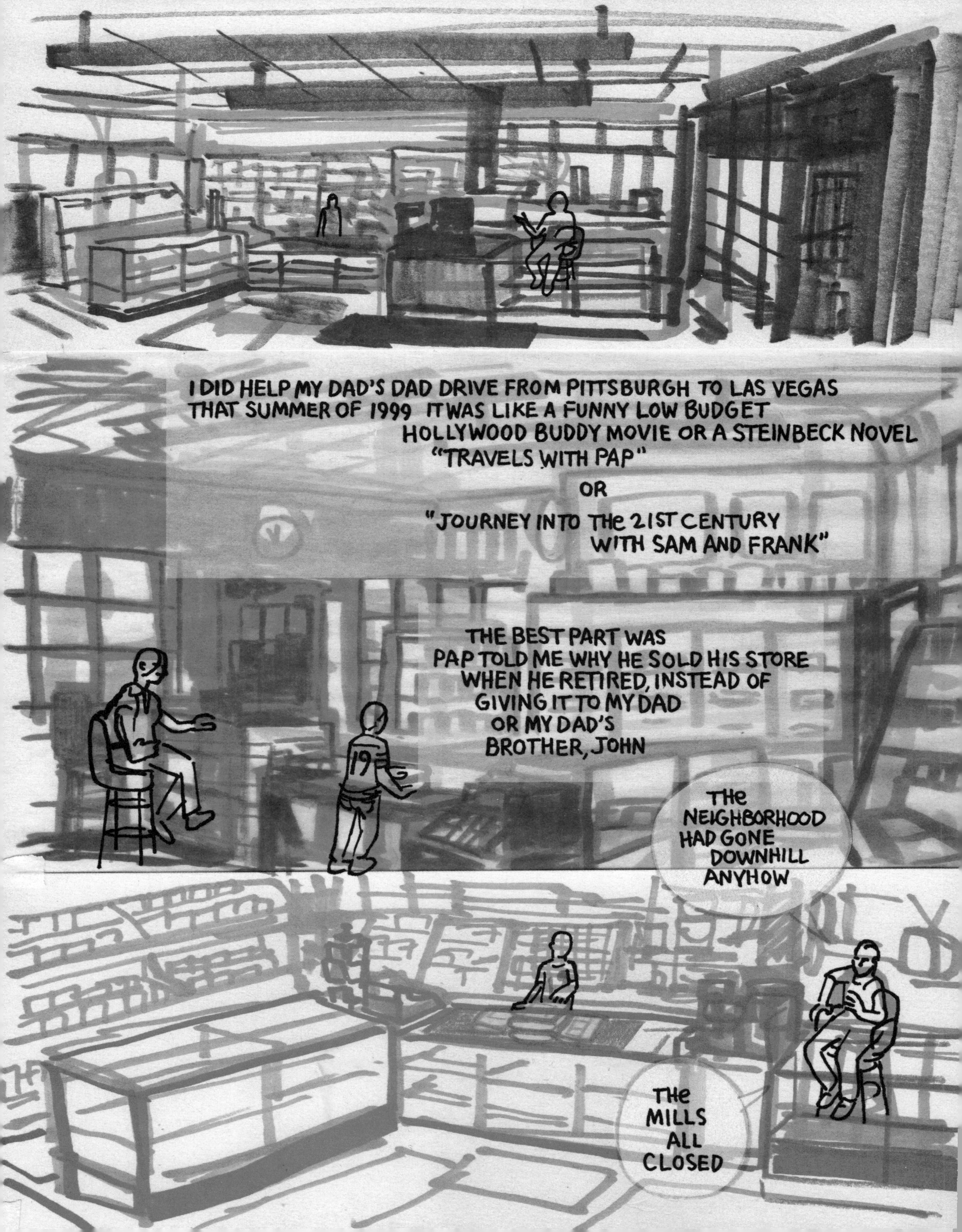
I DID HELP MY DAD'S DAD DRIVE FROM PITTSBURGH TO LAS VEGAS THAT SUMMER OF 1999 IT WAS LIKE A FUNNY LOW BUDGET HOLLYWOOD BUDDY MOVIE OR A STEINBECK NOVEL "TRAVELS WITH PAP"
OR
"JOURNEY INTO THE 21ST CENTURY WITH SAM AND FRANK"
THE BEST PART WAS PAP TOLD ME WHY HE SOLD HIS STORE WHEN HE RETIRED, INSTEAD OF GIVING IT TO MY DAD OR MY DAD'S BROTHER, JOHN
19
THE NEIGHBORHOOD HAD GONE DOWNHILL ANYHOW
THE MILLS ALL CLOSED

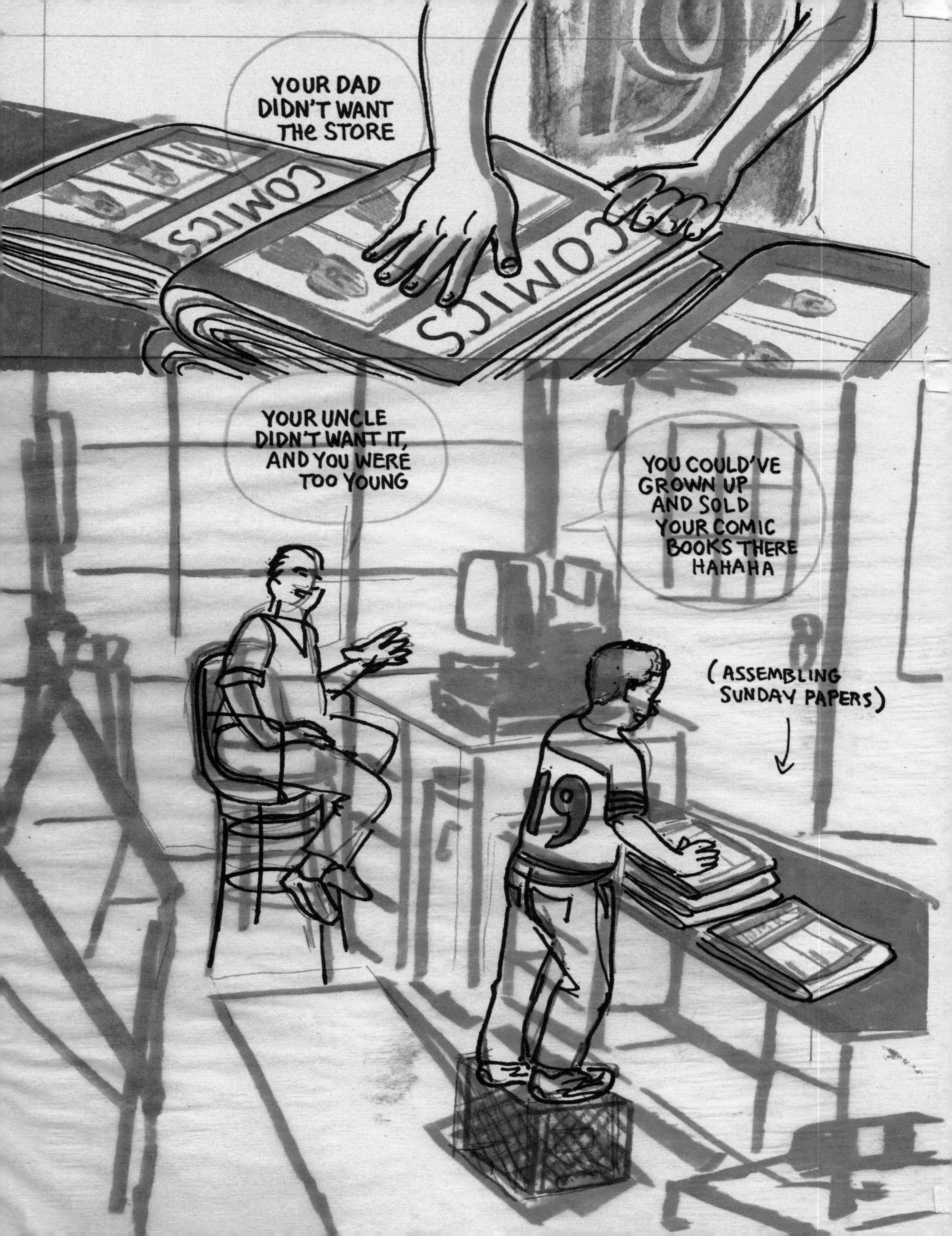
YOUR DAD DIDN'T WANT THE STORE
COMICS
COMICS
COMICS
YOUR UNCLE DIDN'T WANT IT, AND YOU WERE TOO YOUNG
YOU COULD'VE GROWN UP AND SOLD YOUR COMIC BOOKS THERE HAHAHA
(ASSEMBLING SUNDAY PAPERS)
19

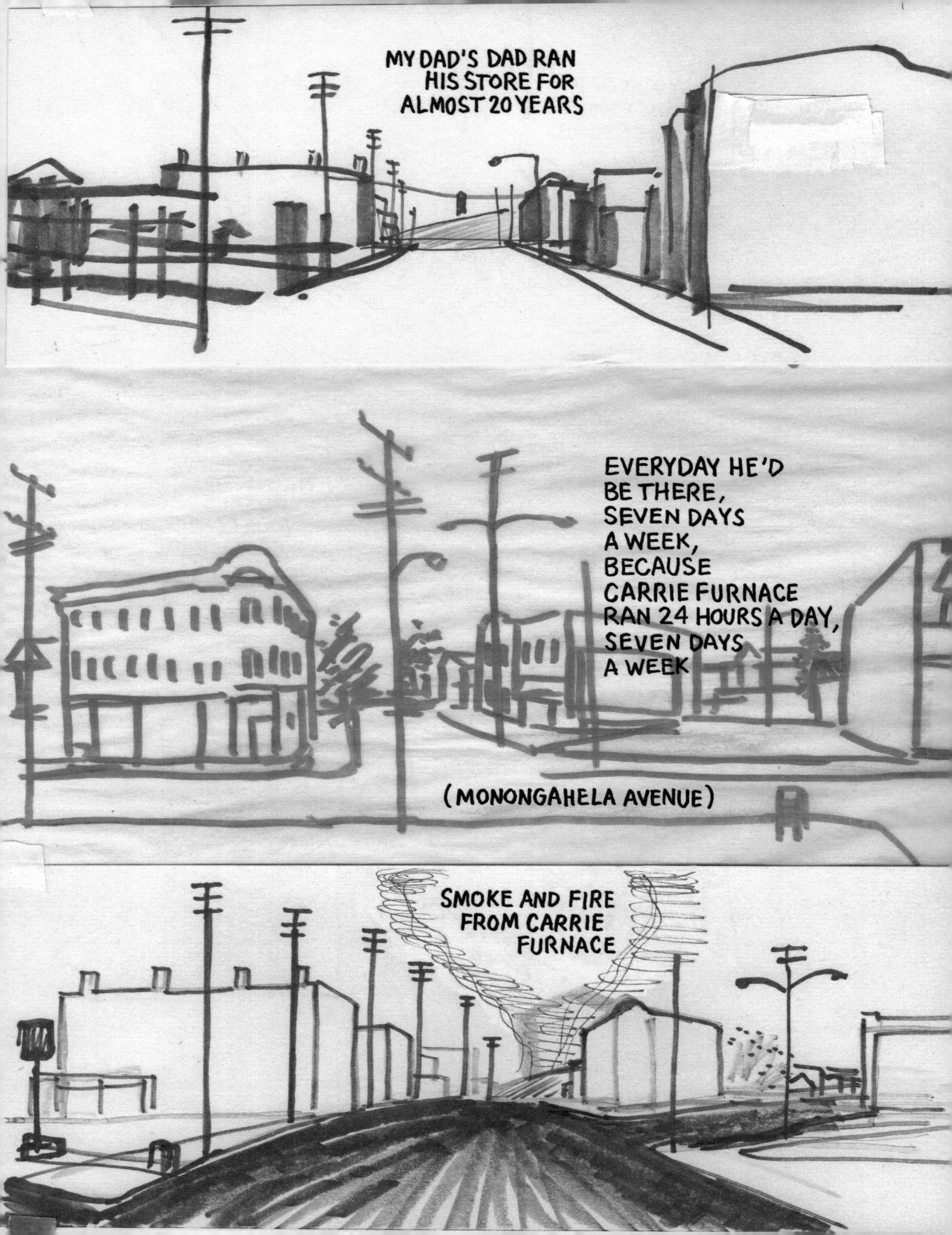
MY DAD'S DAD RAN HIS STORE FOR ALMOST 20 YEARS
EVERYDAY HE'D BE THERE, SEVEN DAYS A WEEK, BECAUSE CARRIE FURNACE RAN 24 HOURS A DAY, SEVEN DAYS A WEEK
(MONONGAHELA AVENUE)
SMOKE AND FIRE FROM CARRIE FURNACE

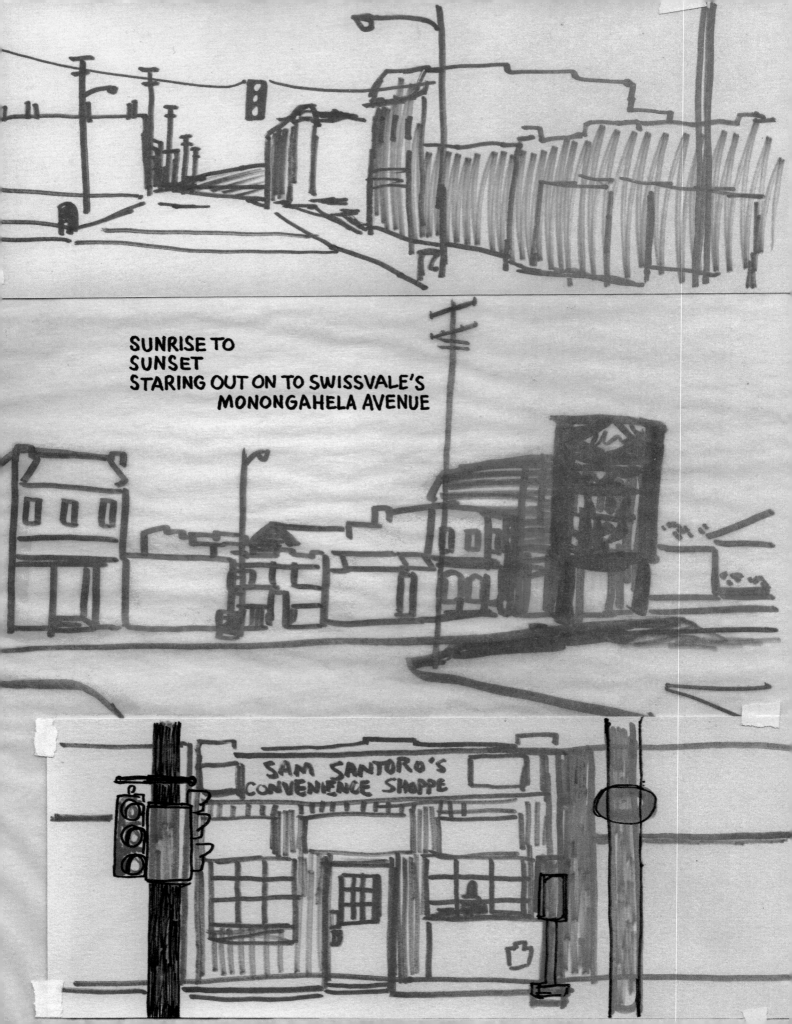

SUNRISE TO
SUNSET
STARING OUT ON TO SWISSVALE'S
MONONGAHELA AVENUE

SAM SANTORO'S
CONVENIENCE SHOPPE

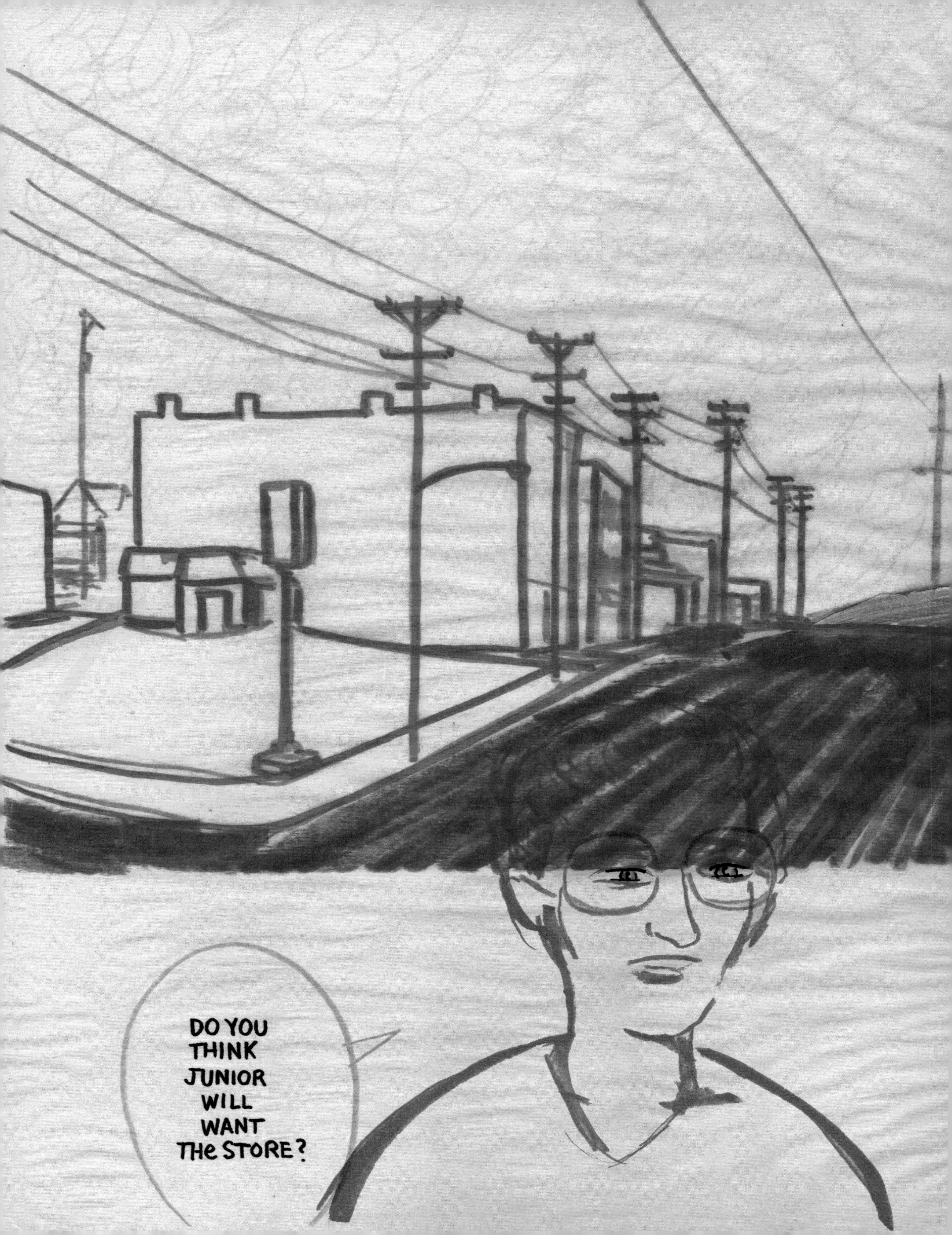
DO YOU THINK JUNIOR WILL WANT THE STORE?

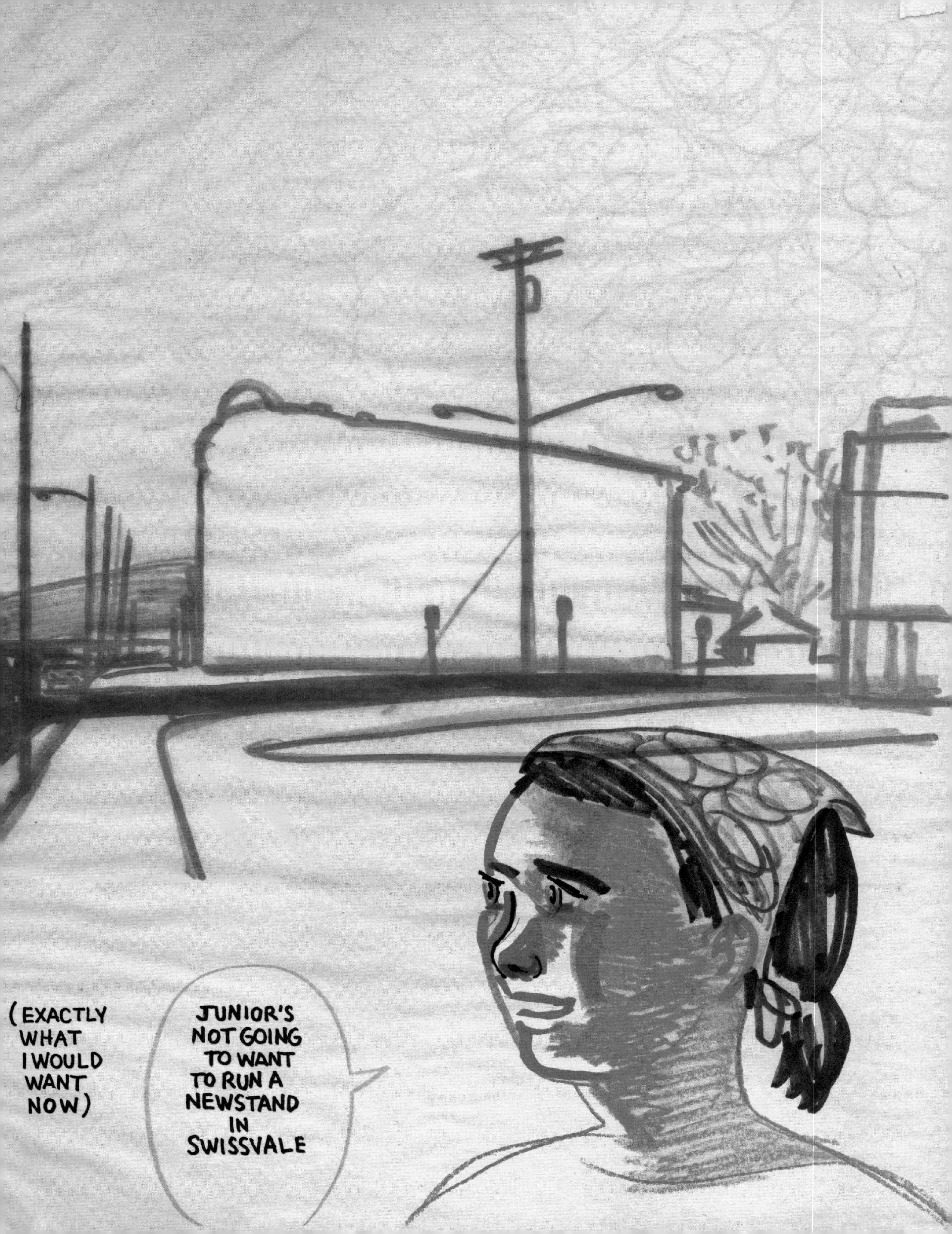
(EXACTLY WHAT I WOULD WANT NOW)
JUNIOR'S NOT GOING TO WANT TO RUN A NEWSTAND IN SWISSVALE

SAM KNEW EVERYONE
HIS SHOPPE WAS THE INFORMATION HIGHWAY
THE REGULARITY OF IT ALL
YOU COULD COUNT ON HIM BEING THERE
OR HERE IN HIS CHAIR

(MOM WOULD
SOMETIMES
BE WORKING 3 TO 6
AT THE STORE
SO PAP COULD
GO EAT)

HOME AT 4 EVERYDAY TO EAT SUPPER
TAKE A NAP AND GET BACK TO THE
STORE BY THE TIME THEY PLAYED
THE LOTTERY ON TV AT 7

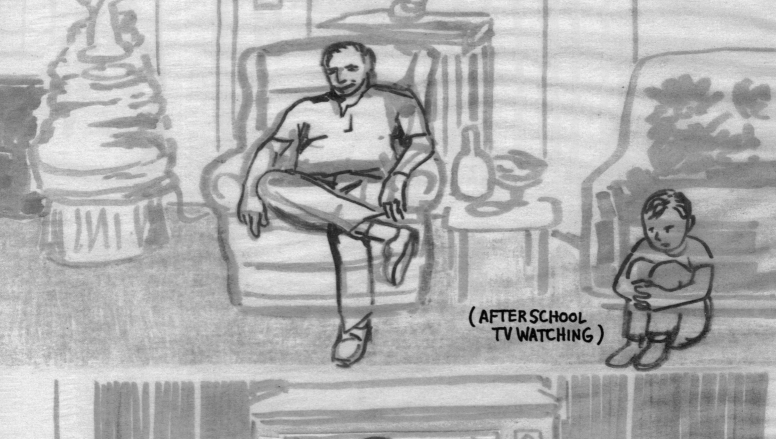

(AFTER SCHOOL
TV WATCHING)

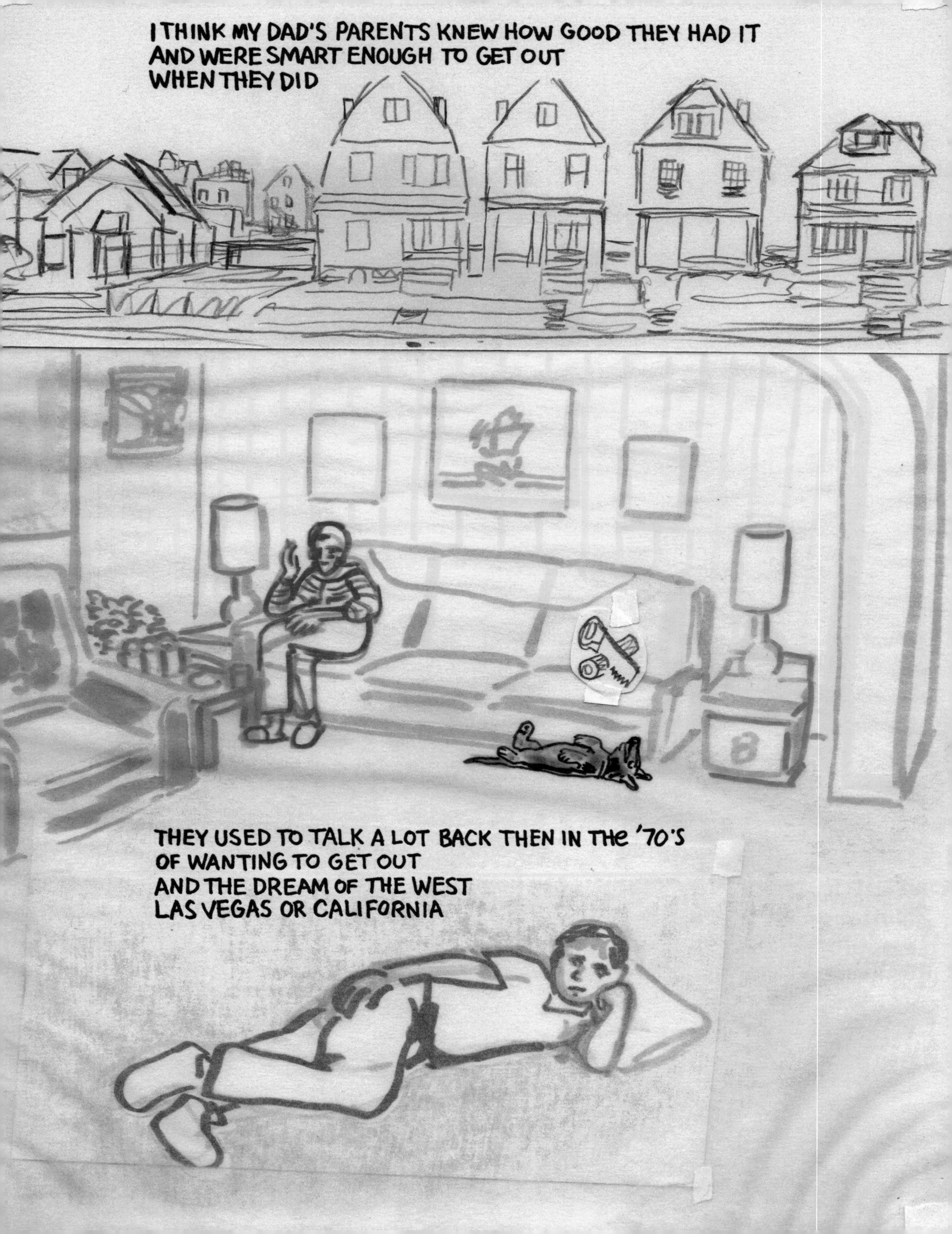
I THINK MY DAD'S PARENTS KNEW HOW GOOD THEY HAD IT
AND WERE SMART ENOUGH TO GET OUT
WHEN THEY DID
THEY USED TO TALK A LOT BACK THEN IN THE '70'S
OF WANTING TO GET OUT
AND THE DREAM OF THE WEST
LAS VEGAS OR CALIFORNIA

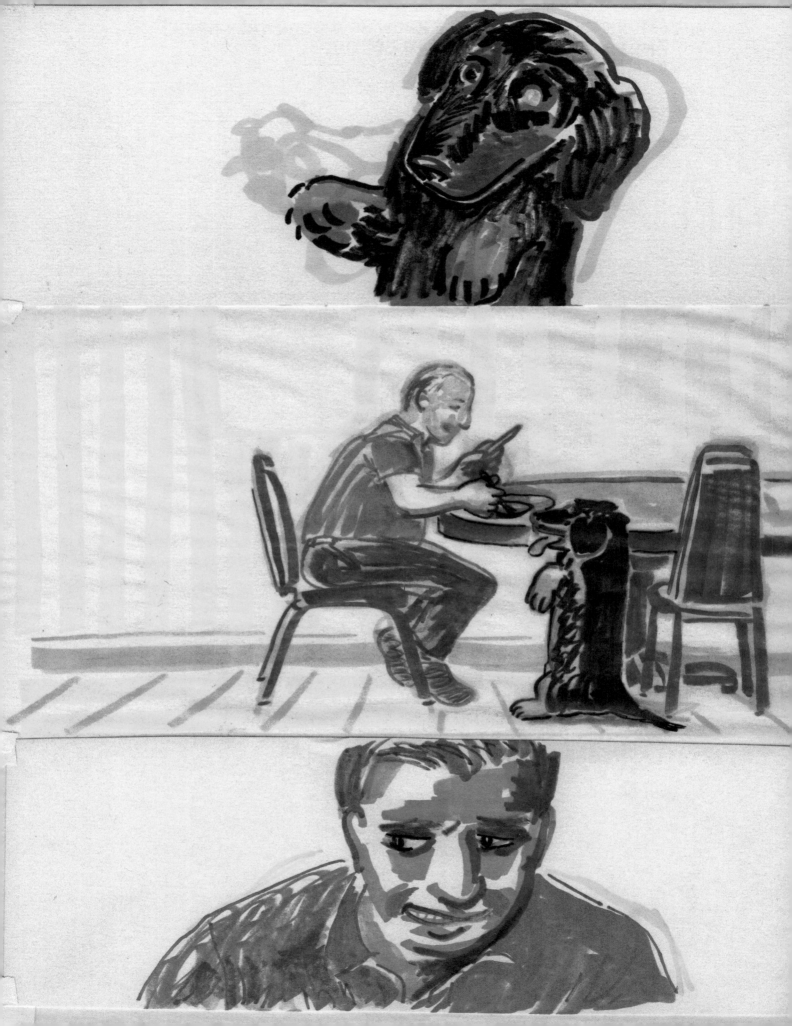

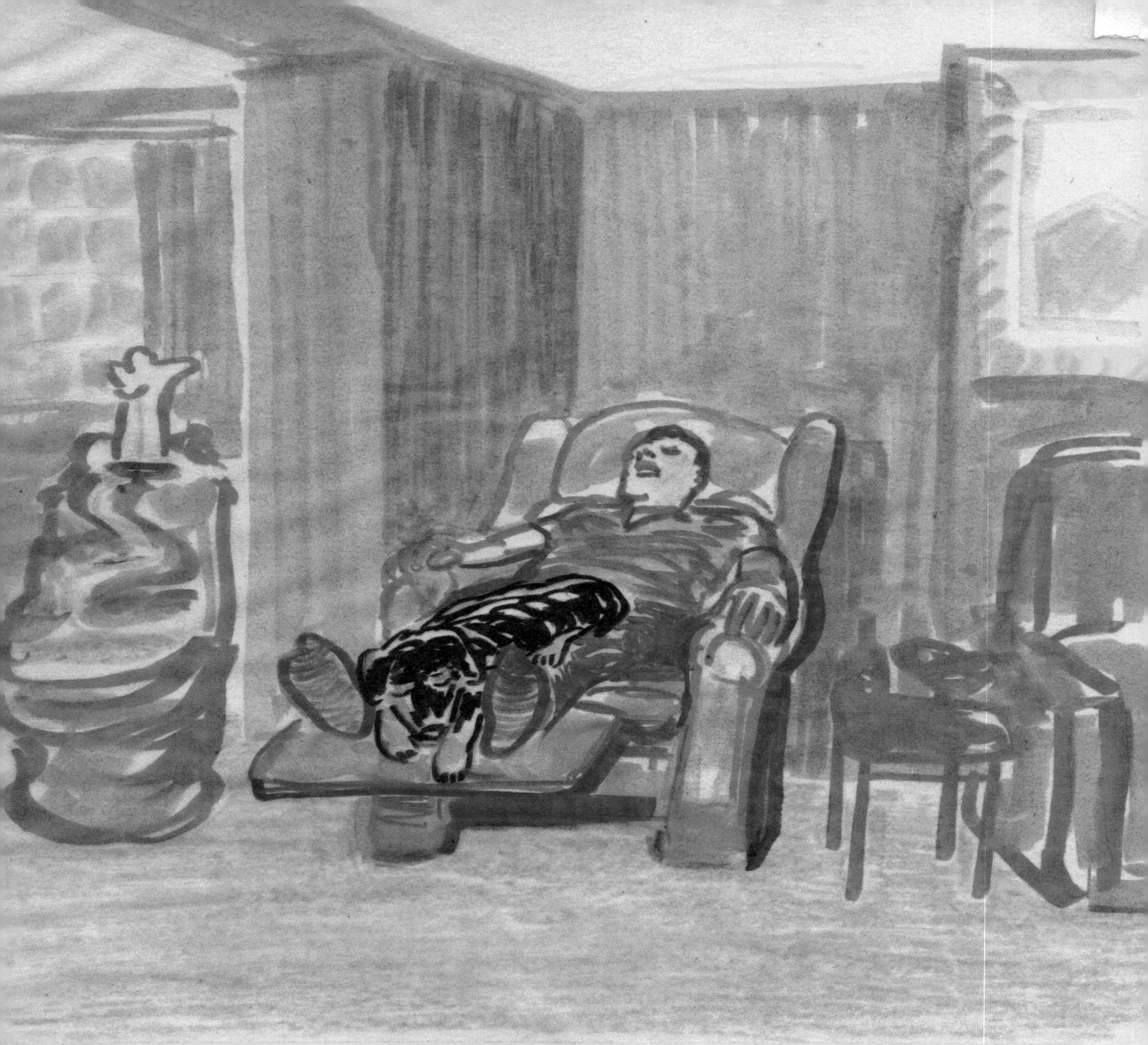

" YOU AND ME WERE A GOOD TEAM", PAP TOLD ME LATER,
WE WERE IN A SIMILAR ORBIT FOR OVER A DECADE,
HE AND MARY WERE ALREADY OUT WEST
WHEN I LEFT PITTSBURGH FOR CALIFORNIA,
SO THEY HELPED ME STAY OUT THERE,
THEIR APARTMENT IN LAS VEGAS
BEING A PLACE WHERE I COULD GO WHEN
I WAS OUT WEST AND MAKING YOUNG MISTAKES

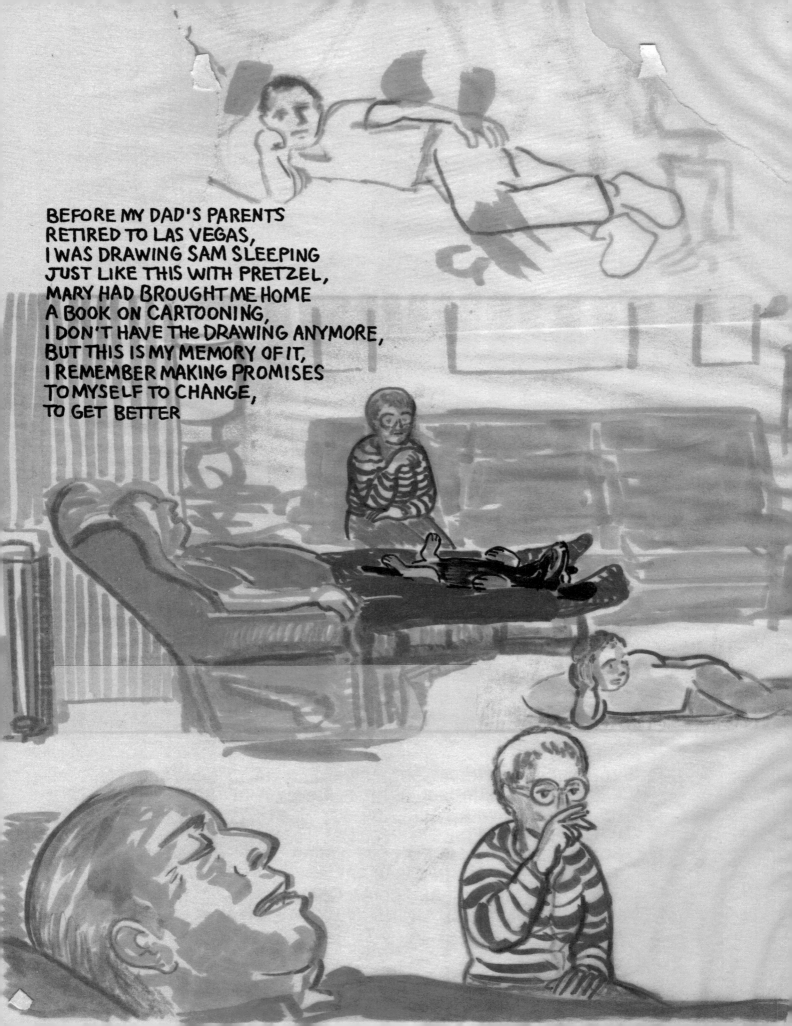

BEFORE MY DAD'S PARENTS
RETIRED TO LAS VEGAS,
I WAS DRAWING SAM SLEEPING
JUST LIKE THIS WITH PRETZEL,
MARY HAD BROUGHT ME HOME
A BOOK ON CARTOONING,
I DON'T HAVE THE DRAWING ANYMORE,
BUT THIS IS MY MEMORY OF IT,
I REMEMBER MAKING PROMISES
TO MYSELF TO CHANGE,
TO GET BETTER

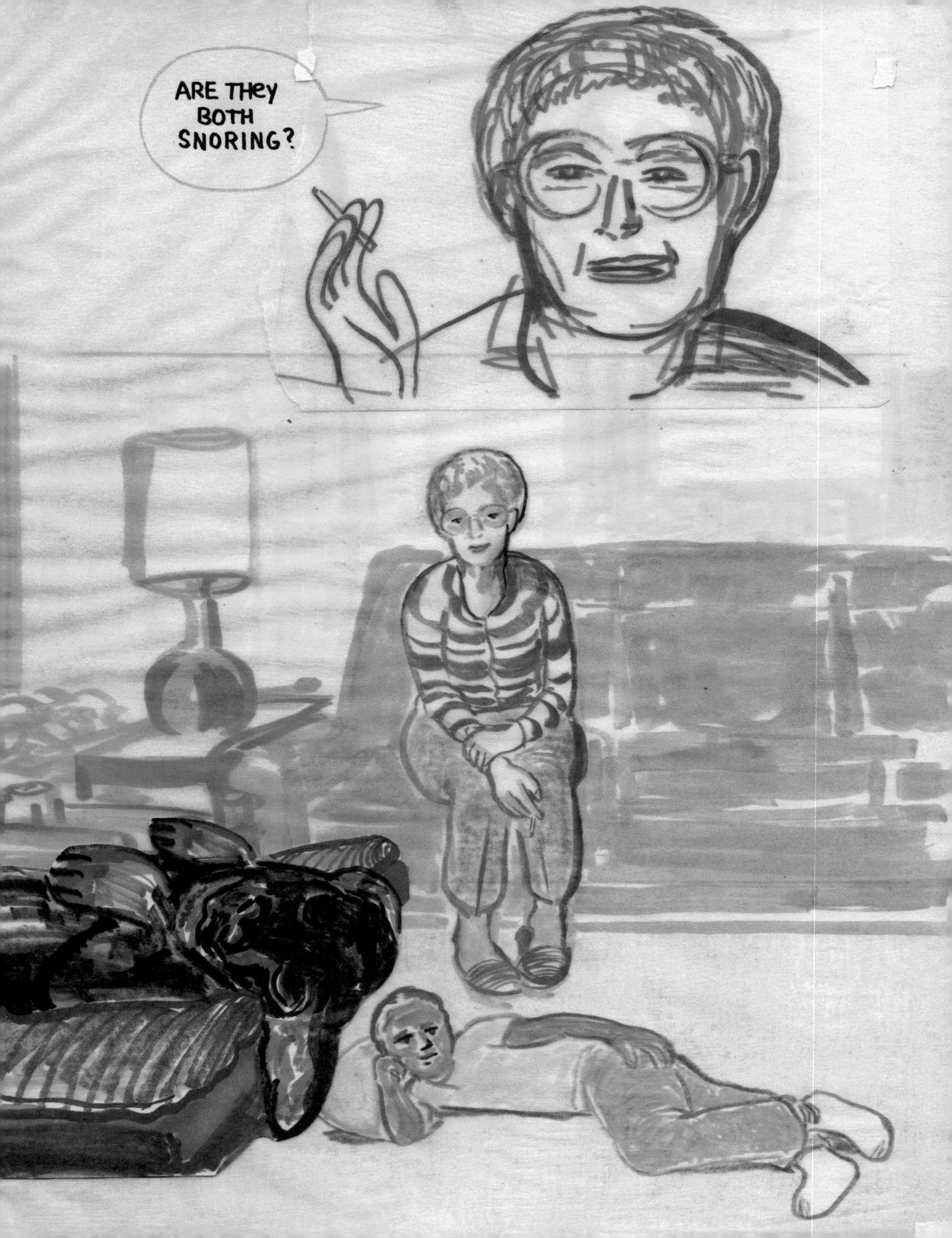
ARE THEY BOTH SNORING?

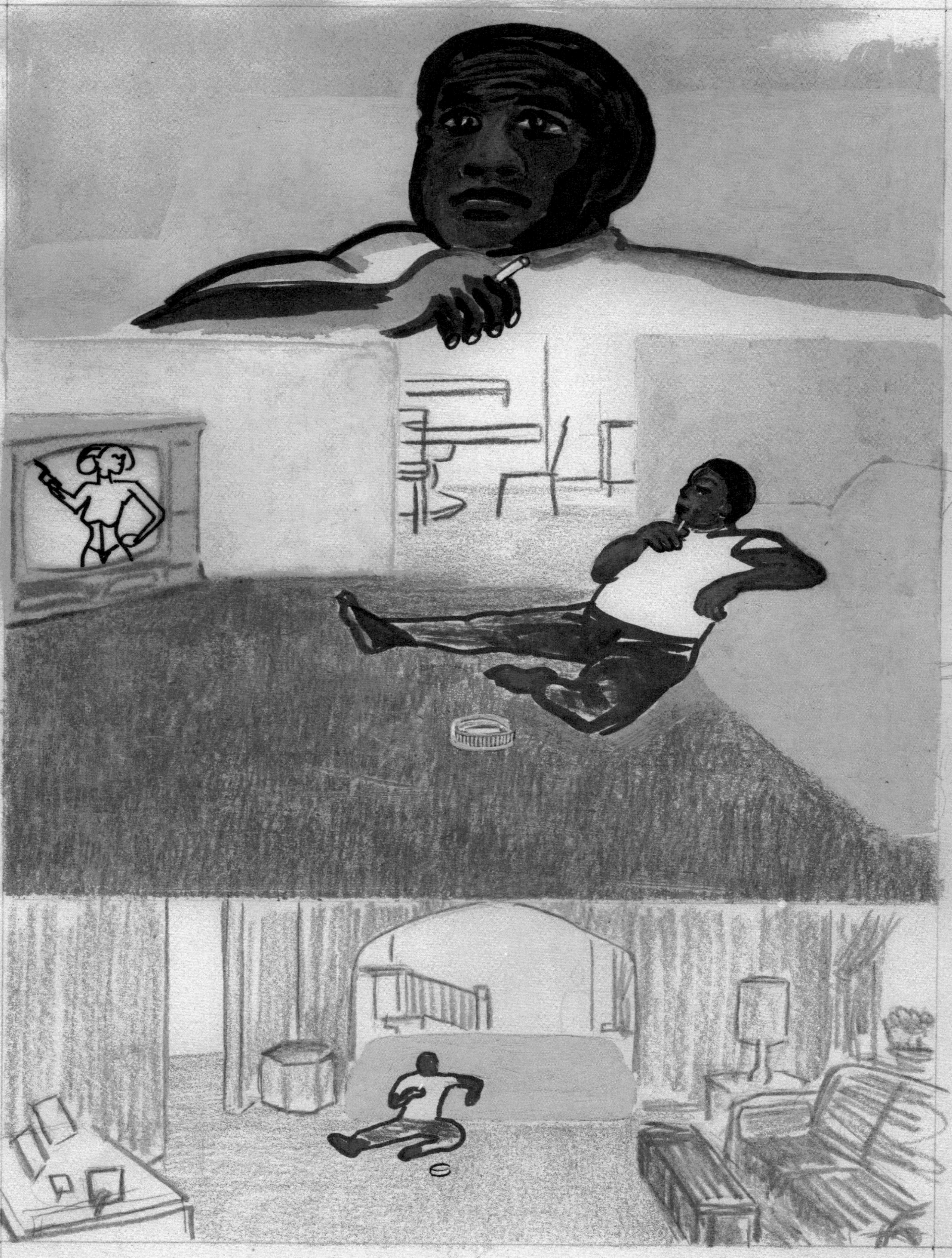

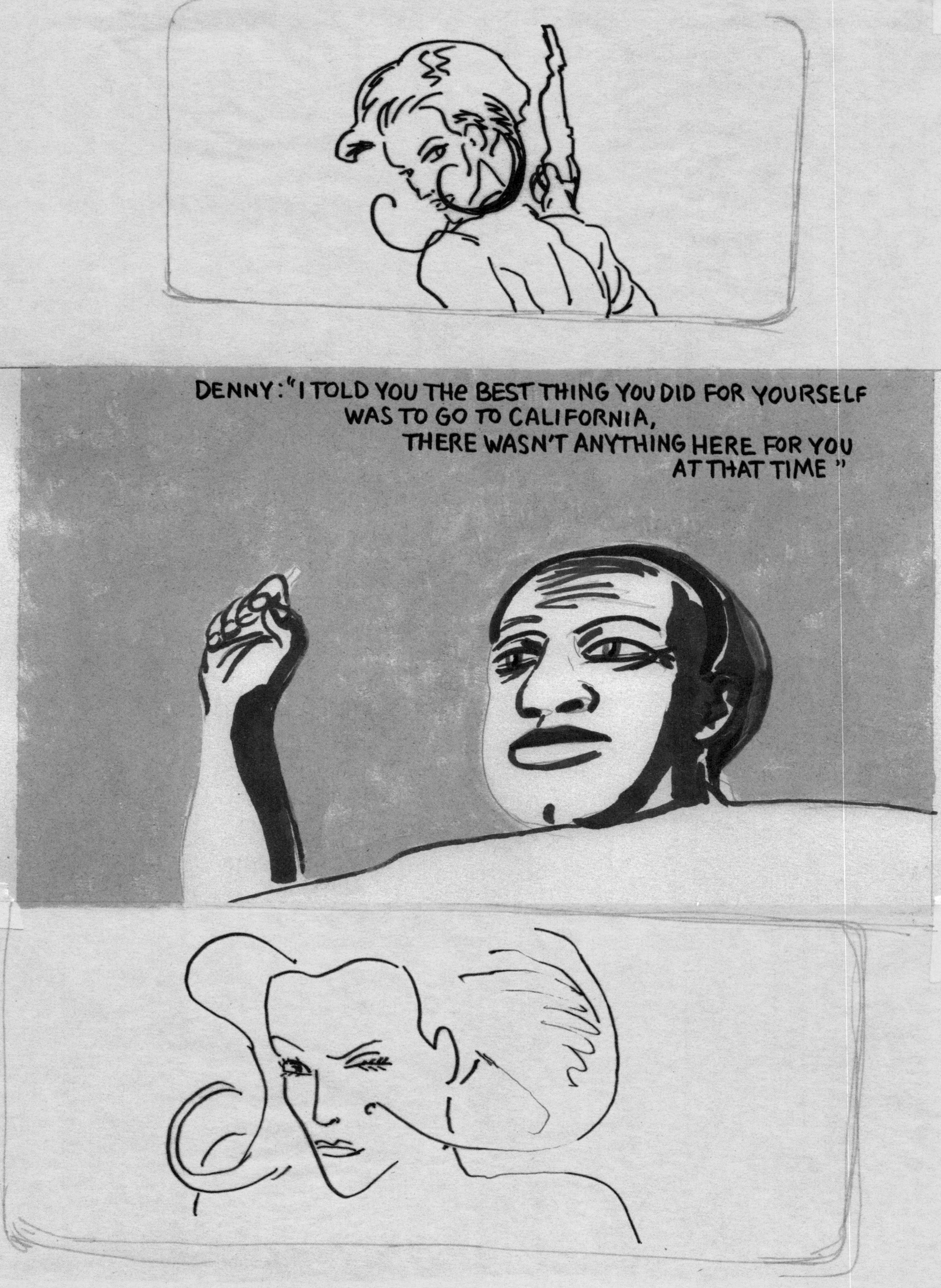
DENNY: "I TOLD YOU THE BEST THING YOU DID FOR YOURSELF WAS TO GO TO CALIFORNIA, THERE WASN'T ANYTHING HERE FOR YOU AT THAT TIME"

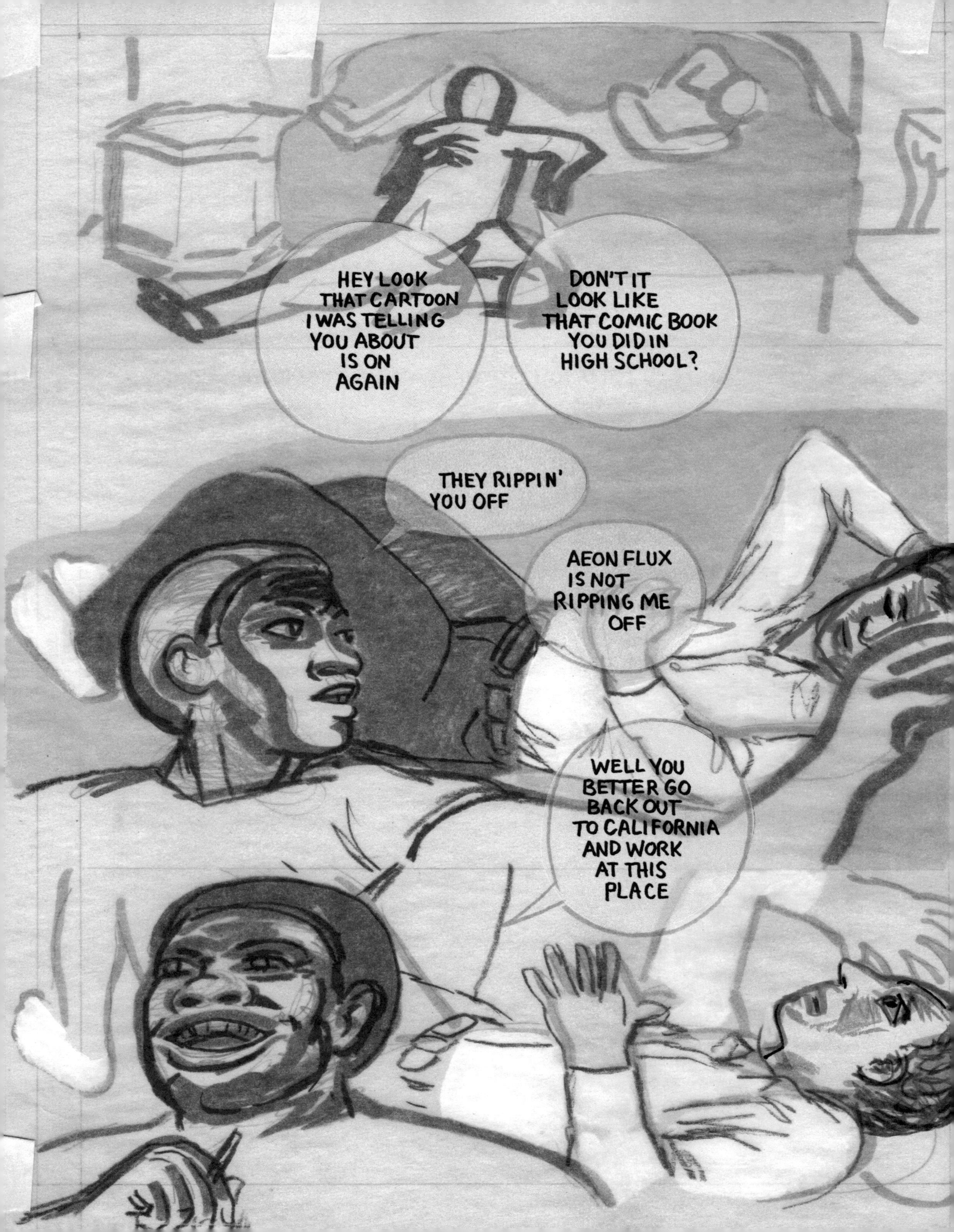
HEY LOOK THAT CARTOON I WAS TELLING YOU ABOUT IS ON AGAIN
DON'T IT LOOK LIKE THAT COMIC BOOK YOU DID IN HIGH SCHOOL?
THEY RIPPIN' YOU OFF
AEON FLUX IS NOT RIPPING ME OFF
WELL YOU BETTER GO BACK OUT TO CALIFORNIA AND WORK AT THIS PLACE

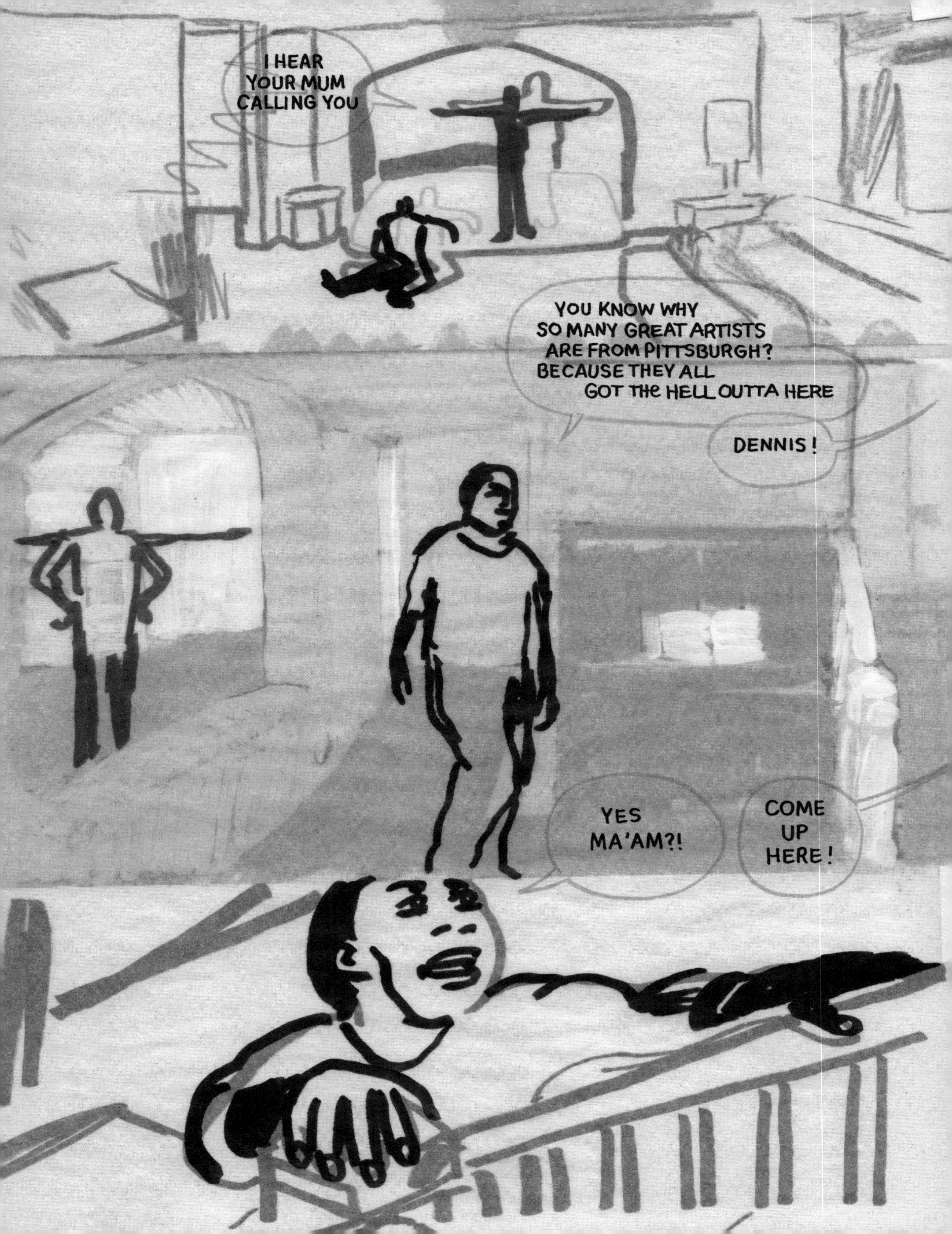
I HEAR YOUR MUM CALLING YOU
YOU KNOW WHY SO MANY GREAT ARTISTS ARE FROM PITTSBURGH? BECAUSE THEY ALL GOT THE HELL OUTTA HERE
DENNIS!
COME UP HERE!
YES MA'AM?!

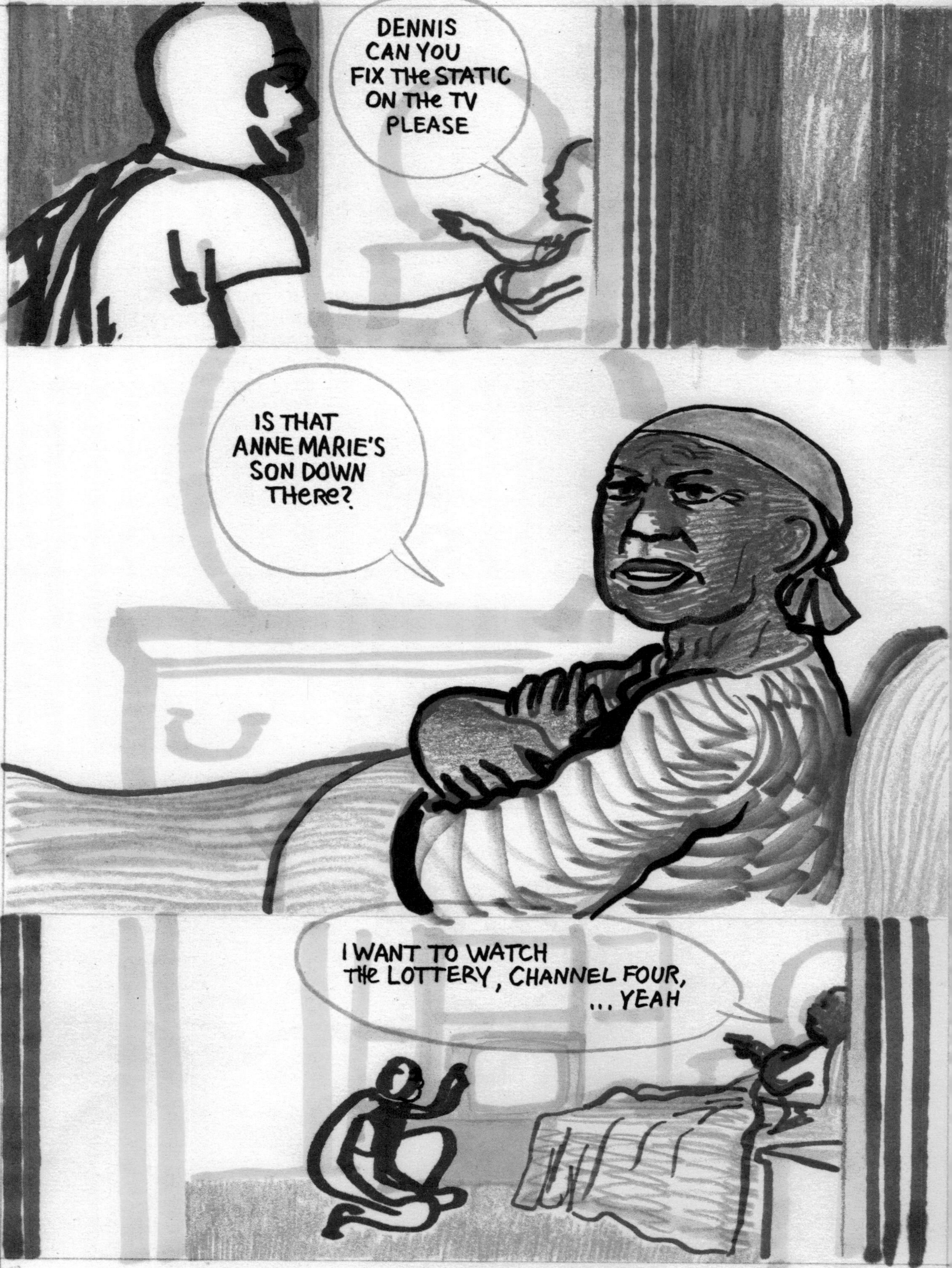
DENNIS CAN YOU FIX THE STATIC ON THE TV PLEASE
IS THAT ANNE MARIE'S SON DOWN THERE?
I WANT TO WATCH THE LOTTERY, CHANNEL FOUR, ...YEAH

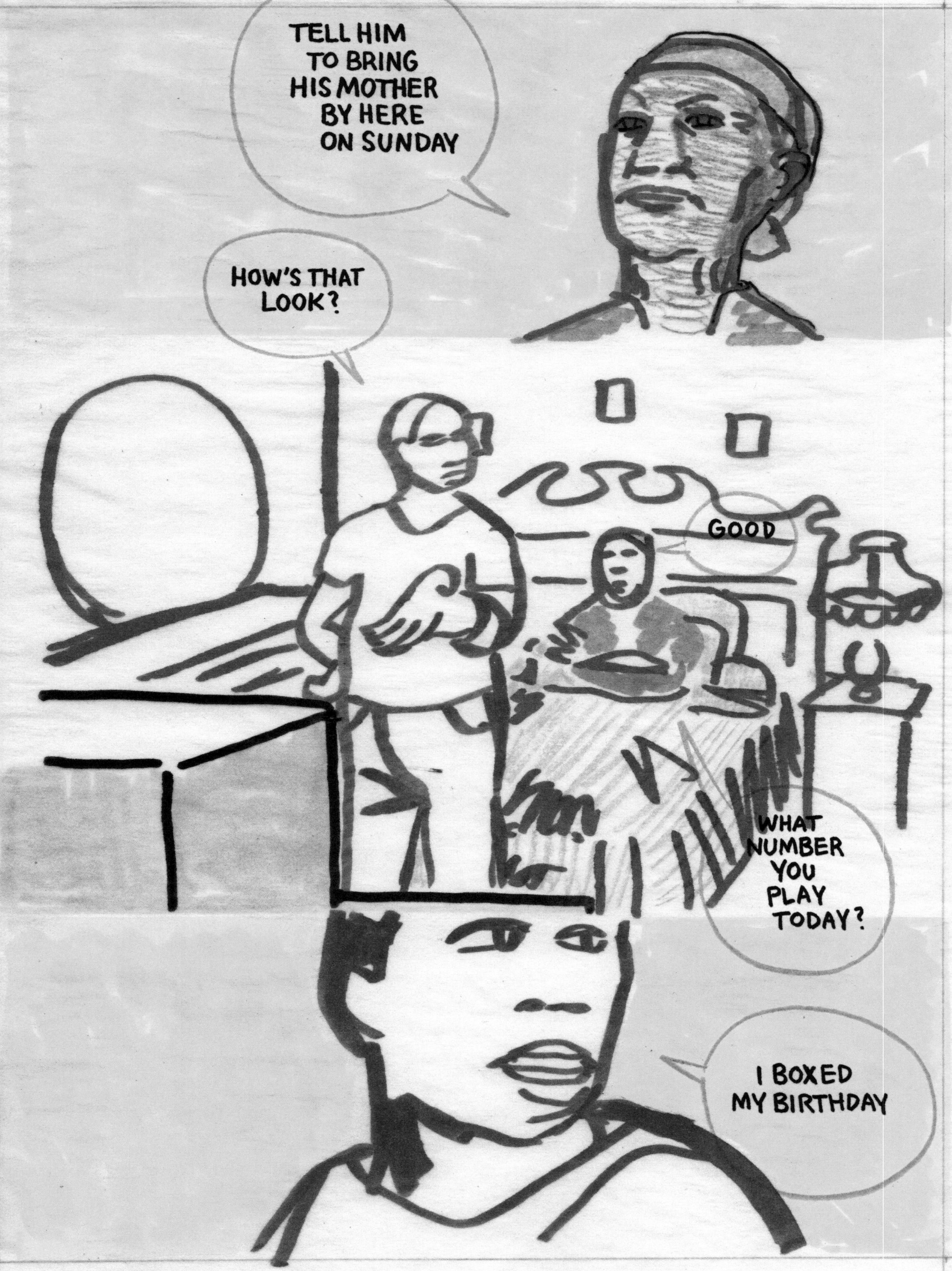
TELL HIM TO BRING HIS MOTHER BY HERE ON SUNDAY
HOW'S THAT LOOK?
GOOD
WHAT NUMBER YOU PLAY TODAY?
I BOXED MY BIRTHDAY

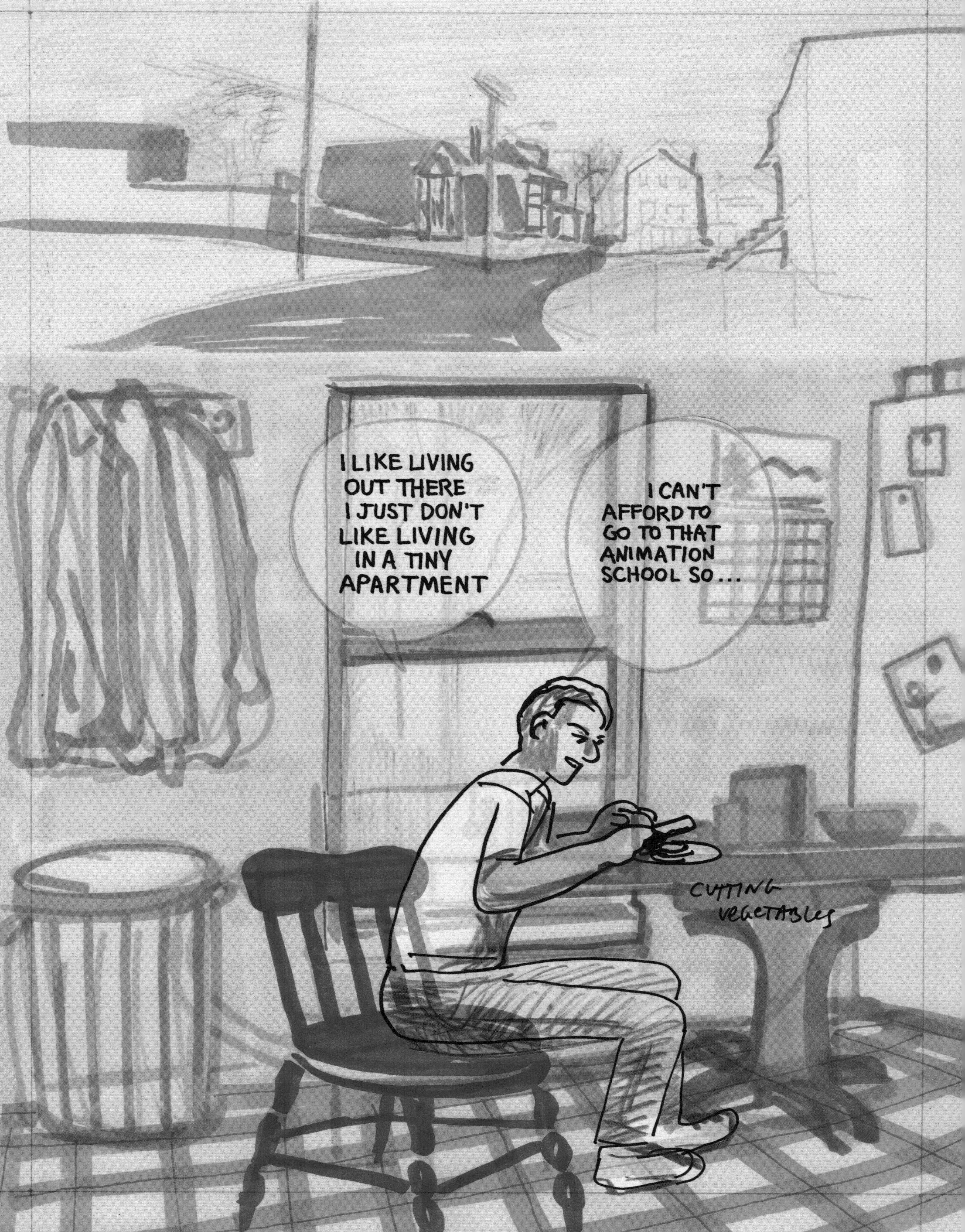
I LIKE LIVING OUT THERE I JUST DON'T LIKE LIVING IN A TINY APARTMENT
I CAN'T AFFORD TO GO TO THAT ANIMATION SCHOOL SO...
CUTTING VEGETABLES

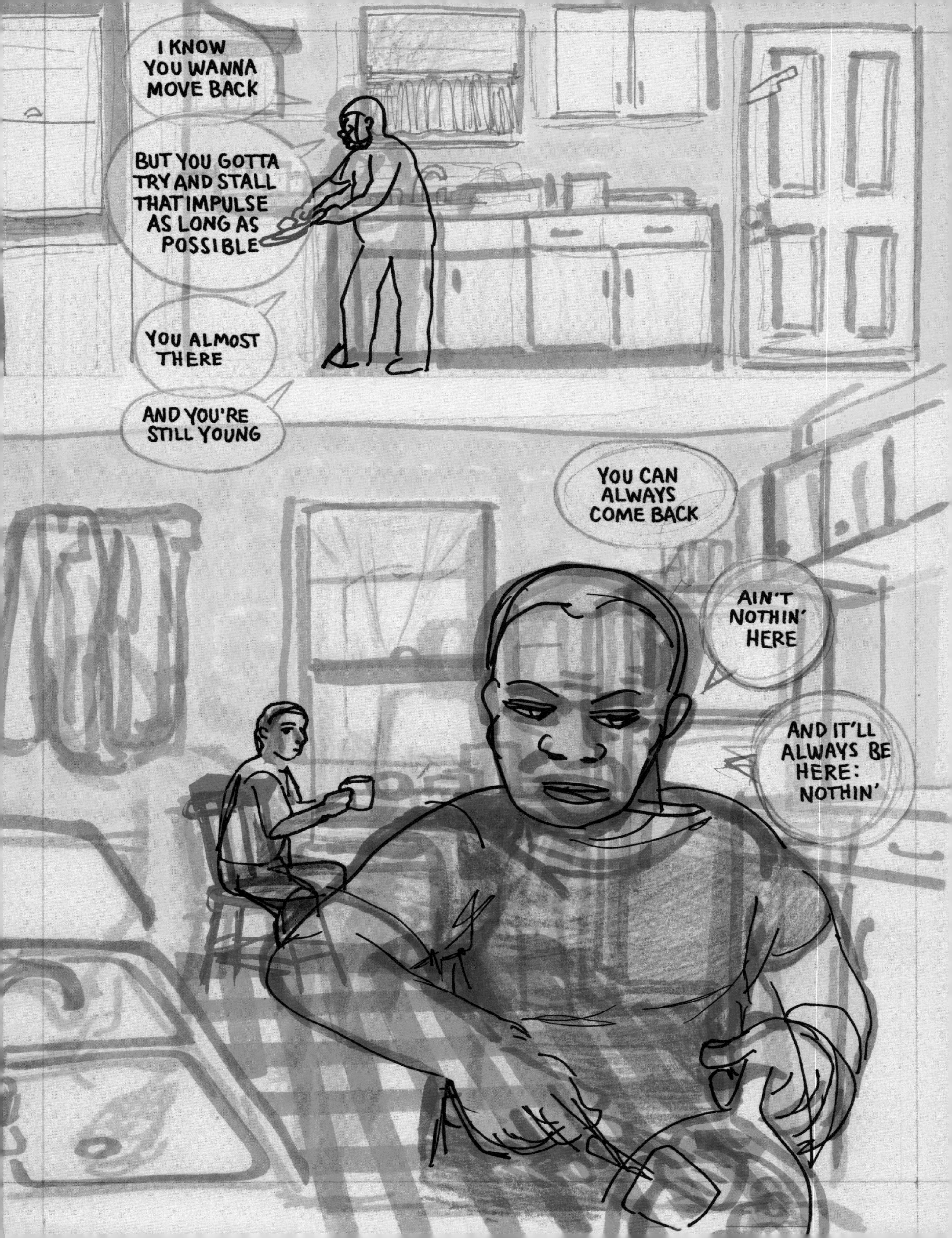
I KNOW YOU WANNA MOVE BACK
BUT YOU GOTTA TRY AND STALL THAT IMPULSE AS LONG AS POSSIBLE
YOU ALMOST THERE
AND YOU'RE STILL YOUNG
YOU CAN ALWAYS COME BACK
AIN'T NOTHIN' HERE
AND IT'LL ALWAYS BE HERE: NOTHIN'

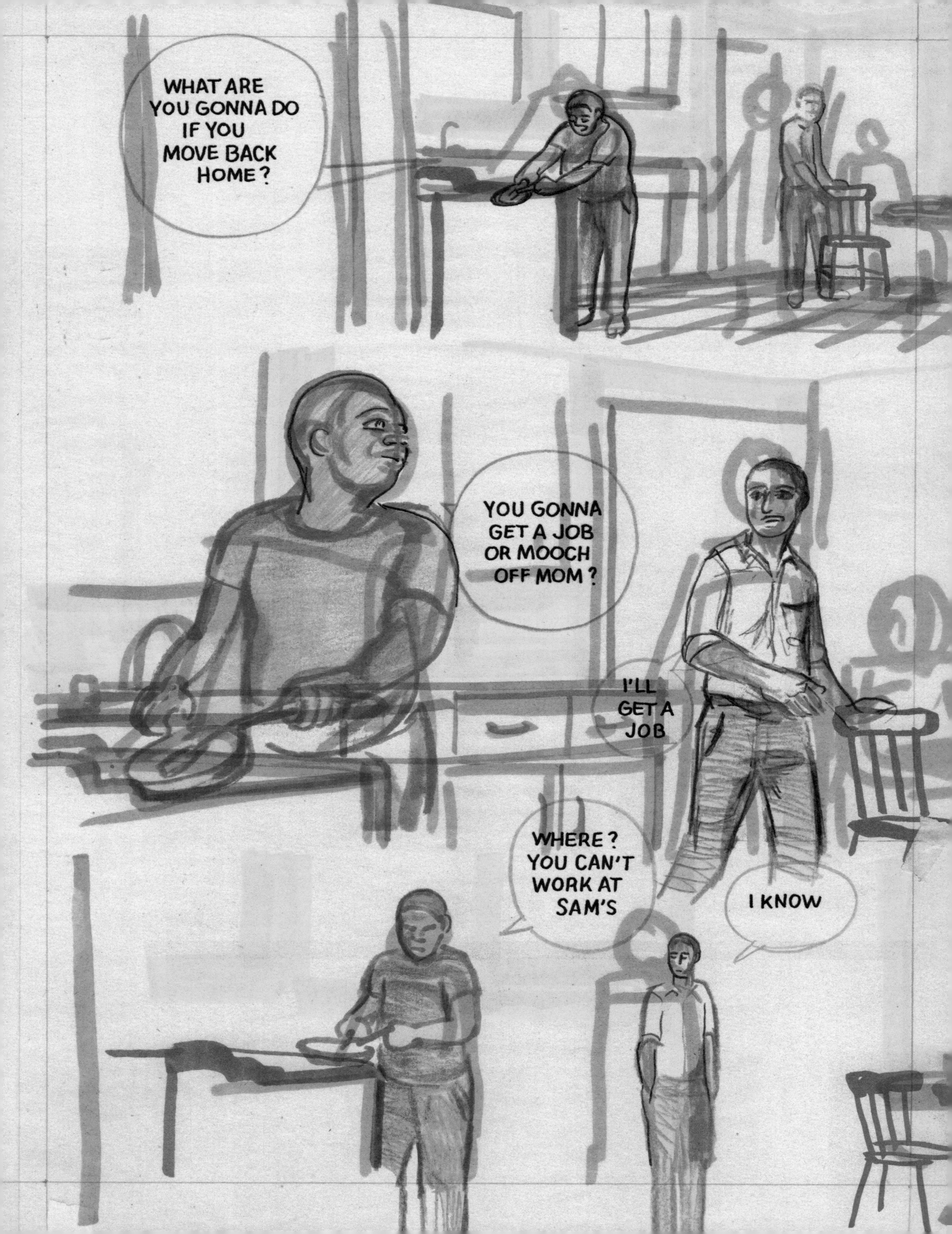
WHAT ARE YOU GONNA DO IF YOU MOVE BACK HOME?
YOU GONNA GET A JOB OR MOOCH OFF MOM?
I'LL GET A JOB
WHERE? YOU CAN'T WORK AT SAM'S
I KNOW

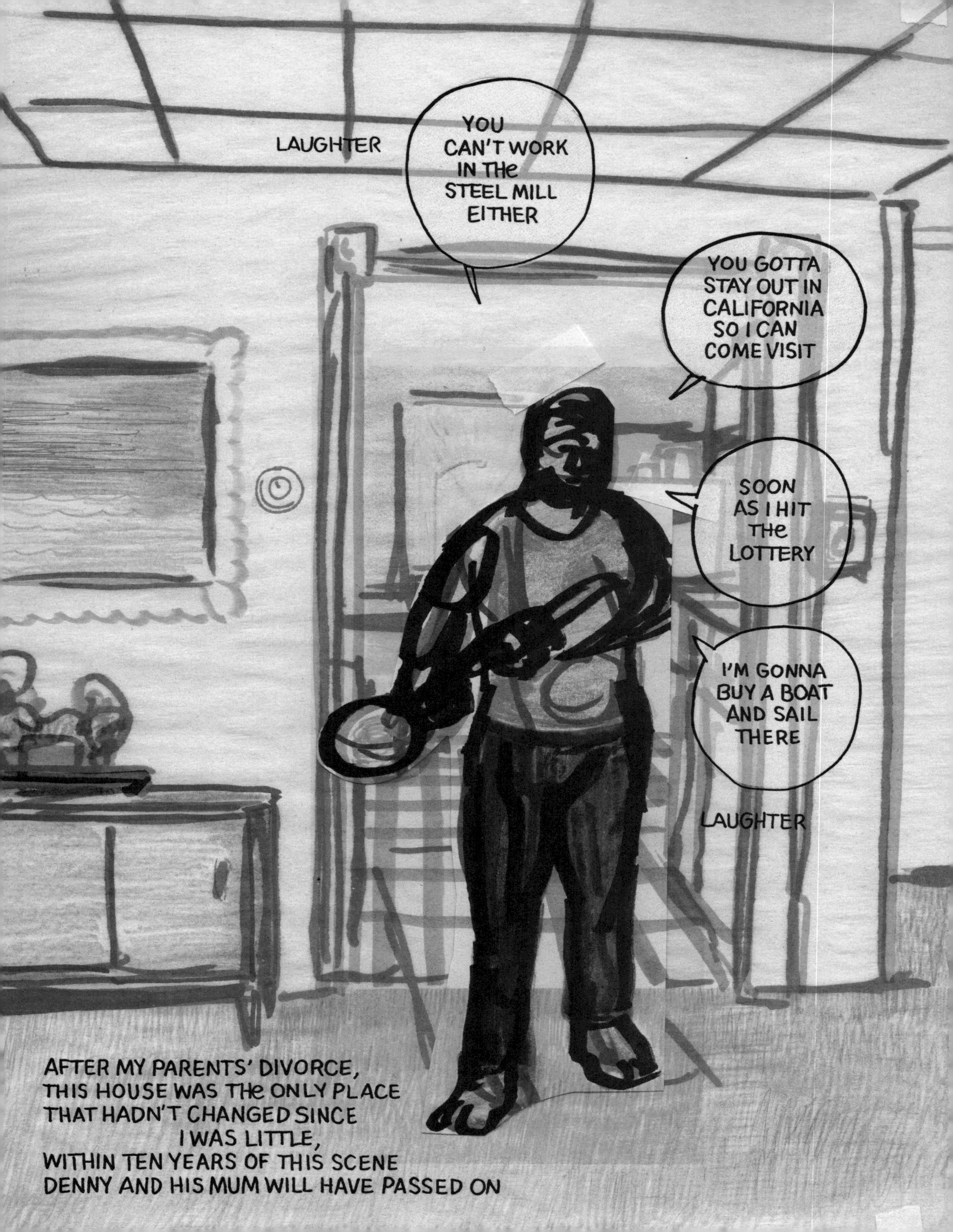
LAUGHTER
YOU CAN'T WORK IN THE STEEL MILL EITHER
YOU GOTTA STAY OUT IN CALIFORNIA SO I CAN COME VISIT
SOON AS I HIT THE LOTTERY
I'M GONNA BUY A BOAT AND SAIL THERE
LAUGHTER
AFTER MY PARENTS' DIVORCE, THIS HOUSE WAS THE ONLY PLACE THAT HADN'T CHANGED SINCE I WAS LITTLE, WITHIN TEN YEARS OF THIS SCENE DENNY AND HIS MUM WILL HAVE PASSED ON

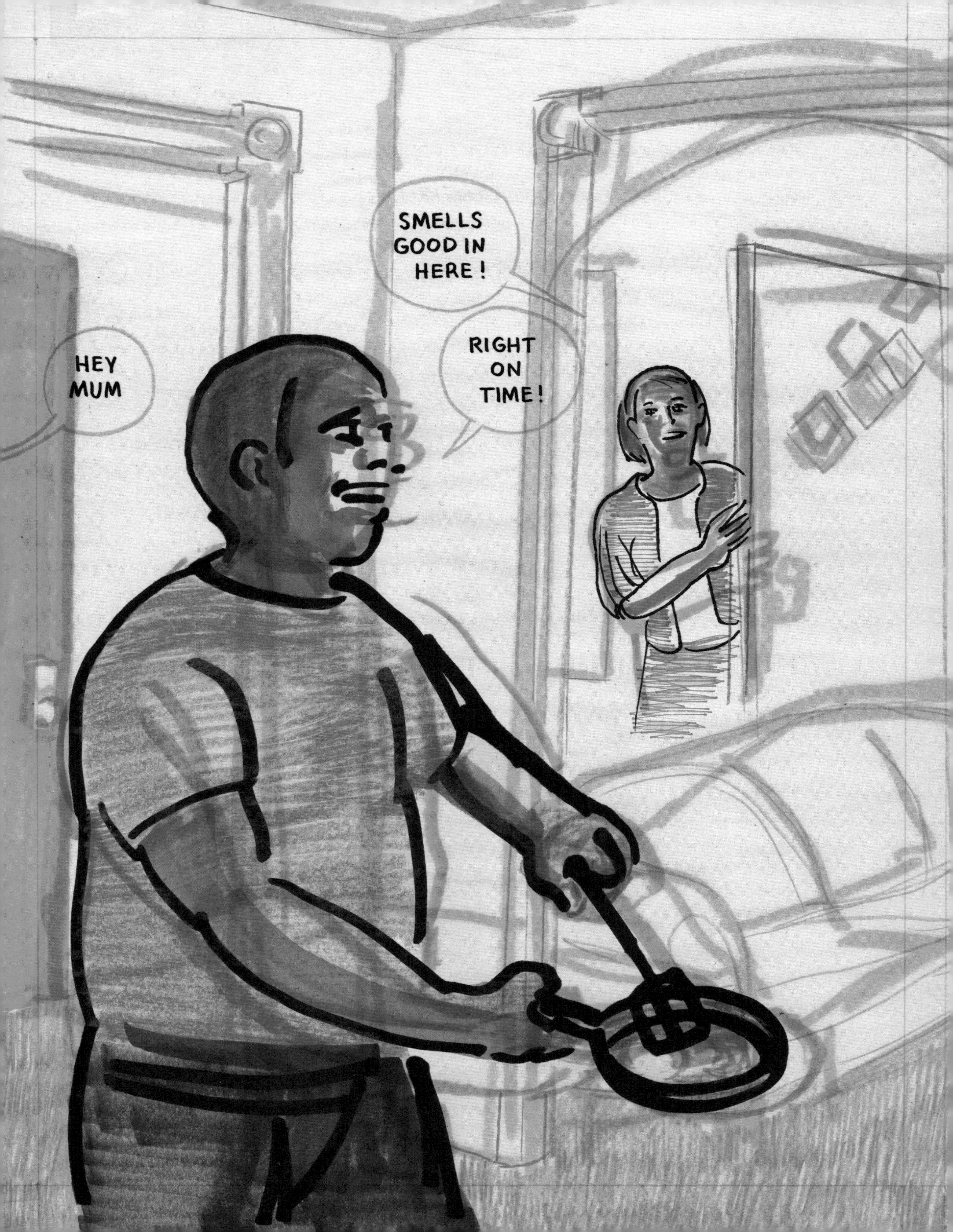
HEY MUM
SMELLS GOOD IN HERE!
RIGHT ON TIME!

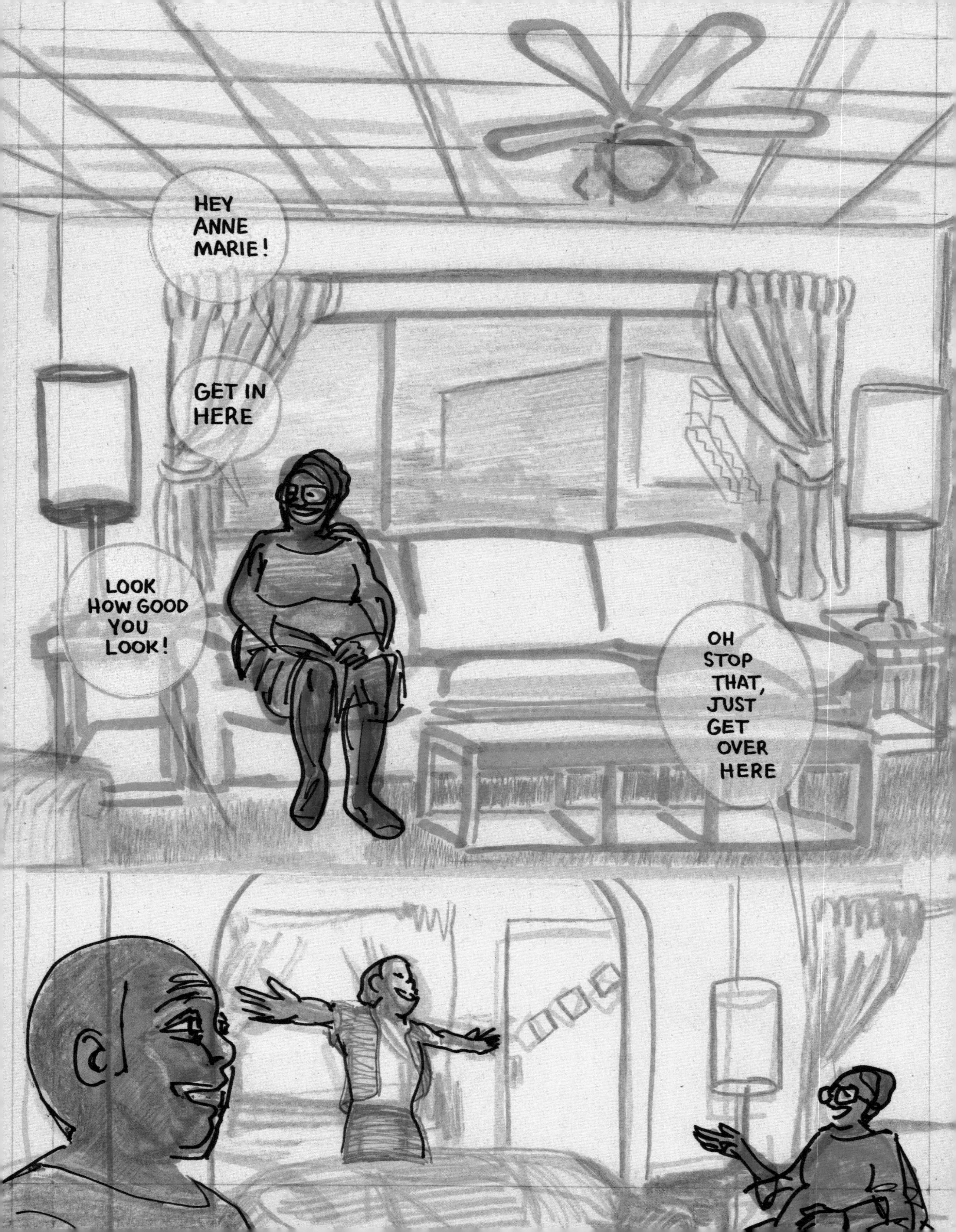
HEY ANNE MARIE!
GET IN HERE
LOOK HOW GOOD YOU LOOK!
OH STOP THAT, JUST GET OVER HERE

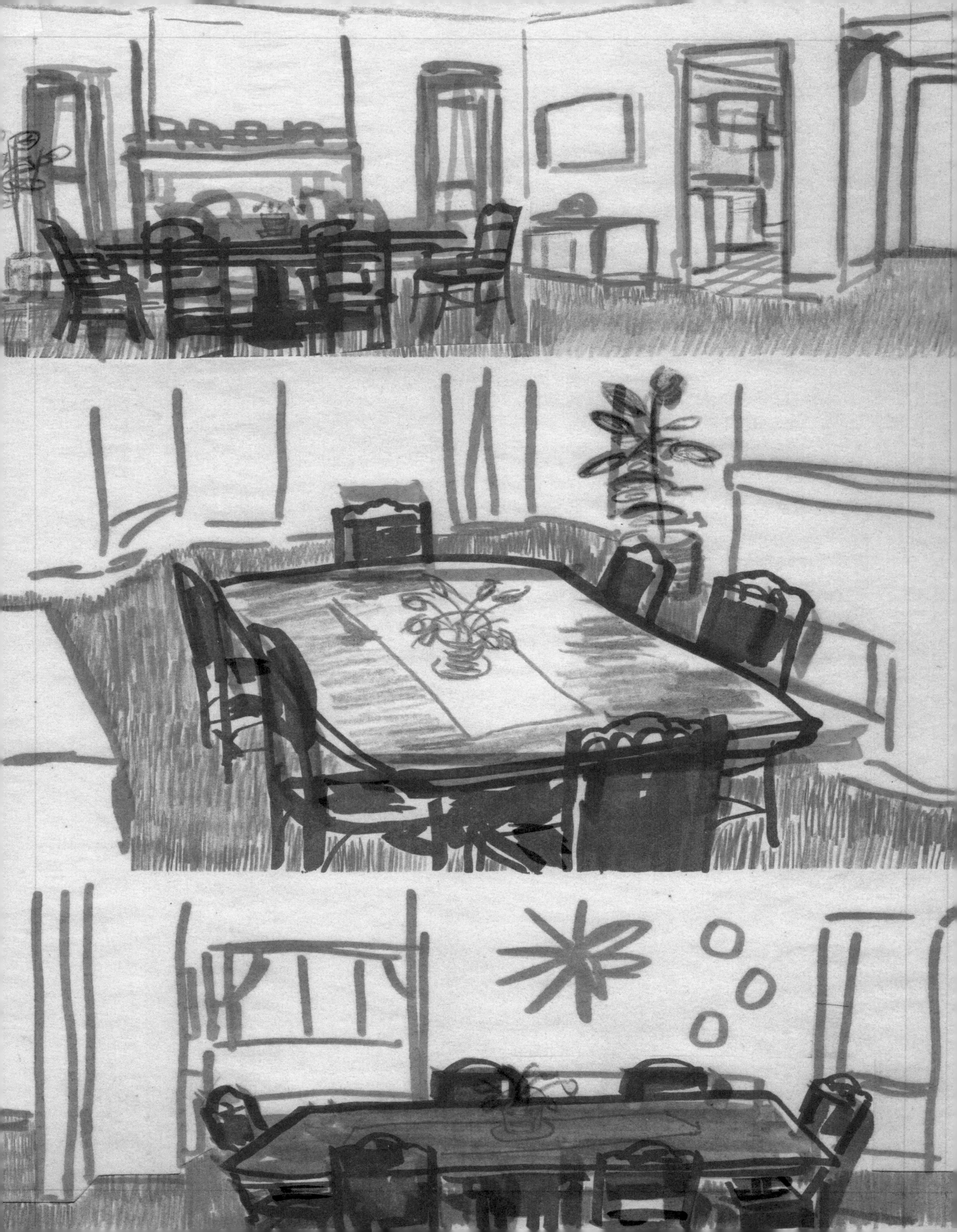

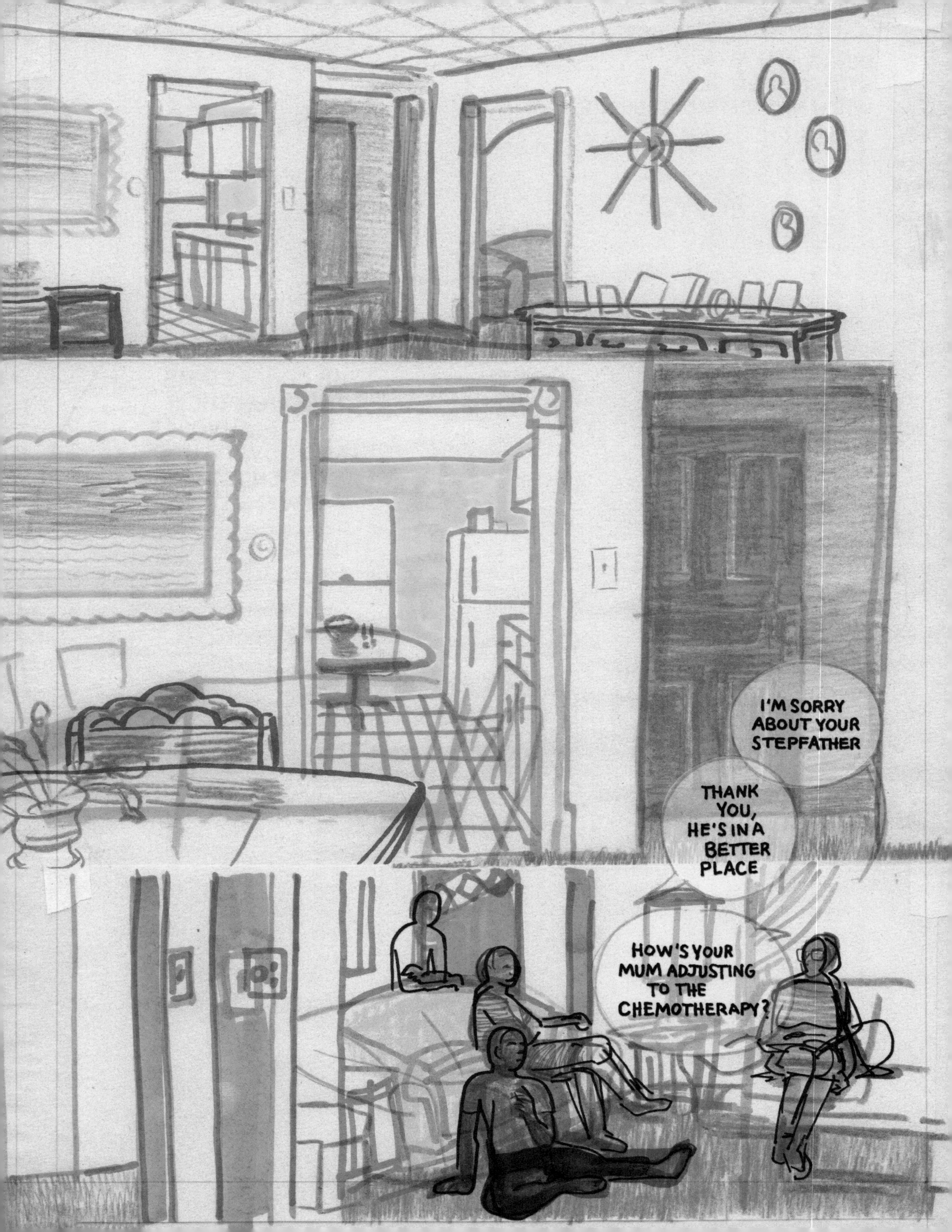
I'M SORRY ABOUT YOUR STEPFATHER
THANK YOU, HE'S IN A BETTER PLACE
HOW'S YOUR MUM ADJUSTING TO THE CHEMOTHERAPY?

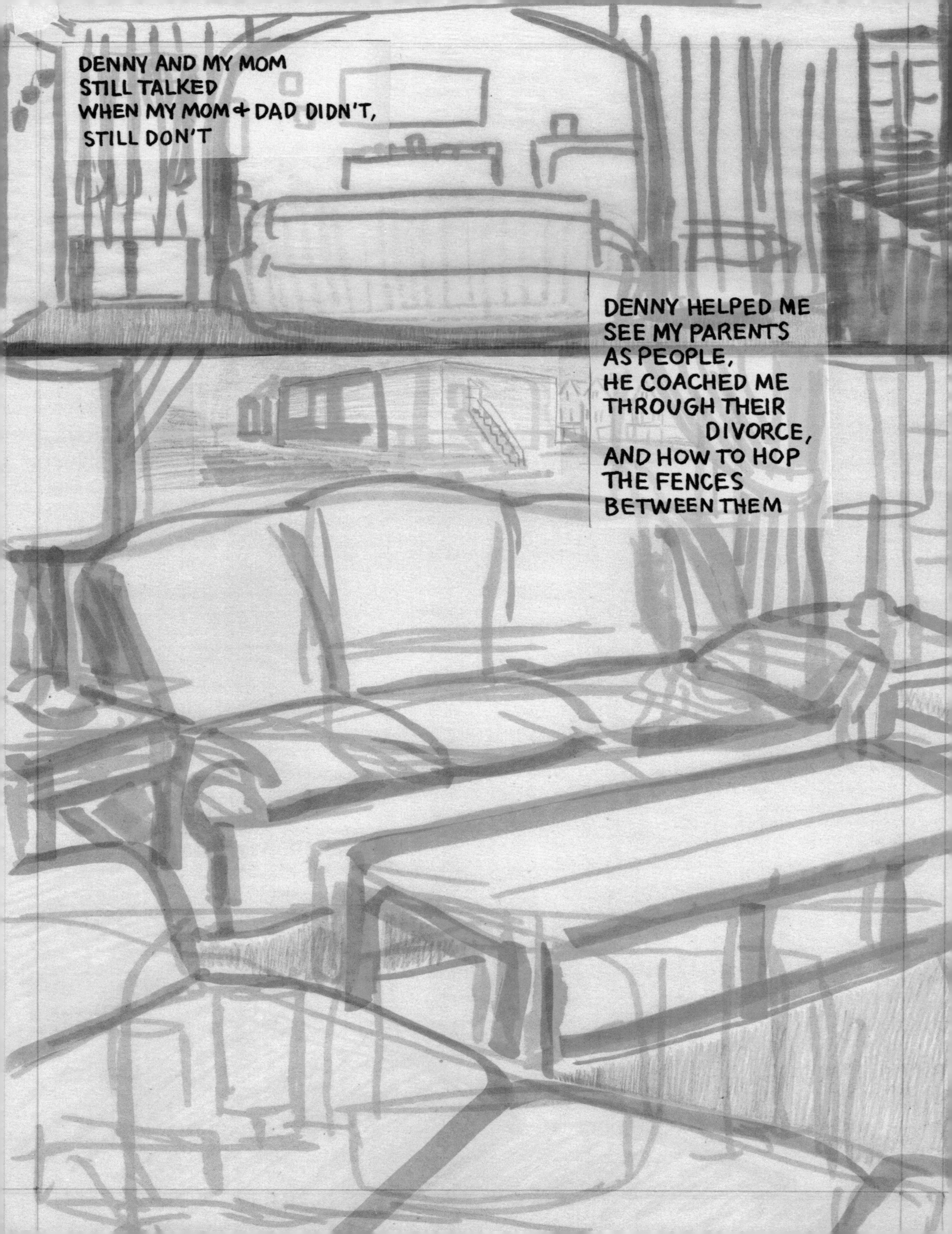
DENNY AND MY MOM STILL TALKED WHEN MY MOM & DAD DIDN'T, STILL DON'T
DENNY HELPED ME SEE MY PARENTS AS PEOPLE, HE COACHED ME THROUGH THEIR DIVORCE, AND HOW TO HOP THE FENCES BETWEEN THEM

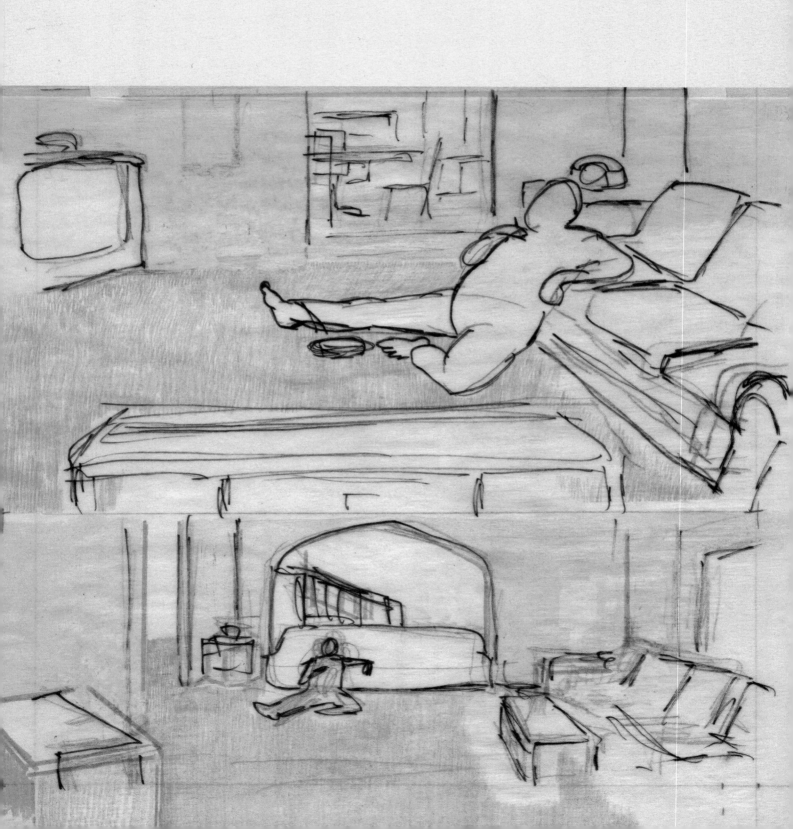

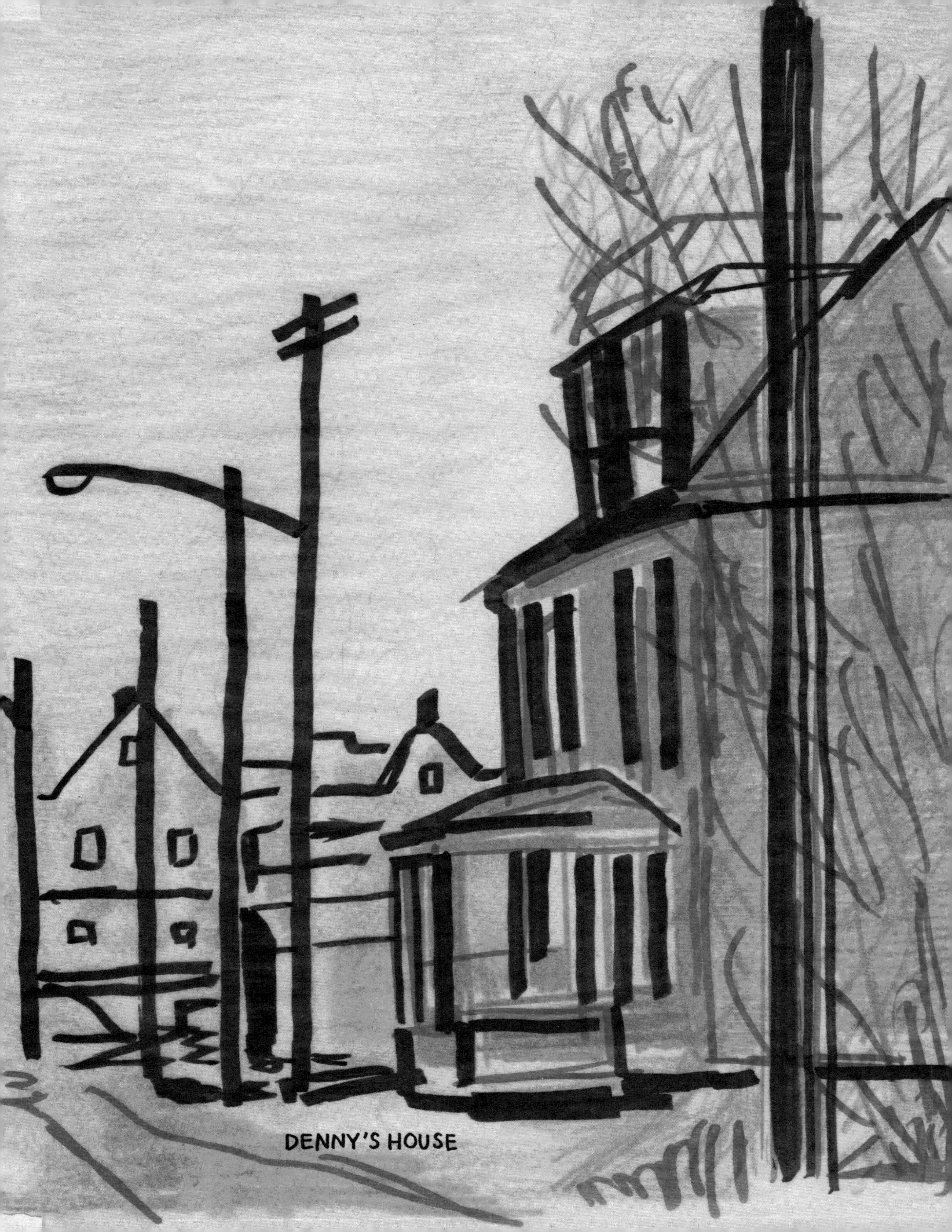

DENNY'S HOUSE

BOTH DENNY & MY MOM
STAYED CLOSE TO HOME
TO TAKE CARE OF FAMILY

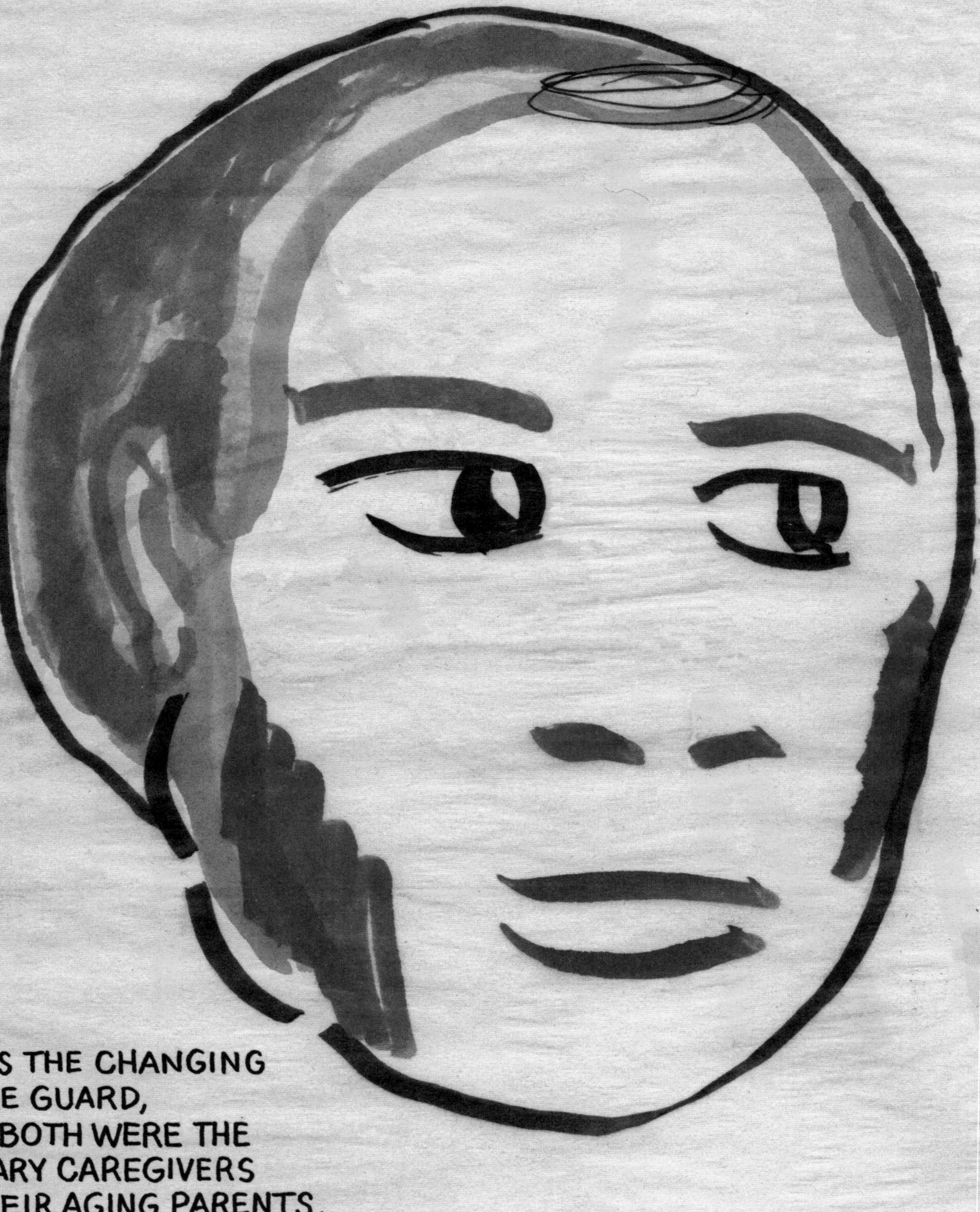

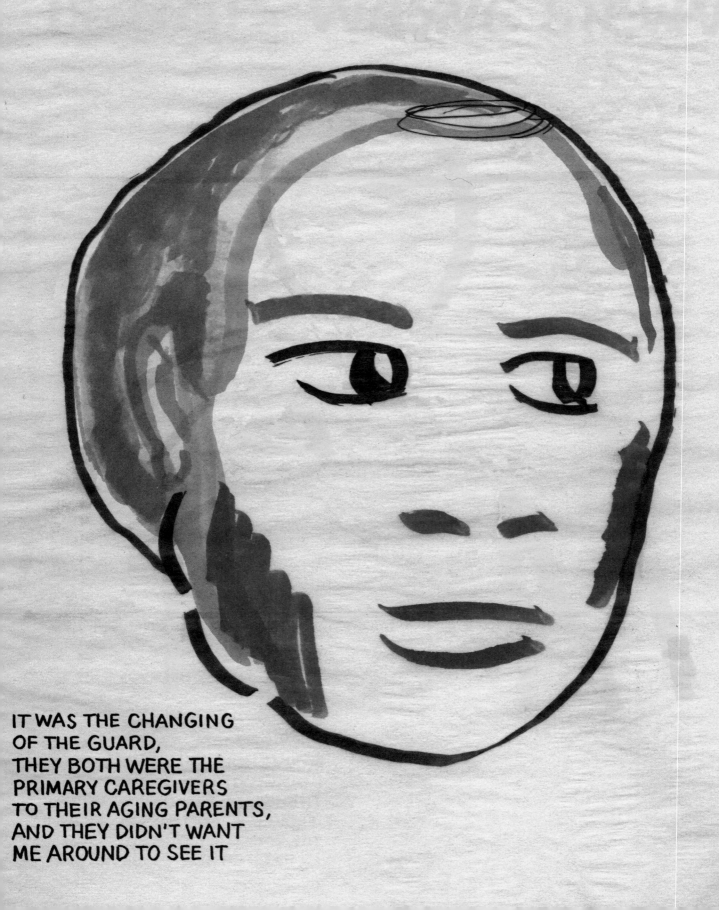

IT WAS THE CHANGING
OF THE GUARD,
THEY BOTH WERE THE
PRIMARY CAREGIVERS
TO THEIR AGING PARENTS,
AND THEY DIDN'T WANT
ME AROUND TO SEE IT

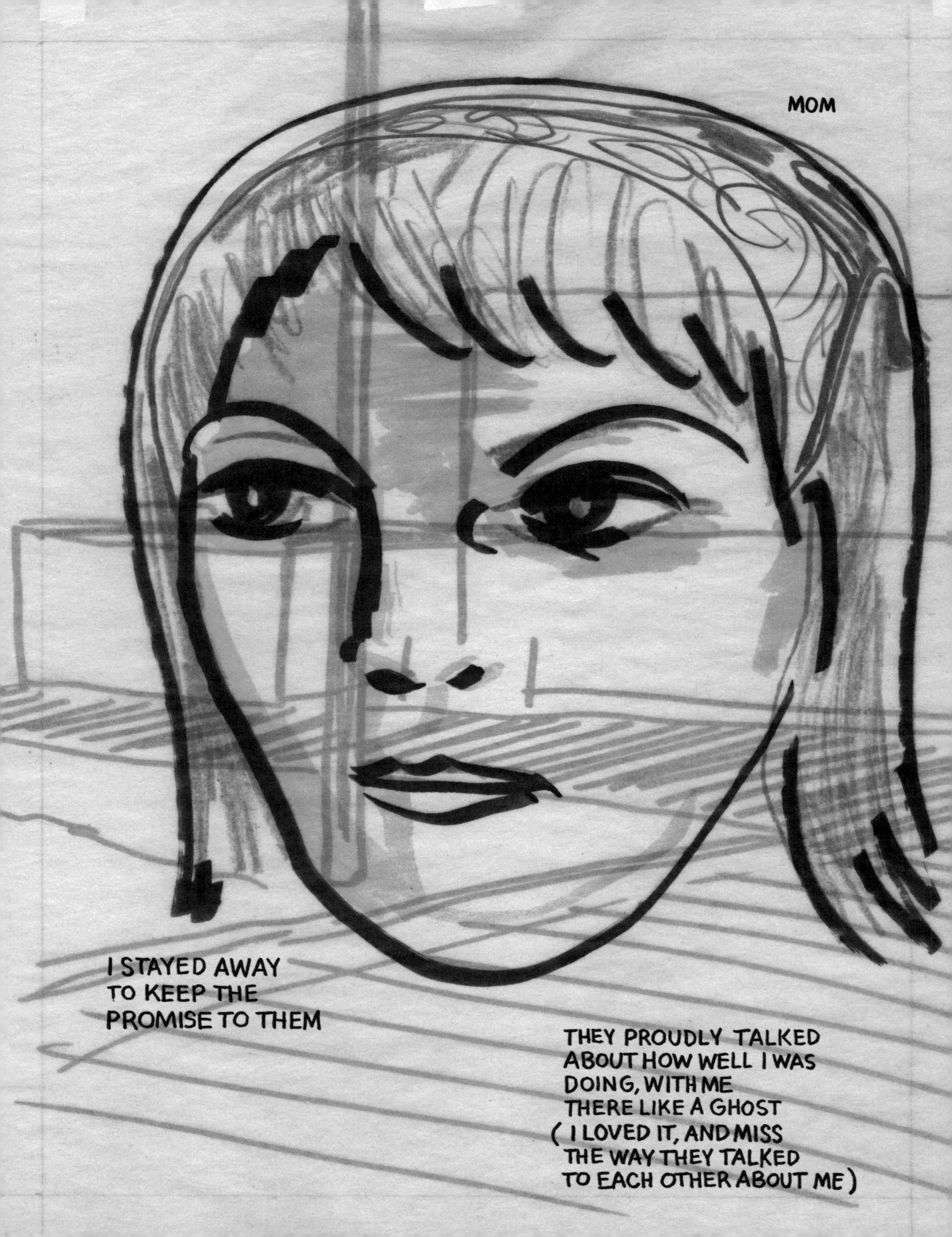
MOM
I STAYED AWAY TO KEEP THE PROMISE TO THEM
THEY PROUDLY TALKED ABOUT HOW WELL I WAS DOING, WITH ME THERE LIKE A GHOST (I LOVED IT, AND MISS THE WAY THEY TALKED TO EACH OTHER ABOUT ME)

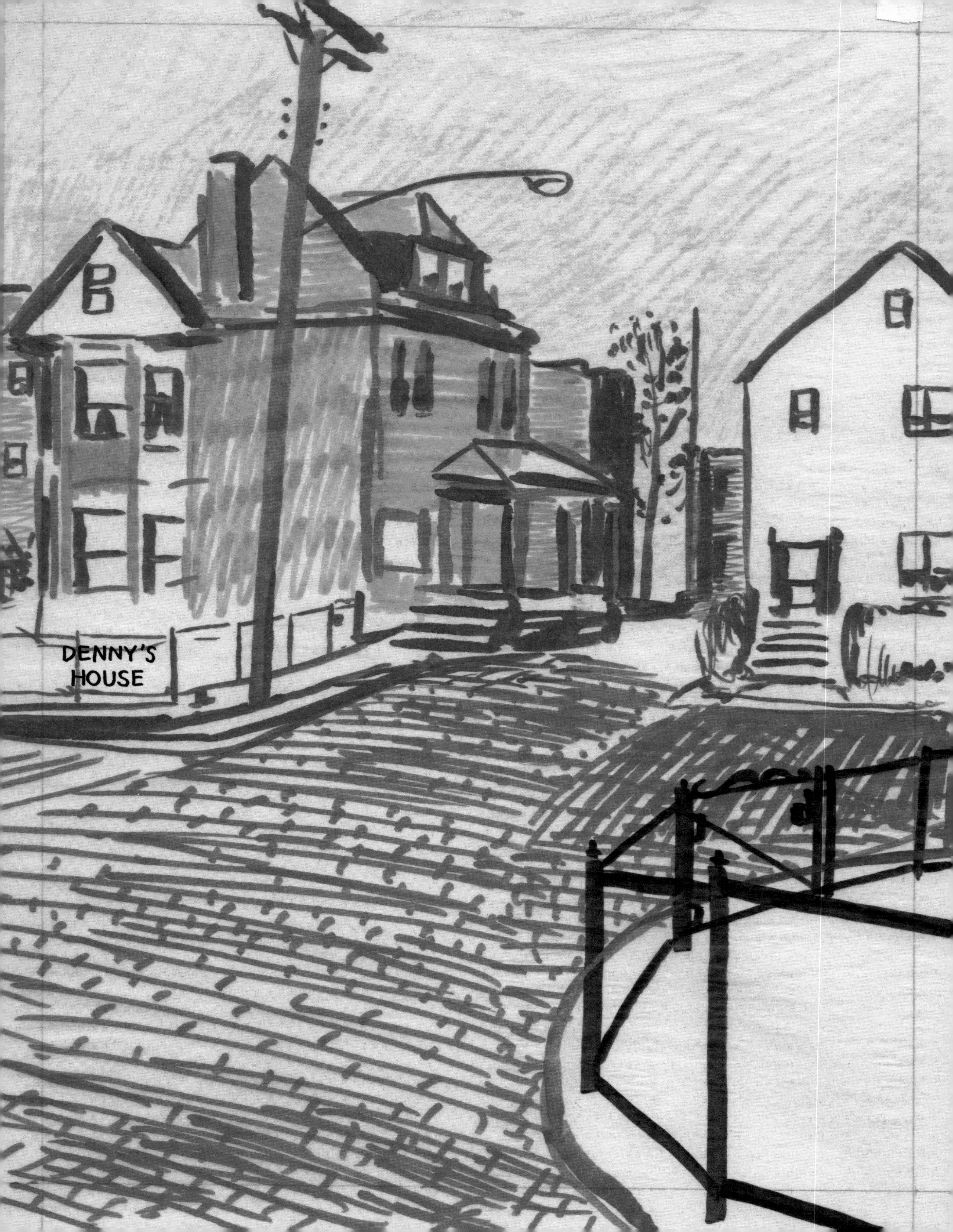
DENNY'S
HOUSE

FRANKIE
(MY DAD)

ANNE MARIE
(MY MUM)

JUNIOR
(ME)

PRETZEL!

I WAS THE FIRST GRANDCHILD ON BOTH SIDES,
SPOILED ROTTEN FOR BLUE COLLAR PITTSBURGH STANDARDS

MY MOM'S BROTHERS, MY UNCLES, WOULD REMIND ME
OF HOW EASY I HAD IT WHEN THEY GOT DRUNK,
THEIR BITTERNESS ABOUT LOSING THEIR REAL DAD
WAS HIDDEN FROM ME BENEATH THEIR ANTICS

LIKE THE TIME THEY SHOT ARROWS OFF OF THE PORCH
AT MIDNIGHT, INTO THE ALLEYWAY GARBAGE CANS

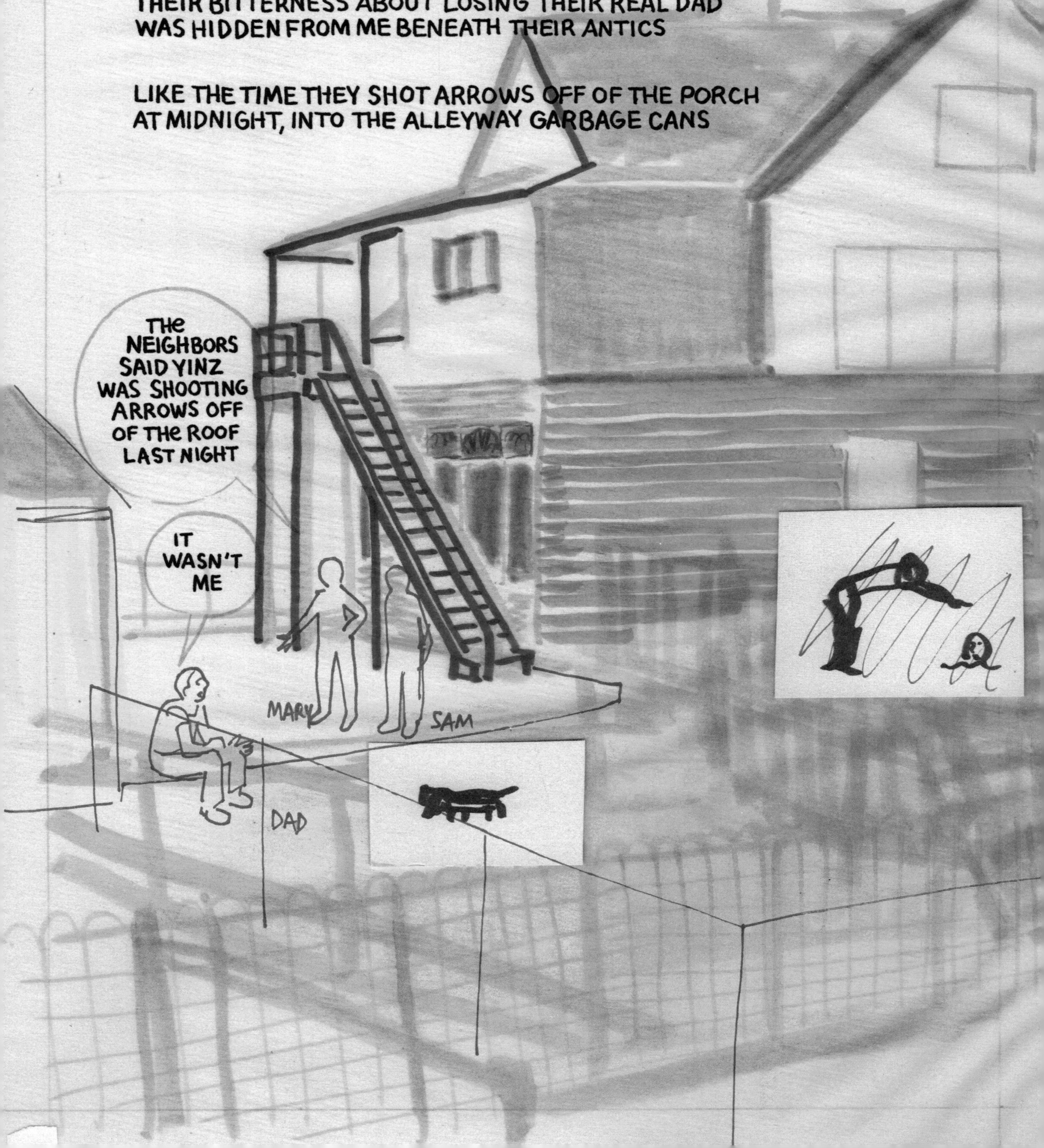
THE NEIGHBORS SAID YINZ WAS SHOOTING ARROWS OFF OF THE ROOF LAST NIGHT
IT WASN'T ME
MARY
SAM
DAD

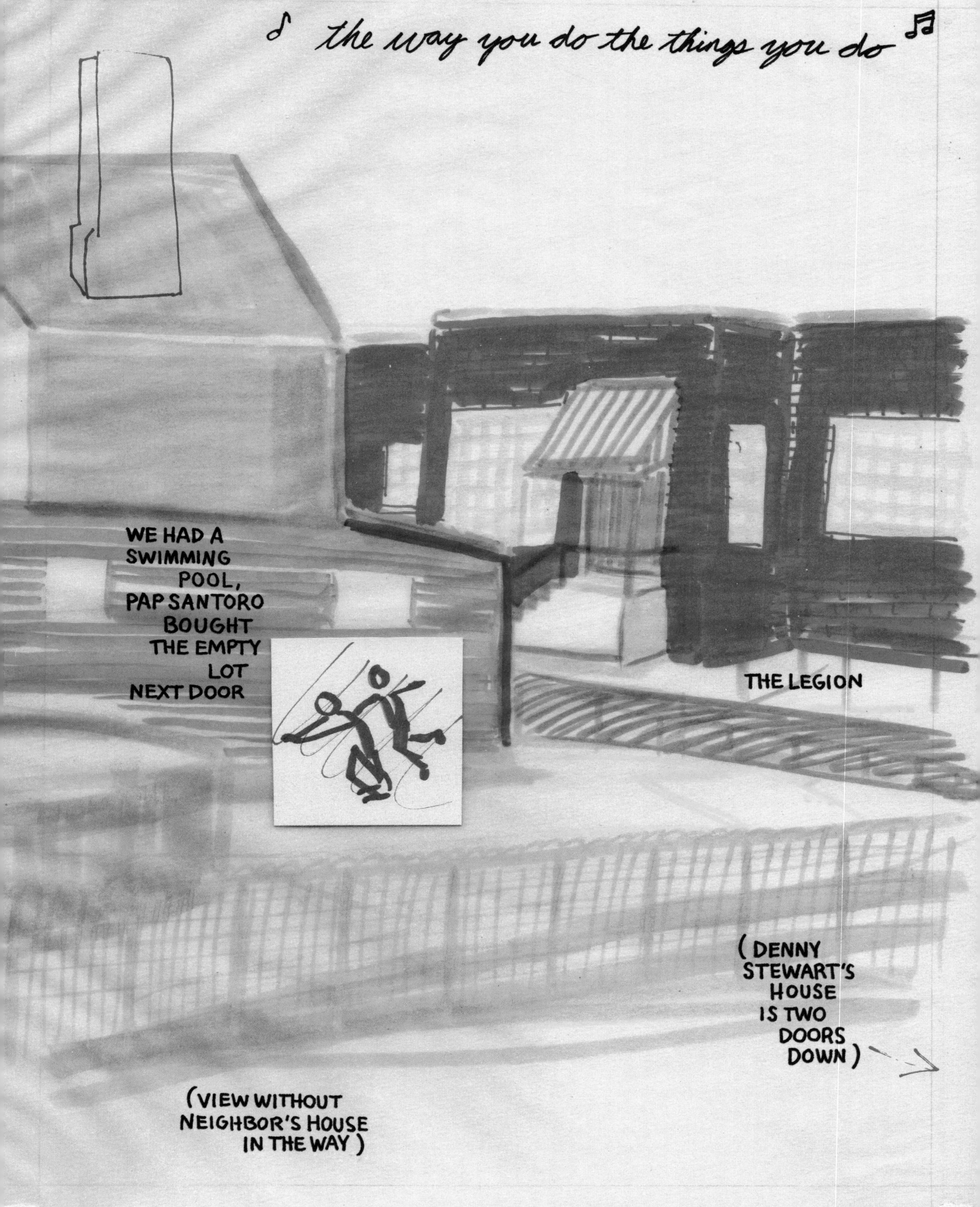
the way you do the things you do
WE HAD A SWIMMING POOL, PAP SANTORO BOUGHT THE EMPTY LOT NEXT DOOR
THE LEGION
(DENNY STEWART'S HOUSE IS TWO DOORS DOWN)
(VIEW WITHOUT NEIGHBOR'S HOUSE IN THE WAY)

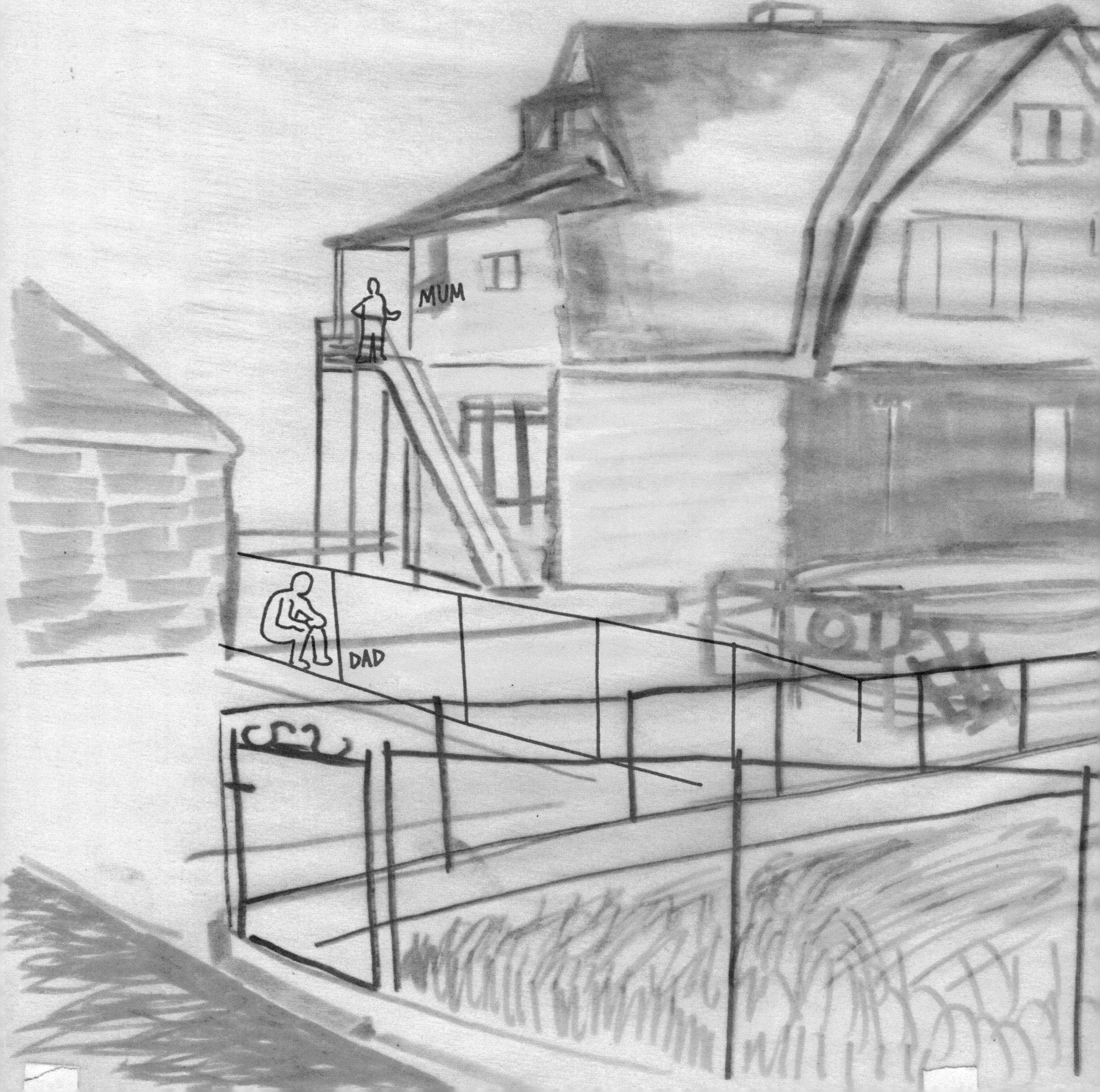
MUM
DAD

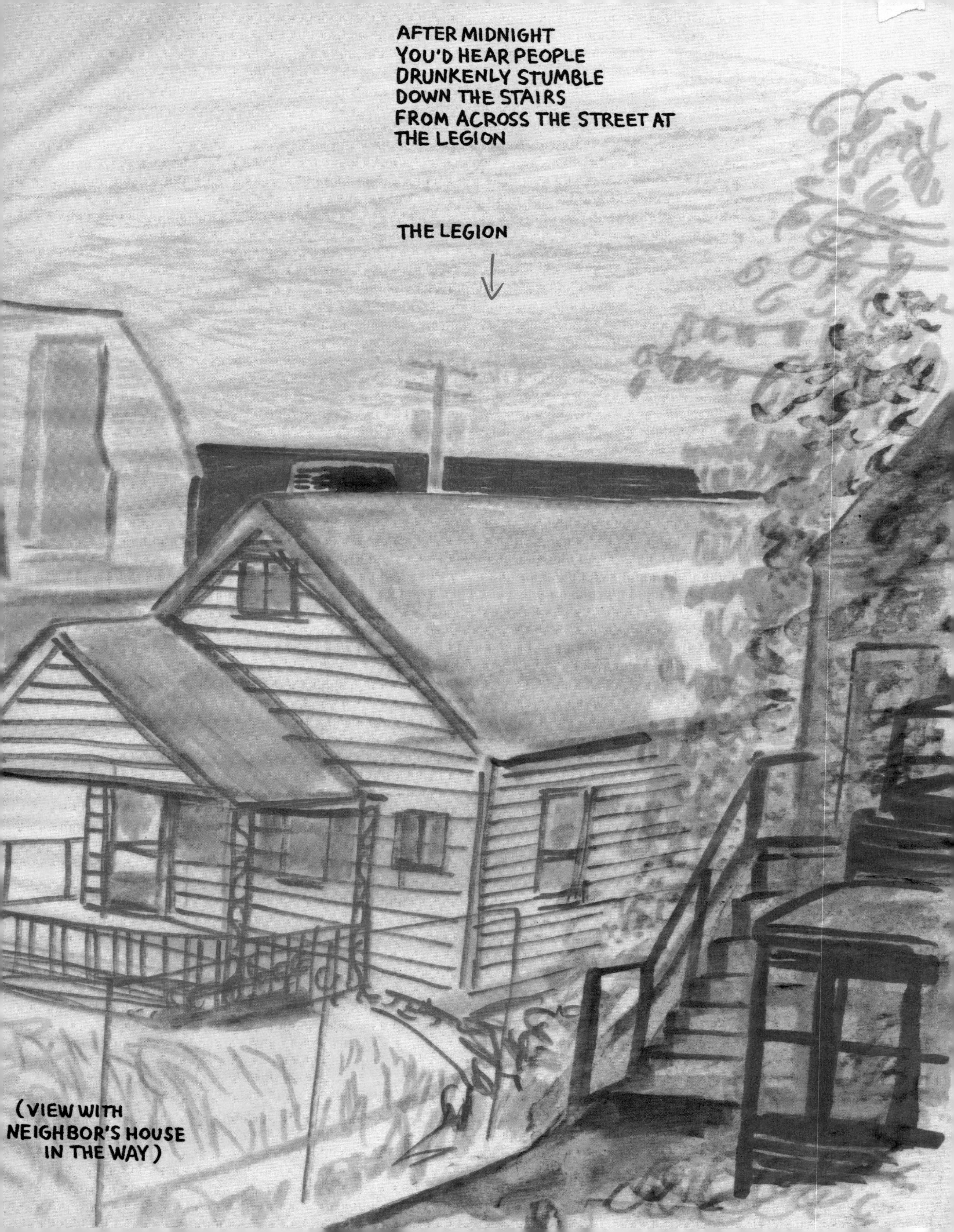
AFTER MIDNIGHT
YOU'D HEAR PEOPLE
DRUNKENLY STUMBLE
DOWN THE STAIRS
FROM ACROSS THE STREET AT
THE LEGION
THE LEGION
(VIEW WITH
NEIGHBOR'S HOUSE
IN THE WAY)

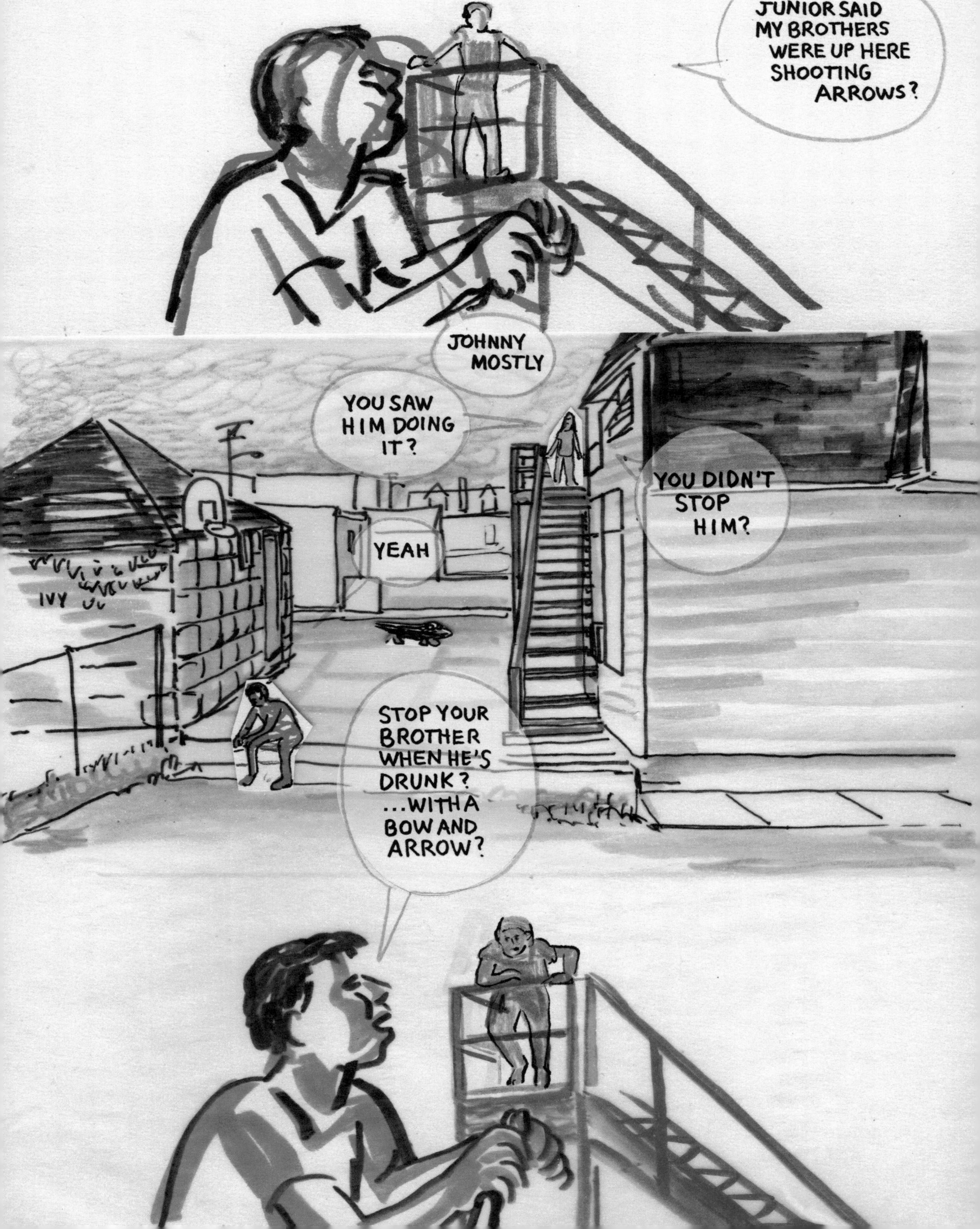
JUNIOR SAID MY BROTHERS WERE UP HERE SHOOTING ARROWS?
JOHNNY MOSTLY
YOU SAW HIM DOING IT?
YEAH
YOU DIDN'T STOP HIM?
IVY
STOP YOUR BROTHER WHEN HE'S DRUNK? ...WITH A BOW AND ARROW?

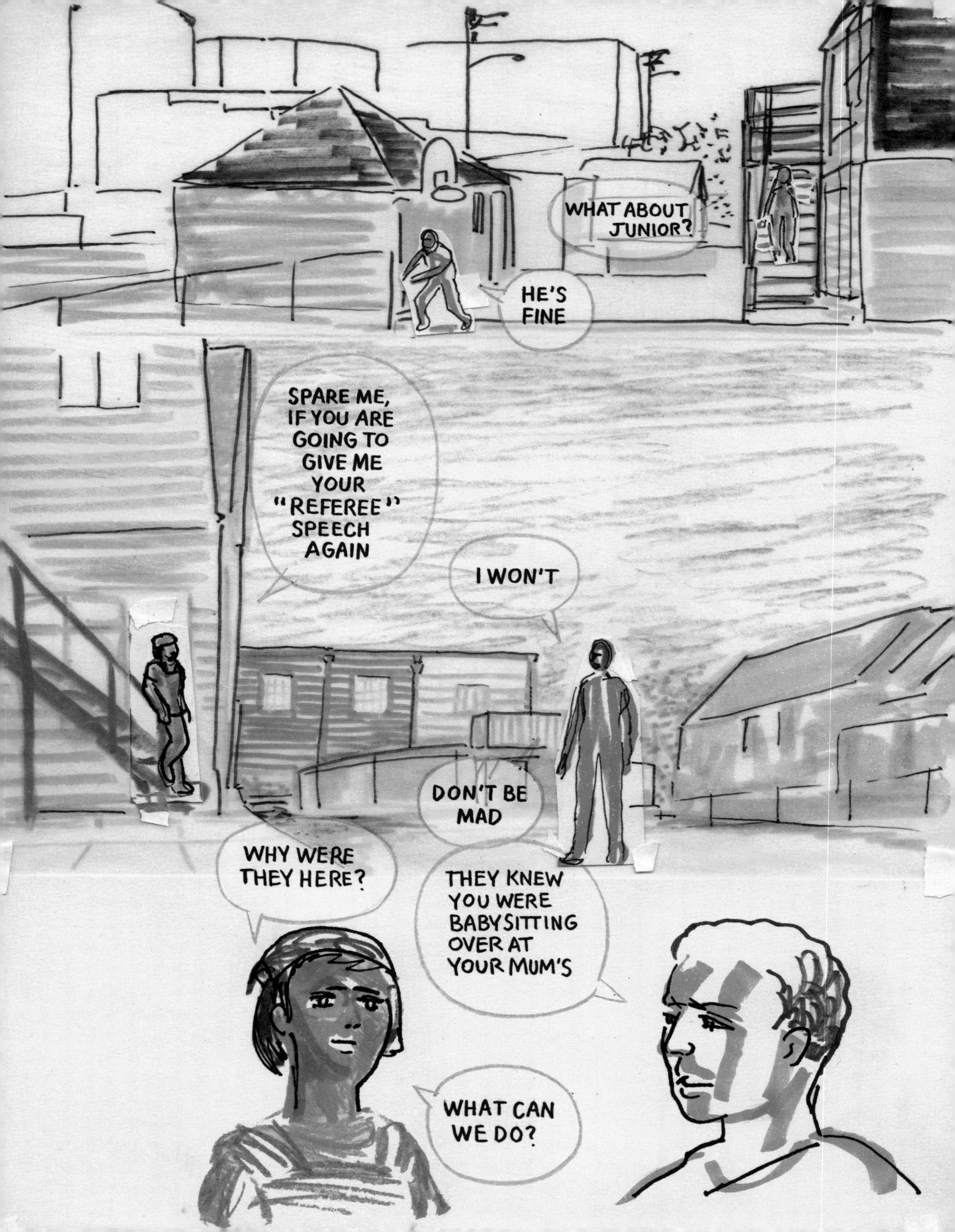
WHAT ABOUT JUNIOR?
HE'S FINE
SPARE ME, IF YOU ARE GOING TO GIVE ME YOUR "REFEREE" SPEECH AGAIN
I WON'T
DON'T BE MAD
WHY WERE THEY HERE?
THEY KNEW YOU WERE BABYSITTING OVER AT YOUR MUM'S
WHAT CAN WE DO?

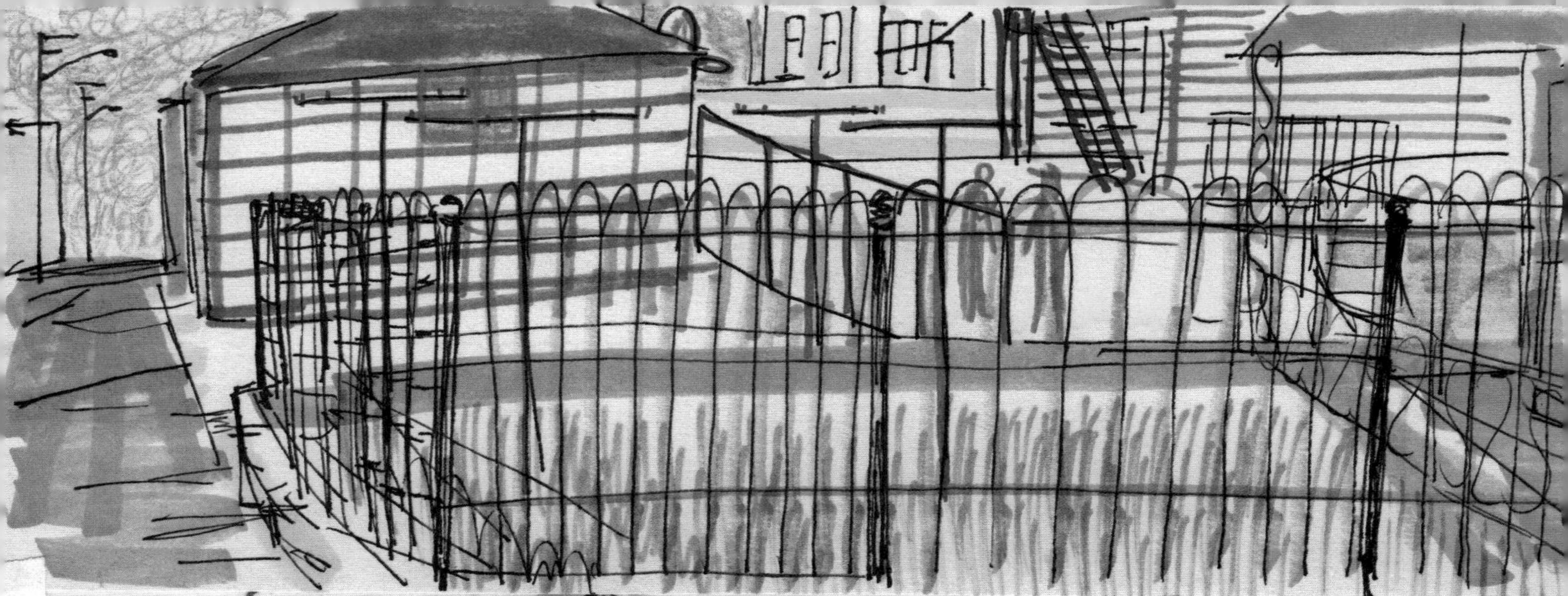

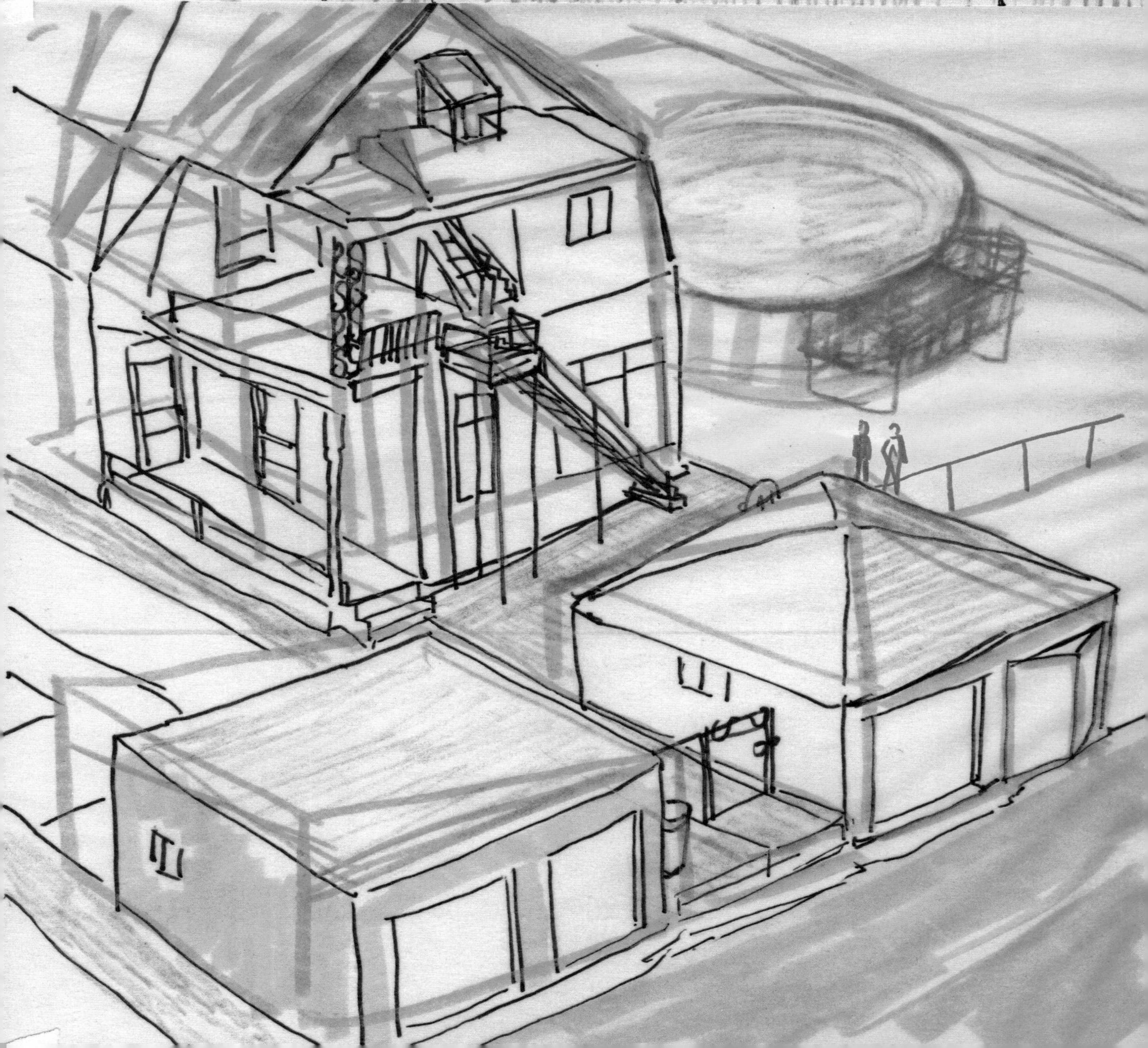

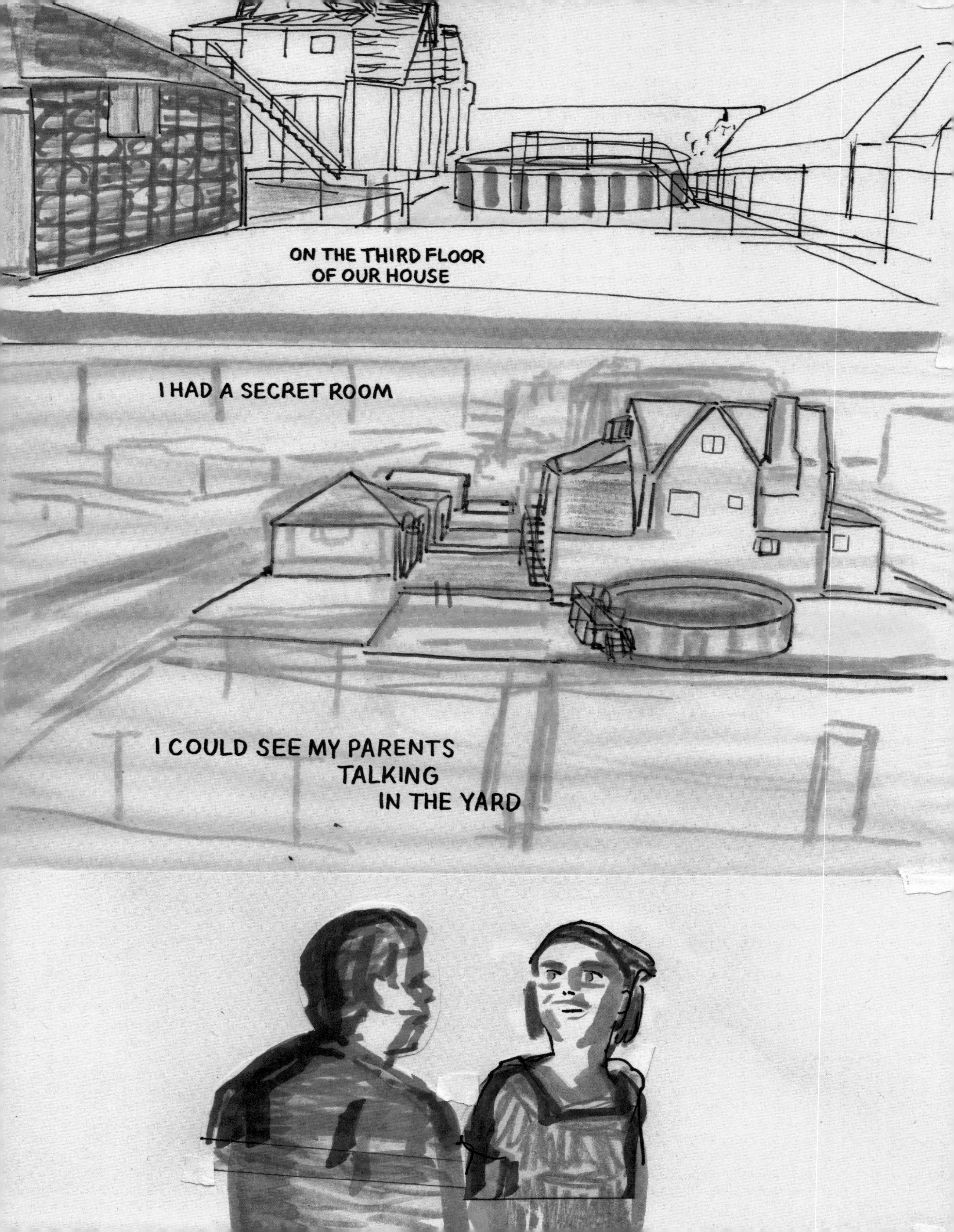
ON THE THIRD FLOOR OF OUR HOUSE
I HAD A SECRET ROOM
I COULD SEE MY PARENTS TALKING IN THE YARD

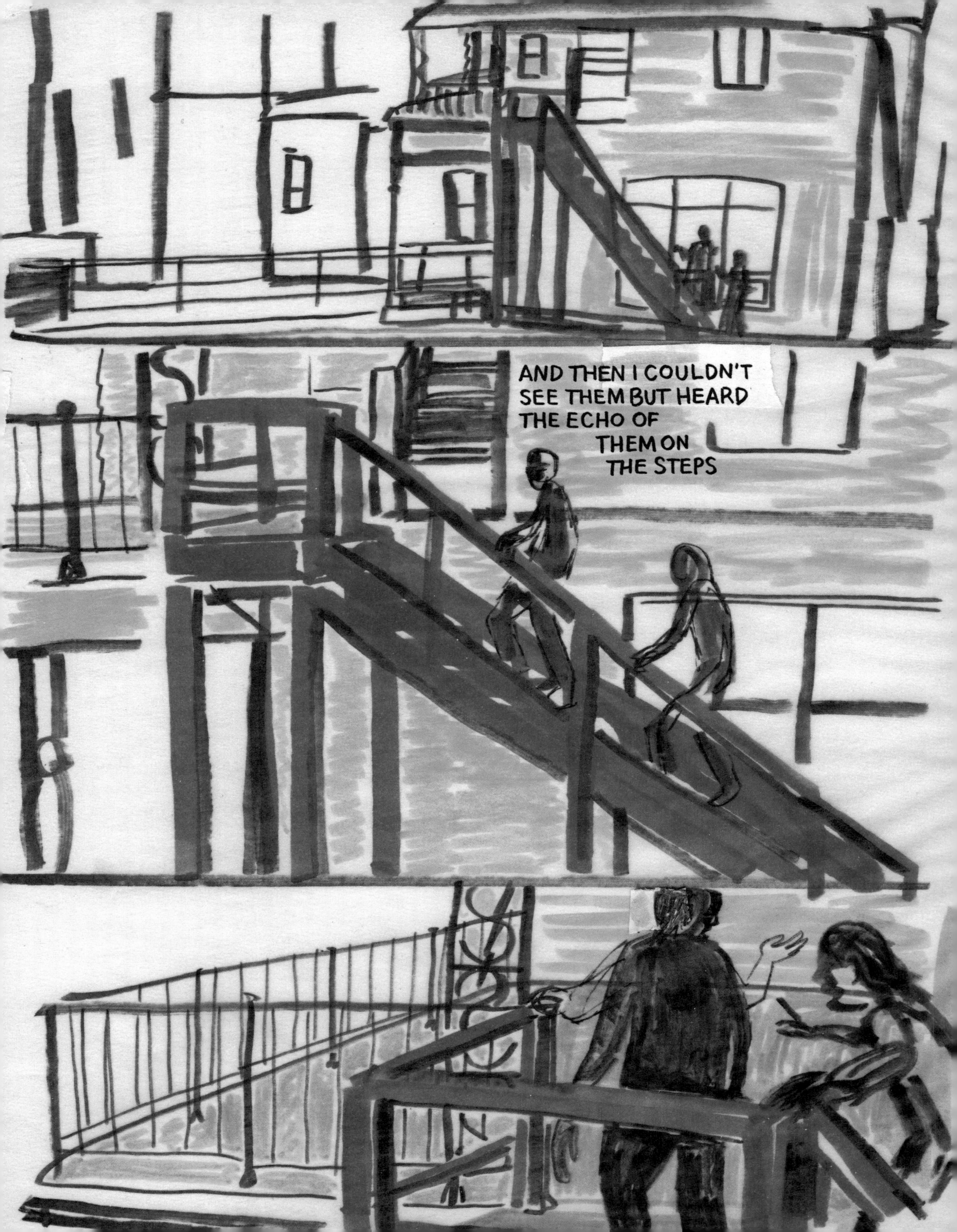
AND THEN I COULDN'T SEE THEM BUT HEARD THE ECHO OF THEM ON THE STEPS

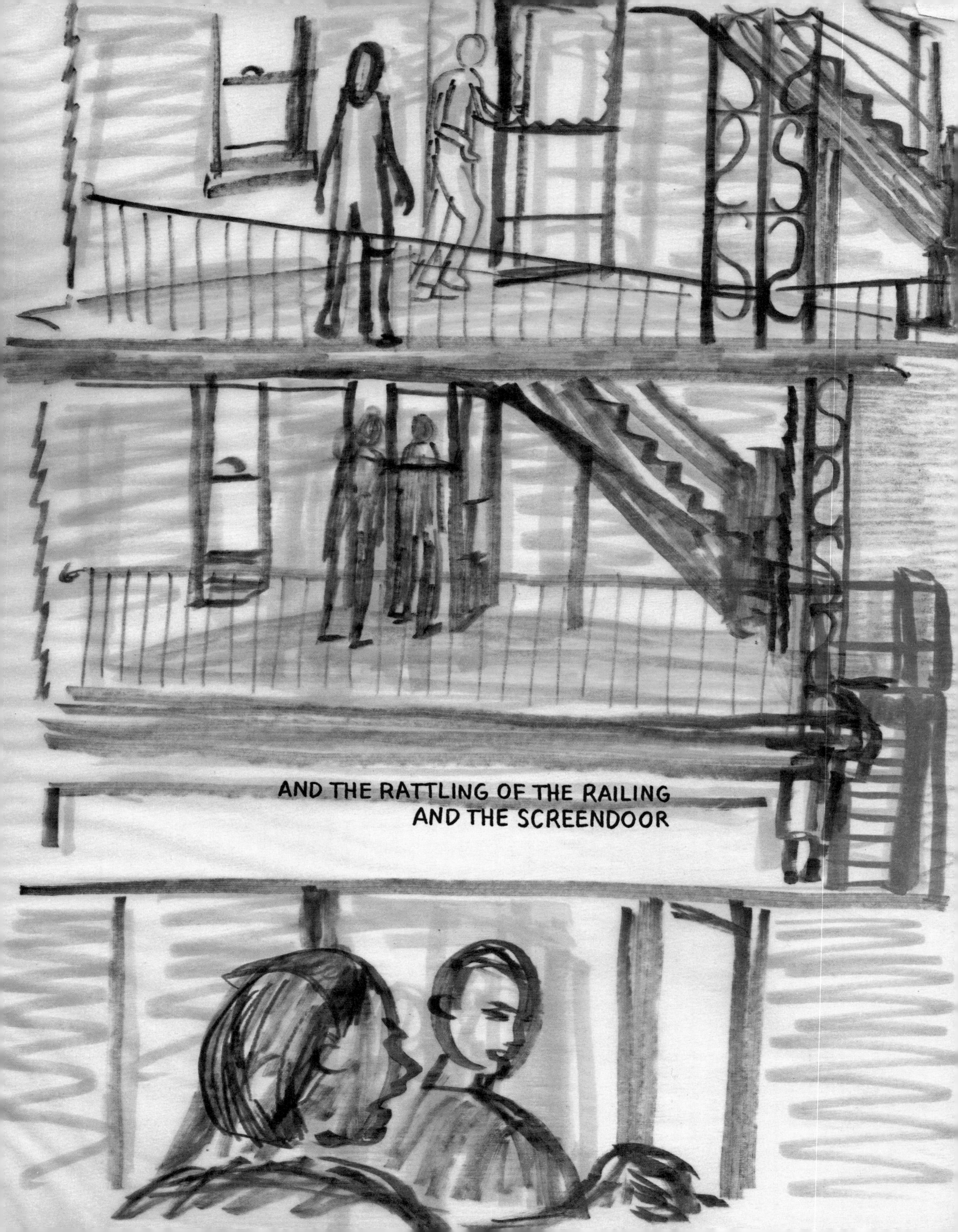
AND THE RATTLING OF THE RAILING
AND THE SCREENDOOR

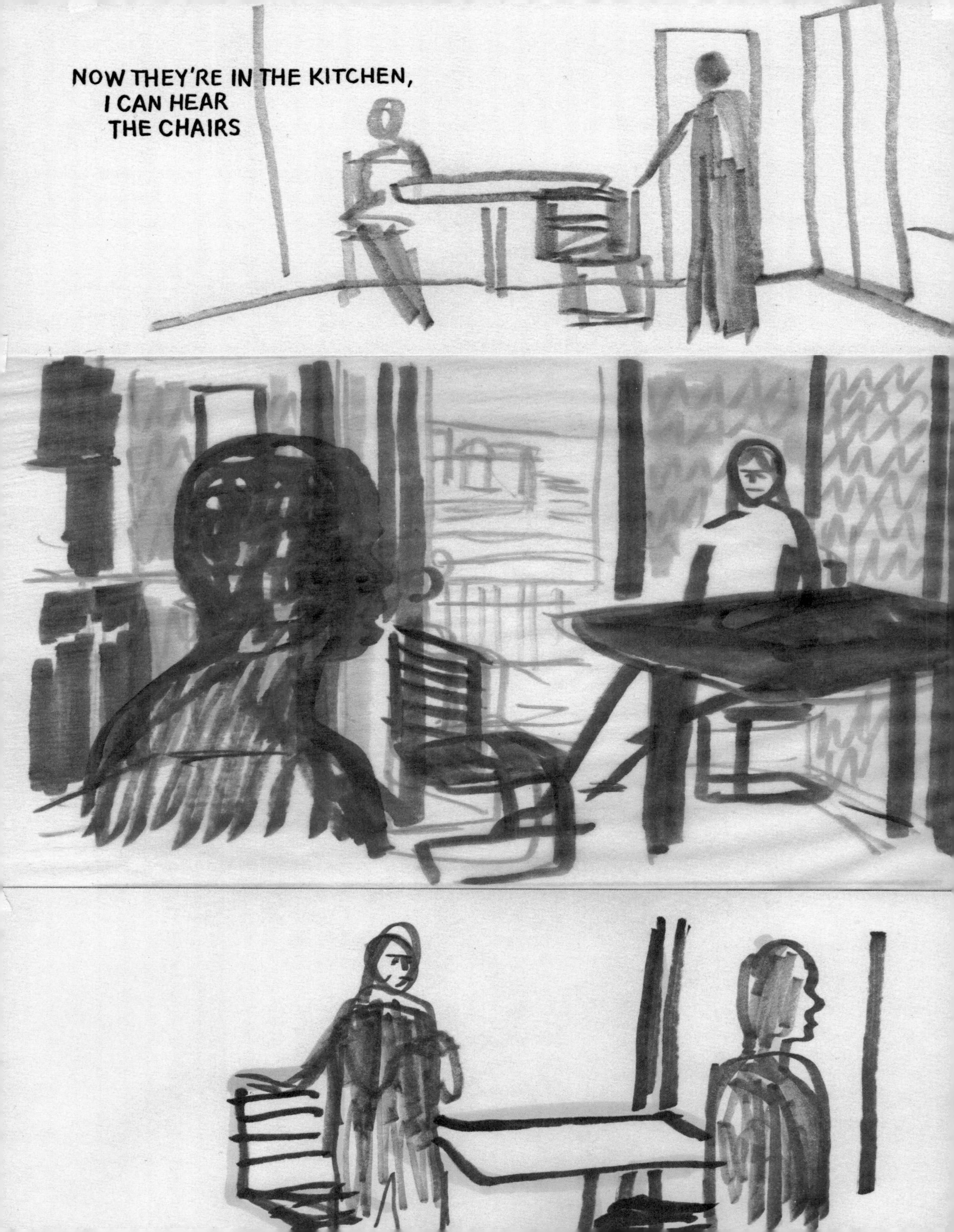
NOW THEY'RE IN THE KITCHEN, I CAN HEAR THE CHAIRS

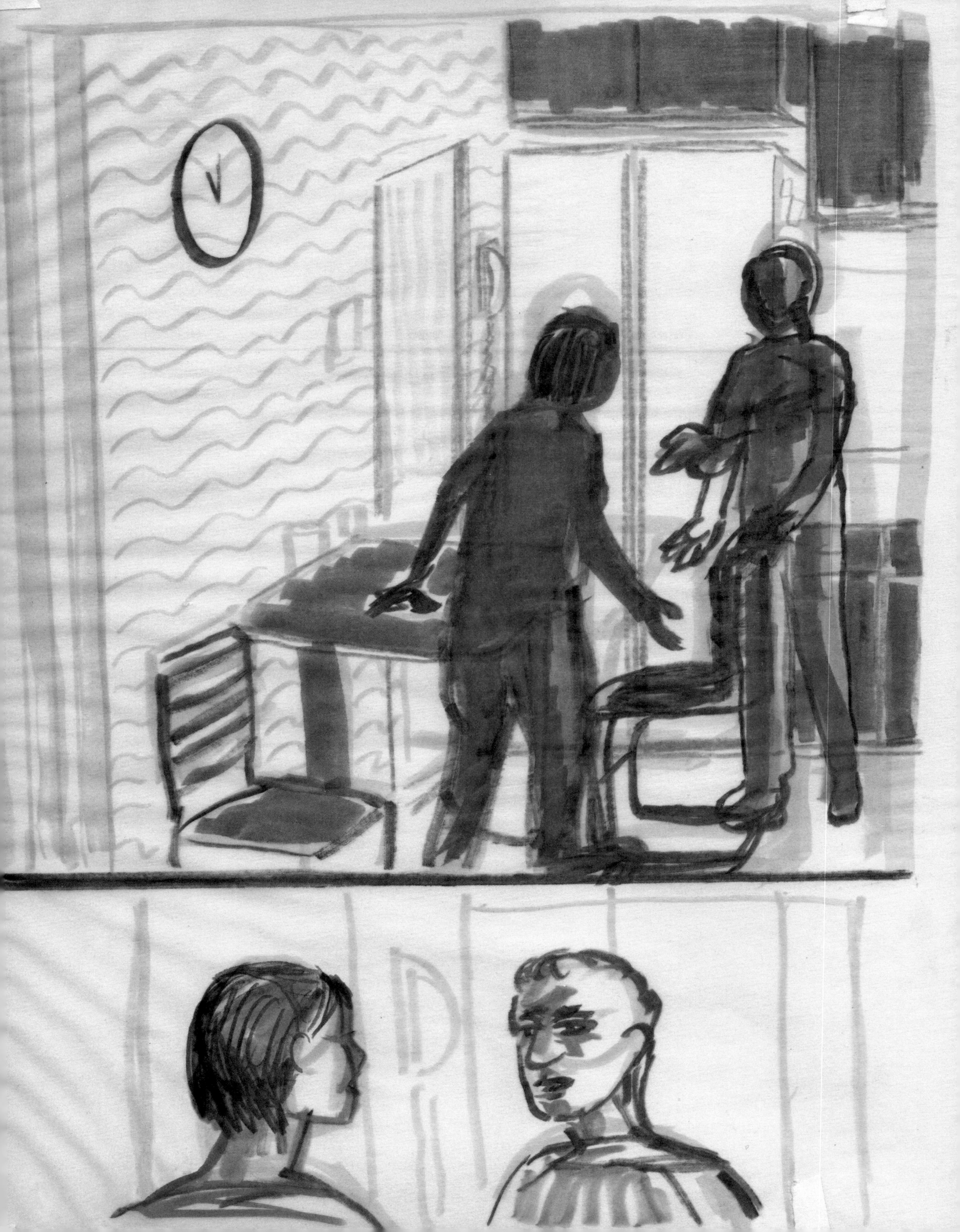

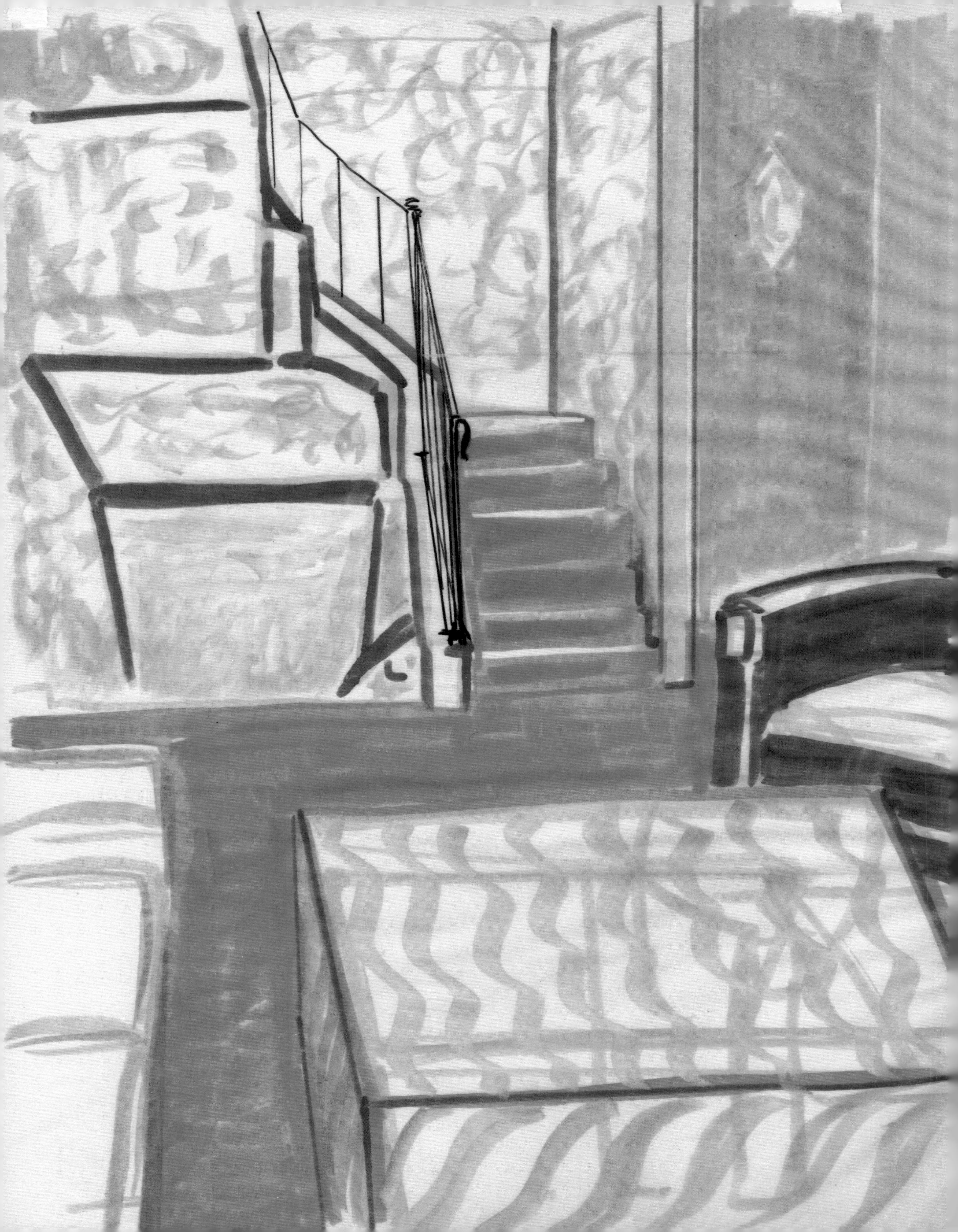

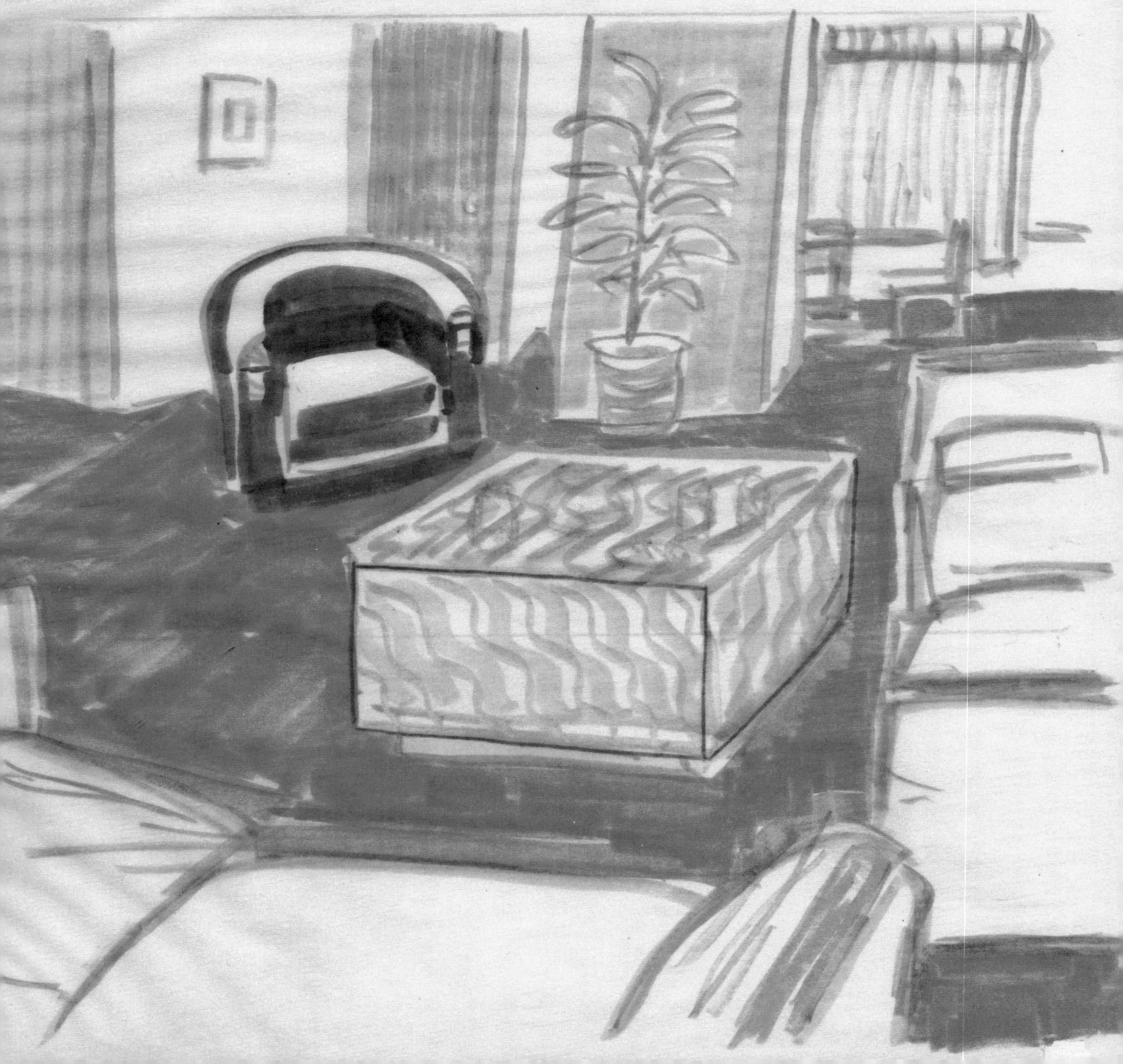

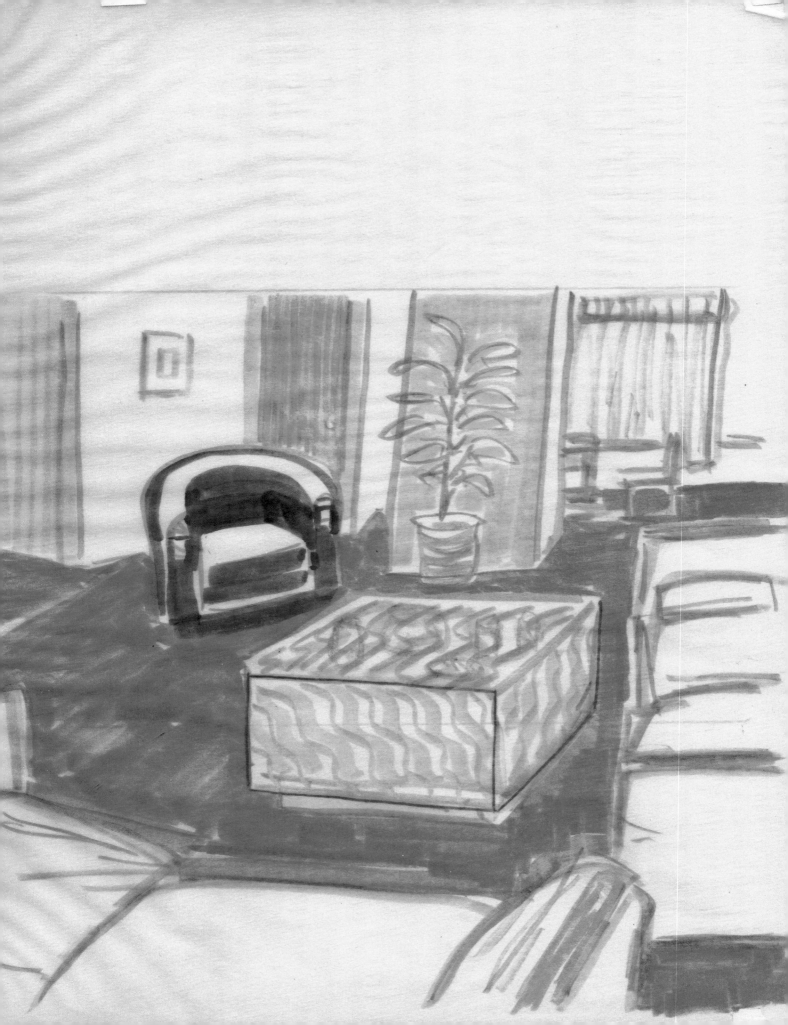

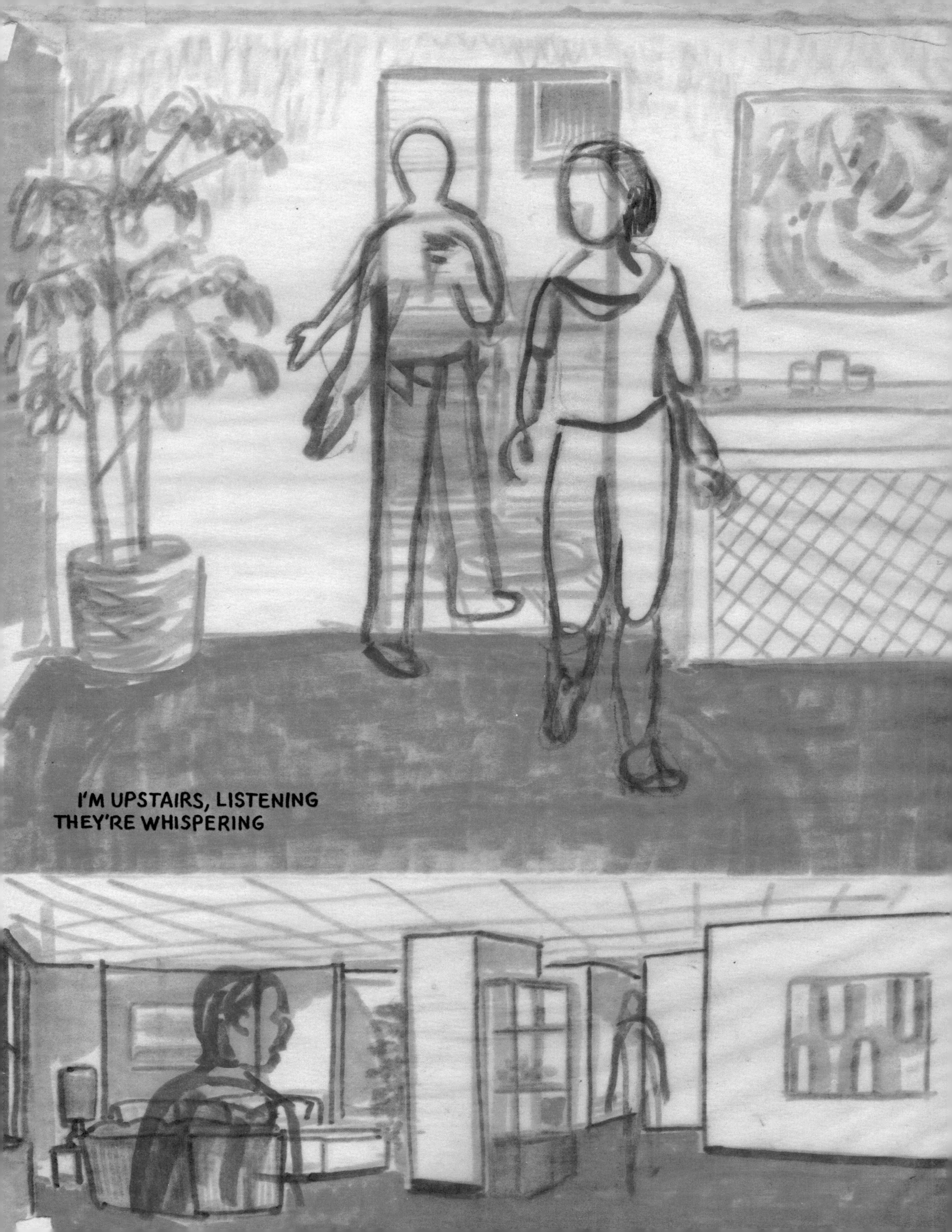
I'M UPSTAIRS, LISTENING
THEY'RE WHISPERING

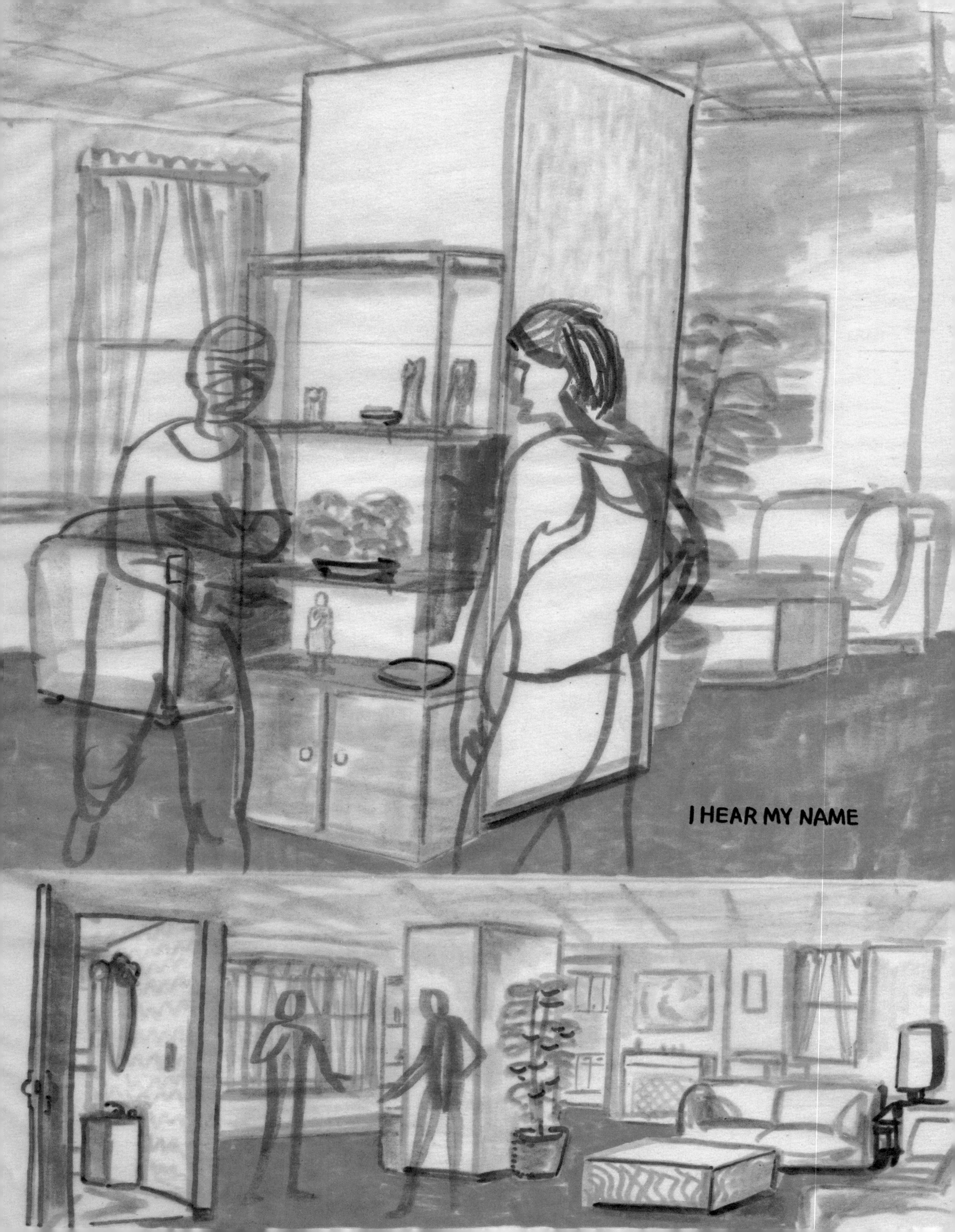
I HEAR MY NAME

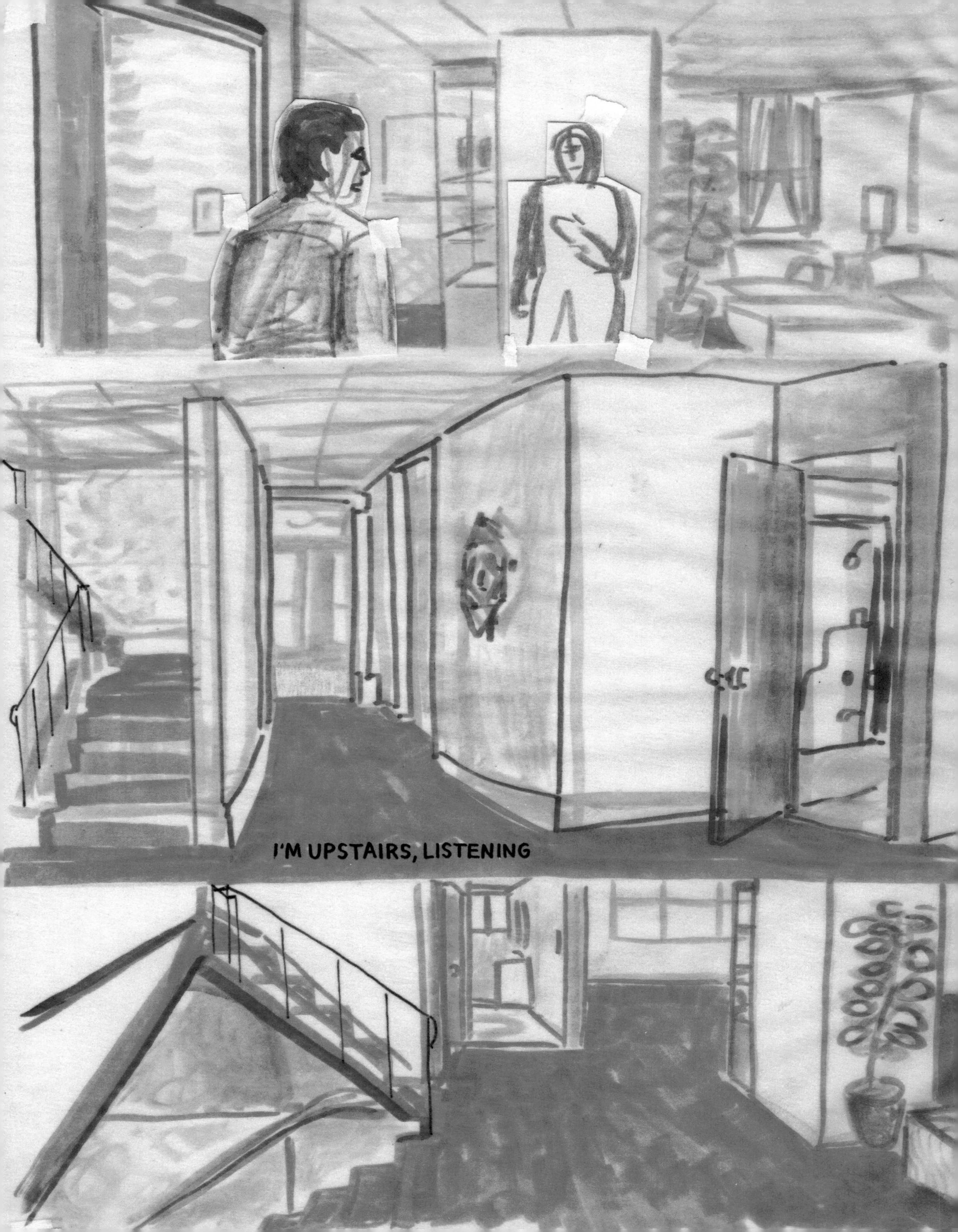
I'M UPSTAIRS, LISTENING

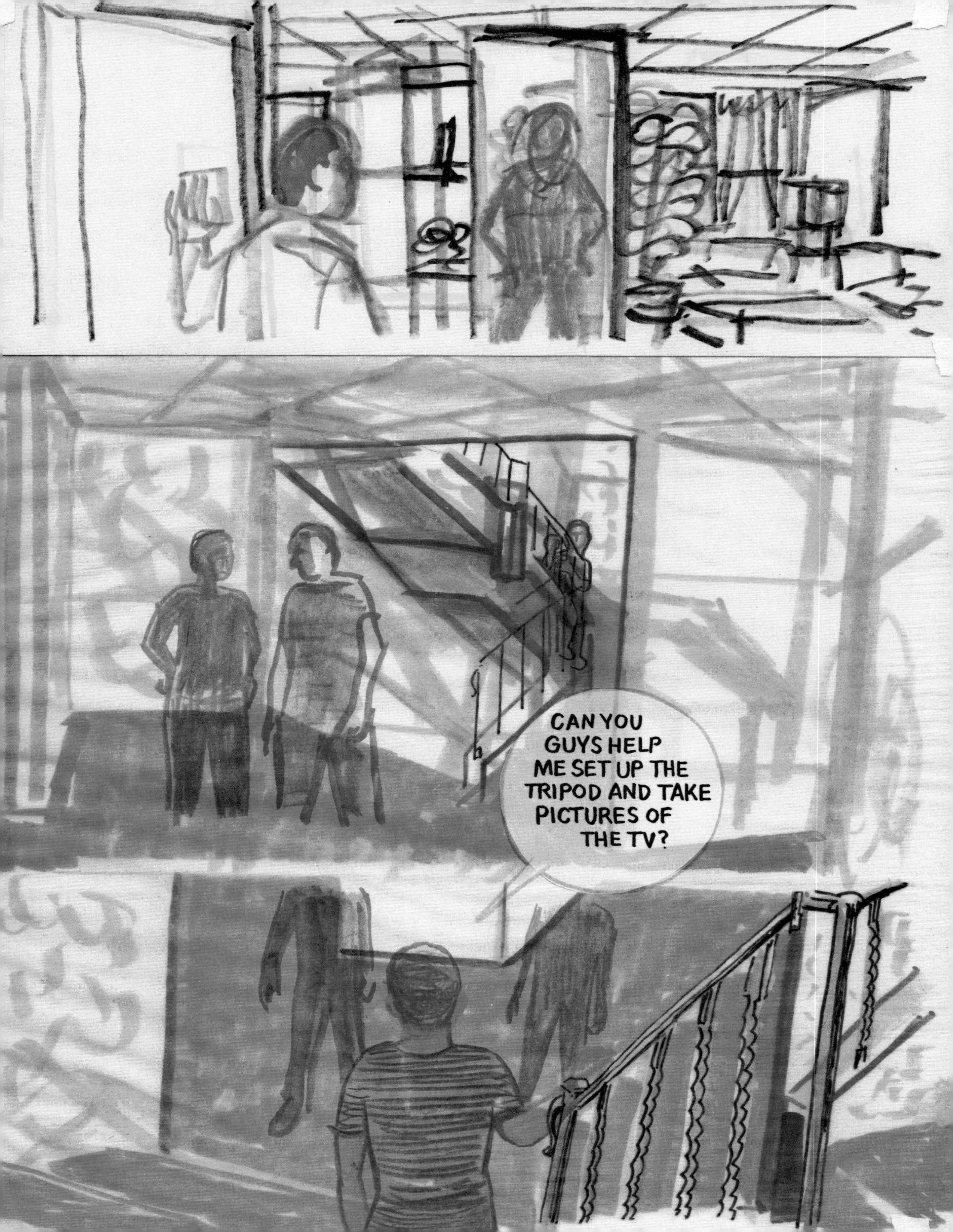
CAN YOU GUYS HELP ME SET UP THE TRIPOD AND TAKE PICTURES OF THE TV?

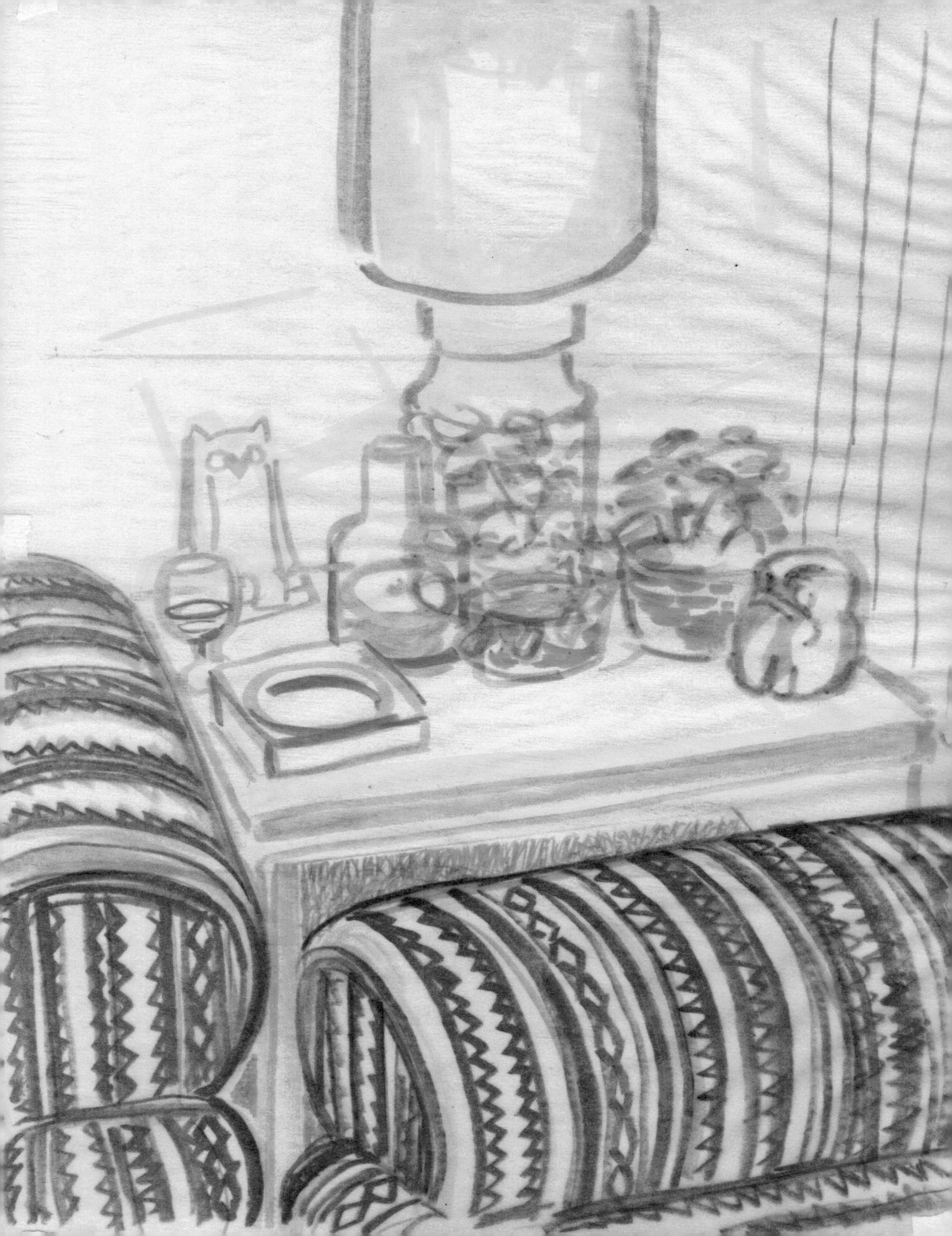

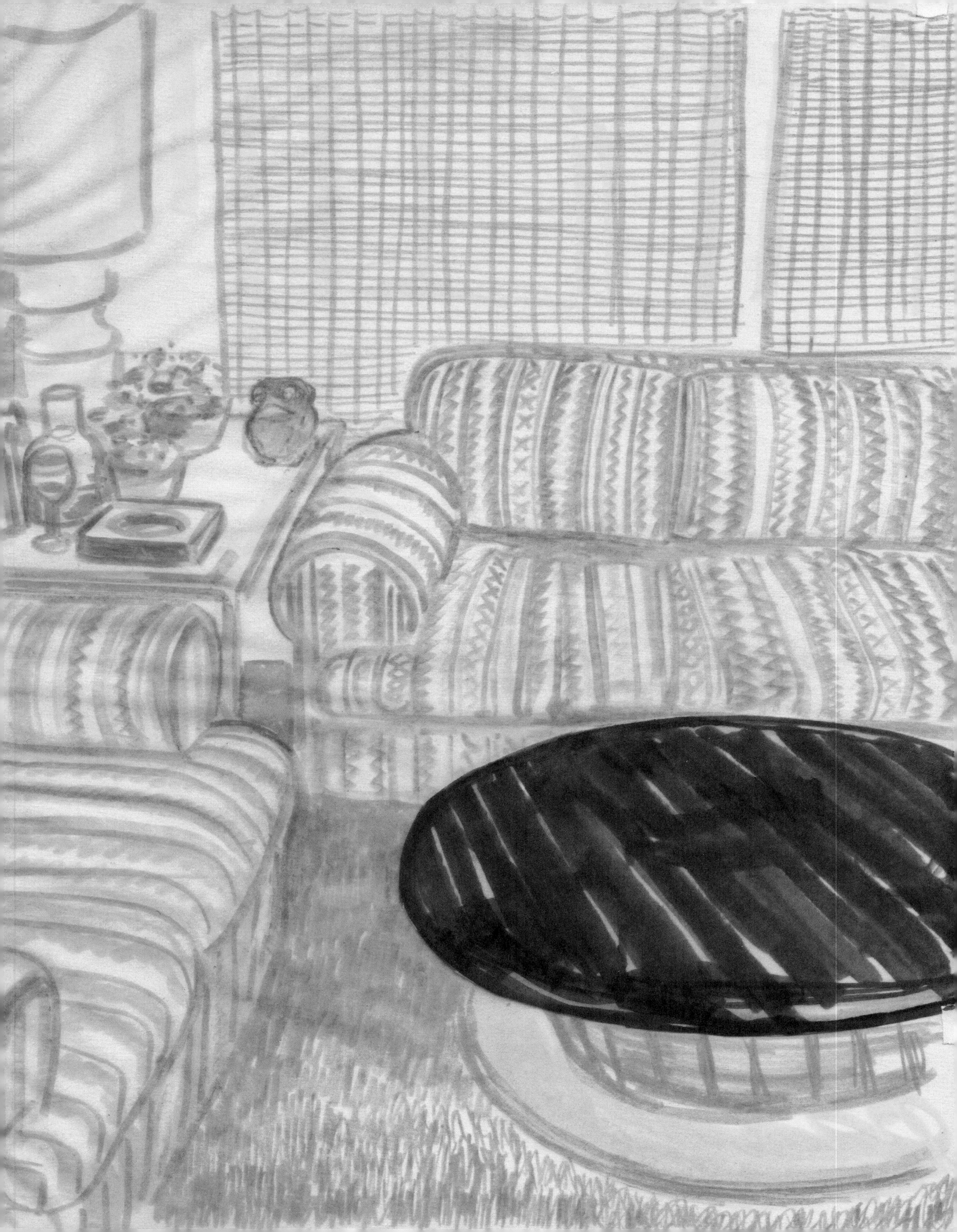

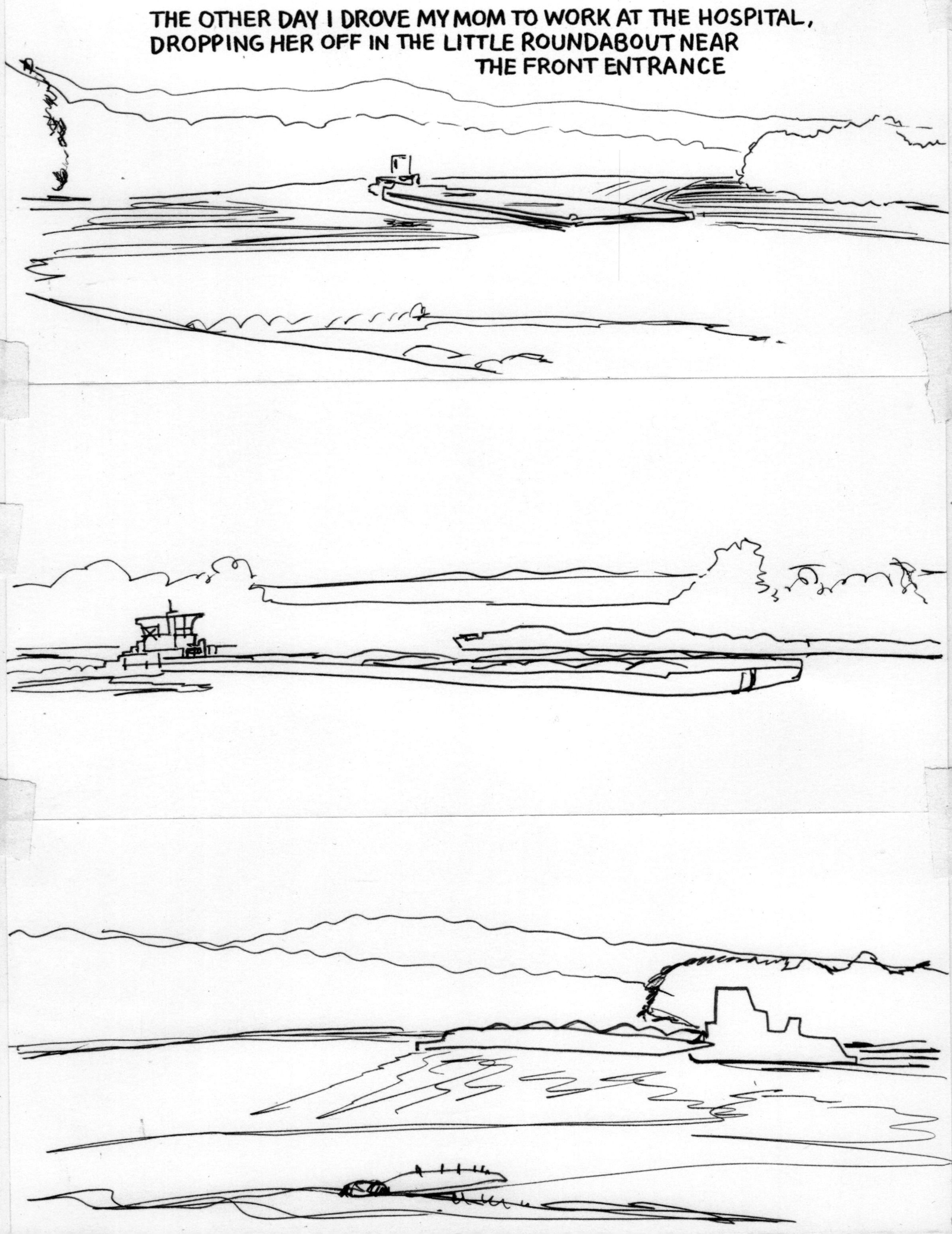
THE OTHER DAY I DROVE MY MOM TO WORK AT THE HOSPITAL, DROPPING HER OFF IN THE LITTLE ROUNDABOUT NEAR THE FRONT ENTRANCE

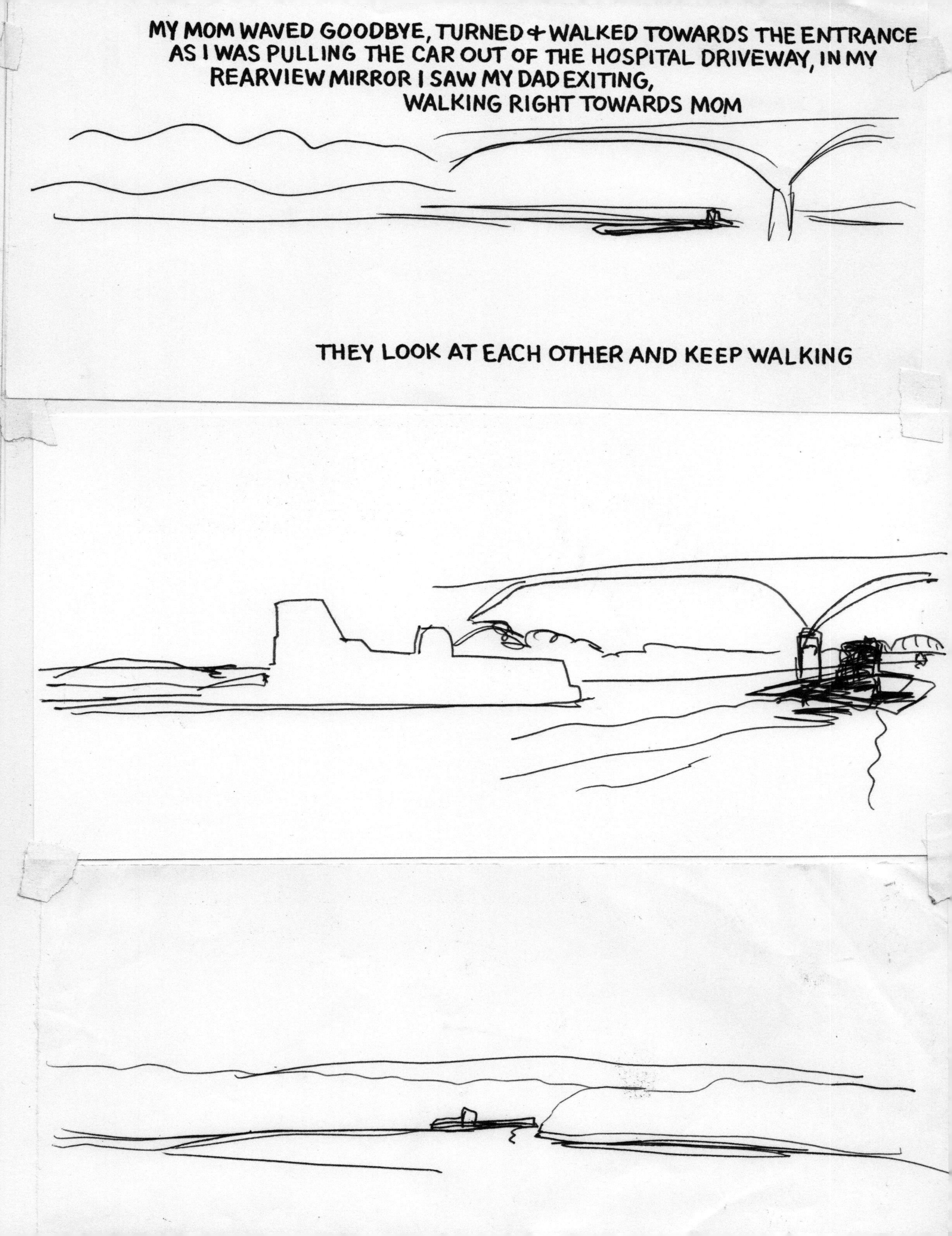
MY MOM WAVED GOODBYE, TURNED + WALKED TOWARDS THE ENTRANCE
AS I WAS PULLING THE CAR OUT OF THE HOSPITAL DRIVEWAY, IN MY REARVIEW MIRROR I SAW MY DAD EXITING,
WALKING RIGHT TOWARDS MOM
THEY LOOK AT EACH OTHER AND KEEP WALKING

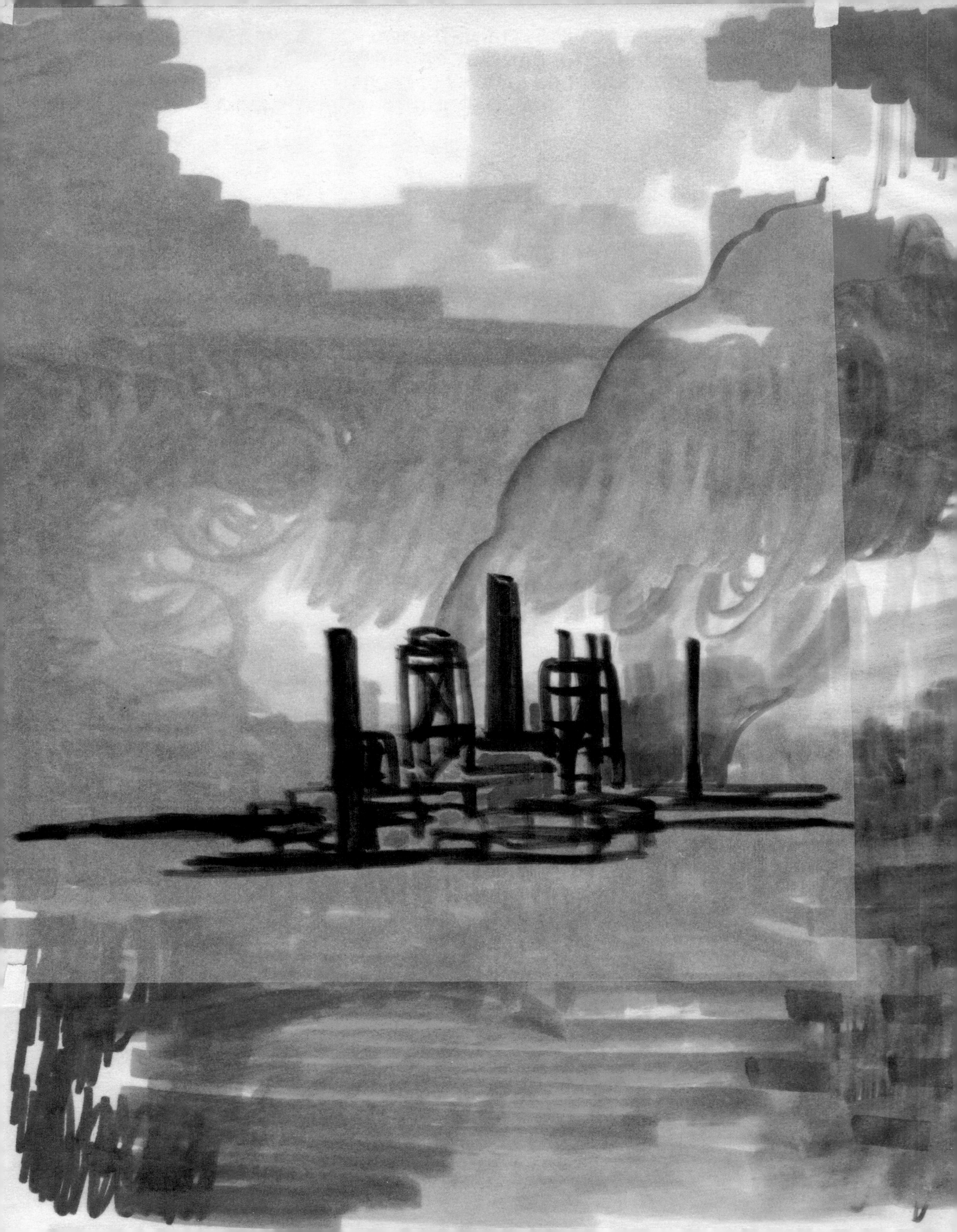

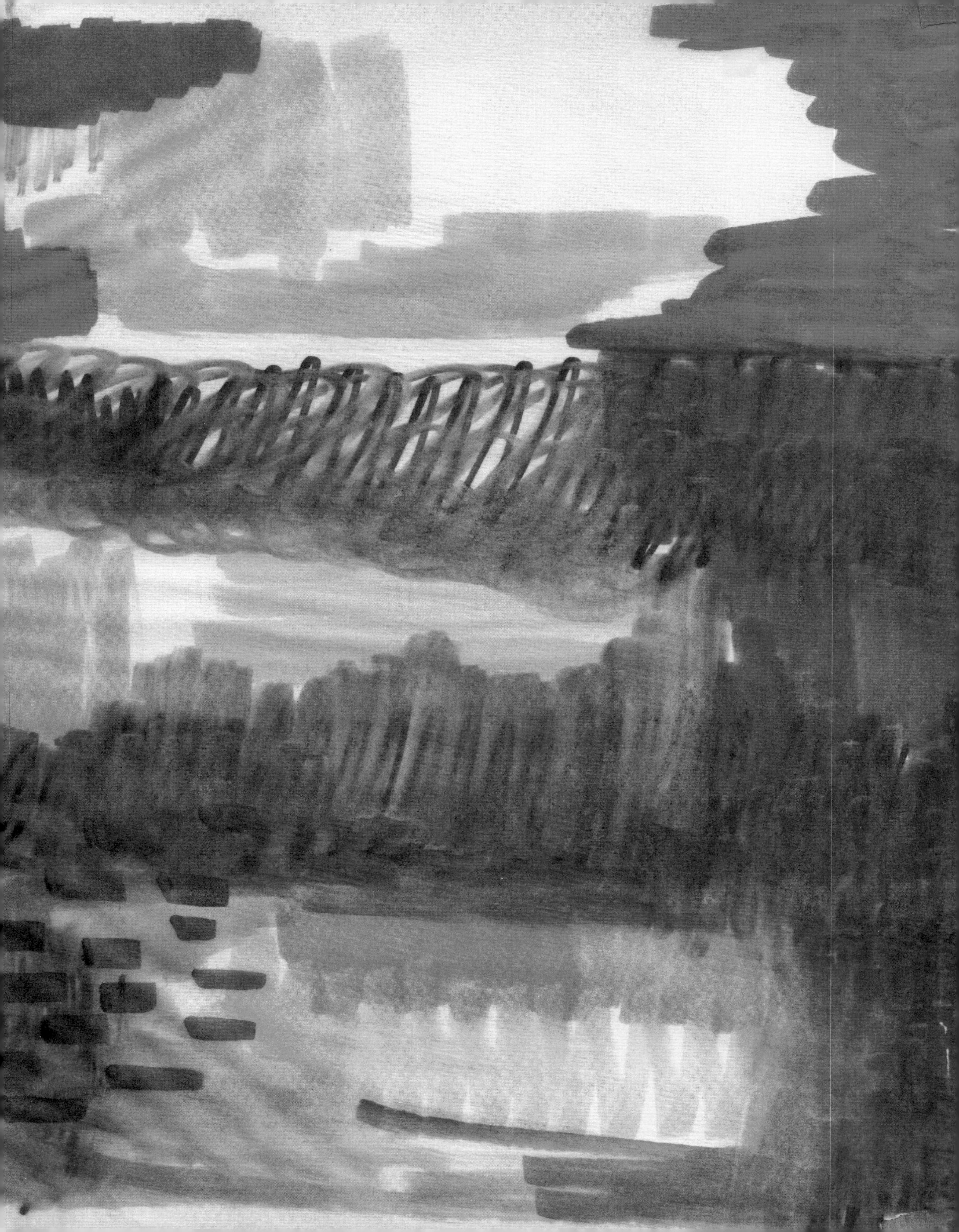

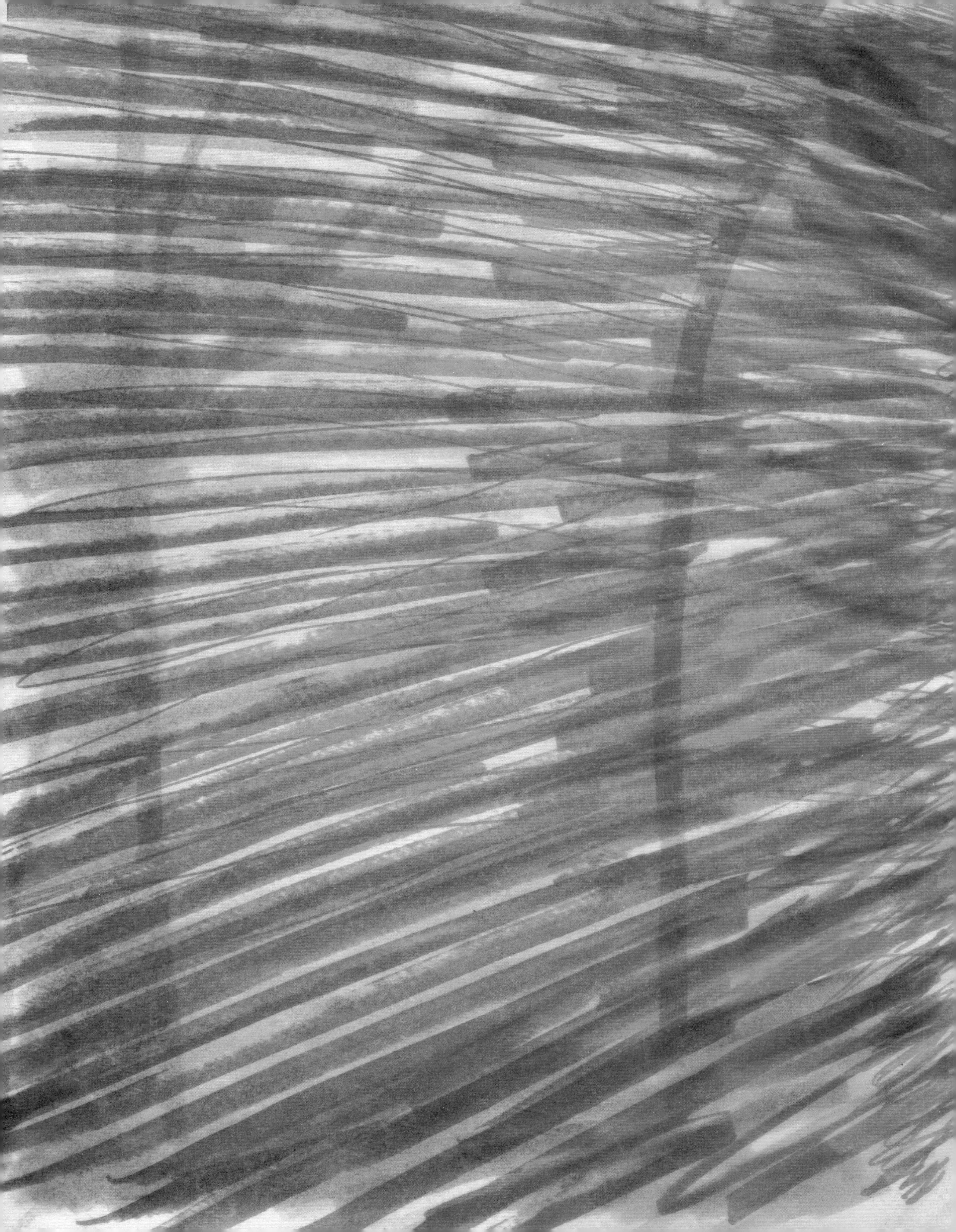

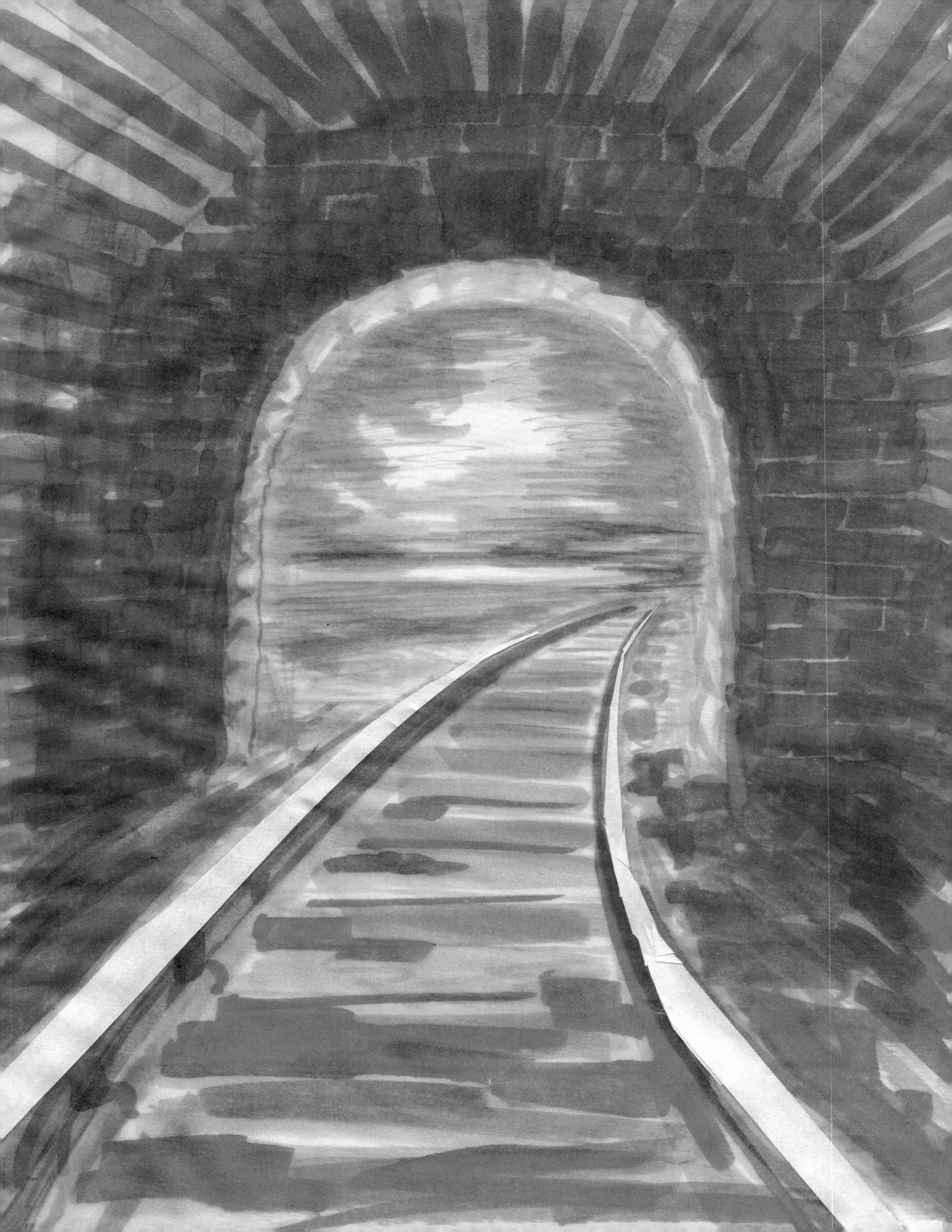

THIS IS A NEW YORK REVIEW COMIC
PUBLISHED BY THE NEW YORK REVIEW OF BOOKS
435 Hudson Street, New York, NY 10014

www.nyrb.com

Copyright © 2018 by Frank Santoro and Éditions çà et là.

A catalog record for this book is available from The Library of Congress.

First published in French by Éditions çà et là in 2018.

Production by Sally Ingraham
Production design by Frank Santoro

Thank you to Serge Ewenczyk for making this book possible.
And thank you to Bill Boichel and Dash Shaw for proofreading.

ISBN 978-1-68137-404-8

Printed in China

10 9 8 7 6 5 4 3 2 1

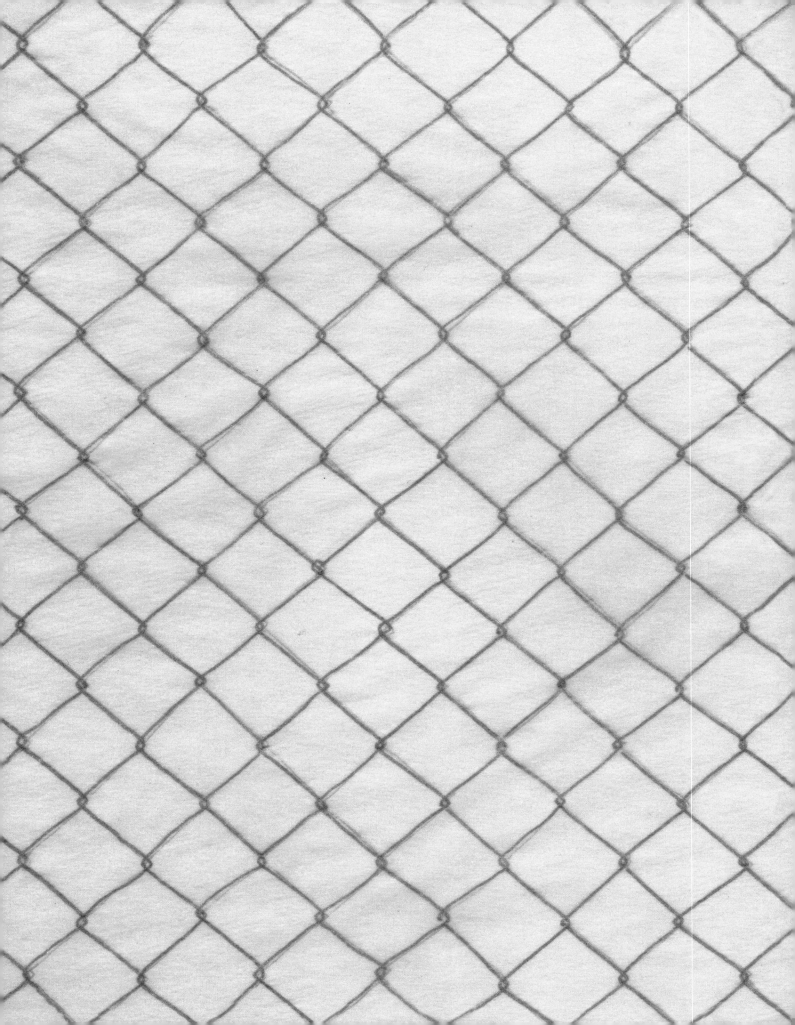

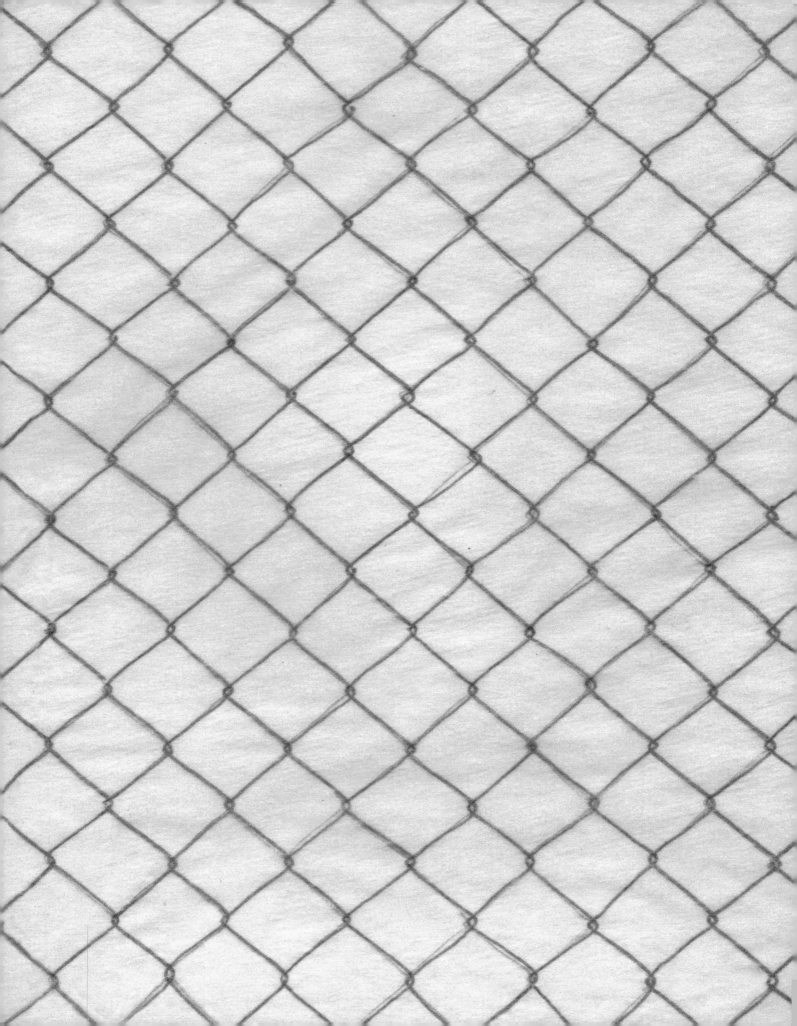